W9-CDP-333

The Minister's Annual Manual
for Preaching and Worship Planning
2012-2013

Logos Productions Inc.
6160 Carmen Avenue
Inver Grove Heights, MN 55076-4422
1-800-328-0200
www.logosproductions.com

First Edition
Twenty-sixth Annual Volume

Compiled and edited by John Indermark

Scripture listings in this publication are from The Revised Common
Lectionary, copyright © 1992 by the Consultation on Common Texts
(CCT). All rights reserved. Used by permission.

Scripture quotations, unless otherwise noted, are from the New Revised
Standard Version of the Bible, copyright 1989 by the Division of Chris-
tian Education of the National Council of Churches of Christ in the USA.
Used by permission. All rights reserved.

Copyright © 2012, Logos Productions Inc. All rights reserved.
Printed by Sentinel Printing, Inc., St. Cloud, Minnesota

This material is fully reproducible, but is for use only within programs of
the purchasing congregation. For other uses, permission must be obtained
from Logos Productions Inc. Contact permissions@logosproductions.com.

Published in the US by Logos Productions Inc.
6160 Carmen Avenue
Inver Grove Heights, Minnesota 55076-4422
Phone: 800-328-0200
Fax: 651-457-4617
www.logosproductions.com

ISBN: 978-1-885361-35-6
ISSN: 0894-3966

Contents

How to Use This Book..10
Preaching as Truth Telling – John Indermark.............................13

Sermons

August 5, 2012
Bread that Perishes, Bread that Endures – William H. Willimon 22
August 12, 2012
Complaining about the Food – John Indermark............................31
August 19, 2012
Who Was Jesus? – William H. Willimon 38
August 26, 2012
To Whom Shall We Go? – John Indermark 44
September 2, 2012
Practicing What We Preach – John Indermark...............................50
September 9, 2012
Good News for the Desperate – William H. Willimon...................56
September 16, 2012
Speaking Openly – Rod Broding...64
September 23, 2012
Why a Child? – Thomas G. Long..70
September 30, 2012
A Cup of Cold Water – Rod Broding 78
October 7, 2012
Let Them Come – Melissa Bane Sevier..84
October 14, 2012
You Lack One Thing – Melissa Bane Sevier 91
October 21, 2012
How to Have Influence – Melissa Bane Sevier 98
October 28, 2012
Blindness and Hope – Melissa Bane Sevier 104
October 31, 2012, Reformation
Held Accountable – Andrea La Sonde Anastos 111
November 1, 2012, All Saints' Day
Making All Things New – Andrea La Sonde Anastos....................117
November 4, 2012
All My Heart and Soul – Andrea La Sonde Anastos......................123
November 11, 2012
Praise for the Passionate – William H. Willimon 130
November 18, 2012
Commissioned as Priests – C. Welton Gaddy 137
November 22, 2012, Thanksgiving
Thanksgiving or Thanxiety? – John Indermark.............................144

November 25, 2012, Reign of Christ/Christ the King
Tell It Again! – C. Welton Gaddy 151
December 2, 2012
The Days Are Surely Coming – John Indermark 158
December 9, 2012
Take Back Your Life and Prepare for God – William L. Mangrum. 165
December 16, 2012
The Nearness of God – William H. Willimon 172
December 23, 2012
For All Who Sometimes Run – William L. Mangrum 178
December 24, 2012, Christmas Eve
Ponder This . . . – William L. Mangrum...................................... 184
December 25, 2012, Christmas Day
Up Close and In Person – William L. Mangrum 191
December 30, 2012
Do You Know Where Christ Is? – David P. Sharp........................ 197
January 6, 2013, Epiphany
Another Way – David P. Sharp 204
January 13, 2013
What We Expect to See – Thomas G. Long................................. 210
January 20, 2013
Abundance – William H. Willimon 217
January 27, 2013
Can We Be One with Christ? – Michael Gemignani..................... 223
February 3, 2013
To the Outsiders – Thomas G. Long.. 229
February 10, 2013
On the Right Track – Jeanette B. Strandjord 235
February 13, 2013
Journeying with Our Eyes on Jesus – Jeanette B. Strandjord 241
February 17, 2013
Remember, Rejoice, Rededicate – Jeanette B. Strandjord 247
February 24, 2013
Take Heart – The Foxes Will Fail – Jeanette B. Strandjord........... 253
March 3, 2013
Church of the Second Chance – Rosemary A. Rocha 260
March 10, 2013
Prodigal Reconciliation – Rosemary A. Rocha 267
March 17, 2013
Holy Adoration – Thomas G. Long... 273
March 24, 2013, Passion/Palm Sunday
The Sincerest Form of Flattery – Rosemary A. Rocha 280

March 28, 2013, Maundy Thursday
Do This in Remembrance – Margaret Marcuson 286
March 29, 2013, Good Friday
Put Away the Swords – William H. Willimon 292
March 31, 2013, Easter Day
Living Easter – Margaret Marcuson 299
April 7, 2013
Free to Serve God – Margaret Marcuson 305
April 14, 2013
They Also Serve Who Stand and Wait – Nancy E. Topolewski 311
April 21, 2013
Show Us Plainly Who You Are – William H. Willimon................. 317
April 28, 2013
Discipleship through Love – Nancy E. Topolewski 323
May 5, 2013
Discipleship by Plums or Pecans?– Nancy E. Topolewski..................... 329
May 9, 2013, Ascension Day
I'm Expected to Do What? – Y. Franklin Ishida 335
May 12, 2013
Prayer, Suffering, and Cutting Corners – John Indermark 341
May 19, 2013, Day of Pentecost
The Spirit's Way – Y. Franklin Ishida 348
May 26, 2013, Trinity Sunday
Bound to the Trinity – Y. Franklin Ishida 354
June 2, 2013
Sing a New Song – John Indermark.. 360
June 9, 2013
Restoring the Natural Order of Things – Clayton Schmit.............. 367
June 16, 2013
Freed in Christ – For What? – David Neil Mosser 374
June 23, 2013
One in Christ – John Indermark 382
June 30, 2013
Spiritual Disciplines Form God's Disciples – David Neil Mosser ... 389
July 7, 2013
The Transforming Power of Christ – Daniel P. Thimell 395
July 14, 2013
God's Love and Ours – Daniel P. Thimell...................................... 401
July 21, 2013
Your Life in Christ – Daniel P. Thimell...408
July 28, 2013
Teach Us to Pray – Daniel P. Thimell 414

Children's Time

8/5/12	Believing in Jesus	22
8/12/12	Living Bread	30
8/19/12	Bread from Heaven	37
8/26/12	Words of Life	44
9/2/12	A Letter from James	50
9/9/12	Jesus Heals	56
9/16/12	Who Am I?	63
9/23/12	Who Is the Greatest?	70
9/30/12	Like Salt	77
10/7/12	Let the Children Come	84
10/14/12	Leave It Behind	91
10/21/12	Servant Leaders	97
10/28/12	Blind Bartimaeus	104
10/31/12	God's Love (Reformation)	110
11/1/12	God's Dream (All Saints' Day)	116
11/4/12	The Most Important Rule	123
11/11/12	What Can We Give?	130
11/18/12	God's Forgiveness	137
11/22/12	Thanksgiving (Thanksgiving)	144
11/25/12	Jesus the King (Reign of Christ/Christ the King)	151
12/2/12	Much Signs	158
12/9/12	Get Ready!	165
12/16/12	Let Us Rejoice!	171
12/23/12	Special Babies	178
12/24/12	Jesus Is Born (Christmas Eve)	184
12/25/12	God's Amazing Gift (Christmas Day)	191
12/30/12	Learning and Growing	197
1/6/13	Special Gifts for Jesus (Epiphany)	203
1/13/13	Jesus Is Baptized	210
1/20/13	Jesus Goes to a Wedding Party	217
1/27/13	Can You Spot Jesus?…	223
2/3/13	Some Didn't Follow	229
2/10/13	God's Glory	235
2/13/13	Ash Wednesday (Ash Wednesday)	241
2/17/13	Giving Thanks	246
2/24/13	Mother Hen	253
3/3/13	Growing and Blooming	260
3/10/13	Lost and Found	266
3/17/13	A Special Gift	273
3/24/13	The Name of Jesus	280
3/28/13	A Meal to Remember (Maundy Thursday)	285
3/29/13	Jesus Dies (Good Friday)	292
3/31/13	The Easter Story (Easter Day)	298

4/7/13	Good News!	304
4/14/13	Completely Changed	311
4/21/13	Do You Know?	317
4/28/13	Job Description	323
5/5/13	Peace Be with You	328
5/9/13	Jesus Goes Home (Ascension)	334
5/12/13	Risky Witness	340
5/19/13	The Spirit Brings Life (Pentecost)	347
5/26/13	Three and One (Trinity)	353
6/2/13	Nicodemus Drama: Singing to God	359
6/9/13	When We Are Sad	367
6/16/13	Measuring God's Love	374
6/23/13	God's Children	381
6/30/13	Growing in God	388
7/7/13	Bearing Burdens	394
7/14/13	The Good Samaritan	401
7/21/13	Mary and Martha	408
7/28/13	Talking to God	414

Appendices

Monthly Prayers for Church Meetings – Charles Somervill ... 418
2012-2013 Writers ... 431
Four-Year Church Year Calendar ... 433
Calendars for 2012 and 2013 ... 434
Index of Sermon Texts ... 435

FREE Children's Sermon Index

Your paid subscription now includes FREE access to the *Children's Sermon Index* – **a database of children's sermons based on the Revised Common Lectionary for each Sunday of the year.** You can search by theme, season of the church year, or keyword.

- **Your activation code is MA363.**
- **Visit www.logosproductions.com** and click on activate my complimentary "Children's Sermon Index" under "online resources."
- Follow the instructions to receive FREE access to the *Children's Sermon Index* for as long as you subscribe to *The Minister's Annual Manual*.

How to Use This Book

Dear Readers of *The Minister's Annual Manual,*

This book contains planning materials for 61 worship occasions from August 2012 through July 2013, plus an article titled "Preaching as Truth Telling" (see pp. 13-18) and a brand new section called "Monthly Prayers for Church Meetings" (see pp. 418-430). We trust you will enjoy using this book throughout the coming year.

What You Will Find in This Resource
The following materials are included for each worship experience:
- Lessons assigned for liturgical preaching
- Speaker's Introduction for the Lessons
- Theme for this service
- Thought for the Day, related to the theme
- Sermon Summary, highlighting thrust of the message
- Call to Worship: to begin community praise and worship
- Pastoral Prayer: a general prayer for the worshiping community
- Prayer of Confession: a prayer confessing our need of God
- Prayer of Dedication of Gifts and Self: an offering prayer
- Hymn of the Day, with background information
- Children's Time for engaging children with the sermon theme
- The Sermon, a homily on one of the day's texts
- Hymn suggestions for opening, sermon, and closing songs
- New this year is a section titled Monthly Prayers for Church Meetings (see pp. 418-430).

The speaker's introductions for the lessons may be read aloud during worship or printed as notes in the bulletin. The Children's Time ideas can be used by pastors or others who lead such a time in worship or as part of the educational program.

Sermon Use
The sermons contained in this book are best used as devotional reading, thought starters, or check points for your own sermon preparation. If you choose to quote from a sermon or base your own sermon largely on the work of others, you owe it to your congregation, and to the writers of these resources, to identify and acknowledge your source.

Lection Guidelines

If you are new to *Minister's Annual Manual,* it may be helpful to review these abbreviations used in the weekly lectionary listings:

RCL = Revised Common Lectionary

SC = Semi-continuous

C = Complementary

RC = Roman Catholic

During the Season after Pentecost, lections marked SC are used by most mainline Protestant congregations. Lections marked C are used by most Lutheran congregations. If you have any questions, please contact us at Feedback@LogosProductions.com.

If you don't ordinarily base worship on the lectionary, these materials will still be useful in planning liturgy and sermons based on specific texts related to the church season. If you are already accustomed to using the lectionary lessons, you will find these materials especially suited for crafting worship.

Many denominations now follow the Revised Common Lectionary, the organizing basis for the resources in this book. You should have no difficulty adapting these materials to your own church calendar. The Consultation on Common Texts asks that we include the following information:

For the Sundays following Pentecost, the Revised Common Lectionary provides two distinct patterns for readings from the Old Testament. One pattern offers a series of semicontinuous Old Testament readings over the course of these Sundays. The other pattern offers paired readings in which the Old Testament and Gospel reading for each Sunday are closely related. In adopting the Revised Common Lectionary, the Presbyterian Church U.S.A., United Church of Christ, and United Methodist Church elected to use the pattern of semicontinuous Old Testament readings. The other pattern of paired readings is found in *The Revised Common Lectionary* (Nashville: Abingdon Press, 1992).

– *The Revised Common Lectionary,* 1992 Consultation on Common
Texts (CCT)

Hymn Resources

Many of the hymns suggested may be reproduced if you obtain a license. A copyright-cleared music license for churches is available through LicenSing at www.licensingonline.org.

More Planning Resources

To assist in your planning, a four-year church year calendar is included in the appendices, as well as calendars for the years 2012 and 2013.

We hope that *Minister's Annual Manual* will enrich your preparation for worship, as well as the congregation's experience of it throughout the year.

– John Indermark, editor
Spring 2012

Using the CD-ROM

Although the book may be the easiest way to read weekly material, if you wish to reprint prayers or worship material in your Sunday bulletin, using the CD-ROM will save you time and effort. As a purchaser of *The Minister's Annual Manual 2012-2013*, you have permission to use and reprint the entire contents of this book. (When quoting portions from the sermons, please credit the author.) Following are some simple hints for using the CD-ROM:

- This CD can be used in both IBM-compatible and Macintosh computers.
- Insert the CD into your computer's CD-ROM drive and select your preferred word-processing application. Click on "File" and then "Open." Be sure the "List Files of Type" drop-down menu says "All Files (*.*)." For additional help, refer to your software manual.
- Select the week of materials you are interested in viewing or copying and double-click on that file.
- Once the file has opened, you will see a plain text version of the manuscript. You may highlight any or all of the information, then copy and paste it into another document – for example, into your worship bulletin.
- Once the material is in place, change the type font and size to match the document.

Preaching as Truth Telling

By John Indermark

Not too many years ago, I did 15 months of pulpit supply at an area congregation during their search for a new pastor. I would not call it an interim per se, as my duties were primarily limited to worship leadership and moderating their monthly board meeting. When the congregation did small-group home meetings in preparation for writing their church profile, however, I did agree to sit in on one of the gatherings. The intent of those meetings was to generate perspectives on the congregation's life, both past history and future hopes. At one point, the topic of conversation shifted to how church conflict got handled in this congregation. Toward the end of the discussion, one of the younger mothers in the church spoke up and said something to the effect of: "Remember, the children are watching." To watching, I would add "listening."

Who Is Listening to Your Sermons, and What Do They Listen For?
I was ordained in 1976. More than once since then, I have heard laments about the demise of preaching, either in its influence or in its quality. Yet over those 35 years, working with small churches of various denominations, I have never come across a congregation that would want to do away with sermons. In fact, when I have been privy to what congregations seek in a new pastor and reflected on such profiles (as alluded to in the previous paragraph), almost without exception "preaching" is ranked at the top of everything else.

Now, a cynical view might be that churches just say that because that is what clergy have indoctrinated them to look for, and that what's really at the top of the "what we want most in our new pastor" list are small group leadership or administrative skills or community involvement or – and perhaps you might fill in the blank with theories (or qualities) of your own. But I am not convinced of the cynic's view. I am convinced that folks really do put a premium on preaching, and not necessarily because they think (rightly or wrongly) that great preaching will grow a church all on its own. To return to that opening story of the cottage meeting and the admonition of that young mother, I believe preaching is still a priority because folks really have an interest – you might even call it a hunger or thirst – for a word that might transform or heal or challenge. They are listening.

In the book of Jeremiah, the king Zedekiah summons Jeremiah from prison and inquires of him, "Is there any word from the LORD" (Jer 37:17). Whether folks in the congregation would phrase it in that way, and even whether all or even most bring that attitude into worship on any given Sunday, "Is there any word from the LORD" serves as the baseline for why you would even presume to think anyone would care what you bring into the pulpit. It also serves as the foundation behind this article's theme: preaching as truth telling. For if the congregants gathered for the sermon bring anything close to Zedekiah's desire to know if there is a word that speaks to this day and situation, then your preaching cannot settle for anything less than truth telling. Truth telling about God. Truth telling about the world. Truth telling about the congregation. Truth telling about ourselves.

Truth Telling about God
During my senior year in university I attended a religious retreat. It was a very intellectually stimulating gathering. Traditional Christian theology was constantly reworked into philosophical frameworks and language to the point where, by the end of the retreat, it seemed we were going to great lengths to avoid mention of God or the "baggage" of traditional language and biblical moorings. I suppose it was an effort to make faith more palatable for modern thought. For me, it led to a conscious decision not to shy away from that language and to ground my own searchings and reflections on God in the biblical narratives. Perhaps that makes me a hopeless traditionalist in Borgian terms. But it has shaped my ministry and preaching in particular as an effort to engage in truth telling about God, grounded in the biblical witness.

What is most true in your experience about God? That should be the core of what you bring to the pulpit in any sermon. Indeed, what you find most true in your experience about God will likely be the filter – or to use a more properly theological term, *the hermeneutic* – through which you listen to scripture and tradition, and from which listening to your preaching will arise. This is not to baptize your experience of God as the one and only possible. To remain viable in ministry and preaching, you are called to continually assess and broaden and test your experience with what others have come to confess, whether in a creed or in a biblical passage or in a heart-to-heart conversation with a parishioner. But in the end, when you step into the pulpit: you owe it to God and you owe it to the congregation gathered to speak in all humility and integrity the truth about the God revealed to us in

14

Jesus Christ; the one who companions us today by the presence of God's Spirit. For if you cannot tell the truth in your sermons about what you truly believe and share your experience of the Holy in life: what exactly are you doing there? And what exactly would you be hoping for the congregation to glean from your words, however creatively or persuasively they are posed? More on this in the final section of this article.

Truth Telling about the World

John Wesley once famously said, "The world is my parish." But one need not be a Wesleyan to grasp the centrality of the world in ministry, including preaching. John 3:16 makes that abundantly clear: "For God so loved the world . . ." The world. The world is not a place to be fled from or condemned, as sometimes seems the case from some pulpiteering. The world is the place of entry for our mission and service. It is where all these fine, sanctuaried words intend to lead us. Why? To tell the truth about the world, which is loved of God. The pulpit is to be a window that enables folks to see the world in its God-loved possibilities, and in seeing to then take action that reflects that love in the most practical and "grounded" of ways.

I know, I know. There are congregations that might prefer pulpits to be less a window and more a blinder, and sermons to be less about the world out there and more about Jesus and the world inside. In those cases, it would seem that a year's worth of sermons strictly from the Gospels would serve a healthy dose of fresh air and new vistas. For where did Jesus engage in ministry if not in the world? Jesus was not a speculative theologian, given to abstract discourse on atonement theories or views of biblical inspiration. Jesus' ministry was not limited to sanctuaries: in fact, the more one listens to those stories, the more it seems Jesus was constantly getting into hot water when he was in sanctuaries.

Allow your preaching the gift of following the logic of John 3:16: to engage in truth telling that the world is the object of God's love, the instigator of Christ's incarnation, and the cause for our being sent as apostles out into our world.

Truth telling about the world, now as then, also needs to be cognizant and vigilant to times and places where the purposes of God's love for the world are thwarted by all manner of evil and oppression and injustice. The pulpit as blinder shelters our eyes from such harsh realities, and bid us keep singing choruses of "What a Friend We Have in Jesus" to assure us all is well. The pulpit as window, however, brings to our attention the truth of conditions outside that go begging for a friend or advocate. The pulpit as window also stirs our will for compassion.

The ministry of Jesus is strongly rooted in the covenantal tradition of Judaism, a tradition that takes seriously not only God's steadfast love and mercy but also God's equally intense desire for justice. In the book of Deuteronomy (whose setting is the preparation of Israel to enter the promised land), this matter is put quite bluntly: "Justice, and only justice, you shall pursue, so that you may live and occupy the land that the LORD your God is giving you" (Deut 16:20). That is a truth that needs telling from the pulpit with each new generation, lest we forget that the love God has for this world is intimately connected with acts of justice. Lest we forget, as some have said, that justice is love enacted for the good of another. The pulpit as blinder – which would have us speak only of love but not justice – jeopardizes the church by calling for only half of a gospel. Love and justice are to be held in tandem, as Jesus once did in his warning to religious leaders of his day: "You tithe mint and rue and herbs of all kinds, and neglect justice and the love of God" (Lk 11:42). Truth telling about the world engages the pulpit in making this link between God's love for the world incarnate in Christ and God's justice exemplified in Christ's ministry and compassion.

Truth Telling about the Congregation
Perhaps you remember the scene in *The Godfather* where Don Corleone visits the mortician, to whom the bullet-riddled body of his child Sonny is taken. "I want you to use all your powers, and all your skills," the Don begins.

Friends, this next element of truth telling may likely require all your powers and skills, in the study and in the pulpit. As a preacher, you are a leader of the congregation. This is true whether you are the solo pastor or an associate of a larger pastoral team. And when you step into the pulpit, you are there to speak truth – not only to the congregation but about the congregation. That is, the message you bear will at its best grow out of your experience of that community of people and the needs of that people on that particular day. So for example, the next time you step into the pulpit, what need or situation is present among and within the gathered folk that needs truth to be told? Will it be the truth of God's comfort and love, offered to folks who might be distressed or hurt? Will it be the truth of God's call to justice or repentance, offered to folks trapped in apathy or sinful acts or attitudes? Will it be the truth of God's all-embracing love, unsettling folks who prefer to limit God's grace to those they choose?

Such truth telling about the congregation hinges on your knowing who and where they are in life, and on an exquisite sense of timing for what word is needed most when. This is nothing new. Read the book of Isaiah, for example. A simple read through, without attention to historical setting, might give the impression that the prophet cannot make up his mind. Is it judgment, or is it hope? The answer is yes. To folks (read congregation) caught up in indifference to the world and injustice around them and by them, it is judgment. But to folks reeling under exile or laboring under the exhausting task of renewal, it is hope. It is not that Isaiah is inconsistent. It is that Isaiah is timely in his preaching.

Truth telling about your congregation from the pulpit is not an excuse for you to berate or make up for your inabilities at other times to call people into account. Truth telling about your congregation requires timeliness on your part. It requires such knowledge and awareness and engagement with them in your common life together that you can recognize what word the times call for. And to recognize what silence the times call for.

Truth Telling about Ourselves

Some years ago, I sat in on the sermons of a colleague of mine. There were times his words truly surprised me, as I heard in his sermons a strong advocacy for inclusion that caught me off-guard. The words suited me, though, for they rang true to my views. Only later did it come to my attention that at least some of his sermons had been lifted almost verbatim from a collection of sermon resources that I had happened to contribute to, and thus had a copy of. My resentment of that plagiarism, however, reached another level when I heard him preach a sermon, after attending a statewide denominational meeting, that contradicted those earlier words preached about inclusion. I felt betrayed – in one sense, lied to in those earlier sermons.

When you step into the pulpit, the congregation expects you to tell the truth: not only about God, not only about the world, not only about them. It expects you to tell the truth about yourself: that is, to speak words that reveal who you are and what you believe. That, to me, is always the danger around using another's sermon, even if it is attributed. It is as if, in my biased judgment, one steps into the pulpit and confesses: I have nothing of my faith or my self to reveal. So here, try somebody else this week.

True enough, there may be weeks where time is so short or perhaps so traumatic for you personally, that you feel you have nothing to say. As to the latter situation, I am not an advocate for routinely dumping on congregations personal agendas in sermon form. But I suspect, as I have on occasions done, there is a time for the congregation to experience the preacher as wounded healer; times when you or someone you love has received heavy news, the disguise of which would be disingenuous in your preaching. Maybe such things are best shared in moments of prayer. But it just may be that the congregation might be engaged in their own journey of faith – particularly when those journeys take difficult directions – by a sermon that disarmingly opens up a part of life that reveals faith is not all certainties and clarities; that laments are every bit as much of our tradition as are thanksgivings, if the psalms are taken seriously.

I say this on a day when I will accompany my wife to a surgical consultation that may lead us who knows where. But that is just the point. I have no idea where – but I do have a conviction regarding "who." For wherever the path leads, we do not journey alone, but in the company of God. God not as cause of everything that happens, but God as the One who will not let us go. And if I were preaching this Sunday, that would likely be the undercurrent of whatever else I would have to say – telling the truth of God's love and companioning, come what may.

What is it you will preach this Sunday? What truth will you bring into the pulpit about the God you follow, and the world of which you are an integral part, and the community that has called you to leadership, and yourself?

People will be listening.

August 5, 2012

10th Sunday after Pentecost (Proper 13)
RC/Pres: 18th Sunday in Ordinary Time

Lessons

Semi-continuous (SC)	Complementary (C)	Roman Catholic (RC)
2 Sam 11:26—12:13a	Ex 16:2-4, 9-15	Ex 16:2-4, 12-15
Ps 51:1-12	Ps 78:23-29	Ps 78:3-4, 23-24, 25, 54
Eph 4:1-16	Eph 4:1-16	Eph 4:17, 20-24
Jn 6:24-35	Jn 6:24-35	Jn 6:24-35

Speaker's Introduction for the Lessons

Lesson 1

2 Samuel 11:26 – 12:13a (SC)

Nathan tells King David a story about a rich man who stole a poor man's lamb. David's rage turns to shock when told that the story reflects his ordering of Uriah's death to take his wife.

Exodus 16:2-4, 9-15 (C); Exodus 16:2-4, 12-15 (RC)

The newly delivered Israelites murmur against Moses in the wilderness. They are hungry. They long for Egypt, where slaves were fed. God offers a gift and a test in the provision of quail and manna.

Lesson 2

Psalm 51:1-12 (SC)

This confession of sin and seeking of a "new heart" is traditionally attributed to David after Nathan confronted him in the Samuel passage noted above.

Psalm 78: 23-29 (C); Psalm 78:3-4, 23-25, 54 (RC)

This portion of the psalm celebrates the gift of manna and quail that sustained Israel in the wilderness.

Lesson 3
Ephesians 4:1-16 (SC/C)
This passage is a call to unity in the Spirit and maturity in Christ, since "there is one body and one Spirit, just as you were called to the one hope of your calling."

Ephesians 4:17, 20-24
Paul calls upon the community to put away the former life for the sake of renewal.

Gospel
John 6:24-35
Confronting crowds who follow him only because he filled their stomachs with bread, Jesus calls them to hunger for the true bread, the bread of life that does not perish.

Theme
God provides the bread needed for faith's journey.

Thought for the Day
What (who) is the "bread" that feeds your life, faith, and hope in ways that endure?

Sermon Summary
In a world all too ready to trade its birthright for a mess of stew, Jesus provides "the bread of life" that brings lasting nourishment and life to the world. Like the crowds in Jesus' day, however, even religious people often prefer having their bellies filled than their souls.

Call to Worship
One: Gather in this place, where grace would feed our spirit's hunger.

All: We come to feed on the grace God gives.

One: Gather in this place, where Spirit would quench our thirsting for God.

All: We come to drink in the joy of God's presence.

One: Gather in this place, and find the One you seek.

All: We come to meet Christ in company with one another.

Pastoral Prayer

God of all Creation, we thank you for the gift of this day: a day you have entrusted to us, a day you promise to journey with us, a day you provide for us what we most need for life. We pray, O God, for those whose lives pass through difficult times and places. For those who hunger, whether for bread or hope, we pray for their filling. For those who face pain of body or spirit, we pray for comfort and healing. We pray for this world: for peace where conflict rages, for justice where oppression rules, for mercy where kindness seems distant. And in offering these prayers, make us mindful that we may be the instruments through whom your Spirit would respond to these needs. We pray in the name and hope of Jesus the Christ, the Bread of Life. Amen.

Prayer of Confession

We confess, O God, that we sometimes settle for filling our lives with things that do not fill, or satisfy, or endure. We may jam activity and busyness into every corner and moment as we can, and still find ourselves empty, anxious, and hungering. And so we come to you. We come having heard those whispers of bread of life. We come wondering if those promises of never hungering again could possibly be true. We come to you. Nourish us with your grace. Empower us for your service. In the name of Jesus, who is life's bread. Amen.

Prayer of Dedication of Gifts and Self

You are the giver of every good gift, Holy One. From your hands we have received life and breath, spirit and senses. Receive now these gifts your people bring. Guide this congregation in the wise and faithful use of these offerings in your service: that as you bring life to us, these gifts may bring life to others. Consecrate the lives of those whose gifts today are but symbols of the giving of self into that same service of Christ Jesus. Amen.

Hymn of the Day
Bread of the World in Mercy Broken

Based upon Jesus' self-description as "the bread of life," this hymn, written by British Anglican priest Reginald Heber, first appeared in print one year after his death. The collection in which it appeared, *Hymns Written and Adapted to the Weekly Service of the Church Year,* had been compiled by the author, but published through the efforts of his widow. This collection became a significant source of 19th-century Anglican hymnody. The hymn, sung in connection with the Lord's supper or on other occasions, can serve as a rich reminder of the Christian's true source of spiritual nourishment.

Children's Time: Believing in Jesus

Ask the children about questions they have asked this week. What did they ask? If they could ask Jesus a question, what would it be? Affirm their curiosity and comment that asking questions is a good way to learn new things.

Explain that in our Bible story today some people asked Jesus a very important question, "What does God want us to do?" Ask the children what they think Jesus said. Affirm their answers and indicate that Jesus gave a very simple answer: "Believe in me."

Explain that to believe in Jesus means to trust him. Comment that when you trust someone, you believe that what he or she says is true. Jesus said many things, but the most important thing he said was that God loves everyone.

Another way to show that we trust someone is to do what he or she asks us to do. What does Jesus ask us to do? Share God's love with others. Exclaim that when we believe that God loves everyone and we share God's love with others, then we are doing what God wants us to do.

Pray with the children, giving thanks for Jesus and his wonderful message of love.

– Sandra Anderson

The Sermon: Bread that Perishes, Bread that Endures
Scripture: John 6:24-35

Presbyterian pastor Ted Wardlaw once told of the day a slicked-up church supply salesman in a three-piece suit came to this office to try and sell him some Bible games for the youth group. The top of the line game was called "Dollars and Sense." It was a board game, much like Monopoly, and the salesman said it was great at teaching children about "Christian economics." The way it worked was, if the players landed on a square labeled "college graduate," they received a certain sum of money, and if they landed on the square named "middle level executive," they received a greater sum of money. But if they were lucky enough to land on the square labeled "company president," they would get a very large sum indeed.

Regardless of the amount of money they received, however, if they gave 10 percent to the "church" square on the board (and here's the alleged lesson in Christian economics), they would reap a bonanza should they land on the "showers of blessings square," being showered in this case with all the money in the game's jackpot.

Wardlaw was, to say the least, not impressed. "I think that's a crass lesson to teach a child," he said to the salesman, "that the word 'blessings' is so easily associated with the word 'jackpot.'"

The salesman did not flinch. Looking Wardlaw straight in the eye, he said, "Yes, Reverend, but isn't that the way the world works?"

Yes, I suppose it is the way the world works. "I'm hungry for a blessing," we say when what we really want is a jackpot. Blessings come as a sign of grace. They are gifts that deepen and enrich our humanity. Jackpots come as a sign of luck, windfalls that give us more of what most people are after – fame, power, fortune. A child in an urban school in Atlantic City who has a passionate and caring teacher has received a blessing: a high roller in the casino down the street who comes up big at the roulette table has received a jackpot. Sadly, given the choice, many of us would happily trade the passion of learning for a few lucky strikes at the roulette wheel. "Yes, Reverend, but isn't that the way the world works?"

This preference for jackpots over blessings is easy to spot, of course, when it comes at us full force and undisguised. The picture of Wall Street financiers working leveraged buyouts of companies whose employees they neither know nor care about, simply to line their pockets with more cash, is easy to decipher. They may say, "Being in the right place at the right time to find this opportunity was a real blessing." But it is no blessing; it's a jackpot, pure and simple. Despite the fact that no one has ever confessed on his deathbed, "I wish I had worked harder on weekends, stayed more evenings at the office, spent less time with my children, poured more of myself into the pursuit of my career," the fact is that countless of us do those things, hustling at warp speed right past life's blessings on our way to some elusive jackpot. "Yes, Reverend, that's the way the world works," and it's fairly easy to spot.

However, it is more difficult to tell the difference between the hunger for a blessing and the lust for a jackpot when it takes a religious form. Take, for example, the crowds, described in John 6, who had been fed by Jesus on the mountainside and who followed him eagerly all the way to Capernaum. At first, we are impressed by their spiritual earnestness. They want to be near Jesus, we say. They thirst for his teaching. They long to deepen their encounter with God. In short, the crowd clearly seems hungry for a blessing.

Actually, no. Jesus discerns their true motive and calls it as he sees it. "You are not looking for me because of the signs of God's presence," he says. "You're looking for me because you got well fed on the mountain." In other words, they weren't after a blessing at all, but a jackpot.

Now, we must be careful here – this is not a simplistic story. This is not the crass account of people who got their bellies filled but who cared nothing for the life of faith, of people who came to church for the potluck supper and not the preaching, who showed up in the sanctuary to make business contacts rather than to sing praises. Not at all. This crowd believes that it is following Jesus for good and true religious reasons. After all, when they had been fed on the mountain, they said of Jesus with one voice, "This is indeed the prophet who is to come into the world" (Jn 6:14).

So why is it that Jesus challenges their motives? In the first place, Jesus perceives that the crowd is following him because he can make their lives better, but on their terms and in their categories. Jesus wants to give them life; they want an improved lifestyle. Many years ago, when I was just beginning my ministry, I managed to save a few dollars from my first paycheck and decided that the wise thing to do was to invest it in the stock market. Inexperienced in such matters, I simply walked into the local Merrill Lynch office and told the receptionist that I was there to make an investment. Quickly sizing me up as a small account, she shuttled me off to the greenest broker in the place. Evidently, he had been trained to make a little small-talk at the beginning with a client, so he asked me what I did for a living.

"I'm a minister," I said, "pastor of a church."

The young stockbroker turned a bit pale. "Give me a lawyer, a dentist, a life insurance agent, anything but a minister," he seemed to be thinking. "What can you say to a minister?" Finally, and with some relief, he thought of something. "I read the Bible when the market's down," he announced triumphantly.

Now there it is - the confusion of a blessing and a jackpot. This broker no doubt thought he was doing a righteous thing, reading the Bible when the Dow dropped. But the presumption was that religion's task – or worse, God's job – is to make his life better, to hold him together when the market faltered, or even to turn the bears into bulls. We do the same thing when we assume that God's role is to make the life that we have designed and planned work out smoothly. "O God," we say, "I have these plans. Make them work." That's not a blessing, but a jackpot. Jesus is not a short-order cook preparing food to suit our whims. He offers not the "food that perishes," but the "food that endures for eternal life" (Jn 6:27).

The "food that endures for eternal life" is, of course, Jesus himself. "I am the bread of life," he tells the crowd (Jn 6:35). This is not perishable bread that feeds a passing whim, but the nourishment of God that feeds our souls. This is not bread that we are supposed to knead and bake, as if we could. This is bread that God gives us as a gift. When the crowd, continuing to be confused, asked Jesus, "What must we do to perform the works of God?" (Jn 6:28), he said in effect, "You cannot 'perform' the work of God. It will transform you, but you cannot perform it. God performs the work of God. You are to believe it, receive it, and live it."

I read recently about a rabbi who died in England. His obituary told of his life, how when he was a young boy, he and his family were prisoners in a Nazi death camp. In the camp, the prisoners were given just barely enough food to survive – some grain, a bit of stale bread, and a few grams of lard each week. Despite their harsh environment, this boy's family continued to observe the Sabbath. Somehow managing to scrounge up a piece of candle and a little food each week, they said the Sabbath prayers and pronounced the Sabbath blessings.

One week, however, there was no candle. So, when the evening came and the Sabbath was at hand, the boy's father took some of their precious lard and molded it around a bit of string. Lighting this makeshift candle, he began to lead his family in the prayers and blessings.

His son was enraged. When the prayers were done, he confronted his father. "How could you do that? How could you waste what little lard we have to make a candle? It's the only food we have."

His father answered, "Son, without food we can live for several days. Without hope, we cannot live an hour."

"Do not work for the food that perishes," Jesus said, "but for the food that endures for eternal life."

– William H. Willimon

Hymns
Opening: Let All Things Now Living
Sermon: Break Thou the Bread of Life
Closing: Guide Me, O Thou Great Jehovah

August 12, 2012

11th Sunday after Pentecost (Proper 14)
RC/Pres: 19th Sunday in Ordinary Time

Lessons

Semi-continuous (SC)	Complementary (C)	Roman Catholic (RC)
2 Sam. 18:5-9, 15, 31-33	1 Kgs. 19:4-8	1 Kgs. 19:4-8
Ps 130	Ps 34:1-8	Ps 34:2-3, 4-5, 6-7, 8-9
Eph 4:25–5:2	Eph 4:25–5:2	Eph 4:30–5:2
Jn 6:35, 41-51	Jn. 6:35, 41-51	Jn 6:41-51

Speaker's Introduction for the Lessons
Lesson 1
2 Samuel 18:5-9, 15, 31-33 (SC)
David had fled Jerusalem in the face of a rebellion led by his son
Absalom. David's followers counseled him not to lead his troops into
battle with the rebels. He stayed back. Absalom did not.

1 Kings 19:4-8 (C/RC)
Elijah's victorious contest with the prophets of Baal resulted in
Jezebel's promise to kill Elijah. In fear, he fled Israel and entered the
Judean wilderness. Alone, and despairing, he prays to die.

Lesson 2
Psalm 130 (SC)
In a time of waiting, the psalmist offers a prayer of trust and hope in
God's steadfast love.

Psalm 34:1-8 (C); Psalm 34:2-9 (RC)
The psalmist offers praise for God's deliverance from fears and
troubles.

Lesson 3
Ephesians 4:25—5:2 (SC/C); Ephesians 4:30—5:2 (RC)
The faith witnessed to in the opening chapters of this epistle now
finds translation into the practicalities of how one is to live. These
verses list imperatives of action in relationship.

Gospel
John 6:35, 41-51 (SC/C); John 6:41-51 (RC)

Jesus' self-revelation of his identity as "the bread of life" evokes connections with the Old Testament gift of manna, not only in the meaning of the gift but also in the expression of complaint.

Theme

God meets our laments with an invitation to live.

Thought for the Day

Faith beckons us to move from complaint – justified or not – to trust in God's life-offering grace revealed in Jesus the Christ.

Sermon Summary

Complaint arises out of dissatisfaction. Lament couples complaint with trust in the one to whom complaint is brought. Some complain about Jesus' claim to be the bread of life. Their complaint stops short of trust. Even so, Jesus leaves the offer of grace open, even to those who complain.

Call to Worship

One: Come to the One who hears our praise and tears, who knows our joys and sorrows.

All: We wait for God, our spirits wait in hope.

One: Open the deep places of your life to God, places of light and shadow.

All: We wait for God, more than those who watch for the morning of a new day.

One: Taste and see that God is good; blessed are those whose refuge is God.

All: We trust in God's steadfast love and great power to redeem.

Pastoral Prayer

You are the One to whom we may bring the whole of our lives, for you know us already. And so we bring to you this day our gratitude for life, grace, and creation. Receive our thanks. And so we bring to you this day what grieves us: children who starve, wars that go on and on, injustice that favors the rich and ignores the poor. Receive our lament. And so we bring to you this day our trust. For you are the One who seeks the good of us and all. You are the One in whose hands rest creation and the future. You are the One whose love is our hope and our home. Receive our trust – and enable us to serve as those through whom you bring answer to prayer and faith to life. In Jesus Christ. Amen.

Prayer of Confession

For spirits closed to the movement and newness you would bring to our lives,
> **forgive us, O God.**

For hearts unwilling to name to you what we complain about among ourselves,
> **forgive us, O God.**

For hands clenched too tightly around the abundance of gifts we enjoy when others go wanting,
> **forgive us, O God.**

For faith that presumes we can only pray about what is good and not lament what is wrong,
> **forgive us, O God.**

May your Holy Spirit grace us with forgiveness that heals, that opens, that encourages, in Jesus Christ. Amen.

Prayer of Dedication of Gifts and Self

God of Manna, who pours out upon us what we need for life, receive these gifts we bring to you and the lives of which they are but symbols and signs. May we give all that we offer with a grateful heart. We pray that you would use these gifts in your service, even as you would receive and commission us in that same service. May we always find our ability and willingness to give growing out of your gracing of our lives. Amen.

Hymn of the Day
I Am the Bread of Life

This is another beautiful hymn emphasizing Christ as the bread of life. Written by Sister Suzanne Toolan, this hymn was first used during a Eucharist service in the Archdiocese of San Francisco in 1967. In addition to the "bread of life" emphasis, the hymn reminds us of the teaching of Jesus that he is also the "resurrection and the life." We also remember that on the last day, Jesus Christ will raise up all who have eaten of the bread of life, believed, and followed him; and that they shall live forever. Having a soloist or choir sing a stanza can be a meaningful and moving introduction to this hymn.

Children's Time: Living Bread

(Preparation: Bring some freshly baked bread)
Show the bread you have brought to the children. Express appreciation for the gift of bread. Break open the loaf and let the children smell it. Break it into smaller pieces and share a piece with each one, being sensitive to those who may have food allergies. While you are doing this, discuss bread: What is your favorite kind? How do you like to eat it? Invite the children to share any experiences of baking bread.

Comment that in our Gospel reading today, Jesus said something interesting about himself. Read or paraphrase verse John 6:35a. (You may wish to set Jesus' words into context by recalling that Jesus had just fed 5000 people.) Ask the children what they think Jesus means by "the bread of life."

Explain that in Jesus' day, bread was very important to people. It was served at almost every meal, it tasted good, it filled empty tummies, and for those people who did not have much food, it kept them alive.

Make the observation that in many ways bread can remind us of Jesus. Whenever we eat bread we can remember how important Jesus is to us. Just as bread keeps us healthy, so Jesus' teachings help us to be strong and to grow.

Pray with the children, giving thanks for Jesus the living bread.

The Sermon: Complaining about the Food
Scripture: John 6:35, 41-51

You may remember hearing the words. You may remember speaking the words: *What? This again! You know I don't like* _____ – and here you can fill in any number of things: broccoli, spinach, rutabaga, salmon surprise (my own personal dread). Complaints about food are as old as school cafeterias and military rations . . . and the Bible. In our Gospel lesson, the people complained about Jesus because he claimed to be the bread of heaven.

It is an intriguing and theologically loaded word that John uses for *complain*. In the Greek versions of the Old Testament, the word in John is the same word used to describe the complaining "murmuring" of the people of Israel in the wilderness. Then, too, the complaint had been about food, or the lack thereof. The taste of freedom did not seem to satisfy. The people wanted better food, even if it came at the expense of slavery in Egypt. "If only we had died by the hand of the Lord in the land of Egypt, when we sat by the fleshpots and ate our fill of bread" (Ex 16:3). Like Elijah under the broom tree, they would rather be dead. And so they complain.

Before we cast accusing fingers in their direction, however: have you ever hungered, really hungered? Sometimes, complaints may be in order. Sometimes, there is good reason to grieve the passing of what has been. The death of Absalom moves David to pour out his heart in the grief of *if only:* "O my son Absalom, my son, my son Absalom! Would I had died instead of you, O Absalom, my son, my son!" (2 Sam 18:33). A great number of the psalms of Israel are laments, whose verses often open with complaints to God of "Why" or "How long?" The faith we inherit from Judaism bares life and emotion before God, even the complaints.

But in practically every case, the laments in the psalms conclude with an affirmation of trust in God. After crying out to God in protest, bewilderment, or wondering, the psalmist avers that hope remains in God. Lament becomes an act of faith, precisely because it holds onto God even in the midst of complaint.

In that sense, the complaints raised in the Gospel lesson against Jesus do not rise to the standard of laments in the psalms. For the murmuring against Jesus does not lead to or seemingly even seek a holding onto him, but rather a letting go. There is distancing here, disengagement. The people complain against Jesus' claim – because they know who and whose he is. They define Jesus solely by family of origin, and thus put limits on who he could be because they know from where he has come. Misunderstanding is a common dynamic in the Gospel of John.

Perhaps what most separates their complaint about Jesus from the positive expression of lament may be seen in Jesus' first words to them. "Do not complain among yourselves" (Jn 6:43). Complaint is one thing when addressed to the individual or group who aggrieves us. At least then there is opportunity for response and dialog. The impression left by Jesus' words is that their complaining had been done without bothering to address him.

When complaint is not shared, how can change come? When we clutch our resentments close to our hearts, not willing to give them a sounding to see if they are valid or can evoke a change – but hold on and nurse them – nothing good will come. Our opinions of those we blame or resent will only worsen, for our conversations are only with others who share our complaints – or if none can be found, we will simply roll those things over and through our minds until they gnaw away at our spirits.

It is likely not coincidental that, at the end of this chapter, the complaining "among yourselves" leads to its logical conclusion. Folks begin to leave. In fact, in verse 60, the complaining has spread. It is not merely Jesus' opponents but "many of his disciples" who separate themselves from Jesus. Complaint can be contagious . . . and deadly to relationship.

Many experiences in life evoke complaint and many times the complaint is justified. In the face of injustice suffered, in the face of pain, whether our own or others, complaint may be exactly what is needed. Lament to God may be the most faithful thing we can do in those moments. Yet, the key is to hold onto the One to whom we cry, to keep together our expression of lament with trust in God. Jesus concludes his words to the complainers, not by slamming a door in their faces but by leaving open the invitation: "I am the living bread that came down from heaven. Whoever eats of this bread will live forever" (6:51). How and why can he do that? Jesus speaks out of the tradition of wilderness murmuring – and wilderness feeding. For when manna falls from heaven, it does not feed only those who remain faithful and trusting. It does not fall only on those who, even if they are hungry, keep their mouths shut and keep their pain to themselves. Manna is given to all, including the murmurers and the complainers.

Such is the nature of God's grace. God seeks our good. And it is that affirmation, and that grace, that allows us to hold together our crying out in lament with our trust in the God who will hear us and receive us – and feed us with grace that will not fail.

– John Indermark

Hymns

Opening: If Thou but Trust in God to Guide Thee
Sermon: Come, O Thou Traveler Unknown
Closing: How Firm a Foundation

August 19, 2012

12th Sunday after Pentecost (Proper 15)
Pres: 20th Sunday in Ordinary Time

Lessons

Semi-continuous (SC)	Complementary (C)	Roman Catholic (RC)
1 Kgs 2:10-12; 3:3-14	Prov 9:1-6	Prov 9:1-6
Ps 111	Ps 34:9-14	Ps 34:2-7
Eph 5:15-20	Eph 5:15-20	Eph 5:15-20
Jn 6:51-58	Jn 6:51-58	Jn 6:51-58

Speaker's Introduction for the Lessons
Lesson 1
1 Kings 2:10-12; 3:3-14 (SC)

The old king, David, is dead. The new king, Solomon, now sits on Israel's throne. Young and inexperienced, he has survived the intrigue that led to his rule. But how will he rule? God offers a choice.

Proverbs 9:1-6 (C/RC)

Proverbs has personified Wisdom before as one who invites individuals to life (1:20-33) and who was present at God's work of creation (8:22-30). Now Wisdom invites others to join her in the banquet she provides.

Lesson 2
Psalm 111 (SC)

This acrostic (each half line opens with a successive letter of the Hebrew alphabet) praises the providential and saving actions of God.

Psalm 34:9-14 (C)

The psalmist reflects on wisdom teachings regarding God's providence and faithful living.

Psalm 34:2-7 (RC)

The psalmist offers praise for God's deliverance from fears and troubles.

Lesson 3
Ephesians 5:15-20 (SC/C/RC)
Paul addresses the Christian community with wisdom teachings that encourage faithful living. This passage prefaces a more extensive "ordering" of the Christian household (5:21—6:4).

Gospel
John 6:51-58 (SC/C/RC)
While John's Gospel contains no narrative of the last supper, this passage brings strong hints of the meal's meaning. Jesus' "flesh" promises life to those who partake of this gift.

Theme
What are we to make of Jesus?

Thought for the Day
If someone were to ask you, "Just who is this Jesus guy, and why is he so important to you?" what would your answer be?

Sermon Summary
What do you make of Jesus? Sometimes he carries on in strange and even disturbing ways. Unwilling to remain a figure of the past, Jesus continues to reach out to us, seeking relationship with us, beckoning us to move our concern from "who Jesus was" to "who Jesus is."

Call to Worship
One: God beckons us to come, with arms opened in love.
All: We thank you, O God, for love that receives us.
One: Christ welcomes us as sisters and brothers, at a table set with grace.
All: We thank you, O Christ, for grace that provides a place for us.
One: Spirit fills us and sends us, in service of the One who calls.
All: Lead us, O Spirit, in our worship and into our living.

Pastoral Prayer

Jesus, just when we think we know you, that we understand you, that we are close to you, you surprise us, shock us, reveal something of yourself and your way to us so that we are confused. When we get close to you and the more we know about you, sometimes it seems as if there is an even greater distance between us. Our ways are not your ways. Yet, in you is life, abundant life. Open us up to the grandness of your mystery, dear Jesus. Give us the courage to walk with you, even in those times when we don't know where you are leading us. Help us to take you in all your mystery, in all your wonder, as you are, rather than as we would have you to be. You have the words of life. Where would we go if we turned from you? Amen.

Prayer of Confession

Holy God, you come to us with such grace in Jesus Christ. Why, then, do we come to neglect the body that is called by Christ's name? Forgive us for that neglect: by our withdrawal in times of confusion and anger, by disunity when your invitations into community become overridden with our ultimatums about community. Restore us to relationship with you and with one another. Renew our discipleship by your Spirit's presence. Lead us to honor your presence and grace by being present and gracious to those with whom we share this life and Christ's calling. In Jesus' name. Amen.

Prayer of Dedication of Gifts and Self

One: For the beauties of creation, for the joys of relationship, for your gracing of our lives:

All: We give you our thanks.

One: For your service in this world, for your children's needs, for earth's hope and renewal:

All: We bring these gifts.

One: Direct the use of these gifts, that they may be instruments of your peace and food for your people.

All: Direct our lives, that we may bear your grace to this world. Amen.

Hymn of the Day
There's a Spirit in the Air

Not many seven-stanza hymns are sung in present-day worship services. This hymn, written by the influential British-born contemporary American hymn writer Brian Wren, should be an exception. The hymn was written for Pentecost in 1974 to celebrate the Holy Spirit at work in our world. Its seven stanzas can effectively serve as a call for Christians around the world to allow the Holy Spirit to fill our praise, guide our thoughts, and change our ways as we seek to influence the world in the name of Jesus Christ.

Children's Time: Bread from Heaven

Encourage the children to tell about some things they have heard that are difficult to understand. Explain that sometimes Jesus said some things that were hard to understand. Recall what Jesus said about being the living bread that came down from heaven (Jn 6:51a).

Mention that when Jesus talked about the bread that came from heaven, he was thinking of something that had happened to the Hebrew people many years before. It was the story of how God gave the people special bread, called manna. The manna was sent from heaven to keep the people alive in the wilderness.

Explain that in many ways Jesus was just like the bread sent from heaven. At the right time, God sent the manna to the people; in the same way God sent Jesus to us. The manna was a sign of God's love, and so is Jesus. The manna gave life and hope to the people, and so does Jesus.

Comment that whenever we celebrate communion we use bread. When we come to God's table and eat the bread, we can remember that Jesus was sent from God to tell us of God's love.

Pray with the children, giving thanks for Jesus who was sent as a sign of God's love.

The Sermon: Who Was Jesus?
Scripture: John 6:51-58

Who was Jesus? What was it like to sit at his feet on the Galilean hillside, to hear his words, to see his signs and wonders? Have you ever longed to be there, to be back there, and actually see and hear for yourself the very words of Jesus?

In a way, that is just what many biblical scholars want to help us do. A few years ago, the much publicized Jesus Seminar attempted to reconstruct the real Jesus, Jesus as he was, through their extensive historical research and historical speculation.

Jesus was a Jew who was from Nazareth in the region of Galilee. Galilee was a marginal region far from the centers of national power like Jerusalem. He was put to death about the year 30 CE by the Roman governor, Pontius Pilate, on the charge of treason. Very few debate these facts. After these assertions, the historically verifiable facts of Jesus become less certain. We have these snapshots of his baptism by John in the Jordan. He was frequently in the synagogue and temple. Perhaps his cleansing of the temple contributed to the movement that led to his execution.

He assembled a group of disciples around him. His teaching was characterized by parables, pithy little stories about the kingdom of God. He seemed to have stressed the justice and righteousness of God in a way that reminded many of the prophets of Israel in the past. Perhaps this was one reason why many felt his message to be threatening and controversial. He criticized those in power and showed gracious compassion for the downtrodden and the oppressed. He preached forgiveness and love of enemies and appeared to disavow violence in any form, even violence against the Romans.

And thus he was killed because he was a challenge to the establishment.

Today's Gospel, John 6:51-58, is one of Jesus' hard sayings.

There are so many times when Jesus demands hard things of us. "Go, sell all that you have and give it to the poor." That's hard. Or, elsewhere, "If your eye causes you to sin, pluck it out." Or, "Be perfect, even as your father in heaven is perfect."

But in today's Gospel, Jesus doesn't demand anything of us other than our faith. Rather, he makes promises. He tells us that he is the bread that has come down from heaven. He is the bread that will satisfy all of our longings. We are to feed on him and we will be satisfied forever.

Isn't it ironic that it is the promise of Jesus that offends here, rather than any of his demands or commands? Jesus promises us that he is the answer to our deepest hungers, that we are to feed upon him and be filled, that he is to be more to us than food and drink – the source of our very lives.

And it scares the wits out of us. In these moments, we consider that perhaps our real problem with Jesus is not so much, "Who was Jesus?" but rather, "Who is Jesus?"

Maybe that's one reason why so much energy is expended on attempts to reconstruct a history of Jesus. If we can make Jesus into a historical figure, a problem of the past, then we don't have to deal with him today. Jesus, in today's Gospel, offends those who stood around him that day. It wasn't that they were gullible, credulous, ancient people and we are skeptical, disbelieving, modern people. It is rather a matter that Jesus is strange.

If he is the "Word made flesh" as this Gospel claimed him to be from the first chapter, God with us, then we ought to be surprised when Jesus is not confusing, not mysterious or elusive. After all, we are not gods. Again and again, in John's words, the "light shines in the darkness," our darkness. He came unto his own and his own did not receive him. It's just hard to believe that God really looks and acts and talks like Jesus. So many were offended by him in the first century and are in our own time.

Sometimes I've heard people say, "I wish I could have lived in the first century and witnessed for myself the work of Jesus, actually seen him face to face." The implication of this desire is that belief would somehow be easier. You could stand face to face with who Jesus was and choose for yourself. But if that were the case, why did more people of that day seem to reject Jesus than follow Jesus?

No, our problem is not that we don't have enough evidence to convince us that Jesus is the Savior of the world. Our problem is that Jesus and his teaching can be difficult and demanding here and now. It is not for us to choose to believe in Jesus on the basis of certain proofs and arguments. It is for Jesus to choose us, to come to us, to speak to us, to reveal himself to us.

That's why you are here this morning. It is not that you did a study of all of the world's alleged saviors and decided that Jesus had the most to offer. It is not that you assembled all of the available historical data and it all added up to Jesus. It is rather that Jesus in some way has come to you, spoken to you, and chosen you to be his disciple.

Just like in the scripture today, Jesus keeps talking to his disciples (that's us), keeps working with his disciples, and keeps speaking and revealing even when they (we) don't understand everything about him.

But understanding isn't the issue. The issue is to keep trying to love Jesus, to follow Jesus, to feed on him, to savor and enjoy him as if we were feeding on the bread of life.

– William H. Willimon

Hymns
Opening: God Himself Is Present
Sermon: Let All Mortal Flesh Keep Silence
Closing: I Was There to Hear Your Borning Cry

August 26, 2012

13th Sunday after Pentecost (Proper 16)
RC/Pres: 21st Sunday in Ordinary Time

Lessons

Semi-continuous (SC)	Complementary (C)	Roman Catholic (RC)
1 Kgs 8:(1, 6, 10-11) 22-30, 41-43	Josh 24:1-2a, 14-18	Josh 24:1-2a, 15-17, 18b
Ps 84	Ps 34:15-22	Ps 34:2-3, 16-17, 18-19, 20-21
Eph 6:10-20	Eph 6:10-20	Eph 5:21-32 or 5:2a, 25-32
Jn 6:56-69	Jn 6:56-69	Jn 6:60-69

Speaker's Introduction for the Lessons

Lesson 1

1 Kings 8:(1, 6, 10-11) 22-30, 41-43 (SC)

> The temple God commanded David not to build has been completed by Solomon. Solomon offers this prayer of dedication, which invites God to hear the prayers not only of Israel but also of foreigners.

Joshua 24:1-2a, 14-18 (C); Joshua 24:1-2a, 15-17, 18b (RC)

> The tribes of Israel stand poised to possess the land long promised. The kept covenant promise of land now summons a renewed covenant choice of whom Israel will serve in this place.

Lesson 2

Psalm 84 (SC)

> The psalmist offers a hymn of thanksgiving for the gift of the temple and God's presence there.

Psalm 34:15-22 (C); Psalm 34:2-3, 16-17, 18-19, 20-21 (RC)

> The psalmist affirms God's ears and eyes and compassion open to the righteous and those who suffer.

Lesson 3
Ephesians 6:10-20 (SC/C)
Drawing on the imagery of the armor and weaponry of an imperial soldier in the service of Caesar, Paul depicts the qualities of spiritual life that are to "equip" those in the service of Christ.
Ephesians 5:21-32 (RC)
Lists of household responsibilities were common in the secular world of Paul's day. Paul uses this device to depict the relationship of wife and husband, a relationship grounded in mutual subjection.

Gospel
John 6:56-69 (SC/C); John 6:60-69 (RC)
Misunderstood words of "eating the flesh of the Son of Man and drinking his blood" have disintegrated into dispute and complaint and abandonment of Jesus. Will the rest walk away – and if not, why?

Theme
Faith may be a gift of grace, but discipleship is a choice of will.

Thought for the Day
Why do you choose to follow Jesus?

Sermon Summary
Choice is foundational to the following of Jesus. The choice is not made once and for all time, but repeated throughout life as we confront situations that ask us again if we will follow. Yet even when our willingness falls short, God remains faithful in God's choice to grace us.

Call to Worship
One: Why have *you* come here?
All: We have come for the hope and wholeness we find in God.
One: But why have you *come* here?
All: We have come because we are pilgrims, and Christ is found on the journey.
One: But why have you come *here*?

All: We have come because this place and these people offer the Spirit's sanctuary.

Pastoral Prayer

Holy God, Living Christ, Present Spirit: Be present to us and to those we name in prayer, whether in words spoken aloud or in sighs of the Spirit too deep to be heard or uttered by us. We are grateful for life's gift: we pray for those whose experience of its giftedness goes tempered by illness, loneliness, violence, or hunger. Lead us to ways that your gracious and loving response to such needs might come through our words and actions and attitudes. Rekindle the joyful opportunity we have to be the body of Christ through whom you reach, touch, feed, lift up, and embrace. For we would follow you, as those who have gone before us, and for the sake of those who wait to learn from us the ways of discipleship. In Jesus Christ. Amen.

Prayer of Confession

Forgive us, O God, when your words and ways seem difficult. Soften us when we harden our views about you and about others into rigid opinions inflexible to Spirit's movement. Refresh us when we parch ourselves and others dry with formulas instead of relationships, with offense taken instead of understanding granted. Remind us through your Spirit that even when we stumble, you are there to renew our spirits, to enlighten our minds, to cast away that which deadens us and others, and to take on that which leads to life in Jesus Christ. We choose to follow Christ, not because we must but because we may. Amen.

Prayer of Dedication of Gifts and Self

Receive, O God, these gifts we choose to render to you through this church. May this congregation choose wisely where and how to expend these gifts in your service. And remind us always how you have chosen to entrust us as stewards with creation's gift, love's grace, and discipleship's call. May our wills tend faithfully to your purposes for us and for all. In Jesus Christ. Amen.

Hymn of the Day
Eternal Ruler of the Ceaseless Round

Considered by some as a hymn of superior merit, this American hymn text was written in 1864 by John White Chadwick for his graduation class at Harvard Divinity School. The next year Chadwick began a 39-year tenure as pastor of the Second Unitarian Church in Brooklyn, New York. An altered text appears in many current hymnals, making this hymn more ecumenically accessible. In this hymn we have a prayer that God would rule in our hearts so that we, by virtue of the Son and the power of the Holy Spirit, may love and do all that we should as we follow and serve.

Children's Time: Words of Life

(Bring a large dictionary)

Show the dictionary to the children. Let them touch it as well as look at it. Say that this is a book all about words. When we need help understanding what a particular word means, we can look in a dictionary. Comment that some words are used often and others hardly ever. Explain that there must be thousands of words in the book.

Mention that in our Bible reading today we hear about some very special words. Set the scene by explaining that Jesus had been teaching the people, and some of them had left because they thought it was too difficult to follow Jesus. Jesus asked his special friends if they wanted to leave him too. Paraphrase Peter's response in verse 68.

Comment that a dictionary is very useful because it has many words in it, but if we want to find the most important words we have to go to Jesus. Jesus has the words that give life and hope. Ask the children and the congregation if they can remember some of the things Jesus said. Affirm all the answers and explain that we can find Jesus' words in the Bible.

Pray with the children, giving thanks for Jesus who gives us words of life.

The Sermon: To Whom Shall We Go?
Scripture: John 6:56-69

The None Zone is the subtitle of a book that explores religious life in the Pacific Northwest. A line on the back cover explains the source of the subtitle: "When asked their religious identification, more people answer 'none' in the Pacific Northwest than in any other region of the United States" *(Religion and Public Life in the Pacific Northwest,* edited by Patricia O'Connell Killen and Mark Silk, AltaMira Press, 2004). One of the points made by the authors from the data collected is that "choice" looms large for those who checked something other than "none." Church affiliation is not a given, not an expectation of tradition. One has to choose.

Then again, that is neither new nor unique to the Pacific Northwest. In Joshua 24, the tribes of Israel stand ready to finally possess the land promised and now conquered. You'd think it would be time to let out a sigh of relief after the 40-year sojourn in wilderness and the battle through Canaan. But no, Joshua says, it's time to choose. Choose the gods of the Amorites; or the gods from where Father Abram and Mother Sarai first set out; or the gods back in Egypt who nearly sucked the life out of you; or choose the God who brought you into this land. Joshua understood that "none zones" are few and far between. The problem for those who would be religious is not the death of gods but their multiplicity – not their absence from contemporary life but the issue of their relevance to it.

I believe that more than a few opt for "none" today based on that last issue: the relevance of God or religious community to their lives. To be honest, the church has sometimes given ample justification to that choice. Folks come looking for spiritual guidance or holy encounter, and walk in on us squabbling over who gets to use the fellowship hall for free and who has to pay. Others come seeking new ways and partners for serving God through serving others, only to find us refusing to budge from comfortable pews and unwilling to risk reserve funds. Some come in search of a place to belong and hear endless debates on who doesn't belong.

"None" can become an understandable choice. Until it comes time for a child to be married. Until it comes time for an elder to be buried. Weddings typically are not performed by "none." Funerals are rarely officiated or hosted by "none." In times of passage and crisis, Peter's response to Jesus in our text from John becomes a lively question: "To whom can we go?" Look around you this morning – and not just at the peculiar furniture and windows that makes this place different from your living room or the Elks lodge. Look around at the memories embedded here of those who have come in hope of finding sanctuary. Perhaps, at some time or another, it was you. Perhaps it was even while your checkmark was still in the "none" box.

"Lord, to whom can we go? You have the words of eternal life" (Jn 6:68). Peter's response arose out of conflict. The troops were deserting. Jesus said things that were difficult to hear, and in John's reporting, "Many of his disciples turned back and no longer went about with him" (6:66). "To whom can we go?" is not a question with only one possible answer – then or now. "To whom can we go?" is not a question to which the church has any monopoly on the response. We live in a culture filled with choices of things to do and movements to follow and gurus to heed.

"To whom can we go?" Perhaps the more important question is to whom *will* we go? Following and discipleship are acts of the will. Peter spoke these words in response to Jesus asking the twelve: "Do you also wish to go away" (6:67). *Wish* is a very weak translation of a verb that means "to will." The world is full of options for religious meaning and affiliation, among which our wills must choose. Religion in the "none zone" simply reminds us that a lot of us live in places where those choices may have less presumptions *of everybody who's anybody goes to the Methodist church in this town.* (Feel free to substitute any brand or flavor, including the currently in vogue "non- (as in none) denominational" one.)

"To whom will we go?" Peter opts for Jesus, in whom he finds words of eternal life. But let us also remember that the willful choices we make concerning faith and following Jesus are not one-time-and-for-all-time matters. Peter chooses to say to Jesus, "You have the words of eternal life" now. And Peter later chooses to say to Jesus, "I will lay down my life for you" (13:37). But then, in a courtyard outside the interrogation place of Jesus, Peter chooses to deny that he knows Jesus. Three times, Peter chooses denial. In the courtyard, Peter discovered "to whom can we go" does have other options. Safer ones. Easier ones. But are those the reasons we follow?

Following Jesus is a choice of the will, made again and again. The good news and grace of it all, however, is that even when our choices and wills betray us, God's grace does not. Grace does not excuse our failings. Grace simply, yet profoundly, receives with open arms those who answer "To whom can we go?" with the choice and will to follow Jesus. Not because it is the traditional thing to do, for that may or may not be true. Not because it is the acceptable thing to do, for that may or may not be true. Not because we will be part of a growing and vibrant community, for that may or may not be true. But because we find in Jesus the words of life, and in those words the grace for living.

To whom will you go?

– John Indermark

Hymns
Opening: Holy God, We Praise Thy Name
Sermon: Lord, I Want to Be a Christian
Closing: O Master, Let Me Walk with Thee

September 2, 2012

14th Sunday after Pentecost (Proper 17)
RC/Pres: 22nd Sunday in Ordinary Time

Lessons

Semi-continuous (SC)	Complementary (C)	Roman Catholic (RC)
Song 2:8-13	Deut 4:1-2, 6-9	Deut 4:1-2, 6-8
Ps 45:1-2, 6-9	Ps 15	Ps 15:2-3a, 3b-4a, 4b-5
Jas 1:17-27	Jas 1:17-27	Jas 1:17-18, 21b-22, 27
Mk 7:1-8, 14-15, 21-23	Mk 7:1-8, 14-15, 21-23	Mk 7:1-8, 14-15, 21-23

Speaker's Introduction for the Lessons
Lesson 1
Song of Solomon 2:8-13 (SC)

This book as a whole contains love songs that some hear as parables of God's love for us. Today's passage contains an invitation to the beloved, set in the context of spring and new life.

Deuteronomy 4:1-2, 6-9 (C); Deuteronomy 4:1-2, 6-8 (RC);

This text serves as the conclusion to Moses' first address to Israel as they are poised on the edge of Canaan. It is an invitation to faithfully observe and do the commandments of God.

Lesson 2
Psalm 45:1-2, 6-9 (SC)

Scholars hold that this psalm is a wedding song, the portions excerpted here are addressed to the king and then to God, the latter of whom is identified with equity and the love of righteousness.

Psalm 15 (C); Psalm 15:2-3a, 3b-4a, 4b-5 (RC)

The psalmist underscores the ethical principles demonstrated in social conduct that God seeks of those who would dwell in God's presence and not be "moved."

Lesson 3
James 1:17-27 (SC/C); James 1:17-18, 21b-22, 27 (RC)
James is a collection of early Jewish-Christian wisdom materials. As with earlier wisdom writings, it emphasizes wisdom not so much as what one knows about God but how one lives in response to God.

Gospel
Mark 7:1-8, 14-15, 21-23 (SC/C); Mark 7:1-8, 14-15, 21-23 (RC)
Jesus turns criticism of allegedly not keeping laws about cleanliness into a critique of attending to God in "words only," while neglecting what one does in life and what one harbors in the heart.

Theme
Be doers of the word and not hearers only.

Thought for the Day
If charged with the crime of being Christian, would our actions provide sufficient evidence to convict us?

Sermon Summary
Faith is not just what we hear or say about God. Christian faith involves how we live and act in response to the God revealed in the Word incarnate, Jesus Christ. Faith's best witness comes in the integrity of word set to deed.

Call to Worship
One: What does God seek of those who seek the Lord?

All: To walk with a clear conscience and do the right thing;

One: To speak truth from the heart and do no harm to neighbors;

All: To stand by one's word even when waffling might be advantageous;

One: To not make another's misfortune a cause for one's own profit;

All: To not use words as weapons;

One: To not put one's judgment up to the highest bidder.

All: Those who do these words will be found in the One they seek.

Pastoral Prayer

Creator God, attend to the words we bring to you in prayer, even as you would shape our actions in faithful response. Hear the words we offer for those who are ill, who face isolation or estrangement. Be present to them in ways that bring healing and wholeness. Hear the words we offer for this church community. May your Spirit form our ministries and shape our witness to your grace and love. Hear the words we offer for this world: for peace, for justice, for compassion. Mold us in word and deed as your servant people, that the faith we offer in sanctuary resonates with the lives we live in workplace, home, and community. We pray in the name of Christ, your Word incarnate. Amen.

Prayer of Confession

Gracious God, it can be easy to coast on the words of faith, basking in your grace – and neglect that those words and that grace come with a purpose for our lives: to change, to renew, to heal, to challenge. Forgive us when we divorce faith from service, grace from ministry. Forgive us when we confuse obsession with words with devotion to your Word. By your Spirit's working inside our lives and communities, restore wholeness to us so that speech and action may flow seamlessly, that word and deed may give common witness to your uncommon grace. The world needs to hear your word in Jesus Christ. May our witness be complemented, not contradicted, by the way we live. This we would pray, and thus we would live, in Jesus Christ. Amen.

Prayer of Dedication of Gifts and Self

Receive, O God, these offerings from our labors, from the work of our hands and minds. Guide this congregation to embody the words of service to which you have commissioned us. As you receive these gifts, receive us into that same service, thus joining our words of praise with deeds of ministry. In Jesus Christ. Amen.

Hymn of the Day
I Sing the Almighty Power of God

Written by Isaac Watts (1674-1748), considered to be the father of the English hymn, this hymn finds its basis in the Genesis account of creation. Watts wrote this for inclusion in *Divine Songs Attempted in Easy Language for the Use of Children,* published in 1715, with the title "Praise for Creation and Providence." The hymn can serve to impress upon worshipers that God is to be seen in God's works and God's Word. We can celebrate this creative power in song. This is not "nature worship" but a confident statement that all of life is in God's care.

Children's Time: A Letter from James

(Before worship, prepare an envelope and piece of paper. On the envelope print, "To all God's people." On the paper print, "Dear friends, If you want to follow in God's way, find out what God wants you to do and then do it! What does God want us to do? Look after others, especially those in need. From James, a servant of God." Fold and put it in the envelope.)
Ask the children if they like to get cards and letters in the mail. Explain that people have been sending and receiving letters for thousands of years. In the early church, people would encourage one another by writing letters about living in God's way. Some of these letters became part of our Bible.

Explain that our Bible reading today is part of a letter written by a church leader called James. Show the envelope and say that it is addressed to the people of God and that means us. Open the letter and read the message. Talk about some of the ways your faith community is looking after those in need. How might we help?

Pray with the children, asking God to help you as you learn to follow in God's ways.

The Sermon: Practicing What We Preach
Scripture: James 1:17-27

Do as I say, not as I do.

Have you ever been tempted to lay that line on someone? The problem with the phrase is the mixed signals it sends. On the one hand, it can be an honest expression that we don't always live up to our expectations. On the other hand, it may give the impression of approving double standards of behavior. Telling a son or daughter not to do drugs while the parent goes on abusing alcohol is not likely to carry much freight. "Do as I say and not as I do" can create a mindset that assumes when one becomes an adult, one is free to have one's actions contradict one's words.

Perhaps the best antidote to the abuses of "Do as I say and not as I do" resides in another proverb: *Practice what you preach.* If the words are good enough to say, then they're good enough to do. It is interesting that the antidote contains within it the language of the church. Education teaches, politics persuades – but the church preaches. "Practice what you preach" assumes that there is the possibility of doing the opposite: of not practicing the preaching, of not putting into action the words of faith. That should come as no surprise to anyone, especially given the tendency to sometimes limit questions about faith to questions about words. Consider, for example, the typical question one might ask about joining a church. In my experience, "What do you believe?" far outnumbers "What do you do?" in such inquiries. Now we may assume that in knowing what is believed we will know what is being done. But that isn't necessarily the case. Words can be differently interpreted and acted upon. Or, they can be flat out ignored. "Practicing the preaching" means that the words of faith are expressed in the actions of faith as best we are able by the Spirit's leading.

You can search through biblical concordances and never find Jesus, Moses, or anybody else in the biblical witness commanding us to "practice what you preach." Our text in James is about as close as those words come to being said outright: "Be doers of the word, and not merely hearers" (Jas 1:22). James's theme is more inclusive, for some might say that "practicing what you preach" is limited to the responsibility of preachers. There is a certain truth to that. Those set apart by the church in ordained ministry do have expectations placed upon their lives for modeling their words. Having said that, however, is not to declare that only clergy have a responsibility of seeking consistency in words and actions. James does not call upon us to be "doers of the word and not preachers only." James calls us to be "doers of the word and not hearers only." Consistency between word and action, between preaching and practice, is the responsibility of everyone in the church. God's word – whether we preach it or hear it – is the word we are to do, the word we are to express in our actions.

James describes the difference between hearing and doing by using parallel illustrations. The one who is only a hearer of the word is like someone who stares at herself or himself in a mirror. There are ways in which the word of the gospel is like a mirror held up before us. In its light, we see not only who we have been and who we are, but also who we can be by the grace of God. To hear that word is to look into that mirror. But to only look in a mirror is to accomplish no change. The one who only hears is able to walk away and forget, untouched by the experience. An alcoholic can be shown exactly what is happening to her or him. But unless the word heard gets inside and acted upon, he or she will walk away from that mirror image unchanged. The end result of only hearing in James's text is deception. The word literally means to "reason wrongly." To be a hearer only is to mislead oneself.

In contrast, the one who is a doer of the word also looks into the mirror held up to us in the word God speaks and in the Word God made incarnate in Jesus Christ. Instead of observing and then "going away," that person "perseveres." Instead of forgetting what was seen, that person keeps at the hard but necessary task of acting out the mirror's vision in daily life. The vision given by God's word does not dissolve in the mist of unutilized memory. Rather, it becomes the blueprint for one's own words, actions, and decisions. The living Word incarnate in Christ and revealed to us through scripture is a word not just taken to heart but acted out in life. The end result for the doer of the word is not deception but blessing.

For James, "Do as I say and not as I do" is not an adequate philosophy. It may express the weakness that will at times surface in our lives – the gap between the words of our faith and the actions of our lives. However, we cannot be content to leave the matter there. We are called to be doers of the word, practitioners of the gospel we preach.

Integrity is a good word to sum up the desired relationship between our words and our actions, our profession and our practice of the faith. This kind of integrity makes it possible for us to affirm "Do as I say and as I do," not out of self-righteous pride but out of the simple truth that faith's best witness is the doing of Christ's word. For in our doing of that word lies the purpose of God for us and the blessing of God upon us. Amen.

– John Indermark

Hymns
Opening: I Would Be True
Sermon: Jesu, Jesu, Fill Us with Your Love
Closing: Lord, Whose Love through Humble Service

September 9, 2012

15th Sunday after Pentecost (Proper 18)
RC/Pres: 23rd Sunday in Ordinary Time

Lessons

Semi-continuous (SC)	Complementary (C)	Roman Catholic (RC)
Prov 22:1-2, 8-9, 22-23	Isa 35:4-7a	Isa 35:4-7a
Ps 125	Ps 146	Ps 146:7, 8-9a, 9b-10
Jas 2:1-10 (11-13), 14-17	Jas 2:1-10 (11-13), 14-17	Jas 2:1-5
Mk 7:24-37	Mk 7:24-37	Mk 7:31-37

Speaker's Introduction for the Lessons

Lesson 1

Proverbs 22:1-2, 8-9, 22-23 (SC)

This passage from Proverbs reminds us to care for the poor, and in so doing we will be blessed as well. God's concern for those who are poor, disenfranchised, and oppressed is evident throughout scripture.

Isaiah 35:4-7a (C/RC)

The prophet Isaiah serves as God's messenger, telling all to have faith that God will deliver them from affliction. The prophets in Hebrew Scriptures generally comfort the afflicted and afflict the comfortable.

Lesson 2

Psalm 125 (SC)

One of a group of psalms (120-34) called "Songs of Ascents" that are associated with pilgrimages to Jerusalem. The psalmist interestingly calls upon God to do good to those who are good, a reversal of what might be expected.

Psalm 146 (C); Psalm 146:7, 8-9a, 9b-10 (RC)

The psalmist offers praise to God for providing deliverance and justice to those in need. The psalm contrasts the God who may be trusted with earthly rulers "in whom there is no help."

Lesson 3
James 2:1-10 (11-13), 14-17 (SC/C); James 2:1-5 (RC)
James is a series of moral teachings and wisdom sayings directed to Jewish-Christian congregations. Departing from Paul's assertion that salvation is by faith alone, James contends that faith is reflected by one's actions.

Gospel
Mark 7:24-37 (SC/C); Mark 7:31-37 (RC)
The Gospel of Mark includes numerous accounts of Jesus' miraculous healings. Despite Jesus' attempts to remain inconspicuous, people of various origins seek his healing touch and reveal Jesus' ability to heal.

Theme
Jesus calls the church to minister to all in need.

Thought for the Day
The Syrophoenician woman asserts her plea for healing, refusing to be put off even by Jesus. Jesus responds to this outsider's need – would we?

Sermon Summary
Jesus attracted great numbers of people who were at the end of their rope, desperate, needing compassion and love in the worst way. Jesus still attracts such people. If the church would be faithful to Jesus, we must be open to those in desperate need, whatever their need, whoever they are.

Call to Worship
One: O Lord, we come to you seeking healing.
All: Great is your faithfulness.
One: We know our destiny is in your hands.
All: Great is your faithfulness.
One: Our confidence is based on your love and mercy.
All: Great is your faithfulness. Amen.

Pastoral Prayer

Lord Jesus, you are always full of mercy. Through your healing acts, you made your love known to us. You reached across boundaries and reached out to those who were desperate. Help us to come to you in our need, to reach out to you in our pain. Also, help us to bring hurting, desperate people to you so that they might also be blessed by your love. Open our ears, remove our impediments, and feed us as children of God. Amen.

Prayer of Confession

Gracious God, healer of all, despite the witness of your wonders, we find ourselves searching for healing. We deplore our addictions and find ourselves immersed in their powers. We suffer afflictions and continue trying to heal ourselves. We often ignore your healing powers. In our hearts we know that you are the source of all that is good, yet our heads lead us into confusion and doubt. Too often we put our lives in jeopardy forgetting that we, indeed, reap whatever we sow. Now we come to you in humility, begging you to strengthen our faith. Feed us with the crumbs of your goodness that we might resist temptations and avoid what is evil. Restore us and forgive our sins. Help us to rely on you, that we might again delight in your will and walk in your ways. Amen.

Prayer of Dedication of Gifts and Self

Heavenly Provider, we give you thanks and praise for your vigilance over the lives of your people. You have redeemed us from the consequences of our own sin through the gift of your Son, Jesus Christ. Your gift of life eternal prompts us to be grateful in our prayers and generous in our giving. Our hearts abound in thankfulness and our lives reflect your goodness. Use your powers to instill in us the need to give. Amen.

Hymn of the Day
Jesu, Jesu, Fill Us with Your Love

While serving as a missionary to Ghana, Thomas Colvin (born in Glasgow, Scotland, 1925) translated a series of native hymns into English. This simple and spiritually stimulating Ghana folk hymn is one of the most popular of his 24 translations published by the Iona Community in 1968. It speaks of our neighbors as "rich and poor, black and white, near and far." This hymn illustrates Christ's example of true servanthood. Colvin suggests that a variety of available percussion instruments be used with the congregation's singing of this tune. The ideal tempo will not be too slow.

Children's Time: Jesus Heals

Invite the children to close their eyes and listen carefully. Ask: What can you hear? Listen once more, what else can you hear?

Have some conversation about the sense of hearing. What kinds of things do you hear everyday? Being sensitive to those who are hearing impaired, ask the children to imagine what it would be like if their ears didn't work well. How would life be different? Comment that the Bible story today is about a man who could not hear anything at all.

Tell the story about Jesus healing the man who was deaf and mute in Mark 7:31-37. Comment that the man was healed because some people asked Jesus to help. Explain that these people had heard many stories about Jesus and knew he could heal with just a touch or a word.

Comment that just like the people who brought the man to Jesus, we can ask Jesus to help those we know who are sick. We do this through prayer.

Ask the children to think about the people they know who are sick. Pray, holding up those who need God's healing touch in their lives.

The Sermon: Good News for the Desperate
Scripture: Mark 7:24-37

The account of the healing of the Gentile woman's daughter has parallels in both Matthew and Mark. In Mark's Gospel, the woman at the center of the account is called a Syrophoenician woman. In Matthew's Gospel she is called a Canaanite woman, but it is the same woman.

Here is the situation: Jesus is operating just beyond the borders of his own land, on one of those very infrequent occasions when he does get outside of the limits of Israel. No sooner has he gotten over the border into a land not populated principally by Jews, those people who do not observe the laws of Judaism, when he is confronted by an unhappy parent. Unhappy is too soft a word for this woman's condition. She is desperate.

This mother's daughter is grievously vexed with a demon. That means some physical and psychological aberrations affects this girl. We don't know what it is, but it was grievous. And she is vexed, and the mother is tormented.

The woman comes to Jesus. The way she addresses him is very interesting, because it is very formal. Hardly ever in the New Testament account do we find such formality used. How do we account for the woman saying, "Have mercy on me, Lord, Son of David" (Mt 15:22). His own disciples call him "Master," less frequently "Lord," sometimes "Rabbi." But this woman, being an outsider, not knowing, as it were, what the ground rules were, gives him the whole works.

Remember, she is an outsider and she knows it. She needs help in the worst kind of way, so she comes to Jesus in utter supplication. When I go to the traffic court to see if there's any way to get my speeding fine lessened, I'm all, "Judge, I mean, Your Honor, Your Grace, Your Royal Highness . . . " I'm desperate to flatter the judge in the hope that this will help me get what I want out of him. So the woman says, "Have mercy on me, Lord, Son of David" (Mt 15:22). And he answers her not a word.

I know the usual interpretation: Jesus is testing this woman's faith. But I don't really find that a very satisfying explanation. I can't think of a time in the New Testament when Jesus puts people's faith to some sort of test. Jesus doesn't play with people in need, testing them to see how far he can push them until they go over the edge. And yet, there it is: Jesus doesn't acknowledge or answer her.

Not only does Jesus not answer her, but when she pesters the disciples to needle him for an answer, Jesus finally comes back with an answer worse than silence. He says, "I was sent only to the lost sheep of the house of Israel" (Matt 15:24). In other words, "Sorry, you don't fit into my plans for the day. You are not a member of the right club. I am way out here, beyond the borders. You are not an Israelite. You are an outsider, a nonbeliever."

But this woman is not to be put off too easily. And finally Jesus speaks to her, well not really to her, but speaks about her. Jesus says, "It is not fair to take the children's food and throw it to dogs" (Mk 7:27). That would probably be taken as an insult anywhere, but in that part of the world, it is particularly tough language.

"Dog," in that part of the world, is not a statement about our cute, cuddly house pets. "Dog" means those disgusting scavengers that live in the streets, living off garbage. Nevertheless, Jesus says, "it is not fair to take the children's food and throw it to the dogs."

This woman is not to be put off so easily. She comes right back at Jesus. She is resilient, pushy, and determined to get a hearing. She says, "In our houses, even the little puppies that scramble around on the beaten floors, even they can have the crumbs that fall off the family table." And now Jesus marvels, as he said to those about him, "I have not seen such faith – no, not in Israel."

He doesn't say, "I haven't seen such desperation, and I've seen a lot of needy people, in Israel or anywhere else." He says, "I haven't seen this kind of faith, even in Israel." Faith. The problem with this woman is that she is not of the faith; that is, she is an outsider. She knows nothing of the beliefs and traditions of Israel. Yet Jesus says that she is a paragon of virtue.

How does she move from no faith, outside of faith, to be recognized by Jesus as full of faith?

We say so casually, "I follow the Christian faith," or "I have faith in Jesus." By that we usually mean something like we adhere to Christian beliefs, that we model our lives on certain Christlike precepts.

But this woman has done none of that. She has simply been desperate, at the end of her rope, utterly without hope – unless Jesus reaches out to her. We have the feeling that in that moment when she presses in upon Jesus, and he turns toward her, this is the center of faith. When human need becomes desperate, heated, white-hot and frantic, when human need and divine compassion meet, this is faith.

We church-type people usually don't think of faith in that way. We say things like, "In order to have faith, you must believe '1, 2, 3.'" We have all kinds of hurdles and requirements: intellectual, creedal, historical, ecclesiological, sometimes even aesthetic and sociological. We are the guardians of faith, the ones who let everyone know what has to be done in order to be certified as having faith.

Theology is fine. Knowledge of biblical precepts is essential. Yes, but faith is also a matter of somebody being desperate enough to reach out, and perceptive enough to reach toward Jesus. Some of you know that deep faith because you have come to Jesus, not for a pleasant discussion of spiritual matters, but rather because you needed a miracle in the worst sort of way.

Maybe the problem with too many of us is that we are fairly well fixed, not too miserable, certainly not desperate. But there is something about Jesus that is close company with the desperate. She doesn't know much about religion. All she can say is, "Please, help." And then it happens.

This woman moves from stilted, formal address to being shoved forward by the tough words of Jesus. She gets the guts to blurt out, "Please, help." And then it happens.

She makes a leap of faith, leaping out of her desperation, into the embrace of Jesus. Her daughter is saved. Anything less than her leap, her desperately hopeful, faithful leap, is less than the fullness of faith. If you're not too desperate right now, just file this away until later. Someday, life being what it is, you'll be in the place of this gutsy, faithful woman. Remember this story.

And someday, maybe today, this Sunday, there are folk who are in church, with Jesus, because they need a miracle in the worst sort of way. They may not have all our answers, know all that we know, but today's Gospel suggests that they are close to the heart of Jesus. Their presence here is a reminder of the seriousness, the resourcefulness, the riskiness of the love of Jesus.

The woman says, Lord, never mind about the puppies or the fact that I am a heathen. My daughter is sick, help. And Jesus says, "This is the beginning place, this is why I have come into the world." It may not be the end of a journey with Jesus, but this is where the journey begins.

– William H. Willimon

Hymns
Opening: Seek Ye First
Sermon: Healer of Our Every Ill
Closing: Go My Children, with My Blessing

September 16, 2012

16th Sunday after Pentecost (Proper 19)
RC/Pres: 24th Sunday in Ordinary Time

Lessons

Semi-continuous (SC)	Complementary (C)	Roman Catholic (RC)
Prov 1:20-33 or Wis 7:26—8:1	Isa 50:4-9a	Isa 50:4-9a
Ps 19	Ps 116:1-8	Ps 116:1-2, 3-4, 5-6, 8-9
Jas 3:1-12	Jas 3:1-12	Jas 2:14-18
Mk 8:27-38	Mk 8:27-38	Mk 8:27-35

Speaker's Introduction for the Lessons
Lesson 1
Proverbs 1:20-33 (SC)

The book of Proverbs gives insights on coping with life. These moral and religious instructions, written primarily for Jewish youth, speak as a prophet making strong threats against those who do not listen.

Isaiah 50:4-9 (C/RC)

The servant brings a word of comfort to the weary Israelites. With a strong emphasis on obedience, the servant is confident of God's support and vindication.

Lesson 2
Psalm 19 (SC)

The psalmist combines praise of God's glory in creation and the gift of Torah, along with seeking God's forgiveness and a closing petition for God to find the psalmist's words and thoughts acceptable.

Psalm 116:1-8 (C); Psalm 116:1-2, 3-4, 5-6, 8-9 (RC)

The psalmist offers thanksgiving for deliverance from some unidentified crisis that threatened death and a closing ascription of praise to God's mercy and graciousness.

Lesson 3

James 3:1-12 (SC/C)

James emphasizes the need for us to "tame the tongue," which he names a "restless evil."

James 2:14-18 (RC)

While the writings of Paul emphasize the importance of faith, James stresses the importance of works, which should emanate from faith. Proclaiming that God shows no partiality, James stresses the need for impartiality among us.

Gospel

Mark 8:27-38 (SC/C/RC)

What begins as an ordinary journey for the disciples moves to a startling revelation. Jesus' provocative question, "Who do you say that I am?" causes each of us to consider our own answer to this important question.

Theme

Jesus speaks openly about what it means to follow him.

Thought for the Day

"Those who want to save their life will lose it, and those who lose their life for my sake, and for the sake of the gospel, will save it" (Mk 8:35).

Sermon Summary

Jesus speaks openly to his disciples and his followers regarding what is in store for him, as well as what it means to be a disciple of Jesus Christ.

Call to Worship

One: We have come here today to worship the One who has saved us from our sins.

All: "You are the Messiah," Peter answered.

One: We thank you, Jesus!

All: "You are the Messiah," Peter answered.

One: We praise your name.

All: **"You are the Messiah," Peter answered.**
One: Our hope rests in you, Jesus.
All: **"You are the Messiah," Peter answered.**
One: Jesus, you have called us to follow you.
All: **"You are the Messiah," we answer.**

Pastoral Prayer

Gracious God, you have shown us in Christ's example what it means to deny ourselves and take up your cross. Thank you for bringing about our salvation. You are the way, the truth, and the life for all. Show us, then, the way you would have us travel as your disciples. Ground us in your truth, and keep us from mistaking it with our opinions, religious or political or otherwise. Remind us that life in you grows not out of fear but out of trust. In Christ you came to show us the true way of living. In Christ you embodied the way of living truth. And that is why we come to you, O God, for there is no one else in whom life and truth abide for all time to come. In Jesus Christ. Amen.

Prayer of Confession

As we come before you, O Christ, we want to speak confidently that you are the Messiah. We give you thanks and praise that through the power of the Holy Spirit you give us the courage to speak boldly. Words of proclamation may come to our lips, but so often our actions lack consistency with our speech. We confess that we are fearful of what it means to follow you. We regret our tendency to put ourselves ahead of others. We desire to repent, but we know that true repentance comes with a cost we'd rather avoid. We beg your forgiveness for our reluctance to follow. Have mercy on us. Give us confidence in you and make us willing and eager to follow you regardless of the cost. Amen.

Prayer of Dedication of Gifts and Self

O God, you have given us life eternal.
    What may we offer in return?
O God, you sustain us through the bounty of the earth.
    What may we offer in return?

O God, you have given us the Holy Spirit as a comforter.
What may we offer in return?
O God, you have provided for every one of our needs.
What may we offer in return?
Strengthen us to offer ourselves as a thank-offering. Amen.

Hymn of the Day
New Every Morning
Written by British Anglican pastor John Keble, this hymn is drawn from
the opening 16-verse poem of his famous work *The Christian Year,* first
published in 1827. While emphasis is given, particularly in stanza five,
on the denying of self to follow Christ (Mk 8:34), the hymn strongly
highlights the freshness of God's daily blessings. Stanzas one and two are
reminiscent of Lamentations 3:22-23: "The steadfast love of the Lord
never ceases . . . they are new every morning." The tune MELCOMBE has
been generally associated with the hymn since 1861.

Children's Time: Who Am I?
Invite the children to play "Who am I?" Choose someone from the congregation that the children would know. Give a few clues, such as "I play
the organ and I have brown hair – who am I?" Invite the children to guess
the identity of the mystery person.

Comment that in the Bible story today Jesus wasn't playing a guessing
game, but he did ask his disciples a similar question, "Who do people
say that I am?" Ask the children to tell how they would describe Jesus to
someone else.

Explain that Jesus' friends had been listening to what the people had
been saying about Jesus. Many people thought that Jesus was Elijah, or
one of the other prophets, come back to life. Some people thought Jesus
might be John the Baptist in disguise! Jesus then asked his disciples, "Who
do you say that I am?" Invite the children to guess what the disciples said.

Paraphrase Peter's response in verse 29. Peter knew that Jesus was sent
from God to tell of God's love for everyone. Comment that this is a great
way to describe Jesus.

The Sermon: Speaking Openly
Scripture: Mark 8:27-38

"How am I doing?" he asked hesitantly. I panicked. I knew what he was asking. I knew he was looking for reassurance. But I could see the quality of his work was lacking. What was I to say – "It could be better"; "Fine"; "OK."? Speaking openly requires not only precision in language and some degree of courage; it also requires speaking truth.

Jesus spoke openly whether he was speaking to the Pharisees or a Gentile, his enemies or his closest friends. And Jesus spoke openly and plainly to his disciples.

When Jesus began to speak openly with his disciples about what was to come, they were unable to accept his words. They probably were stunned. Suffering? Rejection? And be killed? No way!

"This simply could not be," they may have reasoned. "There must be some mistake. We must have heard incorrectly." Their concept of a messiah did not include suffering, rejection, and murder. Nothing could be more foreign to their understanding.

In disbelief, Peter, speaking for the rest of the disciples, pulled Jesus aside and began to reprimand him. For three years, these disciples had witnessed miracle upon miracle. They had seen Jesus give sight to the blind and hearing to the deaf. They had witnessed the exorcism of demons, the forgiveness of sins, the calming of the sea, the raising of the dead. They had observed the compassion of this man, even when he was exhausted. They had seen Jesus expose the hypocrisy of the Pharisees and cure the lepers. Surely this man was the one of whom the prophets spoke. Suffering? Rejection? Killed? No way!

Perhaps some doubt crept into their thinking at this point: "Have we followed the wrong one? Have we left our homes and families and jobs to follow someone who isn't what we thought?"

The degree of Peter's protest demonstrates how Jesus' teaching about his mission and his fate represented a new way of thinking. A new direction in the way of Jesus was being forged. A new view of discipleship was required.

We all understand how ambiguous messages can be misunderstood. But when someone speaks openly and directly as Jesus did here, there is little room for misunderstanding. The problem is that, despite their relationship with Jesus, the disciples did not understand what Jesus was really about. Somehow they had missed the point.

Of course, the disciples had a preconception of what a messiah should be. The scriptures they had heard from their childhood told them of one who would be God's chosen one, one in whom God delighted. This one would bring forth justice and blot out their sins. This one would open the eyes of the blind and redeem the lost. Had they not witnessed all this in Jesus? Of course they had. The disciples could repeat the prophecies of Isaiah and the others by heart.

Is not this the fast that I choose:
to loose the bonds of injustice,
to undo the thongs of the yoke,
to let the oppressed go free,
and to break every yoke?
Is it not to share your bread with the hungry,
and bring the homeless poor into your house;
when you see the naked, to cover them,
and not to hide yourself from your own kin? (Isa 58:6-7)

"Yes," the disciples would say to one another. "We have seen these things taking place." But did they miss the prophecies of Isaiah and the others who spoke of one who would be despised and rejected; one who would be oppressed and afflicted; one who would be wounded for our transgressions, crushed for our iniquities; a man of suffering and acquainted with grief? Did they miss that the messiah would enter Jerusalem, "humble and riding on a donkey" (Zech 9:9)?

The disciples' concept of Jesus' identity and mission was much like the crowd that followed Jesus. Despite the clarity with which Jesus spoke, the disciples just didn't get it.

What do you think the atmosphere in that room was like as Jesus began to expound on what the future would hold? I imagine Peter's face must have paled, his composure evaporated. Peter must have felt like a pebble instead of a rock. Peter's response caused a response in Jesus that must have cut deeply into the disciples: "Get behind me, Satan! For you are setting your mind not on divine things but on human things" (Mk 8:33).

From there Jesus lays it on the line quite openly about what it takes to be one of his disciples. "Those who want to save their life will lose it, and those who lose their life for my sake, and for the sake of the gospel, will save it" (Mk 8:35). It is a three-point plan. Deny yourselves. Take up your cross. Follow me.

Unlike the disciples, some of the religious leaders of his day understood. There were elders who understood and fumed. There were priests who understood and spit on the ground. There were scribes who understood and shouted, "Blasphemy!" Some grasped his call and knew his mission – though in opposition. And the truth of Jesus' words was so threatening to the religious and political powers of that time that they decided to kill him. That is just what they did. Fulfilling what the prophets had forecast, they looted his clothes, mocked his name, and crucified him.

This leaves us to decide just as the disciples and the crowds had to decide. Jesus asks each one of us, "Who do you say that I am?" The answer and what happens next is up to you and to me.

– Rod Broding

Hymns
Opening: Rise, Shine, You People
Sermon: Praise and Thanksgiving
Closing: Now Thank We All Our God

September 23, 2012

17th Sunday after Pentecost (Proper 20)
RC/Pres: 25th Sunday in Ordinary Time

Lessons

Semi-continuous (SC)	Complementary (C)	Roman Catholic (RC)
Prov 31:10-31	Jer 11:18-20 or Wis 1:16–2:1, 11-22	Wis 2:12, 17-20
Ps 1	Ps 54	Ps 54:3-4, 5, 6-8
Jas 3:13—4:3, 7-8a	Jas 3:13—4:3, 7-8a	Jas 3:16—4:3
Mark 9:30-37	Mark 9:30-37	Mark 9:30-37

Speaker's Introduction for the Lessons
Lesson 1
Proverbs 31:10-31 (SC)

> This wife, the personification of wisdom, is lauded as one who demonstrates a series of worthwhile characteristics. Among other virtues, she "opens her hand to the poor and reaches out her hands to the needy."

Jeremiah 11:18-20 (C)

> This is the first of Jeremiah's six personal laments and reflects Jeremiah's deep conviction to serve God.

Wisdom of Solomon 2:12, 17-20 (RC)

> Called a "covenant of death," these words foretell what tests and traps await the Righteous One who is to come.

Lesson 2
Psalm 1 (SC)

> This wisdom psalm reflects upon the endurance of those who delight and meditate on Torah and the transiency of the wicked. Some take this psalm and Psalm 2 as summaries of the psalter's chief themes.

Psalm 54 (C); Psalm 54:3-4, 5, 6-8 (RC)

> The psalmist prays for his own deliverance along with the destruction of his enemies.

Lesson 3
James 3:13—4:3, 7-8a (SC/C); James 3:16—4:3 (RC)

James expands the meaning of wisdom, culminating in the proclamation that true wisdom is a gift from God. A series of admonitions encourages us to resist worldly wisdoms and draw closer to God.

Gospel
Mark 9:30-37 (SC/C/RC)

After hearing Jesus' teaching about what is to come, the disciples are concerned about who is the greatest among themselves. Taking a child in his arms, Jesus reminds all that greatness is accomplished through serving.

Theme

"Whoever wants to be first must be last of all and servant of all" (Mk 9:35).

Thought for the Day

In God's eyes, our greatness is determined by our willingness to serve those considered by humankind as the least.

Sermon Summary

Jesus calls his followers to live the life of a servant, to show kindness and hospitality to the lowly and the outcast. In doing so, they will not only discover the true path to greatness but will also be drawn more intimately into the life and presence of Christ.

Call to Worship

One: Like trees planted by streams of water are those who take God seriously.

All: Like chaff driven by wind are those who think they are the center of the universe.

One: So take delight in the ways and words of God.

All: And take flight from those who live as if the world is beholden to them.

Pastoral Prayer

Holy God, we give you thanks and praise for your word. We thank you for the marvels of creation, and for the gift of children. Remind us that greatness lies not in puffing ourselves up and casting large shadows that have the effect more to chill than to impress. Rather, restore in us the embrace of greatness in servanthood, in acts not of self-congratulation but hospitality to those who come our way, young and old, rich and poor, gay and straight, all your children, all our sisters and brothers. This we pray in the name of the Child who was and is the Christ. Amen

Prayer of Confession

O God, we ask your forgiveness for all of the ambitions, selfishness, and envy that are still a part of your church. In Jesus Christ, you poured out your life on behalf of the world, and we are worried about parking and pews and who gets to use the church's tea set. Refresh us, O God, with a vision of a life so caught up in your purposes that we become beacons of hospitality, welcoming others as you have welcomed us. Give to us, O God, what we cannot give to ourselves: the confidence of those who know in our hearts that we belong to you. Then, and only then, can we lose the protectiveness of self, open ourselves to others, and enact the kindness of Christ in the world. We pray this prayer in the name of Jesus Christ, who held children tenderly in his arms, even children like us. Amen.

Prayer of Dedication of Gifts and Self

Almighty God, thank you for your goodness and lovingkindness, given to us and to all whom you have made. Accept our gifts this day. Make us more aware of your mercies so that we praise you with our lips and also with our works. Lead us in paths of holiness and righteousness all of our days. Amen.

Hymn of the Day
The Church of Christ in Every Age

The late Fred Pratt Green (1903-2000) is considered by some to be the most important hymn writer of Methodism since Charles Wesley. Although a British Methodist pastor, Green's influence as a hymn writer has gone far beyond the walls of Methodism. Most recent hymnals in North America include his hymns. This hymn, written in 1969, calls the church to be an agent of change and reconciliation in the world. It reminds us that we, as the church, "have no mission but to serve in full obedience to our Lord." Perhaps using an already familiar LM hymn tune for the singing of the hymn will facilitate its introduction.

Children's Time: Who Is the Greatest?

(Bring some pictures of some well-known cartoon superheroes. Place the pictures on a sheet of newsprint.)
Converse with the children about the characters and invite some discussion about which one is the greatest and why. Write down the words the children mention such as strongest, fastest, and bravest. If there is disagreement, explain that arguments about who is the greatest are not unusual.

Retell the story of the disciples' argument in Mark 9:33-34. You might use your imagination to present some of the arguments the disciples could have used to defend their position: "I met Jesus first" or "I walked on the water with Jesus."

Mention that when Jesus heard what his friends had been quarreling about, he said something very surprising. Paraphrase verse 35. You may have to explain that a servant is someone who takes care of the needs of others.

Invite the children to name some ways to serve others at home, at school, or at church. Affirm their ideas and comment that every time we serve someone else, we are a hero in God's eyes, and that makes us great.

Pray with the children, asking God to help you as you learn to serve others.

The Sermon: Why a Child?
Scripture: Mark 9:30-37

A good question to ponder about our passage of scripture is this: Why did Jesus place a child in the midst of his disciples? On other occasions, when Jesus wanted to teach something, he told a parable, or held up a coin, or pointed to the birds of the air and the lilies of the field. But this time he took a child and held him in his arms. Why a child?

One possibility is that a child – an innocent child – formed a most fitting contrast to the less-than-innocent attitude of the disciples. Jesus has just announced his passion, that before there is to be any victory, before

70

there can be resurrection, there must be death: "The Son of Man is to be betrayed . . . killed" (Mk 9:31). In sum, Jesus has just proclaimed that his own life involves suffering and the supreme act of sacrifice, and the astounding response of the disciples is to spend the rest of the day sauntering down the road to Capernaum discussing which one of them will turn out to be "most valuable player." Jesus embodies sacrifice; they jockey for position. Jesus announces his own suffering; they argue over reserved parking spaces and who gets to ride first class. Jesus has called them to "deny themselves and take up their crosses," too, but they have instead affirmed themselves and taken up not a cross but the old sandbox debate, "I'm better than you." The disciples are so grotesquely out of line, so in violation of all that Jesus is calling them to do that they need a shocking object lesson. "Here is a child, free of all your adult posturing, manipulation, and finagling," Jesus is perhaps saying. "Take this as an example."

The problem with this view, however, is that Jesus does not actually present the child as an example. In a similar story in the Gospel of Matthew, Jesus does hold up a child as an example: "Whoever becomes humble like this child is the greatest in the kingdom of heaven" (Mt 18:4). But this is Mark, not Matthew, and, as one commentator has observed, "[In Mark] the point lies not in the child's attitude, but in the attitude of others toward him" (Nineham, *Saint Mark,* p. 252).

If the child is not an example for the disciples to imitate, then there must be some other reason why Jesus placed a child in the disciples' midst. Maybe what Jesus is doing is teaching kindness to the vulnerable and innocent. After all, Jesus tells the disciples that the true path to greatness is servanthood (Mk 9:35), and what better way to exhibit servanthood than to care for children, for those who can in no way repay their efforts?

This does move us somewhat closer to the truth of this passage. In the third-century document on church life and order called *Didascalia,* there arises a question about what should happen if a needy stranger should arrive at the church unexpectedly and there is no room for him at the table. The answer is surprising:

> If a destitute man or woman, either a local person or a traveler, arrives unexpectedly, especially one of older years, and there is no place, you, bishop, make such a place with all your heart, even if you yourself should sit on the ground, that you may not show favoritism among human beings, but that your ministry may be pleasing before God (quoted in Gordon Lathrop's *Holy Things).*

In other words, the bishop, the leader, the greatest in the community must sit on the ground if necessary because greatness in kingdom terms is defined not by status or power but by service. So maybe that is why Jesus placed a child in the midst of his disciples, in order to teach them to serve those who are not strong enough to repay them.

But even this insight does not fully plumb the depth of Jesus' action. Children in Jesus' day were not just needy, they were also of low social status. Children in Jesus' day were not Gerber babies, lovely, sweet, and cuddly. They were worth far less to society than adults. Bruce J. Malina and Richard L. Rohrbaugh put it bluntly:

> Childhood in antiquity was a time of terror. Infant mortality rates sometimes reached 30 percent. Another 30 percent of live births were dead by age six, and 60 percent were gone by age sixteen. Children always suffered first from famine, war disease, and dislocation...
>
> Children had little status within the community or family. A minor child was on par with a slave, and only after reaching maturity was he/she a free person who could inherit the family estate. The term `child/children' could be used as a serious insult . . . *(Social Science Commentary on the Synoptic Gospels).*

This now gets us close to the heart of Jesus' action. When Jesus placed a child in their midst, even held the child in his arms, it was not that the child was a cuddly, lovable creature in need of kindness. Rather, it was precisely that the child was unlovable, undesirable, socially unfit.

When John Lewis, a member of Congress from Georgia and civil rights worker who was known as the marcher most often beaten by hostile whites, was asked how he developed his great compassion for the poor and outcast, he pointed to an experience in his childhood. Like many other blacks in the rural South, he was raised in poverty on a farm with no plumbing or electricity in a shack with a dirt yard. His parents put him in charge of the family's chickens, and it was not long before John, a gentle person, was advocating for the chickens, trying to persuade his parents not to kill them for food. He said,

> They seemed so defenseless . . . There was a subtle grace and dignity in every movement they made, at least through my eyes. But no one else saw them that way. To my parents, brothers and sisters, the chickens were just about the lowest form of life on the farm – stupid, smelly, nuisances, awkward, comical birds good for nothing but laying eggs and providing meat for the table. Maybe it was that outcast status, the

very fact that those chickens were so forsaken by everyone else, that drew me to them as well. I felt as if I had been trusted to care for God's chosen creatures (John Lewis and Michael D'Orso, *Walking with the Wind*).

Indeed, when Jesus took a child and placed him in the midst of the disciples, he was placing there "just about the lowest form of life on the farm." Children were weak and replaceable, powerless and worth little. In fact, they were important to no one – to no one except Jesus. Jesus not only placed the child in the middle of his company of disciples, in the midst of his own chosen community, he took the child tenderly in his arms. What Jesus was teaching is not just kindness, but kindness directed toward those who never experience the kindness of the world; not just tenderness, but tenderness toward those who never feel a loving touch; not just hospitality, but a wide welcome toward those for whom all other doors are slammed shut.

But there is one more truth to be discerned, one more profound surprise in Jesus' action. When followers of Jesus stop wrangling among themselves about status long enough to follow their servant master, when followers of Jesus pick up their own crosses and show hospitality and kind-ness to the unlovely and powerless and outcast of the world, they discover that they have not only received a stranger but that they have also received Jesus Christ himself. "Whoever welcomes one such child in my name wel-comes me, and . . . the one who sent me" (9:37). In the words of a song sung by the Sojourners community:

Is there room in this city for the lowly and the poor?
Is there room in this city for the homeless and their friends?
Is there room in this city for the broken little ones?
Well, come in, Jesus Child. We want to make you some room.

–Thomas G. Long

Hymns
Opening: God of Grace and God of Glory
Sermon: Be Thou My Vision
Closing: Son of God, Eternal Savior

September 30, 2012

18th Sunday after Pentecost (Proper 21)
RC/Pres: 26th Sunday in Ordinary Time

Lessons

Semi-continuous (SC)	Complementary (C)	Roman Catholic (RC)
Esth 7:1-6, 9-10; 9:20-22	Num 11:4-6, 10-16, 24-29	Num 11:25-29
Ps 124	Ps 19:7-14	Ps 19:8, 10, 12-13, 14
Jas 5:13-20	Jas 5:13-20	Jas 5:1-6
Mk 9:38-50	Mk 9:38-50	Mk 9:38-43, 45, 47-48

Speaker's Introduction for the Lessons
Lesson 1
Esther 7:1-6, 9-10; 9:20-22 (SC)

Esther demonstrates in story form the certainty of how justice can retaliate against oppression and the need for the oppressed to act with confidence and shrewdness. Here, the wicked leader Haman receives his deserved reward.

Numbers 11:4-6, 10-16, 24-29 (C); Numbers 11:25-29 (RC)

Despite the Israelite's discouragement, God's Spirit came upon 70 of the elders as well as two others who remained in the camp.

Lesson 2
Psalm 124 (SC)

The psalmist offers a joyous thanksgiving for God's deliverance of the whole community that bids Israel to celebrate the humbling truth that without God the end would have been vastly different.

Psalm 19:7-14 (C); Psalm 19:8, 10, 12-13, 14 (RC)

The psalmist praises the Torah (law) of God in humility that seeks God's acceptance of the words and meditation that flow out from us.

Lesson 3

James 5:13-20 (SC/C)

The practical nature of this letter ends with a series of pastoral concerns, culminating in the assertion that God's truth leads to righteousness.

James 5:1-6 (RC);

These verses contrast godliness with worldliness and demonstrate the futility of putting one's own faith and emphasis in the things of this world.

Gospel

Mark 9:38-50 (SC/C); Mark 9:38-43, 45, 47-48 (RC)

We are forewarned that the seriousness of our sin cannot be ignored without risk of eternal punishment. We are encouraged to work for others for the good of the kingdom.

Theme

Do not discourage the good that is done by those outside the church.

Thought for the Day

Much good is accomplished in this world by those who claim no allegiance to Jesus Christ.

Sermon Summary

The stark words of Jesus warn us of the gravity of our sin. We are not called to judge others in their efforts to do good, but rather join them in ministry – remembering that "whoever is not against us is for us" (Mk 9:40).

Call to Worship

One: Your word, O God, revives the soul.
All: The law of God is perfect.
One: You make wise the simple.
All: The decrees of the Holy One are sure.
One: You enlighten our eyes.

All: The commandment of God is sure.
One: The ordinances of the Sovereign One are true and righteous.
All: More to be desired are they than gold.

Pastoral Prayer

Gracious God, source of all goodness and mercy, we give you thanks for your care and keeping. Continue to bestow on us your love and devotion. Strengthen your church that we might be witnesses of your glory by the good that others see in us. Remind us, O God, that we are not the only providers of good in the world. Help us to look with favor upon other helpers and offer assistance where it is desired and needed. Keep us from being prideful of our works, but mindful that all we have is a gift from you. Teach us to share. In the name of Jesus Christ we pray. Amen.

Prayer of Confession

You, O Christ, are the vine; we are but branches. We have difficulty remembering that. You, O Christ, are the cornerstone; we are but bricks. We often forget that, too. You, O Christ, are perfect and whole; we are woefully incomplete. So, in our helplessness and weakness, we cast ourselves upon the altar of your mercy. Turn our inadequacies into powers that will benefit others, and motivate us to care for your environment. Support our efforts and the efforts of others to relieve misery in the world and keep our world safe from destruction. Replace our tendency to destroy with a desire to build. Transform us from haters into healers. In your name, we pray. Amen.

Prayer of Dedication of Gifts and Self

Mighty Creator, you have made all that exists. You have blessed us beyond measure. And so, we offer ourselves to your service and dedicate our lives to the care and redemption of all you have made. We return to you this portion of what you have first given us. Receive our gifts of time, talent, and treasure for the sake of Christ, who offered himself for us. Amen.

Hymn of the Day
Where Cross the Crowded Ways of Life

Written by American Methodist pastor Frank Mason North in 1903, this American hymn is one of the earliest social gospel hymns. It promotes Jesus' teaching to offer the cup of living water to all and to honor all who do so in his name. The author's long ministry in New York City opened his eyes to situations of social neglect, including the many ways that human needs and civil rights can be ignored. These images enabled him to provide us with a powerful expression of Christian concern that may be applied in our time.

Children's Time: Like Salt

(Bring some salted and unsalted crackers. Be mindful of possible food allergies) Ask the children (and keep an eye for signals from their parents) if any of them are allergic to salt. Invite those who are not to try both kinds of crackers, while offering those who may be allergic double shares of the unsalted crackers.

Talk about the difference between the two. While they are eating, have some conversation about salt: When do you use salt in your family?

Talk about some of the ways in which salt is used to make our lives better. For example: Salt is used to prevent food from spoiling. It is used in factories to help make paper and plastic. It is used in the process of making brightly colored fabrics. Admire some of the colors in the children's clothes, noting that without salt those beautiful colors would just rinse away in the washing machine.

Explain that in our Bible reading today, Jesus said that we should be like salt in the world. As followers of Jesus we can add the flavor of God's love to our world and make it a better place for everyone to live. What kinds of things could our church family do to share God's love and help others?

Pray with the children, asking for help as you share God's love this week.

The Sermon: A Cup of Cold Water
Scripture: Mark 9:38-50

"It is better for you to enter life maimed . . ." (Mk 9:43). Shocking words. These dire warnings of Jesus shock us. This blunt and devastating language helps us recognize Jesus' hatred of sin. Now, obviously this hand chopping, eye plucking, and foot severing would never work, if for no other reason than that we don't have enough body parts to keep up with "missing of the mark," as some interpret the literal meaning of one of the New Testament's key words for sin. Besides, after all this dismembering, we'd still have our thoughts and tongue to control. And, as far as I can determine, we haven't done too well on that count either. No, do not take these words of Jesus as literal commands, but view them as a way to see ourselves for what we really are – sinners in need of redemption. In his love for us, Jesus wants us to see the ramification of our acts, thoughts, and attitudes.

Our destination should not be hell, but heaven. In fact, in times of biblical antiquity, hell was never unanimously believed to be a place or state of eternal punishment. It was often regarded as the necessary impasse of the soul when it had to reckon with its misdeeds and rebellion. While nearly every religion believes in the existence of a hell, not every religion considers hell to be a place of punishment. For some it is a form of purgation, a process of purification. Hell is universally described as "fire" because fire cleanses, and fire is painful. Pain and purification are always linked together.

God does not desire that we perish, but that "everyone . . . be saved and . . . come to the knowledge of the truth" (1 Tim 2:4). Our problem is that we insist on our own way instead of God's. That was the problem with John in our text today. John was so sure that any exorcism had to be done by Jesus or the disciples that John stopped this unknown exorcist because he didn't belong to "the group." When John told Jesus what he had done, Jesus' response was a surprise.

"Do not stop him" Jesus commanded, "for no one who does a deed of power in my name will be able soon afterward to speak evil of me" (Mk 9:39). Then Jesus announces, "Whoever is not against us is for us" (9:40). Whoever is not against us is for us! Exclusivity among his followers was something Jesus could not tolerate. The disciples tried to define and limit those who could work so that God's will might be done. The lesson here is that we should not build barriers around those who can do God's work. From Jesus, it is obvious that it matters more that the work gets done than who does it.

We can see a similar self-centeredness in the church today. Egos abound – sometimes among denominations; sometimes among synods or conferences or parishes; sometimes among or within congregations. Who is going to get the credit? Who gets the final say? Jesus says that "who" is not the issue. The issue is that the job gets done. Someone has said that when no one is concerned about who gets the credit, a lot can be accomplished.

God works within the church; God also works outside the church. Everyone can be a worker in the kingdom of God. For "whoever is not against us is for us."

All the world is God's creation. "The earth is the Lord's and all that is in it," the psalmist proclaims (Ps 24:1). Let's not limit the work that God desires. As the hymn "There's a Wideness in God's Mercy" declares, "For the love of God is broader than the measures of our mind."

It is easy for us to confuse the means with the end. It is the end that should determine the means and those who work toward that goal. The churches' approval is nonessential. What matters is that God's will gets done. We are not to be obstructionists or obstacles to that endeavor but partners in it.

The church has no monopoly on God's grace or on God's will. In addition to sanctifying the work of God by all who labor on God's behalf, we are obligated to accept those who wish to work with us. If all sinners are not welcome in the church, then none of us belong. And, who among us is called to be a judge of that? Whom do we stop at the door? To whom do we say, "You don't belong here"?

The wonderful news is that acceptance of others does not dilute our own faith. Jesus made it clear that it is not our task to "separate the weeds from the wheat." Who among us is qualified or even able to tell the difference? (I have enough difficulty in my garden doing that!) God the creator has made us all. Claim that. Ponder that. Rest in that.

More wonderful news is that we are not obligated or limited to doing only "big" works. Our call is not to eliminate single-handedly all the world's poverty or injustices or illnesses. We are called to "bloom where we are planted." We are to do "mustard seeds'" worth of good. Every little bit helps. Even an action as small as a cup of cold water given to one who thirsts is remembered. Jesus tells us that when we do a good work to another, we do the kindness to him.

So, we don't judge. We minister. And we welcome those who may not be part of us. We join together in our efforts to do whatever we can to fulfill the mission Jesus gave us. We work hand in hand offering our energy, our time, and our possessions, even a cup of cold water. Amen.

– Rod Broding

Hymns
Opening: I, the Lord of Sea and Sky
Sermon: We Are All One in Mission
Closing: There's a Wideness in God's Mercy

October 7, 2012

19th Sunday after Pentecost (Proper 22)
RC/Pres: 27th Sunday in Ordinary Time

Lessons

Semi-continuous (SC)	Complementary (C)	Roman Catholic (RC)
Job 1:1; 2:1-10	Gen 2:18-24	Gen 2:18-24
Ps 26	Ps 8	Ps 128:1-2, 3, 4-5, 6
Heb 1:1-4; 2:5-12	Heb 1:1-4; 2:5-12	Heb 2:9-11
Mk 10:2-16	Mk 10:2-16	Mk 10:2-16 or 10:2-12

Speaker's Introduction for the Lessons

Lesson 1

Job 1:1; 2:1-10 (SC)

This book deals with a question that has concerned both ancient and modern thinkers: why is there suffering in the world when it seems so unfair? This passage sets the scene for the rest of the book.

Genesis 2:18-24 (C/RC)

The Lord, deciding that the human God created should have a partner in life, creates a woman from the man's side. This passage moves the people of God to an understanding of oneness.

Lesson 2

Psalm 26 (SC)

The psalm blends a cry for deliverance with love expressed for the place of God's dwelling and gathering there in community with others.

Psalm 8 (C)

This psalm celebrating God's gift of creation lifts up the youngest among us as sources of praise for God's majesty.

Lesson 3

Hebrews 1:1-4; 2:5-12 (SC/C)

The anonymous author opens this letter (addressed to those who have been persecuted) with a firm statement about the superiority of Christ above all creation.

Hebrews 2:9-11 (RC)
To a suffering church, these words from an anonymous author must have brought great comfort – Christ himself suffered and calls all of them brothers and sisters.

Gospel
Mark 10:2-16 (SC/C); Mark 10:2-16 or 10:2-12 (RC)
The Jesus of the Gospels put a high standard on marriage and a particularly high standard on the care and nurture of children. Here he treats children as full human beings loved by God.

Theme
Children are loved by God.

Thought for the Day
Churches often assume children will only "some day" serve and love God. Jesus shows us that children are God's people now.

Sermon Summary
Children, often relegated to the outskirts of our faith, were treated as insiders by Jesus. Jesus wants us to know that there is something to be said for being like children. To be childlike in our faith is to recognize a spiritual truth: we are indeed dependent upon God.

Call to Worship
One: Lord, defend me because I have lived an innocent life. I have trusted the Lord and never doubted.

All: Lord, try us and test us; look closely into our hearts and minds.

One: I raise my voice in praise and tell of all the miracles you have done. I love the temple where you live, where your glory is.

All: Lord, we stand in a safe place. We praise you in the great meeting.

Pastoral Prayer

O great and loving God, who has created human beings for relationship, and who enters into relationship with all your people, we give you thanks for all the people who make our lives interesting and full. Thank you for families who love us, friends who make us laugh, children who show us the delight of discovery, youth who remind us of the importance of asking questions, adults who have much wisdom to share. We pray, O Lord, for those whose relationships are troubled, those who have no one in their lives to love them, those who live in homes where abuse or neglect reign in a twisted and evil departure from your holy design. Teach all of us to seek relationships that are healthy and show us how to reflect your love to those around us. Amen.

Prayer of Confession

Gracious God, whose love is beyond our understanding, forgive us for taking our relationships too lightly, for treating those close to us with coldness, for treating the stranger with contempt. We have not loved wholeheartedly; we have not guarded our words as we should; we have refused to let the interests of others interfere with our own self-interest. Teach us through the example of Jesus how to love, how to share, how to be in community with others. Amen.

Prayer of Dedication of Gifts and Self

Our gratitude for life and its gifts overflows, O Lord, into the giving of ourselves – what we have and what we are. Take these gifts we offer and use them to bless others. Then make of us the type of people who are always looking for ways to share in the name of Jesus. Amen.

Hymn of the Day
Tell Me the Stories of Jesus

Knowing of Jesus' love for children, it is fitting that we sing a hymn that was written in response to children's requests for stories of Jesus. The hymn was written around 1885 by William Henry Parker, an insurance executive who assisted with children's Sunday school work in Nottingham, England. The hymn highlights events in the life and ministry of Jesus. We can imagine being beside Jesus, in language that both children and adults can easily comprehend and sing together. The tune STORIES OF JESUS was written in 1903 as the prize-winning tune in a competition sponsored by the national Sunday School Union of England.

Children's Time: Let the Children Come

(Bring a variety of baby dolls.)
Invite the children to hold the dolls if they wish. Ask the children: "What's great about being a child?" Explain that in Jesus' time, children, even though they were loved by their parents, were not considered very important. But Jesus knew that everyone is important to God and he wanted to teach the disciples about this.

Tell the story of Jesus rebuking the disciples and blessing the children.

Invite some discussion of the story. What do you think the disciples said to each other when they heard what Jesus said? What do you think Jesus said when he blessed the children? What do you think the children said to Jesus?

Comment that Jesus knew that everyone is important to God – children and grown-ups, girls and boys, old and young. We are all part of God's family and that makes us very special. In fact, we are amazing. Invite the children to share this message with the whole congregation. Make a group huddle, have a whisper practice first, face the congregation and shout, "We are amazing!"

Pray with the children, giving thanks for Bible stories that help us understand how important we are to God.

The Sermon: Let Them Come
Scripture: Mark 10:2-16

I started out my adult life as an elementary school teacher, so I feel I have a fairly strong understanding of and appreciation for children. I've taken courses and read books on childhood development. As a Christian educator and then pastor, I have watched individual children grow and develop into teens and adults. As they mature, great physical, emotional, and spiritual changes have come over them. I am always amazed by the miracle of growing up. I love looking at a young adult and thinking, "I remember when you were in the first grade! My, how you've changed!"

Of course, that is no surprise to anyone. We all change as we mature. As children, nearly all of us (except Peter Pan) thought growing up would be a wonderful thing. "When I'm big, I can ride my bike down the street to my friend's house." "When I grow up, no one can tell me what to do." "Someday I can eat chocolate cake for breakfast if I want to!"

Though some would wish to turn back the clock on the aging process, very few would go back to childhood even if they could. Nearly everyone enjoys the independence of being a grown-up.

So if adulthood is the desirable state for nearly all of us, why does Jesus say, "It is to such as these that the kingdom of God belongs . . . Whoever does not receive the kingdom of God as a little child will never enter it" (Mk 10:14-15). Shouldn't Jesus be saying something like, "Aren't they cute? I can't wait until they grow up and can have a mature faith!"

But, as is often the case, Jesus turns our ideas of what ought to be into his better purpose. It's important to see that Mark couples this teaching about children with one about marriage. There is no question that Jesus had a higher view of marriage than some others did in his day. Family ties were important and should not be broken on a whim.

Right upon the heels of this strong statement on marriage, we have a story about children being brought to Jesus for his blessing. The disciples "spoke sternly to them" (10:13). It is unclear whether "them" refers to the adults bringing the children or to the children themselves. In either case, Jesus "was indignant" and responded by declaring that no child should be hindered in such a way. Then, he calls them examples of how to approach and receive the kingdom of God.

It may be hard for us to imagine children as examples. Don't we usually point the children around us to older youth or adults as models of faith and behavior? Children are wonderful, to be sure. They are fun, loving, creative, fresh. But they are also sometimes petty, argumentative, and in need of correction or guidance. Does God want us to be like that?

I believe the answer may be found in that very thing we try to work out of ourselves as we grow: dependence. Every child longs to be able to do things on her own, to make his own decisions. From the time we learn to say no, we say it often as a way of trying to assert our minimal but growing independence. As teenagers we can hardly stand that we still have to get our parents' permission to attend a certain movie or to stay out late with friends. We begin to strive against the fact that we still must rely on parents for financial help and for emotional support. Becoming independent adults means breaking away from those constraints and finding our own way.

However, Jesus wants us to know that there is something to be said for being like children. To be childlike in our faith is to recognize a spiritual truth: we are indeed dependent upon God. Just as a child must rely on others for even the most basic of needs such as food, shelter, love, and security, so do we all truly rely upon God, whether we consciously realize it or not. And the more conscious we are of that dependence, the more we understand what it means to be a child of God.

Like children, we are utterly dependent upon God for everything: for life, for breath, for love, for redemption. It is not that God calls us to be dependent; we already are. God calls us to recognize our dependence.

How would it make a difference in our lives if we were constantly to recognize our dependence before God? If we can live continually, actively in the mindset of dependence, then we are reminded of God's presence in every area of our lives. Though we may try to be cognizant of our physical needs before God, we often forget to remember that we depend on God for our emotional well-being, our relationships with family and neighbor, our ability to get along in the world.

Sadly, it seems the more successful (read: independent) we become – the more we achieve goods, comfort, and influence – the less likely we are to attribute those things to God. When we have more than enough to eat, nice houses, and more than one car in the driveway, we tend to forget who is the source of life itself and its barest necessities. The single parent who has three kids and an unsteady job may be more likely to be aware that everything comes from God than is the person who is financially stable and physically healthy. When need of any kind – a loss, fiscal difficulty, health problems, relational strain – hits us, we are more likely to return to God. That's when we give thanks for the understanding landlord, pray for the healing of a sick spouse, and hope for something good to happen if God wills it.

Those of us who have plenty are no less dependent upon God than those who have little. We may simply have a stronger need to recognize that dependence. That is when we learn to receive the kingdom of God as a little child.

– Melissa Bane Sevier

October 7, 2012
19th Sunday after Pentecost (Proper 22 [27])
RC/Pres: 27th Sunday in Ordinary Time

Hymns
Opening: All Things Bright and Beautiful
Sermon: I Want to Walk as a Child of the Light
Closing: Jesus Loves Me

October 14, 2012

20th Sunday after Pentecost (Proper 23)
RC/Pres: 28th Sunday in Ordinary Time

Lessons

Semi-continuous (SC)	Complementary (C)	Roman Catholic (RC)
Job 23:1-9, 16-17	Amos 5:6-7, 10-15	Wis 7:7-11
Ps 22:1-15	Ps 90:12-17	Ps 90:12-17
Heb 4:12-16	Heb 4:12-16	Heb 4:12-13
Mk 10:17-31	Mk 10:17-31	Mk 10:17-30 or 10:17-27

Speaker's Introduction for the Lessons
Lesson 1

Job 23:1-9, 16-17 (SC)

Job, after listening to his friends' "explanations" of why bad things had happened to him, complains that God's presence has been hidden during the entire ordeal.

Amos 5:6-7, 10-15 (C)

Amos, the shepherd-turned-prophet, rails against the attitudes of injustice and the lack of faithfulness in those around him.

Wisdom 7:7-11 (RC)

All good things come with God's wisdom, a gift more precious than gold and jewels.

Lesson 2

Psalm 22:1-15 (SC)

This psalm of lament cries out to God out of a vivid experience of abandonment: why is God "so far from helping me?"

Psalm 90:12-17 (C/RC)

In the only psalm attributed to Moses, the plea for wisdom combines with a prayer for God to bless "the work of our hands."

Lesson 3

Hebrews 4:12-16 (SC/C); Hebrews 4:12-13 (RC)

The writer of the letter to the Hebrews expresses an exalted understanding of Christ to encourage readers who may be suffering.

Gospel

Mark 10:17-31 (SC/C); Mark 10:17-30 or Mark 10:17-27 (RC)

The Gospel of Mark shows Jesus' love for and challenge to one who questions him. The text moves from a specific person to all the wealthy, then to all persons.

Theme

Faithfulness requires examining heart and motive.

Thought for the Day

Love for God requires digging deeply into our psyches to see what things hinder our faithfulness.

Sermon Summary

Like the man in the story, we enthusiastically run after Jesus, only to find that often we are held back by our own desires and presuppositions. Even though we are imperfect in our obedience, with God real faithfulness is possible.

Call to Worship

One: My God, my God, why have you rejected me? You seem far from saving me, far from the words of my groaning.

All: My God, I call to you during the day, but you do not answer. I call at night; I am not silent.

One: Praise the Lord, all you who respect God. All you descendants of Jacob, honor God; fear God, all you Israelites.

All: God does not ignore those in trouble. God does not hide from them, but listens when they call out.

Pastoral Prayer

O God, whether we are in a time of crisis or of relative normalcy, help us to see all the good things we have received from you. Let us draw our loved ones close and breathe a prayer of thanks for their safety. Let us look around our homes and wonder why we have so much when so many others have little or nothing. Let us put on our clothing and eat our meals and sleep in our beds, and realize how often we take those simple things for granted. We thank you for giving us hearts that are pulled by the needs of others. We pray for those today who are grieving loss, for the elderly and weak, for the sick and depressed, and for those who have lost all hope. Show us how we may share the love of Christ in whatever way we can. Amen.

Prayer of Confession

Loving and forgiving God, you have reached into our souls and have seen us as our true selves. You know where we have been faithful and where we have come up short. Forgive us when we believe we have kept all your commandments, but have forgotten to remember the poor, the weak, the stranger, and the hurting. Instill in us an understanding of your love and grace so that as we are forgiven we may reach out to others and share that same love with them. Amen.

Prayer of Dedication of Gifts and Self

Thank you, O God, for all your good gifts. In response, we bring to you the results of our work and the intentions of our hearts. Receive our offerings and use them for the work of this congregation in your world. Receive our very lives and make us willing servants who are always listening for the call to help those in need. Help us dedicate ourselves anew to efforts of love. Amen.

Hymn of the Day
O Jesus, I Have Promised

This musical prayer of commitment, written for the confirmation of youth, easily serves as an expression of commitment for the congregation. The major focus of the hymn is the dedicated commitment to Christ-centered service. It was written by Anglican priest John Ernest Bode of Cambridgeshire, England, in 1866 for the confirmation of his three children. Although the hymn emphasizes dedicated servanthood, it reminds us that even as Jesus is our master, he is also our friend. As we sing this hymn, we may perhaps identify with the disciples' relationship to Jesus and their desire to "follow him to the end."

Children's Time: Leave It Behind

(Bring a backpack packed to overflowing with things that would not be useful on a day hike [electric kettle, movie] and things that would be [water bottle, sunscreen, map])
Show the packback and explain that you are going on a hike later, so you packed a bag. Lift the bag and exclaim that it's too heavy to take on a long walk. Let the children feel the weight.

Comment that you will have to leave some things behind. Unpack everything and ask the children to help you decide what to leave behind. As the children make their suggestions give some ridiculous reasons for keeping everything. Reluctantly follow the children's directions and repack the bag. Let the children feel the reduced weight.

Explain that in the Bible story today, Jesus was talking to some people about what it meant to be a disciple. Jesus said that if we want to follow him we might have to leave some things – like selfishness – behind. Comment that sometimes it can be hard to decide what is important and what is not as we follow Jesus. As a church family we can help each other decide.

Pray, asking God to help you as you learn more about following Jesus.

The Sermon: You Lack One Thing
Scripture: Mark 10:17-31

Shirley goes to church every Sunday. She teaches a class of four-year-olds how much God loves them. She serves on the mission committee and raises money for both local and international projects. For a year she was on the board of the Habitat for Humanity chapter for her county, spending one night a month and several Saturdays giving her time "for a good cause." As a businesswoman, she sees to it that her small corporation invests wisely and fairly.

Last year, Shirley's mother became ill. Her mother lives a half-hour away, but Shirley went to visit only once over a period of about six months. With no family to help, the mother relied on friends and taxis to get her to the doctor and had someone come in several times a week to look after her. Though the daughter was well-equipped and energetic when it came to helping all sorts of other people, she felt emotionally paralyzed and incapable of responding in the face of her own mother's needs. Events from her past kept her from helping, even though if it had been a neighbor she would have been free with her assistance.

Some people know Bob as a guy who is generous with his money. It's not that he's public about it; he's helped out many in very quiet ways. Bob's church put out an appeal for help for hurricane survivors, and he gave half his salary for the month. An old friend comes by on a regular basis and Bob always pulls out his wallet – the guy has fallen on hard times. At Christmas, Bob responds to every request for money from an agency he respects. He gives money for toys, food, emergency aid, and funds a Christmas party for the nursing home down the street. But, even though Bob has plenty of spare time (he is retired) and is in great health, he never responds to requests for volunteering. He has said no to helping at the Christmas party, to delivering meals, and to working a fund-raiser event for the hurricane survivors. He even avoids conversation with the friend who always needs money. Bob's point of view is that he doesn't have to give his time because he gives his money. He has his own pursuits and interests, and he just likes having his time at his own disposal, without demands from others. Writing a check is easy; giving up a Saturday – that's another thing altogether.

When Bill and Marge discuss their retirement, they realize they will be very comfortable. They plan to travel to Europe and Asia. They want to buy a lake house and a boat. They have good health insurance and long-term care insurance, so they don't worry about their future. They have good relationships with their family members and friends. They work hard at their jobs and are respected in them. They feel they have earned every penny they've made, and they've invested wisely. But they decided long ago to stop giving to charities and those in need. They love to read accounts of churches and not-for-profits who have handled money poorly and illegally; these incidents give them additional reasons never to trust their contributions to any organization. And individuals, they say, like the homeless they pass on their way to work, will just use the money to buy drugs and alcohol. So, they enjoy the financial rewards of their labors and plan how they will spend their retirement income.

When Jesus encountered the man in today's story, Mark tells us Jesus looked at him and "loved him" (Mk 10:21). He was one of us – our neighbor, our co-worker, our fellow pew-sitter; he was us. He was a normal guy, a very good guy who was happy with his life. "Is there anything lacking?" he asked. I think he knew what was lacking. He seemed to be faithful in so many ways. Jesus told him to keep the commandments. "I do all that," he said eagerly. "You know what's required," said Jesus, loving him. "What's the one thing you have trouble with?"

"Give up your money," said Jesus. "Give away all of it to the poor."

"All of it?" he gasped.

"All of it."

This rich man was shocked. Shocked. It was impossible to imagine that, after all he had done for God, there would be this one, enormous, unreasonable thing asked of him.

When he realized Jesus was serious, he went away. He grieved, because he could not believe this would be required of him. He wanted to do all for God, but this was just too much. This was over the edge. Maybe Jesus wasn't from God after all. The God he knew would not require such a thing – possessions are blessings, aren't they?

Jesus watched this man and loved him. And the disciples watched, slack-jawed. If this is true, then who in the world can get into the kingdom? "With God," smiled Jesus, "all things are possible." And he loved them.

Each of us, no matter how faithful we are, has the potential to hold something back. We have the potential of keeping one door of our hearts closed to God. We have the potential to love one thing too much to allow God to use it, because only we know how best it should be used. We have the potential of letting that one thing – small though it may be – grow in importance to such an extent that it overshadows our faithfulness. But we also have the potential of learning to let go of that one thing, of making small beginnings to be more faithful and more open to God and others. We have this possibility because all things are possible with God. And because, even when we are shocked that this one last stronghold must now be opened to God's intrusion, and when we turn away in sadness and grief – grief that we are losing that one last thing – Jesus looks after us and loves us.

– Melissa Bane Sevier

Hymns
Opening: God of Grace and God of Glory
Sermon: Great God, Your Love Has Called Us Here
Closing: Jesu, Jesu, Fill Us with Your Love

October 21, 2012

21st Sunday after Pentecost (Proper 24)
RC/Pres: 29th Sunday in Ordinary Time

Lessons

Semi-continuous (SC)	Complementary (C)	Roman Catholic (RC)
Job 38:1-7, (34-41)	Isa 53:4-12	Isa 53:10-11
Ps 104:1-9, 24, 35c	Ps 91:9-16	Ps 33:4-5, 18-20, 22
Heb 5:1-10	Heb 5:1-10	Heb 4:14-16
Mk 10:35-45	Mk 10:35-45	Mk 10:35-45 or 10:42-45

Speaker's Introduction for the Lessons
Lesson 1
Job 38:1-7, (34-41) (SC)
God's response out of the whirlwind to all Job's questions about suffering consists of more questions.
Isaiah 53:4-12 (C); Isaiah 53:10-11 (RC)
The servant portrayed by the prophet suffers for the people and is exalted by God because of his sufferings.

Lesson 2
Psalm 104:1-9, 24, 35c (SC)
This psalm offers praise and awe at God's presence and work in creation. Scholars suggest connections between this psalm and an Egyptian work called "Hymn to the Aten" (Sun deity).
Psalm 91:9-16 (C)
The psalmist uses the imagery of a sheltering mother bird for her chicks to affirm trust in God's protection of God's people.

Lesson 3
Hebrews 5:1-10 (SC/C)
Jesus, though he suffered greatly, was elevated to the rank of high priest, as was the ancient priest of Salem, Melchizedek.

Hebrews 4:14-16 (RC)
The writer of the letter to the Hebrews exalts Christ to encourage readers who may be suffering.

Gospel
Mark 10:35-45 (SC/C); Mark 10:35-45 or 10:42-45 (RC)
Jesus answers a question about power by teaching that, in God's kingdom, power is of a different sort.

Theme
Power is not what we think.

Thought for the Day
The true power of God's love is expressed in humility.

Sermon Summary
Personal power raises many issues within us. Jesus teaches a different way.

Call to Worship
One: Bless the Lord, O my soul. O Lord my God, you are very great.
All: You are clothed with honor and majesty, wrapped in light as with a garment. You stretch out the heavens like a tent.
One: O Lord, how manifold are your works! In wisdom you have made them all; the earth is full of your creatures.
All: Bless the Lord, O my soul. Praise the Lord!

Pastoral Prayer
Creator God, when we look at all you have made and the great beauty of it, we feel small in comparison. We see your vastness in the sea, hear your power in the wind, experience your genius in the first cry of an infant, know your wildness in the howl of the leopard. We thank you for the blessings of the people we hold dear, the love we experience, the gifts of life and security. May these blessings lead us to reach out to others who have no one who holds them dear, whose lives are empty or unhealthy

or unsafe, who reach out for faith or justice or help and find none. Teach us to love with compassion, to aid while preserving dignity, to share with delight. Amen.

Prayer of Confession

O God of great power, how often we have abused the power you have given us. We have hurt family members; we have ignored the poor; we have refused to share what we have; we have not cared about the feelings of others. Forgive us our sins, show us where we have been wrong, and give us the ability to acknowledge and address those wrongs. Help us to live as people who have much to share. Through Jesus Christ our Lord. Amen.

Prayer of Dedication of Gifts and Self

For gifts of love, O God, we offer our compassion to others. For gifts of possessions, we offer what we have to help those in need. For the gift of time, we offer our days of service. For the gift of life, we offer our selves to be your servants. Amen.

Hymn of the Day
Immortal, Invisible, God Only Wise

The combination of this hymn text with the Welsh tune St. Denio makes for a grand and majestic statement about the splendor of Almighty God. Based on 1 Timothy 1:17 ("To the King of the ages, immortal, invisible, the only God, be honor and glory forever and ever") the hymn provides images of God as unchanging and hidden. Yet, it also presents God as being visible in creation and as the God of righteousness. Walter Chalmers Smith, a Scottish pastor of the Free Church, wrote the hymn in 1867.

Children's Time: Servant Leaders

(Bring a toy crown)
Ask children for ideas about who might wear a crown like this. Ask for a volunteer to wear the crown. When you have crowned your volunteer, ask what he or she would do as a king or queen.

Explain that in the Bible story today two of Jesus' disciples ask Jesus if they could be leaders with him in God's realm. They wanted to be like two kings sitting with Jesus. Comment that they probably wanted to be in charge! Jesus suspected they didn't really understand what he expects leaders to do, so he called the disciples together and began to teach them about being a leader in God's realm.

Paraphrase Mark 10:42-43. Ask the children if they know what a servant does. (If the children don't seem to have a good understanding, describe a servant as someone who works to take care of someone else.) Comment that in God's realm if we want to lead, we have to be servants. Talk about how you might care for the needs of others at home, at school, or in the community this week.

Pray with the children, asking that God would help you become servant leaders.

The Sermon: How to Have Influence
Scripture: Mark 10:35-45

A version of an ancient story is told in many cultures: The monarch is challenged to consider the poor in the kingdom who have sometimes been forgotten. So one day the monarch decides to see what it is like to live as a poor commoner. In disguise, he spends time walking among the poor, seeing what it is like to live under the sometimes oppressive laws of the government. Returning to the palace, the king is changed by the experience, and the state becomes more friendly to those under its rule.

Why has this tale been so popular in so many places for so long? I think it is because people want those in authority to know what it's like to live under that authority. And I think it is because people don't see that kind of understanding very often. This can be true in nations, work environments, even in churches.

Two brothers, followers of Jesus, came to him to ask a question. Mark puts this story in an interesting place – after a couple of chapters in which Jesus has predicted his passion three times and has set a child in front of these same followers as an example of humility. Perhaps we're to see the brothers as waiting, biding their time to ask Jesus this question. They are so interested in what they want to ask of Jesus that they have failed to listen to what he's been saying. "Teacher, we want you to do for us whatever we ask of you . . . Grant us to sit, one at your right hand and one at your left, in your glory" (Mk 10:35, 37).

They had in mind, of course, some earthly or heavenly palace, a throne, a couple of extra scepters, a great deal of authority where they would reign as benevolent yet firm co-leaders with their Lord. The minds of Mark's readers, though, jump forward to the only place in this Gospel where we are given a vision of people on Jesus' right and on his left – the cross and the two thieves who join him there. This is hardly a realization of anyone's definition of glory. If I had to guess, it's not the kind of glory James and John were thinking of when they asked Jesus for a favor. Jesus asked them if they could drink that cup, meaning the cup of suffering; they said of course they could drink that cup, meaning the cup of glory. He told them they would indeed share in his fate.

Now the other ten followers, who had been watching and listening to this conversation, got very angry with the two brothers, and Jesus used the moment to speak to all of them about leadership. It's almost certain Mark chose to record this interchange as a lesson to leaders in the early church of which he was a part.

Don't be like those worldly rulers you see around you, Jesus told them, and they knew what he meant. They could see Herod's palace, the governors, and even the priests who did not consider those over whom they had authority. I'm sure that the Twelve believed they could be different rulers. If they had authority, they'd use it wisely, take care of people; they'd be benevolent rulers.

But for Jesus, leading goes far beyond benevolence. A benevolent ruler waves from the rooftop to adoring crowds. Jesus walked among the crowds so that they pressed upon him and wore him out. A benevolent ruler sends servants to care for important invited guests. Jesus invited everyone to the banquet, then washed their feet himself when they arrived. A benevolent ruler hopes that people will be fed. Jesus broke enough bread and fish to feed a crowd. A benevolent ruler sees that laws are applied as fairly as possible to as many as possible. Jesus taught about God's love as the law by which we live. A benevolent ruler may even give up something for others. Jesus gave his life as a ransom for many.

So, if the followers of Jesus are supposed to move into a different type of leadership role – that of servant – what does that mean?

Ron Heifetz, a leader in the field of leadership training, tells a story of when he and his wife were in England on their way to a speaking engagement. Rosh Hashanah, the Jewish New Year, was approaching, and they had hoped to observe the holiday at a synagogue in London. The day came, however, and they found themselves still in the English countryside, nowhere near a synagogue. On a bit of a whim, they decided to enter a small, empty Anglican church for a time of spiritual reflection. At the front of the church was a crucifix, and Ron found himself in a bit of spiritual conflict. Here he was, a Jew well-aware of the abuses of Christians toward his people, confronted with the figure of Jesus on the cross. Nevertheless, he asked "Reb Jesus" to tell him about the experience of the cross. Suddenly, he asked his wife to go outside with him for a small experiment. They sat together near a tree in the deserted churchyard. He asked her to spread out her arms in a cruciform pose, which they both did. After a few moments, he asked her how she felt, to which she replied, "Really vulnerable." That was it! For this expert in leadership, the experience was a lesson in vulnerability. Jesus was such a great leader because he was open and vulnerable to the experiences of life. (Ronald A. Heifetz and Marty Linsky, *Leadership on the Line,* Harvard Business School Press, 2002, pp. 228-229.)

That is exactly what we see and know from the life of Jesus. He inspires all of us to follow him because he was willing to give up equality with God for a time in order to become one of us; he walked with us and was vulnerable just as we are. That is the kind of leader we should be.

– Melissa Bane Sevier

Hymns
Opening: Celebrate with Joy and Singing
Sermon: Called as Partners in Christ's Service
Closing: Lord, Make Us Servants of Your Peace

October 28, 2012

22nd Sunday after Pentecost (Proper 25)
RC/Pres: 30th Sunday in Ordinary Time

Lessons

Semi-continuous (SC)	Complementary (C)	Roman Catholic (RC)
Job 42:1-6, 10-17	Jer 31:7-9	Jer 31:7-9
Ps 34:1-8 (19-22)	Ps 126	Ps 126:1-2a, 2b-3, 4-5, 6
Heb 7:23-28	Heb 7:23-28	Heb 5:1-6
Mk 10:46-52	Mk 10:46-52	Mk 10:46-52

Speaker's Introduction for the Lessons

Lesson 1

Job 42:1-6, 10-17 (SC)

Job responds to God's message to him. God honors Job and dismisses the responses of Job's friends.

Jeremiah 31:7-9 (C/RC)

God will bring the people of Israel back to their homeland.

Lesson 2

Psalm 34:1-8 (19-22) (SC)

This wisdom psalm, mostly written as an acrostic (each verse except 6 and 22 begin with a successive letter of the Hebrew alphabet) celebrates God's goodness and deliverance.

Psalm 126 (C/RC)

The psalmist offers praise for deliverance from exile (verse 1) and pleads for a new act of restoration.

Lesson 3

Hebrews 7:23-28 (SC/C)

Jesus, the Son of God, is the great high priest of our faith. Here are his attributes.

Hebrews 5:1-6 (RC)
Jesus, though he suffered greatly, was elevated to the rank of high priest, as was the ancient priest of Salem, Melchizedek.

Gospel
Mark 10:46-52 (SC/C/RC)
This is the story of a blind man named Bartimaeus, restored to his sight by Jesus.

Theme
Jesus came to help us through our hopeless situations.

Thought for the Day
Though a situation may seem hopeless, God cares about each person and each situation.

Sermon Summary
Bartimaeus begged by the side of the road. When Jesus saw him, he had mercy on the man's physical situation and also on his emotional and spiritual needs. In the same way, God cares about our needs and gives us hope in the midst of crisis.

Call to Worship
One: I will praise the Lord at all times; praise for God is always on my lips.
All: My whole being praises the Lord. The poor will hear and be glad.
One: Glorify the Lord with me, and let us praise God's name together.
All: I asked the Lord for help, and God answered me, saving me from all that I feared.
One: The angel of the Lord camps around those who fear God, and God saves them.
All: Examine and see how good the Lord is. Happy is the person who trusts God.

Pastoral Prayer

Loving and giving God, you have made us and all things. We thank you for the hope we find in the smallest and grandest of things: an October morning; a baby's cry in worship; a phone call from a good friend; a decent night's rest. When hope is lost, when rest does not come and morning takes too long to arrive, when friends are nowhere to be found, and when life seems empty, speak to us, O God, even as Jesus spoke to Bartimaeus. May your word of kindness and hope bring us back to our feet and enable us to walk with full sight. Today we remember all who struggle with a lack of hope and who long for a decent job, a roof over their children's heads, a day without pain, a life of freedom and security. Show us, we pray, how to bring your hope to them. Amen.

Prayer of Confession

O God of hope, how often we have lived as if there were no hope to be found. We neglect to see Christ in the other person; we do not look for the brightness of Christ's love in the shadows. We have forgotten how to share hope with those in need. Forgive us our short-sightedness, and give us the vision to see you at work in the world around us. And when we see others who are hurting, enable us to find ways of bringing your hope to others. Jesus, Son of David, have mercy on us. Through Christ we pray. Amen.

Prayer of Dedication of Gifts and Self

For gifts of hope, O God, we give you thanks. Enable us to see – in the places we live and work and go to school – the desperate and obvious needs of some, and the silent, hardly noticeable needs of others. Then strengthen our hearts to respond to what we discover. In Christ our Lord. Amen.

Hymn of the Day
O for a Thousand Tongues to Sing

Written by Charles Wesley in 1739 to celebrate the first anniversary of his Christian conversion, this hymn has become somewhat of an "anthem" for Methodist and other Wesleyan churches. Included in most every other hymnal as well, the hymn enjoys a broad ecumenical usage, perhaps making it the most popular of Wesley's some 6500 hymns. Most current hymnals contain from four to seven of the hymn's original eighteen stanzas. In addition to the standard tune AZMON, the hymn tune RICHMOND is often used with this hymn, lending fresh insights to the text. British Methodists often use the tunes LYDIA and UNIVERSITY.

Children's Time: Blind Bartimaeus

Invite the children to play a game of "I spy." Explain how to play the game and start by giving an example, "I spy with my little eye something that is *(name the color)*." The children guess the object. The one who guesses correctly takes the next turn. Play several times.

Explain that you would like to change the game a little. Comment that God has given us many ways to explore the world around us. Suggest that this time you use your ears. Start by giving an example, "I hear with my little ear something that rings." Play several times. If you have time, move on to the sense of touch, "I feel with my hands something that is *(rough, smooth, sticky . . .)*"

Comment that the Bible story today is about a man who could not see anything at all. He had to use his other senses to explore the world. Tell the story about Jesus healing blind Bartimaeus. Ask the children to imagine what it was like to be Bartimaeus after his eyes were healed. What might he like to look at the most? How would his life be different?

Pray with the children, giving thanks for the gifts of eyes, ears, noses, and fingers.

The Sermon: Blindness and Hope
Scripture: Mark 10:46-52

It is hard, sometimes, to preach from the healing stories of Jesus, for in just about any congregation someone sits, wondering, "Why would Jesus heal Bartimaeus, but God seems to ignore my pain?" It's a legitimate question. There is certainly enough pain to go around in this world, and we all imagine that if we were God, we wouldn't allow it. We'd do something about it.

The question of pain is an ancient one, as old as the world itself, and the question never has an answer – at least not the kind of answer we wish we could hear. There is no explanation, no resolution, no key to understanding why Bartimaeus and all of humankind find ourselves in need of physical healing and not receiving it.

Though the healing stories from Jesus' ministry do not provide us with an answer to human pain, or even a promise that, if we have enough faith, we can be healed just like Bartimaeus, they do give us a look into the work and mercy of God.

"Jesus, Son of David, have mercy on me!" (Mk 10:47) cried the blind man beside the crowd, at the fringes of society. This was his place, where his blindness had put him. This was where he could get the only help available to him – handouts from passersby. He cried out, as he always did, for alms. But when he heard that Jesus was in the crowd, his pleas changed. I don't know if he even held out hope for healing or if he expected something else from Jesus. Perhaps he'd heard of other healings. Those who wanted to protect Jesus told the man to be quiet, but he was determined to be heard. "Son of David, have mercy on me!"

That is when we see it: not the answer to all our pain, but one who pays attention. Though others tried to shush the crier, Jesus stood and turned. "Call him here," he said (10:49). And they did. Those who had previously told Bartimaeus (not a little meanly) to be quiet, now followed the merciful example of Jesus: "Take heart; get up, he is calling you" (10:49).

And Bartimaeus did. He didn't just amble, but threw off his cloak, jumped to his feet, and came to Jesus, who asked, "What do you want me to do for you?" (10:51).

"My teacher, let me see again" (10:51). And so it happened. Bartimaeus was healed of his blindness and became a disciple, following Jesus along with the crowd that had, a few moments before, told him not to bother Jesus.

The story of Jesus' healing of a blind man is a story of mercy and hope. There is more emotion in this story than in many others, expressed through both words and actions: the crowd first "sternly ordered" Bartimaeus into silence and later told him to "take heart"; Bartimaeus shouted and cried for mercy, threw off his cloak and sprang to his feet, then followed. Far from refusing to deal with hurting people, Jesus responded to the shouts and cries and enthusiastic hopes of a man in need.

What for us, then?

There is much about the workings of human pain within a community in this story, workings that many will recognize. The blind man, in great need, continually calls out for help, not just on this day but every day. He is there, by the side of the road, asking for aid. Just as we often do, the people walk on by. And some of them try to get him to be quiet. Are they worried Jesus will be disturbed? Or are they using that as an excuse to quiet him because they are disturbed? They are disturbed by the reminder that there is pain in the world; they are disturbed by how close that pain has come to them – close enough to reach out and touch them – and they would just as soon not hear about it.

But the one in need is wise enough not to keep the pain bottled up inside. He shouts; he cries out to Jesus; and Jesus recognizes and responds to his cries.

The crowd's response is interesting, isn't it? Once protective (of Jesus, ostensibly), after they see how Jesus responds, they too turn to Bartimaeus and tell him to take heart, get up, and draw close, because his cries have been heard and Jesus wants to see him.

I see in this story a human being in pain, who thankfully isn't afraid to talk about it, and a community that initially is reluctant to hear his pain but eventually is willing to listen and to help the man get the help he needs. What would it be like in our churches and communities if we encouraged those in pain to talk about it, if we made a space for those who are troubled to be heard? Would we start support groups, open our fellowship hall as a place where social workers could mingle with street people, set up a program for laypeople to visit with the elderly and sick, just to listen? And once we truly listen, we have no other way to go than to begin to show them the mercy and hope of Christ, to encourage them to take heart because Jesus has heard their cries.

No, there may not be an answer to pain and suffering, but there is indeed hope. This is what the community of Christ does: we watch for those by the side of the road; we listen to them; and we offer them hope. Nothing less is expected of us, because we are following the example of Jesus.

– Melissa Bane Sevier

Hymns

Opening: I Greet Thee Who My Sure Redeemer Art
Sermon: Seek Ye First
Closing: We Walk by Faith and Not by Sight

October 31, 2012

Reformation

Lessons
Complementary   Jer 31:31-34   Ps 46   Rom 3:19-28   Jn 8:31-36

Speaker's Introduction for the Lessons
Lesson 1
Jeremiah 31:31-34

> God has offered us an eternal covenant: God's own law written on our hearts so that we do not need to stand separate from God, but can be one with the Most Holy.

Lesson 2
Psalm 46

> Today's psalm inspired Martin Luther's hymn "A Mighty Fortress." Seeking refuge may seem weak to us, but when God is our refuge, therein is our strength.

Lesson 3
Romans 3:19-28

> Although humanity is broken by sin, faith becomes the path by which we can rest confidently in God's righteousness.

Gospel
John 8:31-36

> Jesus calls us out of slavery to sin into the freedom of discipleship.

Theme
The Reformation is not about an event or an era; it is about committed discipleship and the willingness to be who God needs us to be here and now.

Thought for the Day

Once an old woman at my church said the secret is God loves us exactly
the way we are and that [God] loves us too much to let us stay like this,
and I'm just trying to trust that.

— Anne Lamott, *Operating Instructions*

Sermon Summary

We are accountable to God to be persons fitting lightly to our identity
in this moment, so that we can become the vessels and instruments God
requires to bring the realm of shalom to fulfillment. Thus we will never
"be," because we are always "becoming."

Call to Worship

One: We come together not as perfect people,

All: But as people seeking God's re-formation of our souls,

One: Of our hopes and visions,

All: And of our words and deeds.

One: As clay in the potter's hands,

All: We offer ourselves to be shaped anew.

Pastoral Prayer

Reforming God, you offer us the grace of beginning each day anew with
a heart, soul, mind, and spirit freshly born into the universe. Help us to
stop dragging the burdens of past mistakes and past glories behind us, so
that we may be free to become faithful sisters and brothers of the One
who defined himself only by your image in him. Grant us the grace to be
a re-formed people, not once only, but day after day until your peace is
accomplished here on earth as it is in the eternal places. Amen.

Prayer of Confession

Merciful God, we acknowledge all the ways we cling to our old selves and
to the image of you we were called to reveal yesterday. We admit our fear
of losing the comfort of what we have been. We confess our resistance to
accepting the new self you are offering and the image of you we are called

to reveal today. Forgive us our anxiety and inspire us to trust so that we can hold ourselves lightly, letting go of the outworn and receiving the new self you are continually promising. Amen.

Prayer of Dedication of Gifts and Self

Accept these gifts, Gracious God, offered back to you from the bounty you have shared with us. Form them into tangible hope for your needy world and re-form us to become ever more bounteous givers. Amen.

Hymn of the Day
A Mighty Fortress Is Our God

Here is another popular hymn that transcends denominational boundaries. "*Ein feste burg ist unser Gott*" was written by German Reformation leader Martin Luther, probably between the years of 1527 and 1529. The German text has been translated into more than fifty languages, including some 100 English versions. Based on Psalm 46, the hymn expresses confidence in God and may be used as a source of strong encouragement for the advancement of the entire church. Singing the tune EIN FESTE BURG in a joyful, moving tempo allows an expression similar to that associated with Luther's original rhythmic setting of the tune.

Children's Time: God's Love

(Bring a large hoop)
Ask the children to tell you what shape the hoop makes. Gather around the ring and observe that there is no beginning or ending to the circle. Trace the ring with a finger and observe that a circle just goes on and on and on. Encourage the children to join you saying "on and on . . . "

Comment that this circle reminds you of God's love. God's love has no beginning and no end. God has always loved us and always will. Even when we make a mistake, God still loves us. Just like a circle, God's love for us goes on and on. Express excitement that God loves us no matter what.

Ask the children to search for circles in the church. Comment that every time we see a circle we can remember God's amazing love for us. Mention that today is Reformation Sunday. On this day we celebrate the lives of people through the ages who wanted to share the good news of

God's love. If you have time, you might want to tell the story of Martin Luther or other reformers who have influenced your church.

Pray with the children, giving thanks for the good news of God's love.

The Sermon: Held Accountable
Scripture: Romans 3:19-28

Here in the epistle to the Romans, Paul wrestles with an old, old issue for the Christian community: Are we under the law or under grace? Are we saved by our own works or by God's unconditional love? For a long time, I worried about this, and I broke out in a cold sweat every time I needed to preach one of these texts because the preacher is always – to some greater or lesser extent – translating. The idiom of another time and place must be made accessible in the language of the time and place in which we find ourselves right now, so that the light of scripture is reflected into the corners of our daily lives.

Law or grace? Our own works or God's unconditional love? We ask this as if pinning it down to one thing that is essential for faithful living. We ask as if it is – or needs to be – the same thing for everyone. Or as if it is the same for each person at all times in his or her life.

Are we under the law or under grace? Yes, we are. Does our salvation depend on our own works or God's unconditional love? Yes, it does. It depends on both.

This is Reformation Day. It is assuredly a celebration of an historical event that has marked our own faith journeys. But if that is all it is, the remembrance has failed in its true purpose. When we speak of reformation, we are speaking not only of an event or of a time in the life of the corporate church, but also of an ongoing process within our own individual hearts, minds, souls, spirits. We are speaking of the process of being shaped by God – reshaped and reshaped yet again as a potter shapes clay. Here the clay becomes a chalice, there a basin. Here, a pitcher or a flowerpot; there, a statue. It is shaped now for the sacred; then, for the mundane. What is necessary today will not be tomorrow. The vessel needed yesterday is not the one needed today.

What remains unchanging is that we who call ourselves followers of Jesus are accountable to God to be shaped as God needs. We are accountable to God to be God's servant people, to be available to God for God's use to bring the divine realm to fulfillment. We are accountable under the law and under grace. We are accountable in our works and as the recipients of God's unconditional love.

We have it from the Gospel according to Matthew that Jesus said, "Do not think that I have come to abolish the law or the prophets; I have come not to abolish but to fulfill" (5:17). We are accountable for what we have heard, learned, and done as a result of being graced to receive prophetic wisdom. In some things we will act as persons transformed and in others we won't. Yet even under the weight of sin, we are accountable to God to resist despair and to embrace confidence, because God promises that in the divine universe death and sin are not the last word – abundant life in the resurrection is the last word. We are accountable to God to act on God's behalf, reflecting the divine image that God entrusted to us in our creation.

We are accountable to God to be people of faith, not merely people of belief. A faithful disciple is not in a passive or abstract relationship with God. Rather, a faithful disciple is anticipatory and eager. That means we are beings in the process of becoming. I'm not sure that the term "Reformation Day" does justice to what we are about. Perhaps "Reforming Day" describes it better. We are a people covenanted with God to being formed and re-formed as many times as God needs us to be.

We are not spiritual infants. We should not cling to our image of God as a baby clings to a favorite blanket, shrieking in terror if anyone tries to take it away. We are spiritual adults growing into the full maturity of Christ, able to meet God as God chooses to become. We are not concrete, operational children fiercely resisting any and every change of language, liturgy, hymnody, and ministry that God offers through the wild tempest of the Spirit blowing through human history. We are spiritual adults, able to recognize and embrace that God is bigger than all our thoughts, our words, our ideas, our theories, and our doctrines. God may choose to be revealed through the least expected persons and the most radical notions, just as God has always done.

We are a people being re-formed in the thought of the Holy One. We are useless to God unless we are malleable enough to be reshaped by the divine hands and the divine vision for the service God needs here and now. In another place Paul says, "I have become all things to all people, that I might by any means save some" (1 Cor 9:22b). On this Reformation Day, looking back at our life since last October 31, have we acted as persons committed to such wholehearted service? Have we acted as persons willing to give up the comfortable and the familiar to meet God's needy people in the words and deeds they require here and now? Or have we resisted all re-formation? Can we say with Paul that we are willing to become now Jew, now Gentile, now radical, now conservative, now foolish, now wise? Or must we acknowledge that our own opinions and our self-illusions are more important to us than God's startling word and holy image in our lives?

As we sit in prayerful quiet with these questions, I invite you to inhale God's divine breath that animated creation and, thus, to hold yourself as lightly as breath exhaled at rest. I invite you to still yourself into an attentive tranquility where the echoing silence of God's word can name you into new being and, thus, resonate with more profound harmony. I invite you to risk the grace of transformation from who you are to who you might become. In the name of God, may it be so.

– Andrea La Sonde Anastos

Hymns
Opening: The Church of Christ in Every Age
Sermon: God Is Here
Closing: We Walk by Faith

November 1, 2012

All Saints' Day

Lessons

Semi-continuous (SC)	Complementary (C)	Roman Catholic (RC)
Wis 3:1-9 or Isa 25:6-9	Isa 25:6-9 or Wis 3:1-9	Rev 7:2-4, 9-14
Ps 24	Ps 24	Ps 24:1-2, 3-4, 5-6
Rev 21:1-6a	Rev 21:1-6a	1 Jn 3:1-3
Jn 11:32-44	Jn 11:32-44	Mt 5:1-12

Speaker's Introduction for the Lessons

Lesson 1

Wisdom 3:1-9 (SC/C)

God watches over the souls of the righteous forever.

Isaiah 25:6-9 (SC/C)

Isaiah describes God calling the people to a feast on the mountain where death will be swallowed up forever.

Revelation 7:2-4, 9-14 (RC)

This vision includes the multitude of the saints rejoicing before the throne of God, praising God and worshiping with angels and elders.

Lesson 2

Psalm 24

The earth is the Lord's, sings the psalmist, and we are invited to contemplate entering God's holy temple.

Lesson 3

Revelation 21:1-6a (SC/C)

John offers a vision of the new heaven and the new earth and the joy that will wipe away all sorrow.

1 John 3:1-3 (RC)

We have been granted the greatest of gifts in being received by God as God's own children, which, in time to come, will reveal us to be like God, reflecting the divine image.

Gospel
John 11:32-44 (SC/C)
Jesus comes to Martha and Mary in their time of grief.

Matthew 5:1-12 (RC)
This passage is the beatitudes – Jesus' mandate to the community he calls to walk in God's ways – as recorded by the Gospel of Matthew.

Theme
God is already making all things new.

Thought for the Day
Eternity is not something that begins after you are dead. It is going on all the time. We are in it now.

— Lily Dougall, "The Undiscovered Country"

Sermon Summary
God has called us into a new creation right here, right now. God has called us to be saints of God now and here. Our baptism births us anew and commissions us for that vocation.

Call to Worship (in unison)
Come, sisters! Lift up your heart and mind with me!
Come, brothers! Lift up your soul and strength with me!
Come! Let us climb the holy mountain.
Come! Let us join the company of those who seek the God of Glory.

Pastoral Prayer
Alpha and Omega, you are our beginning and our end. You are our pathway and our goal. You are companion and journey. Help us to see through the veil of time to the eternal now in which your hope for creation already exists, whole and holy. Guide us to live as citizens of that new heaven and new earth in this time and place and, in so doing, to bring your shalom to radiant fulfillment. Amen.

Prayer of Confession

Holy and merciful God, we often are more ready to admire the saints than to imitate them – to praise them than to follow where they have led. We give our lives to the pursuit of success, pleasure, and self-aggrandizement, rather than spending ourselves for the sake of the kingdom. We are rich in earthly things but poor in the coin of heaven; we have filled our bellies with food that perishes but have not hungered and thirsted after justice. But in Christ and the saints, you have set before us a better way. Forgive our sinful and selfish choices. Renew and inspire us that we may once again set our feet on the path of holiness and service; through Christ our Lord. Amen.

Prayer of Dedication of Gifts and Self

Create in us such wise and generous stewardship of your gifts that these offerings may become new life for those to whom they are committed. Amen.

Hymn of the Day
For All the Saints

As we sing this hymn we are praising God for the Christian believers who have lived and died in all eras of history. We are giving thanks for those who have fought the good fight, remained faithful, and now live in bright array. We are reminded of the vastness of the family of saints, as gathered from the earth's widest bounds and ocean's farthest coast. Anglican bishop William W. How, in the year 1864, based this hymn on the Apostles' Creed statement: "I believe in the communion of saints." The tune SINE NOMINE by Ralph Vaughan Williams provides a powerful musical expression when sung with energy and rhythmic drive.

Children's Time: God's Dream

Have a brief conversation about dreams: What was the best dream you ever had? Comment that the Bible has many stories about people who heard God's voice in a dream.

Hold up a Bible and show the children how to find the book of Revelation. Explain that many years ago God shared a dream with John. It was a wonderful dream about the kind of world God wants for us. Paraphrase verses 3-4.

Invite the children to imagine what it would be like to live in a world where there was no sadness and everyone loved each other. What might it be like?

Comment that today is All Saints' Day. On this day we celebrate the lives of all the people who followed in God's way and worked to make the world a better place. These people wanted to see God's dream come true. (If you have time, you might want to give an example of someone who worked hard to bring God's love into the world.) Invite the children to name ways we might make our world a happier place to live.

Pray, giving thanks for all those who show us how make the world a better place to live.

– Sandra Anderson

The Sermon: Making All Things New
Scripture: Revelation 21:1-6a

In this vision of John of Patmos, God proclaims something we mortals have a difficult time comprehending. God does not say, "See, I am making all things better." God does not say, "See, I am making all things bigger . . . " or "different" or "beautiful" or, even, "perfect." God does not say, "See, I am changing all things." God says, "See, I am making all things new."

God is saying that everything we have understood about the creation in which we are currently living is or will be (it isn't clear what the correct verb tense is here) no longer valid. God is describing the creation the prophets were trying to tell us about when they talked about the lion lying down with the lamb and the child putting her hand in the adder's nest. This is the creation that doesn't make any sense under the rules as we understand them. This is the creation that Jesus was trying to explain to us when he talked about the owner of the vineyard hiring the workers at different times of day, but paying them all the same (abundant) wages, and about the first being last, and about a servant monarch. This is the creation that just doesn't compute in our worldly economies or earthly power structures.

It's hard for us to understand this new universe because we have only our human experience to inform us. No matter how hard we try, we can't imagine something beyond the laws of physics of the universe in which we live. We may think we are imagining truly new things, but I defy you to start from nothing and create something that you don't have to describe as "like an armadillo but with eight arms and fur." But *new* means a creation without fur or eight arms or sound, and we simply can't get there from here via the brain synapses and neurological pathways we already have!

"And the one who was seated on the throne said, 'See, I am making all things new.'"

Perhaps we will just have to wait until we are there to comprehend – whatever *comprehend* means in that universe. Perhaps we will just have to be where all things are new in order to understand it. And maybe it is just not important to worry about it at the moment.

There is, however, something that I suspect God really needs us to work on understanding right here and right now, on this specific All Saints' Day in the year of our Lord 2012. This is the day on which we annually remember and honor the saints of God, those people most of us consider extraordinary and rare, people like Francis and Mary (any one of them) and Mother Teresa of Calcutta, or like Paul or the martyrs of Uganda or Japan or New Guinea, or someone like the Venerable Bede or Clare or Dominic or Bernard. "What amazing people," we think to ourselves. "This is what it is like to be real disciples." We think how lucky we are to have such role models. And somewhere deep in our subconscious, where we truly believe our thoughts are masked even from God, we heave a huge internal sigh and think, "Thank God I am not religious enough to be among them!"

Uh, uh, uh . . . Put that thought away right now. Because guess what? If you are a baptized Christian, God is simply waiting for you to offer your name to be put on the calendar along with all the rest of them. "Wait," you say, "what is this about baptism and sainthood?" In baptism you and I and the person beside you in the pew were all made new. We were not made bigger, better, different, more beautiful, more perfect; we were not even changed (in the way most of us use that word), we were made new. We were told that in entering the waters of baptism, we died to the old self; and in rising from those waters, we were born anew of one being with Christ. We are told that we have been rooted or grafted to a different vine entirely. We are new creatures of a new creation. The fact that we are given the amazing baptismal present of being allowed to inhabit this creation for the purpose of incarnating that newness here and now seems to be part of God's plan for making "all things new" one creature at a time. That means you and me, folks.

"And the one who was seated on the throne said, 'See, I am making all things new.'"

See, I am making all things new. On this All Saints' Day, we are not only remembering and honoring those who chose to believe that they were new and to live as if they were new, we are reminding ourselves and each other that God is waiting for us to believe it and live it, too. I have said this before and I suspect I will say it many more times before I preach my last sermon: the saints of God are not some other people who lived in some other place or some other time. We – you, me, our parents, our children, our friends and, yes, even our enemies – are the saints of God. The difference between Francis or Mary and me is that they took up the vocation to which they had been commissioned . . . and I am still thinking about it.

What am I waiting for? This seems the ideal day to stop waiting and to say yes to the One who created me and then created me anew. It seems the ideal day for any of us who are still waiting to accept our sainthood, to stop dragging our heels, to start dancing with the angels and that great company of witnesses who surround us and uphold us.

My friends, my fellow saints of God, look! Listen! God speaks, "I am making all things new . . . It is done!" May it be so. Hallelujah! Hallelujah!
– Andrea La Sonde Anastos

Hymns
Opening: Give Thanks for Life
Sermon: O Holy City, Seen of John
Closing: O Day of Peace

November 4, 2012

23rd Sunday after Pentecost (Proper 26)
RC/Pres: 31st Sunday in Ordinary Time

Lessons

Semi-continuous (SC)	Complementary (C)	Roman Catholic (RC)
Ruth 1:1-8	Deut 6:1-9	Deut 6:2-6
Ps 146	Ps 119:1-8	Ps 18:2-4, 47, 50
Heb 9:11-14	Heb 9:11-14	Heb 7:23-28
Mk 12:28-34	Mk 12:28-34	Mk 12:28b-34

Speaker's Introduction for the Lessons
Lesson 1
Ruth 1:1-8 (SC)

> The opening of this book introduces Naomi and the life events
> through which she becomes the means for Ruth, a Moabite woman,
> to journey to Judah and eventually become an ancestor of Jesus.

Deuteronomy 6:1-9 (C); Deuteronomy 6:2-6 (RC)

> Moses tells the people to keep God's commandments as they pass
> into the land promised to them, carrying the commandments in their
> hearts and teaching them to their children.

Lesson 2
Psalm 146 (SC)

> The psalmist offers praise to God while cautioning against putting
> trust in "princes." The psalm closes with celebration of God's justice
> and reign.

Psalm 119:1-8 (C)

> This is the opening 8-verse stanza of 22 such stanzas that meditate on
> the gift of God's Torah and the wisdom it brings.

Psalm 18:2-4, 47, 51 (RC)

> This psalm celebrates God's joyful delivery from death and destruc-
> tion.

Lesson 3

Hebrews 9:11-14 (SC/C)

The personal sacrifice of Christ is infinitely preferable to the animal sacrifices previously offered; this sacrifice purifies all things for all time.

Hebrews 7:23-28 (RC)

Jesus is described as high priest, eternally available as an intercessor for humankind because, unlike the priests of Levi, Christ is recognized permanently by God.

Gospel

Mark 12:28-34 (SC/C/RC)

Jesus converses with one of the scribes about the two great commandments. This episode contradicts the simplistic understanding that all the religious authorities were enemies of Jesus.

Theme

God has no other hands than ours.

– Dorothee Sölle, *Suffering*

Thought for the Day

Disciples live the blessing that was, is, and will be in each moment that unfolds. They do not wait for some other life; they live holiness now.

Sermon Summary

To love God with our whole hearts, minds, souls, and strength is our true vocation. Our vocation is made manifest through loving the sisters and brothers that God has put beside us with our whole hearts, minds, souls, and strength.

Call to Worship

One: We come with what strength we have of heart, mind, and soul,
All: To learn to love the God who first loved us into being.
One: In joy, God returns that love with abundance,

All: Through the hands and hearts of our neighbors. Praise God from whom all blessings flow!

Pastoral Prayer

You call me your servant.
Grant me the grace this day to speak every word with your voice,
To greet each person with your compassion,
To make each decision with your wisdom,
To see every opportunity with your vision.
In every breath I take, may others see your glory revealed. Amen.

Prayer of Confession

Self-giving God, you loved us by taking on the fullness of our humanity.
We confess that we would rather forget what you taught us about being
fully human! We confess our halfhearted love of our neighbor, our mind-
less grasping after pleasure, our soul-numbed response to another's need,
our weak excuses in the face of injustice. We pray for forgiveness, but we
also pray that we may be awakened, startled, shocked into remembering
that others will know you through our actions. Amen.

Prayer of Dedication of Gifts and Self

Bless the offerings we bring, beloved God, that they may reflect not our
imperfect love but your boundless charity. May our hearts and souls be
graced in the giving, as we have been graced by receiving from others.
Amen.

Hymn of the Day
Spirit of God, Descend upon My Heart

Written by Irish pastor George Croly in 1867, this hymn recounts the
Holy Spirit's descent on Christ's baptism and at Pentecost. It also offers a
prayerful request for personal indwelling of the Spirit. This prayer is not
for a dramatic display but simply for the Spirit to "take the dimness of my
soul away." The fourth line of the fourth stanza presents a request that
may not be too popular, when we sing, "teach me the patience of unanswered prayer." Sing the hymn with a sense of quiet confidence, growing
in intensity on the final stanza in singing of our commitment to God.

Children's Time: The Most Important Rule

(Bring three large paper hearts and a marker)

Invite the children to think of some important rules or laws where you live. (You may have to recruit the help of some of the adults.) Do you have any family rules? Is there any rule that is more important than any other?

Open the Bible and mention that in today's Bible story Jesus talks about the two most important rules of all. Tell the story of Jesus' conversation with the Pharisees.

Show the three hearts and ask the children what Jesus said about love. Who are we to love? Print one of these words on each heart: God, Self, Others.

Explain that the first rule about love was a commandment written in the Hebrew Scriptures. This meant it was very special to Jesus and all Jewish people. Jesus added the second commandment because he knew it was very important for us to love one another.

Hold up each heart in turn and invite the children to name ways that we might show love to God, to ourselves, to others. Observe that there are many different ways of showing love.

Pray with the children, asking God to help you as you learn to love God, others, and yourselves.

The Sermon: All My Heart and Soul
Scripture: Mark 12:28-34

Listen, my sisters and brothers, to the words of that long-ago scribe of Israel. Listen to the words of one person whose heart was yearning to share in the life-giving teaching of Rabbi Jesus while he was traveling the dusty roads of the countryside with his followers and preaching. Listen to the scribe: "'To love one's neighbor as oneself' – this is much more important than all whole burnt offerings and sacrifices"(Mk 12:33b).

We are drawing near the end of the long season of Pentecost and preparing ourselves in these November days to conclude one liturgical year and begin a new one. In these final weeks of Pentecost, the gospel moves decisively toward apocalyptic readings. Our hearts and souls are invited to dance and to pray in *kairos* (God's paradoxical time), holding side by side the expectant longing of Advent and a prayerful consideration of the end time (the time not of the incarnation but of the second coming of Christ.) In that context, this encounter sits on a fulcrum between past and present: between the ancient riches and wisdom of Judaism in which Jesus was steeped, and the yet-to-be riches and wisdom of the Christian way that he visioned with his disciples.

It can be far too easy for 21st-century Christians to assume that every time Jesus spoke to the religious authorities there was conflict and antagonism. This, in turn, encourages many faithful churchgoers to believe that Jesus taught that Judaism was no longer valid as a path for God's covenanted people. Such misunderstanding of scripture leads some to disdain the spiritual wealth of Jewish practice and learning, or, even worse, to scapegoat Jews and permit in themselves an anti-Semitism that breeds violence.

We need to look again at our preconceptions. This dialog is not hostile; on the contrary, it is built around the blessing of tradition (represented by the scribe) on the new teaching that God is offering (represented by Jesus). The scribe invites Jesus to express the deepest, most holy truth of his belief and practice. Jesus responds with the Shema, one of the principle statements undergirding Judaism – a proclamation of the Holy as the center from which all creation flows and toward which all creation looks, "Hear, O Israel, the Lord our God, the Lord is one!" Then, in what is almost a duet, Jesus and the scribe trade additional statements about how God's people respond to God's outpouring, each building on the choices of the other in a soaring proclamation of what the kingdom of shalom will be like.

The passage ends with Jesus gathering the blessing from his past and casting it over the future. He tells the scribe, "You are not far from the kingdom of God" (12:34). What was the statement of the scribe that brought this blessing? Listen! "'To love one's neighbor as oneself' – this is much more important than all whole burnt offerings and sacrifices."

Whatever else can be said about burnt offerings and sacrifices, they are personal and individual, they are an offering back to God from me on my own behalf, from you on your behalf. Yes, burnt offerings and sacrifices were sometimes (in times of famine or exile or at the High Holy Days) made for the whole people; but 99 times out of 100, they were pretty private and pretty exclusive.

Jesus, standing firmly rooted in the prophetic Jewish tradition, was not about being private and exclusive! Jesus was about community. Jesus was about discovering the presence of God in community. Jesus was about Immanuel – God with us. The scribe doesn't say, nor does Jesus, that burnt offerings and sacrifices don't have their place. They do. A sacrifice is a way I practice with God what God is training me to do: love others.

Think of it this way: Have you ever watched a parent and child play what I call the "Give-Give Back" game? The parent gives the child something (a book, a blanket, a toy) and then asks for it back. The child gives it back and the parent says, "Thank you." Then the parent holds it for a moment and asks, "Would you like it back?" The child reaches for it and the parent prompts, "What do you say? Thank you?" The child attempts the words. The parent invites the child to offer the object again and says, "Thank you!" and the game continues. Some time later (weeks, months) the parent and child are with another child and now the parent invites the child to give the book, blanket, toy to the "neighbor." The initial game was practice for this much more important skill of sharing.

Most of us have seen this parenting technique so often that we don't think about how strange it is. Why should the parent say, "Thank you"? The object came from the parent in the first place! The child didn't buy this object or earn it. But each time the parent receives the object, she or he says, "Thank you!" We understand that the parent is modeling gratitude and inviting the child to mimic it. The parent is teaching the child how to receive with grace and how to give with generosity.

In the same way, a sacrifice or a burnt offering is God's way of teaching us how to receive with grace and give with generosity. God invites us to practice this easier generosity (giving back to God directly) so that we will mature into our real vocation, which is practicing generosity with one another – with friend and stranger and, yes, with enemy. Listen! "'To love one's neighbor as oneself' – this is much more important than all whole burnt offerings and sacrifices."

This Gospel reading is about the end time. It is about what that holy commonwealth will be like. In that glorious realm, the One God will be loved and praised with all our hearts and all our minds and all our souls, and every neighbor will be loved as we love ourselves. What Jesus was about in his earthly ministry was teaching us that "then" is really "now." There is nothing about "then" that we can't be doing right now. We are not far from the kingdom because it is among us, around us – beneath, above, and before us – in the neighbor we dare to love. May we live what we await. Amen.

– Andrea La Sonde Anastos

Hymns
Opening: As Those of Old Their First-Fruits Brought
Sermon: Here I Am, Lord
Closing: Go Forth for God

November 11, 2012

24th Sunday after Pentecost (Proper 27)
RC/Pres: 32nd Sunday in Ordinary Time

Lessons

Semi-continuous (SC)	Complementary (C)	Roman Catholic (RC)
Ruth 3:1-5, 4:13-17	1 Kings 17:8-16	1 Kings 17:10-16
Ps 127	Ps 146	Ps 146:7, 8-9, 10
Heb 9:24-28	Heb 9:24-28	Heb 9:24-28
Mk 12:38-44	Mk 12:38-44	Mk 12:38-44 or 12:41-44

Speaker's Introduction for the Lessons
Lesson 1
Ruth 3:1-5, 4:13-17 (SC)
Naomi urges her daughter-in-law Ruth to seek a husband in order that she might have some security in life. Ruth becomes the wife of Boaz and they become the ancestors of King David.

1 Kings 17:8-16 (C); 1 Kings 17:10-16 (RC)
This story of Elijah and the widow at Sidon recounts a miracle in the midst of famine.

Lesson 2
Psalm 127 (SC)
The psalmist affirms that human labor relies upon God for purpose and fulfillment, as well as the gift of rest from labor.

Psalm 146 (C); Psalm 146:7, 8-9, 10 (RC)
The psalmist offers praise to God while cautioning against putting trust in "princes." The psalm closes with celebration of God's justice and reign.

Lesson 3
Hebrews 9:24-28 (SC/C/RC)
The letter to the Hebrews compares Christ to a great high priest who intercedes for us with God.

Gospel
Mark 12:38-44 (SC/C/RC)

Jesus notes a widow who offers all that she has for the temple treasury and sees her as an example of unrestrained generosity.

Theme

The path to joy winds through extravagant, reckless self-denial.

Thought for the Day

"We always attract into our lives whatever we think about most, believe in most strongly, expect on the deepest level, and imagine most vividly."
— Shakti Gawain, *Reflections in the Light*

Sermon Summary

A poor woman, with very little to give, gives all that she has and is praised by Jesus. Sometimes our acts of reckless, thoughtless, and extravagant emotion are our best acts. Jesus calls us to recklessly, extravagantly, and passionately throw away all that we have and follow him.

Call to Worship

One: It is not enough to gather in this sanctuary made by human hands,

All: Because God is calling us to make all the world a holy sanctuary.

One: We come in to be strengthened to go out,

All: So that, at the end of time, all creation will be ready to be born again, whole and glorious.

Pastoral Prayer

Loving God, you willingly sacrificed yourself so that we could learn that not even death will separate us from you. You remind us again and again that our sins are already forgiven and redeemed and that Christ comes again not to judge but to save. You invite us to lay aside the fears that hold us back from becoming your whole and holy servant people. Grant us the confidence to believe your promise and to accept your invitation so that the commonwealth for which we wait eagerly may become reality in this world today. Amen.

Prayer of Confession

Lord Jesus, we want to follow your way, but we confess that we hold back. You call us to be your disciples, but we don't want to risk all and walk with you. We are cautious, fearful, and timid in our affections. You are bold, decisive, and brave in your love for us. Give us a spirit of boldness! Make us reckless, wild, and brash in our determination to have more abundant life. Inflame our desire for you, to walk with you, to serve you completely and extravagantly, and to love you with all that we are and all that we have. Amen.

Prayer of Dedication of Gifts and Self

Gracious God, what you have given abundantly for the good of all, receive back from overflowing hearts and open hands as a gift of salvation for those in need. May you bless us with the same fullness that we give. Amen.

Hymn of the Day
Seek Ye First the Kingdom of God

In the year 1971 contemporary American singer/songwriter Karen Lafferty was inspired to write the first stanza and music of this scripture song after attending a Bible study on Matthew 6:33. The second stanza appeared as an anonymous addition in 1980. The song became popular in the Jesus movement of the 1970s and early 1980s, helping to pave the way for today's contemporary Christian music movement. The text and simple tune call our attention to the eternal things of God and away from the material things of this world. This provides a convenient way of memorizing scripture; thus, the term "scripture song."

Children's Time: What Can We Give?

(Bring offering plates and offering envelopes to show. If needed, bring paper and pencils. Arrange for a slip of paper to be inserted with each worship bulletin.)
Have some conversation around the offering part of worship. Most parishes or congregations have a time in their worship service for the taking up and dedication of the offering.

Ask the children what they think the offering is for. Say, "Do you ever wonder why we call it `offering'? It's a special time to stop and think about all that God has given to us, and to say, `Here, God, I'm offering something back to you.'"

Talk about the many ways we can give to God. Some people talk about offering God our time, our talents, and our treasure. God knows that all of us have time, talents, and treasure that we can share. The offering is a part of that – a way of saying "Thanks, God, for all we have received from you. We want to be givers, too, by sharing in the work you do in the world."

If you have time, invite everyone together, both children and adults, to write down or draw one thing (besides money) that they could offer of themselves to put in the offertory plate. Assure them that these will be presented during the offering. (Alternative: Find a way to include the children in the offertory part of the service. One way of doing this would be to change the order of the service, just this once, to make the offertory part of the children's time. You could even include them in all the activities that take place during this time – collecting, and receiving – and giving thanks.)

The Sermon: Praise for the Passionate
Scripture: Mark 12:38-44

Being interviewed about seminary education and preparation of future clergy, Dean Greg Jones of Duke Divinity School was asked, "What quality do you want most in future clergy?"

Dean Jones responded, "I think, passion. I would look for passion. I'm looking for students who have a passion for ministry, a desire for God, and a love for the church."

"Passion?" I thought we were Christians. We are against passion!

No. Paul says that the three greatest human attributes in the world are "faith, hope, and love" (1 Cor 13).

Aren't all of these emotions, passions, and desires?

The emotions, the passions, get a bad press in the history of human thought. The pre-Socratic philosophers thought that there was a role in human thought for the passions. Heracleitus saw the world as in constant flux. Our lives are the result of struggle between competing forces. Human beings are in constant conflict between reason and emotion – and this is good. The conflict itself produces truthful living. The goal of the well-lived life is to achieve a good mix of reason and emotion, a healthy tug and pull between these two opposites.

But when you get two philosophers like Plato and Aristotle, reason takes over – cool, dispassionate, and thoughtful reason. In Plato, for instance, there is the idea that, within the same human soul, the soul is divided into three parts. There is a rational part, which ought to be the dominant part, thought Plato. Then there is the appetite and the spiritual part. Our appetites and our spiritual strivings make us excited and agitated. The goal of life is to foster reasonableness that holds our appetites and strivings in check. But it is clear that, for Plato, reason is the dominant human characteristic. The purpose of philosophy for Plato is to make sure our reason has its way with us.

Thus, Plato has his famous image of the human soul as a chariot pulled by three horses. The three horses are reason, appetite, and spirituality. For the chariot to go forward, all of these three horses must be pulling together. And for that to occur, reason must be the dominant one, leading the other two.

Plato's teacher, Socrates, often warned his students not to be carried away by emotion. Moderation is the best way. You can take this as an axiom for most of Western philosophy – don't get carried away with emotions. Plato's student Aristotle stressed that the good life is the life of moderation. In all things, strive for the golden mean, the middle way, neither too far to the right nor to the left. A good society is dependent upon a large middle class, said Aristotle. Extremes, whether they are the extremes of wealth and poverty, or the extremes of flux and order, are to be avoided. Seek, in all things, the moderate, balanced, middle way.

But think, you rational, bloodless philosophers, of how our emotions give our lives substance and meaning! Might it be that emotion is not the opposite of thought but rather another, perhaps even more complex way of thinking? One of the ways we perceive the world, move into reality is through our emotions – joy, sadness, ecstasy, heartache, grief, and love.

Even the grammar of our language has a negative view of emotions. We say that our emotions get the best of us. One is struck by jealousy, paralyzed by fear, overwhelmed with emotion. One falls in love, is madly in love, green with envy, fighting mad, or insane with jealousy.

With emotions we are "bewitched, bothered, and bewildered," as the song says.

We become the victims of emotions. We say, "I'm sorry, I just got carried away."

Emotions involve suffering. The very word *passion* means "suffering." The very word expresses the idea that feelings take us off in the wrong direction. In Buddhism, the Sanskrit word for emotion is *affliction.*

Aristotle urged us to aim for the golden mean. We are to aim for that state in life where we are balanced, not too much on the one side or the other – our reason rules.

Years ago, during one of the presidential elections, William Buckley and the author Gore Vidal were offering color commentary on the nomination process during the political convention. Throughout their time together, Vidal kept taunting Buckley. Finally, Buckley, as we say, lost it. He let forth a string of insults and invective against Vidal.

Later, Buckley was quoted as saying, "He won." That is, Buckley lost it, gave in to his emotions, and thus allowed Vidal to defeat him.

Isn't it interesting that we say, when we have given in to our emotions, that we lost it? To be a mature, thoughtful human being, one cannot lose it; one cannot give in to emotions. Thus, the Greeks conceived human life as a long process of the utilization of reason and the suppression of emotion.

But then, here comes Jesus. An old lady passes by the temple treasury as people are putting their offering in the coffers. It isn't just that she gave but that she gave everything she had. All. Others gave more money, but she gave a greater proportion of what she had.

Why did she give it all? We are not told. Jesus simply notes the effusive, extravagant nature of her giving. She gave all, this poor widow. The one who had the least gave the most.

Why? What was her reason for giving? Perhaps there was no reason, because what she did was quite beyond mere reason. Perhaps she got carried away in her religious devotion; I've known folk who have.

If you ask them about their Christian commitment, how did they decide to follow Christ, you will find it was not so much a matter of their decision. It was an emotion, a feeling, or an extravagant example of someone carried away. Perhaps being a Christian, for many of us, is not a matter of decision and deliberation but a matter of feeling, a matter of the affections.

I fear that sometimes those of us in mainline Protestant Christianity may have over-rationalized the Christian faith, presenting Christianity as a matter of belief, principle, and ideas. There are churches that keep reminding themselves that it's a matter of the affections, something that you feel in your heart before it gets in your head.

I know a woman who grew up in an atheistic home. She had no church background at all. She lived most of her life quite happily with no Jesus, no Christian faith.

Then, at age 41, in her words, she found Jesus. She began attending church every time the doors opened. But she did not limit her piety to the church. She began a ministry among the poorest of the city's poor. She began inviting homeless families into her home. Her life was consumed with thoughts of how she might show her love for Jesus.

To us, it seemed a bit, well, extravagant. She seemed, to some, out of control.

Perhaps she had come under the control of another who had released in her energy, vitality, and passion beyond the bounds of our measured faith. She put us in the mind of another extravagant, passionate woman long ago. Jesus tends to do that to some people. Has he ever had that effect on you?

– William H. Willimon

Hymns
Opening: Joyful, Joyful, We Adore You
Sermon: There's a Wideness in God's Mercy
Closing: Jesu, Jesu, Fill Us with Your Love

November 18, 2012

25th Sunday after Pentecost (Proper 28)
RC/Pres: 33rd Sunday in Ordinary Time

Lessons

Semi-continuous (SC)	Complementary (C)	Roman Catholic (RC)
1 Sam 1:4-20	Dan 12:1-3	Dan 12:1-3
1 Sam 2:1-10	Ps 16	Ps 16:5, 8, 9-10, 11
Heb 10:11-14 (15-18), 19-25	Heb 10:11-14 (15-18), 19-25	Heb 10:11-14, 18
Mk 13:1-8	Mk 13:1-8	Mk 13:24-32

Speaker's Introduction for the Lessons

Lesson 1

1 Samuel 1:4-20 (SC)

Amid gross misunderstanding – barrenness was wrongly considered spiritual disfavor and sincere prayer was falsely equated with drunkenness – God's servant, Hannah, received assurance of God's favor.

Daniel 12:1-3 (RC/C)

Though no one knows the time and circumstances of the final reality of history, we can be certain of God's identity as loving deliverer, even in the midst of the most trying circumstances.

Lesson 2

1 Samuel 2:1-10 (SC)

The song of Hannah confesses the power of God employed for the sake of justice and equity.

Psalm 16 (C); Psalm 16:5, 8, 9-10, 11 (RC)

The psalmist affirms the providential care of God that makes life possible.

Lesson 3

Hebrews 10:11-14 (15-18), 19-25 (SC/C); Hebrews 10:11-14, 18 (RC)

Through the ministry of Christ, God removed for all time the need for any intercessor to stand between God and us in order to secure forgiveness for our sins. No more offerings for sin are required.

Gospel

Mark 13:1-8 (SC/C); Mark 13:24-32 (RC)

Using the language of apocalyptic literature to describe disturbing developments related to the end time, Jesus assures his followers that not even the worst that happens can invalidate the promise of God's word regarding salvation.

Theme

Our identity as followers of Christ is that of priests to each other.

Thought for the Day

The priesthood bestowed upon us by Christ takes the form of a blessing as we claim our individual access to God and the form of a responsibility as we serve as priests to each other.

Sermon Summary

Jesus, the great high priest, commissions us to serve as priests offering forgiveness, exuding confidence, confessing hope, prompting love, and providing encouragement to one another.

Call to Worship

> One: Our hearts are glad, our bodies secure, and our souls rejoice.
> **All: We bless you, O God.**
> One: You, O God, show us the path of life and grant us the pleasures of living.
> **All: We worship you, God, and sing your praises now and forever.**

Pastoral Prayer

Holy God, sustain within us the praise appropriate to you as creator and redeemer. Strengthen us by the teachings of your written word. Energize us through our realization of your forgiveness. Stretch the reach of our compassion by extending the breadth of our vision of need. Elicit from us actions of generosity and helpfulness. And, please God, keep vital our prayers and actions by the fidelity of your presence with us, that we may seek to be as faithful, healing, and loving in our lives as was Jesus in his life. Amen.

Prayer of Confession

O God, sometimes that for which we want to pray is buried so deep within us – mired in fear, sunk in embarrassment, wedged in sorrow – that we cannot find and form words to convey it. For some of us, the subject about which we long to speak to you is wrapped in so much hurt that to give words to it seems to be more painful than we can stand. Dear God, you have promised that when we cannot voice our prayers, you will understand our pained groans, our deep sighs, and even our silence. So, look into our souls, God. Please sense the tremors of our spirits. Touch the turbulence of our thoughts. Listen to our silence. Interpret the emptiness of the space where ordinarily words fit, and know the reality of our lives that exists beyond where words form. Hear our prayers, O God. Amen.

Prayer of Dedication of Gifts and Self

Though, in our giving, we never can come close to equaling the ultimate offering made by Jesus, O God, we do seek to emulate Jesus by offering to you right now – for your glory and for the good of others – all that we are and all that we have. Amen.

Hymn of the Day
O Love, How Deep, How Broad, How High

Having the organ or other instrument announce this hymn in a majestic manner introduces us to an in-depth description of Christ's self-sacrificing love. The hymn is an 1854 translation by Anglican minister Benjamin Webb of an anonymous 15th-century Latin hymn. The hymn illustrates Christ's deep, broad, and high love through his incarnation, baptism, ministry, passion, death, resurrection, and exalted reign. We enjoy a grand climax of directed praise and thanksgiving as we sing the sixth stanza's "all glory to our Lord and God . . . " The name of the tune DEO GRACIAS (once named AGINCOURT) means "thanks be to God."

Children's Time: God's Forgiveness
(Bring a small whiteboard, dry-erase markers, and eraser)
Talk briefly about the board and show the children how it works. Explain that you like to use the board because you don't have to worry about making mistakes. Draw a simple picture and make an obvious mistake, then erase it. Comment that the wonderful thing about the whiteboard is that you can try over and over again. The eraser always works.

Comment that this whiteboard and eraser remind you of God's love. Sometimes in our lives we make mistakes. *(Write "oops!" on the board.)* We forget to live in God's loving ways. When that happens all we have to do is ask God to forgive us and God erases the mistake. *(Erase the board.)* We can start over and try again.

Comment that the Bible tells us that God will forgive us every single time we ask. *(Write the word "oops!" on the board several times and invite the children to take turns erasing the board.)* We get a fresh new start every time. Isn't God's love amazing?

Pray with the children, giving thanks for God's amazing love.

The Sermon: Commissioned as Priests
Scripture: Hebrews 10:11-14, 19-25

Reading the exquisite promises from the writer of Hebrews makes me a bit uncomfortable. Oh, to be sure, I am grateful beyond measure for affirmation of the truth about Christ's priestly work – its singular sufficiency for everybody, its comfort and assurance personally, its revolutionary promise regarding forgiveness. Then I ponder the implications of this blessing – the responsibility that is mine as a beneficiary of Christ's offering. The ministry of Jesus has become my ministry and yours. We have been made priests. We are priests called by God and commissioned by Christ. We are priests to each other. And what a priesthood it is!

Frankly, my first reaction to this realization of priesthood was a sense of heaviness imposed by an anticipation of more responsibilities stacked on top of an already large pile of duties. After further reflection, however, I realized that the basic issue here is not more tasks to be assumed but a basic identity to be embraced and enjoyed – a recognition of who we are that prods us to be all we can be, all that God created us to be. That understanding of our priesthood births a sense of excitement and expectation.

Though not included among the readings today, 1 Peter 2:9-10 and 4:8-11 read like an insightful commentary on the Hebrews text. Christ, who extended grace to us, in turn appointed us as stewards of grace. Just as we received mercy from him, we are to extend mercy to others. Having been blessed by the unique priestly ministry of Jesus, we also have been charged to bless others through our shared ministry as Christ-appointed priests. The author of 1 Peter writes with a clarity that leaves no room for doubt or confusion regarding our identity and ministry: "You are a chosen race, a royal priesthood . . . Once you were not a people, but now you are God's people" (1 Pet 2:9-10).

What does this mean? Since Jesus has offered the ultimate sacrifice and cleared the way for us to relate to God personally, what is left for us to do? What is the nature of the priesthood to which we have been called? Look carefully – the characteristics of this priesthood are enumerated by the author of the Hebrews text.

First, Jesus commissions us to a priesthood of forgiveness (Heb 10:18). What we see in Jesus points us to the nature of God and to the nature of our lives as the people of God. In other words, what Jesus did, we are to do – namely, serve as facilitators of forgiveness.

Be forewarned that, at times, this can be scandalous work. Almost everyone can name somebody whom they think does not deserve forgiveness. Jesus, though, reveals to us the God who is not a moralist, not an accountant, not a rules maker, not a power broker, not a law enforcement officer, but a graceful lover eager to take the burden of sin off people's backs. Such an identity for God combined with such a ministry from Jesus must inform our priestly efforts.

No priest of God rightly can withhold from an individual who has sinned that which God freely offers to everybody, that for which Jesus made the once-and-for-all offering described in the Hebrews text. To withhold the grace of God from a person who has sinned is a sin every bit as serious as the sin to which the withholding is a response. Acting as a miser of grace contradicts ministry inspired by the priesthood of Jesus.

Second, Jesus commissions us to a priesthood characterized by humble confidence (10:19). The work of Jesus fills us with confidence regarding our ability to experience forgiveness and our opportunity to engage God in the "holy of holies" of life. Herein is all of the authority that we need to function as priests to each other. Confidence, however, must not be confused with arrogance. Our responsibility is to serve each other, not to try to play God or to take on the authority of Jesus in relation to each other.

Knowing with confidence the all-sufficient work of Jesus allows us to speak boldly about Jesus – commending him to others – and to serve others compassionately in Jesus' name without attempting to take unto ourselves work that only Jesus can do. So confident are we of Jesus that humbly we refrain from judging other people and proclaiming who is and who is not acceptable to God.

Third, Jesus commissions us to a priesthood of hopefullness (10:23). What good news we have been given to share with people! God keeps promises, and the promise of the work of Jesus is forgiveness, reconciliation with God, and meaning in life for all of us.

Some years back I spent a good deal of time among hurricane survivors – people for whom hope seems scandalous. Life has not been easy for these folks. Things have gone badly for them. Depression seems more fitting than positive expectation. Such individuals will not listen to an easy optimism or be moved by promises based only on hunches.

Among priests commissioned by Jesus, the substance of hope consists not of a Pollyanna view of the future but of a realistic view of the past. Look what God has done through Christ. Consider the provisions made for us in the priestly ministry of Jesus. We have every reason to live with vibrant, expectant hope and to encourage others to do the same.

Fourth, Jesus commissions us to a priesthood provocative of love (10:24). Because we have been loved so lavishly, we love responsibly. To experience the love of God through the revelation and actions of Jesus is to live by love ourselves and to seek to prompt love among others.

Virtually nothing in this whole Hebrews passage on priesthood makes sense apart from recognition of its foundation of love. Both the gift of God and the offering of Jesus were profound expressions of love. Our subsequent priesthood reeks with a lack of authenticity if both its words and actions are not transparent to a similar love within us and a desire for such love within others.

Finally, Jesus commissions us to a priesthood that is encouraging (10:25). To us is given the happy responsibility, rooted in the love of God and the grace of Jesus, of enabling others to feel better about themselves, to see previously unrecognized possibilities in their lives, and to face the future with eager anticipation. Conversely, any priesthood that trades primarily in prohibitions, judgment, negatives, and condemnation is not the priesthood commissioned by Jesus.

Our commission as priests is accompanied by a positive promise. Though we work every day at the responsibilities assigned to us by Jesus – offering forgiveness, exuding confidence, confessing hope, prompting love, and providing encouragement – we need not worry about the success of our efforts. The results of our priestly work already have been assured by the one who calls us to this work and makes us strong in the faith that allows us to live as the righteous people of God. Thanks be to God! Amen.

– C. Welton Gaddy

Hymns
Opening: Love Divine, All Loves Excelling
Sermon: There's a Wideness in God's Mercy
Closing: Called as Partners in Christ's Service

November 22, 2012

Thanksgiving Day (U.S.A.)

Lessons

Semi-Continuous (SC)	Complementary (C)	Roman Catholic (RC)
Joel 2:21-27	Joel 2:21-27	Deut 8:7-18
Ps 126	Ps 126	Ps 67:2-3, 5, 7-8
1 Tim 2:1-7	1 Tim 2:1-7	1 Cor 1:3-9
Mt 6:25-33	Mt 6:25-33	Mk 5:18-20

Speaker's Introduction for the Lessons

Lesson 1

Joel 2:21-27 (SC)

> The prophet Joel calls the people of God to exultant praise, sure that even pestilence and war fail to prevent a proliferation of blessings and goodness from God. Let there be no doubt that God is among us.

Deuteronomy 8:7-18 (RC)

> This passage reminds the people of Isreal not to forget God when they experience prosperity.

Lesson 2

Psalm 126 (SC/C)

> The psalm offers a community song of thanks for God's transformative acts of restoration and homecoming.

Psalm 67:2-3, 5, 7-8 (RC)

> The psalmist prays for God's blessing upon the people while confessing God's saving power among all the nations.

Lesson 3

1 Timothy 2:1-7 (SC/C)

> The joy of thanksgiving is made full when we obey God as revealed in the scriptures and give thanks for other people.

1 Corinthians 1:3-9 (RC)

> Thanksgiving for other people inexorably leads into thanksgiving for Christ who strengthens people with spiritual gifts and sustains them

to the end of life, and thanksgiving for God who is faithful to all of us beyond measure.

Gospel
Matthew 6:25-33 (SC/C)
Jesus described God as the faithful provider and the great caregiver. Acknowledging this identity of God stills anxieties within us and increases our praise and thanksgiving to God.
Mark 5:18-20 (RC)
After his healing from demon possession, a man becomes a witness to Jesus' power.

Theme
Let gratitude trump anxiety today.

Thought for the Day
All that we have and all that we are is a gift from God – and an opportunity to lift up the lives of others.

Sermon Summary
Thanksgiving calls us out of anxiety and into gratitude expressed in words of thanks and actions of service.

Call to Worship
One: It is good to give thanks to God.
All: How great are God's works!
One: It is good to give thanks for God's steadfast love and faithfulness.
All: We will worship God with thanksgiving!

Pastoral Prayer
Great loving and giving God: What are we to do when it is time to give thanks and not all is well? Deliver us, God, from a chauvinistic gratitude that says, "We are thankful that we are so much better off than other

people." Spare us the thanksgiving of cynicism that says, "This is probably as good as things can ever be, so we are thankful." Mute the thankful impulses in our hearts that have been stirred by pessimism that says, "There is nothing we can do but give thanks; it doesn't matter much anyway." O God, nurture within us sensitivity to your love and the resources of your presence that, even in the worst of situations, we may know how to give thanks for your gifts. Amen.

Prayer of Confession

O God, sometimes, most of the time, actually, we feel caught between competing emotions – between praise and protest, between gratitude and cynicism, between optimism and despair, between thanksgiving and complaints. The dilemma is not merely a subjective one; our lives are pulled in diametrically different directions. We feel spiritually stretched as if on a rack. Relief looks possible only if we relieve the tension and go with one emotion alone. But such a mode of relief poses problems for our integrity; we can't simply close our eyes to difficulties in order to mouth praises. Yet, total cynicism is not a possibility because we know that underneath that which fills us with anxiety are realities that properly evoke gratitude. Great God, enable us to tolerate ambivalence and speak to you as honestly about our thankfulness as about our complaints. God, help us, please. Amen.

Prayer of Dedication of Gifts and Self

O God, you have blessed us with gifts beyond measure and love that defies understanding. We give you now a portion of our possessions, a promise of our devotion, and the commitment of our lives, daring to hope that you will feel blessed by us. Amen.

Hymn of the Day
For the Fruit of All Creation

This hymn by Fred Pratt Green originally bore the title "Harvest Hymn" with the opening line, "For the fruits of his creation." The hymn also appears in some hymnals with the title "For the Fruits of This Creation" and in others as "For the Fruits of His Creation." The original hymn was written by Green for the purpose of supplying a fresh text for the hymn tune EAST ACKLAM, composed by Francis Jackson in 1957. First printed in the British publication *Methodist Recorder* in 1970, the hymn has enjoyed widespread use as a thanksgiving hymn with a strong social gospel accent.

Children's Time: Thanksgiving
(Bring a variety of thank-you cards)
Pass around the thank-you cards, and tell how you might use them to write thank-you notes. Ask: How else might you say thank you to someone? Has anyone said thank you to you this week? How did you feel when that person thanked you?

Comment that the Bible tells a story about a group of ten people who had a lot to be thankful for. Jesus had healed them, and they went off to tell the good news to others. But one of the ten came back to thank Jesus. Talk about the story: How do you think the man felt when Jesus made him better? Why did he come back to say thank you to Jesus? How do you think Jesus felt when the man said thank you?

Comment that this story reminds us that it's good to give thanks. We can thank other people when they help us, and we can thank God for all the things God has done.

Observe that today is Thanksgiving, a special day when we say thank you for the all the ways God has blessed us. Mention that Thanksgiving Day is just one day in the year, but we can remember to say thank you to God every day.

Pray with the children, giving thanks for all of God's blessings.

The Sermon: Thanksgiving or Thanxiety?
Scripture: Matthew 6:25-33

Some biblical texts are easy to hear but difficult to understand, because they seem rooted in some experience not our own. Other texts are difficult to hear but all too easy to understand, because they read as if God had whispered into the author's ears our biography. For me, this morning's text from Matthew falls neatly though uncomfortably into that latter category.

In three different places there, Jesus challenges the mindset and life-style that is beset with anxiety: "Do not worry about your life . . . . is not life more than food, and the body more than clothing? Therefore do not worry."

Worry. Anxiety. At the grand old age of nine, I vaguely remember a doctor telling my mother with some puzzlement that her son had ulcers. Apparently by nature before, and somewhat by nurture since, I enjoy having things organized and under control. When they aren't, anxiety sometimes results. Now while others of you may not have quite the problem as I have had with fretting over things, I think the tendency to be anxious is fairly widespread among us. If it were not so, Jesus need not have spoken and Matthew need not have preserved these words.

Perhaps that contributes to why this reading from Matthew is so appropriate on Thanksgiving. It is a valuable rendering of the Gospel to any and all who fall prey to more than our share of anxious moments in tending to the details of life. Details that, as the day of Thanksgiving would remind us, are rather secondary when compared to the source and gift of our lives.

Yet another timely aspect of this text is that we are poised to enter that season of the year haunted, with all due apologies to Charles Dickens, by the ghost of Christmas Anxiety. There is *so* much to be *done* in the coming weeks: presents to buy, cards to write, packages to mail, dinners to plan, trips to make, relatives to be remembered . . . And that rush, for some of us, begins with getting ready for what we will do and where we will be and whom we will host and what we will eat in a few hours. If a person is not careful, the preparations soon overtake and surpass, if not totally overwhelm the holiday itself – be it Thanksgiving or Christmas. Little wonder that this week inaugurates the time of year for which counselors and mental health clinics and suicide prevention lines brace themselves for a wave of crises. For more than any other, this is the season when people are most easily disappointed – and most deeply depressed. With all the time and energies and finances spent in getting things just right, our expectations can easily soar beyond reality. And when the time finally arrives to gather 'round the table or sit beside the tree, and we find ourselves wondering why we feel so exhausted and why we don't enjoy things like we used to . . . of such things are the fruits of anxiety. Fruits that give no nourishment and provide no satisfaction but only deepening hunger. So where do we find rest – which, given today's context, might also be rendered, where do we anchor our thanks-giving? Consider some of the things proposed by Jesus in today's passage:

It is the rest, and thanks, of discovering our anxieties add nothing to the length, nor depth, nor breadth of our lives. "Can any of you by worrying add a single hour to your span of life?" (6:27). These concerns need not control us, since they add nothing to us.

- It is the rest that comes from taking in the sights and sounds and gifts of creation – in the imagery of Matthew 6, the birds of the air and the lilies of the field. It is the rest that comes by perceiving in their existence the hand of God's care and providence, so we may go on to trust in that same care and providence for our own lives.

- It is the rest that comes from gaining such new perspective to our lives: that what we get by hustle and bustle is not all there is to life. For as the text affirms, isn't life more than food, and the body more than clothing? Or to consider it specifically in the light of Thanksgiving: isn't the family more than well-stocked tables and window-dressed appearances that would make Martha Steward envious?

On a day when we celebrate God's providence with our thanks, it is good to be reminded that while it's a pleasant experience to have plenty of food to choose from and a closet of clothes to match occasion and need, such things are truly secondary and even incidental to the meaning of Thanksgiving. For to put first things first, the text presents the perspective that we are valued of God, valued more than the birds that are fed so freely and the fields that are beautifully clothed so by God. A valuing that, in turn, encourages our love of and compassion for those with whom we share this gift of God's providence.

After all, it is one thing to be anxious over what we will eat and quite another to be anxious over whether we will eat. It is one thing to be anxious over what we shall put on as clothing and quite another to be anxious over having clothing period. For those of us who need not be anxious in these things, thanksgiving can take the shape of alleviating the anxiety of those who have real cause to wonder where the next meal or sheltering roof will come from.

For as we engage in such actions, we do not just remove another's anxiety over food or clothing or shelter. We may play unseen roles in helping them know they are loved and valued. And for those who are crippled by feeling they are unloved and without value even in the midst of their

plenty, our acceptance of them for who they are – not what they have
– may be the best gift we have to offer.

As you gather with family and friends, or perhaps as you face this day
by yourself, take these words of Jesus to heart. Words about birds and lilies
and getting first things first. So that in your busyness – or perhaps in your
loneliness – you do not succumb to anxiousness. So that in reveling in the
gifts enjoyed in abundance, we do not forget the needs of those who may
lack in many things – but not in God's love for them. Thanksgiving calls
us to remember the important things in life: the Creator who cares for all
with grace and love, the gifts of providence entrusted to bring joy to us
and to those whose lives God enables us to touch. Thanks be to God!

– John Indermark

Hymns
Opening: We Gather Together
Sermon: We Praise You, O God
Closing: God, Whose Giving Knows No Ending

November 25, 2012

Reign of Christ/Christ the King(Proper 29)

Lessons

Semi-continuous (SC)	Complementary (C)	Roman Catholic (RC)
2 Sam 23:1-7	Dan 7:9-10, 13-14	Dan 7:13-14
Ps 132:1-12 (13-18)	Ps 93	Ps 93:1a, 1b--2, 5
Rev 1:4b-8	Rev 1:4b-8	Rev 1:5-8
Jn 18:33-37	Jn 18:33-37	Jn 18:33-37

Speaker's Introduction for the Lessons
Lesson 1
2 Samuel 23:1-7 (SC)
> Through words attributed to King David, his last words we are told, this popular ruler of Israel describes the essence of civil leadership – a ruler who fears God, a ruler that advances justice.

Daniel 7:9-10, 13-14 (C); Daniel 7:13-14 (RC)
> With mind-boggling metaphors and fiery images, the writer of Daniel describes how all realms of sovereignty will pass away until the realm of God's rule is established forever.

Lesson 2
Psalm 132:1-12 (13-18) (SC)
> The psalmist calls on God to remember the promises of the Davidic covenant and dynasty.

Ps 93 (C); Psalm 93:1a, 1b-2, 5 (RC)
> This enthronement psalm celebrates God as sovereign, bringing the image of waters (originally a symbol of chaos that God tamed in creation) to thunder God's praise.

Lesson 3
Revelation 1:4b-8 (SC/C); Revelation 1:5-8 (RC)

The book of Revelation opens with a cosmic burst of praise for the Messiah. Christ is recognized as supreme among all who rule and lauded as the sovereign who loves us, frees us, and calls us into a realm of obedient service to God.

Gospel
John 18:33-37 (SC/C/RC)

In response to Pontius Pilate's concern about the reign of Christ, Jesus explains that the realm of his rule is not in this world. Indeed, all who know the truth understand the nature of Christ's reign as well as the nature of his identity as a ruler.

Theme

A review of the life of Christ prompts affirmation of the sovereignty of Christ.

Thought for the Day

The reign of Christ is a reign of love.

Sermon Summary

According to Jesus, dominion is shaped by compassion. Love is supreme – king or queen, if you will. Its goal is a fellowship of redemption. Its strategy involves forgiveness and reconciliation. Its mode of operation is humble service.

Call to Worship

One: Lift up your heads, people of God. Behold the King of glory.

All: Who is this King of glory?

One: The Lord of hosts, the eternal God, is the King of glory.

All: We lift our heads, we bow our knees, and we open our hearts to worship the King of glory, our God, graceful and mighty.

Pastoral Prayer

O God, we celebrate the reign of the Christ who wipes away our tears and joins our laughter, comforts our grief and draws us into joy. Keep us always mindful of the sovereignty that allows us to experience intimacy with Christ in the shadows of our lives as well as in the sunlight, when spiritually lost in a wilderness even as when gloriously found in a service of worship. Make us ever mindful of the provisions inherent in a realm in which the governing law is the spirit of love, and a beloved community in which all are included is the goal of every person devoted to the Christ. Amen.

Prayer of Confession

We are so busy, God. Our calendars are so full. Why, we don't even have time for you – to study, to worship, to commune, to serve. Thank you for having time for us, God. Forgive us for any momentary lapse in our recognition of your providence. Forgive us as well for a presumption of busyness that leaves no time for focused experiences with you. How foolish can we get? Please, God, stop us, quiet us, and make us be still. Grant us the courage to say no to any commitment on our calendars that leaves us without time to meditate, to pray, to worship, to count our blessings, to confess our sins, to realize that we are not alone, to express our love for you – to be reborn. Amen.

Prayer of Dedication of Gifts and Self

Divine Giver of all that is good, we seek freedom from the cultural philosophy of possessions as power and money as a means of control. That is why we dedicate to you not only who we are but what we have, praying that you will use our possessions, our money, and, indeed, our very lives as instruments of compassion and service for the betterment of others and for your glory. Amen.

Hymn of the Day
Jesus Shall Reign

This hymn is a paraphrase of the second part of Psalm 72, written by Isaac Watts. It was included by Watts in his *Psalms of David, Imitated in the Language of the New Testament* in 1719. One of Isaac Watts's major contributions to English hymnody is his Christian interpretation of psalms. Although Psalm 72 is a prayer for the king of Israel, Watts makes Jesus the subject of his paraphrase. Even though Watts intended his psalm paraphrase as an adaptation to address the circumstances of 18th-century Christians, it applies just as easily to the Christians of the 21st century.

Children's Time: Jesus the King

(Bring a paper crown for each child and a children's book that has a story about a king or queen)
Show the book and ask the children to tell you what they know about queens and kings: What do they do? Where do they live? What do they wear?

Explain that in Jesus' time the people of Israel had been hoping and praying for a long time. They wanted God to send a new king to lead them. God heard their prayers and sent Jesus, but Jesus was not the kind of king the people expected. Discuss this notion by asking: Was Jesus born in a palace? Did he sit on a throne? Did he have a golden crown to wear? Did Jesus boss people around? What kinds of things did Jesus do? Comment that Jesus was a very different kind of king.

Observe that today is Reign of Christ/Christ the King Sunday. It's a time to remember what kind of leader Jesus was and how we can follow his example.

Give each child a paper crown to wear as a reminder to love and help others like Jesus did.

Pray with the children, giving thanks for Jesus the king, who came to show God's love.

The Sermon: Tell It Again!
Scripture: John 18:33-37

Some years back, I had the good fortune to share worship leadership responsibilities with the outstanding African American actor and musician Jester Hairston. We took the theme for the service from the gospel song that is almost synonymous with Jester's name – that wonderful, rollicking choral piece, "Amen." Likely you know the rhythm and the text: "A-a-amen, a-a-amen, a-a-amen, amen, amen." This piece of music reviews the life of Jesus from beginning to end, following every reference to history with the ringing refrain "amen," meaning "let it be so" or "so be it."

The whole story of Jesus' role in salvation history is right there in Jester's words – Christmas morning, Easter, "talkin'," baptizin'," prayin'," and savin'." There is a recognition of deepest sorrow, knowing that Jesus was led before Pilate and an exclamation of "Hallelujah" recognizing that Jesus rose and lives forever. The whole gospel story is there and every part of it is followed with a resounding "Amen."

In the more formal liturgy of Christians gathered in public worship, the grand story of salvation unfolds through a pilgrimage guided by the worship-oriented road map through time that we call the Christian year – Advent, Christmas, Epiphany, Lent, Holy Week, Easter, Pentecost, and the long stretch of spirit-filled Ordinary Time following Pentecost. On the calendar of the Christian year, today is designated "Reign of Christ Sunday" or "Christ the King Sunday." Significantly, this is the last Sunday of the church year, the Sunday before the entire cycle begins again with the First Sunday of Advent. The message is quite clear – after a review of the entire sweep of the major events in the life of Jesus, we sound a soaring "amen" and laud Christ as the sovereign of all history, as well as of our personal lives.

In that spirit – reflecting on the scope, spirit, and substance of the ministry of Jesus – people of Jesus' day who were well-versed in ancient hopes and prophecy immediately began to apply to Jesus the expectations of spiritual dominion and political sovereignty. This association, I am sure, motivated those who gave the title "Christ the King Sunday" to the last Sunday of the church year. It was a spiritual conclusion, a personal conviction, and a liturgical affirmation.

Yes, followers of Jesus properly called him "Lord," a term that acknowledged his sovereignty. Yes, the Gospel writers dramatized Jesus' dominion over all creation. However, neither the dominion nor the sovereignty of Jesus was of the nature envisioned in ancient hopes and desired by the earliest disciples.

Look carefully at the conversation between Jesus and Pilate reported in the Gospel text for today. From this exchange, there is much to learn that can prevent the exalted title of "King" from distorting the meaning of Jesus' ministry and leading to misunderstanding about the nature of Christianity.

A political sovereign named Pilate interviewed the spiritual leader named Jesus, who was accused of political crimes that warranted capital punishment. When Pilate quizzed Jesus about his kingship, Jesus insisted that Pilate make up his own mind about the identity and the authority of the one standing before him. Freedom prevailed. Jesus would have it no other way.

Faith is never about compliance with a decree from sovereignty. Authentic belief can never be imposed, compelled, or forced. Faith is always a consequence of a decision made with free will.

In his conversation with Pilate, even as at other pivotal moments in his life, Jesus turned the traditional understanding of religion upside down. According to Jesus, the story of salvation is not about individual success, personal elevation, national supremacy, political authority, or social-cultural superiority. In the way of Jesus, dominion is shaped by compassion. Love is supreme – king or queen, if you will. Its goal is a fellowship of redemption. Its strategy involves forgiveness and reconciliation. Its mode of operation is humble service.

The story of God's work in the world consists both of hope and despair – not hope in the absence of despair, but hope in the face of despair and, often, through despair. The soaring carols of joy evoked by Jesus' birth did not mute haunting echoes of Rachel weeping for her children. Simeon and Anna celebrated Jesus' presentation in the temple, though each had more years behind them than in front of them to enjoy the fulfillment of the hope that they had held tenaciously for a lifetime. Jesus' inviting message of freedom and inclusion lofted across the plains and hills of Galilee amid harsh exclamations of prejudice, strident calls for exclusion, and ugly acts of hatred. Many of the same voices that sought to shout the good news of Jesus' resurrection must have been hoarse from their earlier shouts demanding Jesus' crucifixion.

Do you see the implications of this truth? Do you catch a glimpse of what all of this means? Our worst moments do not disqualify us as recipients of God's grace. Indeed, God's grace is for people mired in their worst moments. Our suffering does not occur outside the realm of God's love. Often God's love finds its most memorable expression in suffering or through suffering.

The story of God's work in the world enables us to realize that the essence of meaning in our lives resides not in what we can do but in all God can do in us, through us, and with us. Then, it becomes clear to us that what we receive from God – the hope, the strength, the encouragement, the assurance – is available nowhere else, from no one else. No other story can make the promises and deliver the fulfillment that can be found in God's story.

As we look back over the dramatic sweep of God's story of salvation – seeing love with flesh on it; sin as an opportunity for forgiveness; suffering as a cradle for hope; war as a context in which to discover the meaning, importance, and ways of peace; darkness as a prelude to light; and the sufficiency of faith in all situations – we find that it is almost too much for us. We don't know whether to laugh or to cry.

Thoughts of Jester Hairston's music rush in again. After the whole story has been told and affirmed by exciting outbursts of "Amen," the lyrics of the music rush to declare, "Sing it over." Our sentiments precisely! Like a two-year-old child having heard her favorite bedtime story, we say passionately, "Please tell it again." This time, not only do we want to hear it, we want to live it. And so, laughing and crying at the same time, we begin to tell the story again – singing it and living it. Amen. So be it! Amen.

– C. Welton Gaddy

Hymns
Opening: Lift Up Your Heads, O Mighty Gates
Sermon: Crown with Your Richest Crowns
Closing: Amen, Amen

December 2, 2012

1st Sunday of Advent

Lessons

Semi-continuous (SC)	Roman Catholic (RC)
Jer 33:14-16	Jer 33:14-16
Ps 25:1-10	Ps 25:4-5,8-10,14
1 Thess 3:9-13	1 Thess 3:12—4:2
Lk 21:25-36	Lk 21:25-28, 34-36

Speaker's Introduction for the Lessons

Lesson 1

Jeremiah 33:14-16 (SC/RC)

God promised a leader to establish righteousness and bring safety and salvation to the people of God. And God keeps promises.

Lesson 2

Psalm 25:1-10 (SC); Psalm 25:4-5, 8-10, 14 (RC)

The psalmist prays and waits for the knowledge of God's ways and mindfulness of God's mercy and love in the face of opponents.

Lesson 3

1 Thessalonians 3:9-13 (SC); 1 Thessalonians 3:12—4:2 (RC)

The fondest hope among Christians involves being together, growing in holiness, pleasing God, and abounding in love.

Gospel

Luke 21:25-36 (SC); Luke 21:25-28, 34-36 (RC)

Through many signs, sayings, parables, and actions, Jesus offers assurance that God's word will remain and redemption will come. He urges all to stay alert so as not to miss any aspect of the advent of God.

Theme

God's promises for justice and the Just One will be kept.

Thought for the Day

Advent offers a season of preparation for the God who comes: in the child of Bethlehem, in the Lord at history's end.

Sermon Summary

Advent confronts us with what we will make of God's promises of a future day. Advent's promises challenge us not to give in to the apathy and distrust often bred by our contemporary experiences of promises broken in society and relationships.

Call to Worship

> One: The days are surely coming –
> **All: Will you believe that, and in believing open to the signs of God's new day?**
> One: They are days when God will fulfill promises made –
> **All: Will you trust that, and in trusting live on the basis of promise?**
> One: God will execute justice and righteousness in the land.
> **All: Will you be God's partner, will you be God's instrument?**

Pastoral Prayer

God, we hesitate to complain, but this morning we must tell you that Advent seems a bit out of place in our world right now. Some of us are hurting so badly that we find it unreal to speak of hope. Many of our friends, grieving the absence of members of their families, flash angry resentment when they hear comments about a reign of justice or peace. And frankly, when love can be such hard work, we sometimes find it easier to settle for just a little kindness and the possibility that someone might like us. So if you insist on Advent, God, please remind us why we should expect you to come into this world and help us. And remind us, as well, that while we are waiting for the baby Jesus in the manger and the Lord of history at time's end: that you are already here, and that you have a habit of using the likes of us to bring hope to another and exhibit justice in our own relationships – and to love as we are loved. In Jesus the Christ, whose coming we would prepare for. Amen.

Prayer of Confession

God of hope, a fight is raging in our souls. We are finding Advent pushing our credibility. You know us. We live in a world in which skies don't open, stars don't guide, and people don't stop what they are doing to go to see a baby, to greet the Messiah, or to do anything that they (that we) don't want to do. Our cynicism has a headlock on our faith. Our spirituality is gasping for breath. We need a serious encounter with holiness. The best that we can do at the moment is to offer a simple but sincere prayer. If this is not enough, please forgive us. Come among us, God. Come, O long-expected Jesus. Amen.

Prayer of Dedication of Gifts and Self

O God, on the front edge of a season marked by the frantic selling and buying of gifts among people concerned that each gift will be big enough, attractive enough, and expensive enough to impress and please the recipient, give us wisdom regarding the value of what we give to others and to you. We give our love to you and, in the name of the Christ, we give a portion of our possessions to be used as expressions of your love to other people. Amen.

Hymn of the Day
Lo, He Comes with Clouds Descending

This Charles Wesley hymn emphasizes the second appearing of Jesus Christ on the earth. It was first printed in Wesley's *Hymns of Intercession for All Mankind* in 1758 under the heading "Thy Kingdom Come." Wesley may have written this hymn as a "refinement" of a hymn by Moravian hymn writer John Cennick. The tune HELMSLEY has most always been associated with this hymn. It first appeared in John Wesley's tune book *Select Hymns and Tunes Annext* (2nd edition, 1765) under the name OLIVERS. Realizing the tune's longevity, some authorities believe the tune may be the greatest musical achievement of Methodism.

Children's Time: Much Signs

Invite the children to look around the church and spot changes in your worship space. What is different this week? Take a quick tour around the church to look at Advent decorations. Explain that all these changes are signs that something special is coming. Ask the children if they know what it might be. Affirm all answers and explain that in the church, Advent is a special time of waiting as we get ready to celebrate Jesus' birthday.

Have some conversation about other signs at church, in the community, or at home that tell us that preparations for Christmas are underway. Conclude your discussion by observing that there are many signs telling us that it's time to get ready to welcome Jesus.

Explain how Jesus promised that one day he would return, but no one knows when that will be. Jesus told his followers that they needed to get ready for his return. We can get ready by living the way that Jesus taught us. When we do that, we become living signs pointing to Jesus!

Pray with the children, giving thanks for this special Advent waiting time.

The Sermon: The Days Are Surely Coming
Scripture: Jeremiah 33:14-16

The days are surely coming. With those five words, Jeremiah opens his testimony to God as keeper of promises. With those five words, we enter this season of Advent. But a bit of clarification is in order. The days are surely coming is not some early scriptural reference to the unstoppable march of shopping days to the 25th of December when, ready or not, the holiday arrives. The same march of days that sometimes drains us rather than empowers us for the festival at its end. The days are surely coming points instead to the time when God's promises will be kept. Christmas serves as both sign and foretaste of that keeping. The days are surely coming declares that the realm of the future is ultimately the realm of God. And Advent? Advent offers a season of preparation for the God who comes: in the child of Bethlehem, in the Lord at history's end. Advent proclaims the days are surely coming not out of a sense of fearful dread for what looms out of our control, or from an apathetic observance of the same-old same-old, year in and year out: Advent proclaims the hope that history moves toward a goal whose name is redemption. Such is the promise of God for the days surely coming.

But what kind of days are they to be? Jeremiah offers a fundamental word about the future by declaring a fundamental word about the God in whose hands it rests: "The days are surely coming when I will fulfill the promise I made to the house of Israel and the house of Judah." Jeremiah reveals that the God whose coming we await in Advent is, first and foremost, the keeper of promises. Someone whose word will be kept, someone whose word can be trusted.

Promise keeping is, arguably, an increasingly lost art. Or maybe, promise keeping has *always* been an underdog. Certainly in the public arena, the keeping of promises runs a distant second to the making of promises – and that may be a charitable assessment. Persons seeking public office too often promise whatever is necessary to gain election, hoping no one will put together a collection of sound bytes at re-election time of promises not kept. Worse yet is the cynicism bred as a result. When the issue of some non-fulfilled promise is raised, the reaction often runs: "Well, what did you expect?" Without expectations placed upon them, promises are voided of power, and those who make them escape accountability. I have no doubt that the debasing of promises in political life affects the way promises are viewed and held in other arenas. Historians may well judge that one of the most devastating legacies of the last quarter of the 20th century and into this decade of the 21st has been the cynicism and outright disdain bred for a host of institutions. Perhaps we can recall the slogans employed over this time, sometimes out of our own mouths, that have been symptomatic of this. *Question authority. . . Don't trust anyone over 30 . . . Big government is the enemy of democracy.* An ethic of suspicion has become the accepted norm: whether of voters for politicians, or parents for teachers and administrators, or laity for clergy, or congregations for denominations. And vice versa applies in each case. With distrust comes apathy, a lowering of expectations for those we disdain. Why should we expect them to keep promises when we don't believe what they say?

When it becomes natural to assume promises will be broken without raising protest, we contribute to an atmosphere that devalues the bond of our words among us. For in the end, a promise is no more than our word, the most fundamental way we have of expressing to others who we are. When our word cannot be trusted, can we be trusted?

Days of promise breaking, and the equally devastating ignoring of promises as if they do not matter, are not limited to our era. "The days are surely coming . . . when I will fulfill the promise I made" (33:14). When Jeremiah first offered these words to Jerusalem and Judea, the ones entrusted with the care of that people were found to be utterly lacking in the keeping of their vows. Jeremiah elsewhere laments the twisted words of prophets and priests – and the resulting perversion of expectations: "The prophets prophesy falsely, and the priests rule as the prophets direct; my people love to have it so" (5:31). He holds up the kings of Judea to similar judgment for having distorted their calling to shepherd the people into an opportunity to feed upon them. So when God declares himself through Jeremiah to be One who will fulfill promises, that word comes intentionally couched in the current language of government and societal order. "I will cause a righteous Branch to spring up for David; and he shall execute justice and righteousness in the land . . . Judah will be saved and Jerusalem will live in safety" (33:15-16). The promise God will keep has to do with fairness and equity in human community. Where the previous branches of David's line faltered, God promises a new branch to take up the cause of justice once more. The future will be different, Jeremiah declares, because it will be a place and time where promises are kept.

In Advent, we encounter Jeremiah's words through the prism of the manger. The ancient light of David's righteous branch shines through the birth in Bethlehem, David's city – and through Joseph, a Davidic descendant. So we see in Christmas one part of God's promise unfolding. But not all the way. Those days of which Jeremiah spoke did not fully arrive in Bethlehem, nor even upon Calvary. We still long for the not yet promise of justice executed in the land. We still yearn to live in places of absolute safety. Those days are surely coming, says the Promise Keeper. The issue of Advent is: how do we await their coming?

Does Advent christen us as those who may take a wait-and-see attitude, sitting back in padded pews while we passively wait to see what God will do? No. To proclaim God as the keeper of promises involves us in the unfolding and fulfilling of those very promises. It is not enough to say we long for God's day of justice and equity, only to be indifferent to cries for justice and fairness among us. It is not enough to say we yearn for God's promise of safety and salvation, only to be unmoved by those who need sanctuary as a literal matter of life and death.

Whom we say God to be intends to transform how we conduct our lives in response. Advent prepares us for the God who keeps promises by having us become keepers of those same promises. Their fulfillment may stretch far beyond our effort and day. Every generation of the faithful has labored to evidence the signs of God's kingdom in their lives and world – and they have done so without history drawing to a close or the promises being exhausted. So it is with us.

The days are surely coming.

– John Indermark

Hymns
Opening: Hail to the Lord's Anointed
Sermon: Watchmen, Tell Us of the Night
Closing: Come, O Long-Expected Jesus

December 9, 2012

2nd Sunday of Advent

Lessons

Semi-continuous (SC)	Roman Catholic (RC)
Bar 5:1-9 or Mal 3:1-4	Bar 5:1-9
Lk 1:68-79	Ps 126:1-6
Phil 1:3-11	Phil 1:4-6, 8-11
Lk 3:1-6	Lk 3:1-6

Speaker's Introduction for the Lessons

Malachi 3:1-4 (SC)

> The prophet indicates God's weariness with Israel's cynicism. God speaks: A messenger is coming. Indeed, who can stand in the presence of Yahweh?

Baruch 5:1-9 (SC/RC)

> God will lead Israel with joy, in the light of God's glory.

Lesson 2

Luke 1:68-79 (SC)

> In the *Benedictus* of Zechariah, the aged prophet rejoices at the birth of his and Elizabeth's son, John, with words that celebrate God's redemptive purposes in the coming of a prophet and a savior.

Psalm 126:1-6 (RC)

> This song of thanksgiving both celebrates return from exile as well as calling upon God for continued works of restoration and transformation.

Lesson 3

Philippians 1:3-11 (SC); Philippians 1:4-6, 8-11 (RC)

> Paul gives thanks for the Philippian church, but does not merely reminisce. God is still working, he assures them, and God will not stop until history itself culminates in the fullness of Jesus Christ.

Gospel
Luke 3:1-6 (SC/RC)
Luke makes a radical distinction here between the political conventions of nations and the ways of God. God skirts the powerful whom Luke lists and instead picks a messenger from the desert.

Theme
God wants you to step up and live your life.

Thought for the Day
Take back your life from all the personalities and competing interests that have claimed you and prepare for living with God.

Sermon Summary
Our lives are made for God. Most of us, however, live secondhand lives through endless cycles of headline news, celebrity scandal, sporting events, and political intrigue. John the Baptizer preached a message of "personal agency." We are responsible for our lives. It is time we take back our lives and prepare for God to come live in us.

Call to Worship
One: When the Lord restored the fortunes of Zion, then we were like those who dream.

All: Then our mouths were filled with laughter, and our tongues with shouts of joy;

One: Then it was said among the nations, "The Lord has done great things for them."

All: The Lord has done great things for us, and we rejoice!

Pastoral Prayer
We have just begun a new season of watching for your coming, O God, and already some of us are tired. Can we make it until Christmas Eve? Come now and bless us. Look past the disarray of our celebrations and expectations – and bless us. We need you, Holy One of Israel, to shine upon us, to lift us, to bring us up out of the depths and set us again on a firm, dry rock. We belong to you. So come, Lord Jesus, come. Come quickly!

Prayer of Confession

Loving Creator, who hears and listens to all we say and think and feel: hear our confession. We could say that we are too busy, that we have forgotten the "reason for the season," and that our priorities are really out of whack. Perhaps those are true. Even more troubling, when we are honest with ourselves, is that we wonder how and even if you can help us. So hear our prayer and confession, even if we doubt and wonder. And remind us, once again, that our good is what you have in mind – even as our good and the good of this creation is what the promises and hopes of this season hinge on. Come to us, O God, with forgiveness, with renewal, and with the assurance you do not give up on us. In Jesus Christ. Amen.

Prayer of Dedication of Gifts and Self

Blessed are you, O God. Sort through our offerings – where there is vanity and pride, may these gifts advance your kingdom without the stain of our sin. Where these gifts come with needs for love and assurance, grant these in abundance to those of us bent low in shame and hurting. Where these gifts are given without due thought as to the real needs of our world, shake our foundations. Thus we pray, even as we give, in hopes of the transformative power of Jesus Christ. Amen.

Hymn of the Day
Love Divine, All Loves Excelling

This hymn first appeared in Charles Wesley's collection, *Hymns for Those That Seek and Those That Have Redemption in the Blood of Jesus Christ,* in 1747. In addition to being a prayer that emphasizes the indwelling of the Holy Spirit, it is a positive statement of faith in the "joy of heaven to earth come down." This hymn, with its 13 biblical references, illustrates well the way in which Wesley's hymns are so firmly based on theological and biblical themes. Singing the text to an alternate tune, such as BLAENWERN or LOVE DIVINE, can provide a refreshing change from the tune BEECHER, normally used with the hymn in American churches.

Children's Time: Get Ready!

(Bring some items that could be used for sending, receiving, and passing on messages. These might include a message pad, a printed email message, a cell phone text message, and an answering machine).

Have some conversation with the children about these items, noting how these can all be used in conveying a message. Ask the children when they have had to take a message and then give it to someone else. Comment that in our Bible story today we meet someone who brought messages to people from God. Tell the children about John the Baptizer and his special message.

Mention that in the Bible story, the people were getting ready to welcome Jesus. In this Advent waiting time, we also are getting ready to welcome Jesus. Explain that the best way to do this is by living the way that Jesus taught us.

Observe that John's message to the people was never forgotten. It has been passed from one person to another down through the years. Now it's our turn to pass on John's special message. Show the children how to make megaphones by cupping their hands around their mouths. Together call out, "Get ready! Get ready! Jesus is coming!"

Pray with the children, giving thanks for John the Baptizer and his message.

The Sermon: Take Back Your Life and Prepare for God
Scripture: Luke 3:1-6

When I turn on my computer in the morning, I am greeted with headline news. When I pick up the paper, there again are the large print headlines. As I drive to work, the all-news radio repeats the same information, along with traffic and weather. If I watch TV, perhaps at work or in the gym, many of the same headlines will once again clamor for my attention. News, news, news. Everywhere I look there are headlines, bulletins, banners, and pop-up windows.

With no real effort to speak of, I can learn about politicians, rock stars, movie stars, and business moguls. I can locate my discourse and orient my activity on any given day within a frame of reference drawn from a list of celebrity birthdays, "this day in rock-and-roll history," or "soon-to-be-released" cinematic features. However, if I choose to live as a political junkie, rock groupie, or sports fan, my actual life loses significance. My world will increasingly mirror their world. I will dress like them, wear clothes bearing their name, and repeat their jokes and stories. I will mouth their opinions on food, sex, politics, extraterrestrial life forms, religion, and relationships. Of course, my own self will wither in doing so, and eventually die.

Luke draws a similar frame of reference in verses one and two of the third chapter of his Gospel. He positions the major players of his day. Herod, brutal son of the even more brutal Herod the Great, rules Galilee. Brother Philip holds court over two lesser regions. Someone named Lysanias is the governor of Abilene. Collectively, these regions represent the geographic area in which most ordinary peasants of Jesus' day would have lived. Of course, in addition to knowing who ruled over them in the immediate sense, they needed to know that over the entire known world – that is, the ultimate realm of significance – reigned Emperor Tiberius. They also would have known that over the religious life of Israel, Annas and Caiaphas held preeminent power. These two high priests presided over the temple in Jerusalem, the center of the universe according to ancient Jewish teaching. Tiberius, Herod, Philip, Lysanias, Annas, and Caiaphas: these six – together with their wives, children and, as John the Baptist would later discover, their lovers – were the players, the movers, and the shakers.

Of course, no one had explained these important facts to God. God appears to be living out of the wrong frame of reference. God had at least six significant leaders who were available for serving up the "word of God." Even Luke knew this much. There were at least a dozen or more different palaces from which official announcements could have been issued. And, each of these weighty leaders had massive military and police presence throughout the region for enforcing the word of God as official government policy.

It seems like God messed up, and not just in terms of whom God selected to carry the message – who, after all, was John the Baptist? God chose the wilderness as the first forum for issuing the word of God. Jerusalem or Rome would have provided far more extensive coverage and initial public exposure. John the Baptist in the wilderness? It made no human sense. Not only did God pick a poor point man to launch the word of God campaign as well as a sparsely populated and hostile desert venue, God also issued an upsetting press release of rather harsh demands: repentance, baptism, and personal agency.

In a nutshell, that is what God wanted of Israel then and what God wants from us now. God, you see, is not about to excuse our sordid and messy affairs on the basis that we have "died" and let some celebrity have control. God is not going to set aside our sins of omission and commission on the plea that we have not attended to our own life because we've been consumed with the loves, labors, and laughs of politicians and athletes. Giving up our lives for notable religious leaders won't get us any favors either. God gave us life and is quite upset that we've squandered it by handing it over to others.

God wants us to step up and live our life. This is what is termed personal agency. I am responsible for me. You are responsible for you. There is no one else who will be held accountable for you – only you! Only you can live your life in the company of God who formed and fashioned you in God's own image. Only you can shut off the news, tune out the appeals of celebrities, and make haste for the river Jordan. Only you can walk down into the waters, confess your sins, put your head in the hands of John the Baptist, and plunge beneath the running waters of God's unending mercy. Only you can get serious about living your life before God. Take back your life, and prepare for God.

Palaces are unworthy places for announcing this good news. Emperors and governors have no credibility to call people to repentance. Celebrities cannot wash us clean. We need ascetics – what the church calls spiritual athletes – to hear our confession, cut our hair, bathe our bodies, lay balm on our sores, and feed our souls. We need Isaiah, Jeremiah, and Malachi to turn our hearts to God. We need John to lead us to the water.

If we know what is good for us this Advent season, we will quit our office festivities, forsake our political parties, abandon our Christmas-as-usual cycle of gift and drink, and get ourselves down to the nearest river. If we are wise, we will turn off the repetitious cacophony of carols, pick up a prophet, and bow low. In a word, we should begin to take our bodies, minds, wills, and souls seriously. God does; we should too.

"Get ready," John the Baptist says. "Tear down every obstacle between you and God – or God will tear it down. Fill in every ditch between you and God – or God will fill it in. Straighten the blind curves in your attitude and the twisting ways in your behavior toward others – or God will straighten you out. Get to work smoothing God's way home, for God is surely coming home to live in you!"

That is the message of John the Baptist, and his message lives: "Get ready!"

– William L. Mangrum

Hymns
Opening: Praise the Lord Who Reigns Above
Sermon: Comfort, Comfort Now My People
Closing: Lift Up Your Heads, O Mighty Gates

December 16, 2012

3rd Sunday of Advent

Lessons

Semi-continuous (SC)	Roman Catholic (RC)
Zeph 3:14-20	Zeph 3:14-18a
Is. 12:2-6	Is. 12:2-6
Phil 4:4-7	Phil 4:4-7
Lk 3:7-18	Lk 3:10-18

Speaker's Introduction for the Lessons

Lesson 1
Zephaniah 3:14-20 (SC); Zephaniah 3:14-18a (RC)

God's prophet speaks words of hope and encouragement for suffering Israel, telling the people, "I will bring you home."

Lesson 2
Isaiah 12:2-6 (SC/RC)

The prophet offers a song of thanksgiving for God's salvation that evokes trust and the dismissal of fear.

Lesson 3
Philippians 4:4-7 (SC/RC)

"Rejoice in the Lord always," Paul tells an early congregation, "The Lord is near."

Gospel
Luke 3:7-18 (SC); Luke 3:10-18 (RC)

John the Baptizer preaches fierce words to those who come out to the wilderness to hear him preach.

Theme

Smuggling God into the world.

Thought for the Day

"Every day," said Rabbi Nachman of Bratslav, "the glory is ready to emerge from its debasement."

— Annie Dillard, *For the Time Being*

Sermon Summary

Jesus is Immanuel, God with us. Into our isolated, forlorn existence comes a Savior, someone who does for us that which we cannot do for ourselves. He is our hope. As we move toward the babe of Bethlehem, we are encountered by the God who has moved near to us.

Call to Worship

One: Show us your steadfast love, O God, and grant us your salvation.

All: Let us hear what God the Lord will speak, for God will speak peace to the people, to God's faithful, to those who turn to God in their hearts.

One: Surely God's salvation is at hand for those who fear the Holy One, that God's glory may dwell in our land.

All: The Holy One will give what is good, and our land will yield its increase. Righteousness will go before God, and will make a path for holy steps.

Pastoral Prayer

Almighty God, you not only created a world where once there was chaos, you not only brought forth humanity from the dust of the earth, you not only gave us your holy law and your truthful prophets, you also drew near to us. For your advent in our empty world, your light shining in our darkness, your word into our silence, we give thanks. Today, O Lord, give us hearts open and receptive to your advent, spirits expectant for your presence, lives ready to rise up and follow you at your call. Amen.

Prayer of Confession

We speak now to you in truth, God, for you see and know all truth and all falsehood. We are all sitting here in one place, but we are not one. Within a stone's throw of where we sit are those whom we have stoned with our words.

We are eager for the church to do more to help those is need, those displaced, those without. Instead, we find it all too easy to fail to see you in the neighbor beside us – and even at times within us. So grant us your grace: that forgives, that opens, that heals, that renews – and that, in this season, brings hope. In Jesus Christ. Amen.

Prayer of Dedication of Gifts and Self

Most high and holy God, in the quietness of the night, when we are most afraid, when we face overwhelming difficulty, we make promises to you in return for your assistance. This morning we acknowledge that you need nothing from us, for you are complete and without need. Still, we are grateful. So, accept in the precious name of Jesus Christ our lives, our loves, our hopes, our dreams, our plans, and our gifts. Take us and use us for the sake of this world so loved by you that you sent your Beloved. Amen.

Hymn of the Day
Hark! The Glad Sound! The Savior Comes

This excellent Advent hymn text has maximum impact when coupled with a suitable tune. Most congregations will catch on to the tune RICHMOND more readily than they will to BRISTOL, the tune often associated with this text. The hymn's author is Philip Doddridge, a British Congregational minister. The hymn was first published in 1755, four years after his death, although it's believed to have been written in 1735. While not as popular today as it once was, this hymn lends itself quite well to 21st-century worship, reminding us that "He comes the broken heart to bind, the bleeding soul to cure."

Children's Time: Let Us Rejoice!

(Bring a small bell or jingle bell loop for each child. Thread a couple of large jingle bells onto a pipe cleaner and form the pipe cleaner into a circle.)
Comment that today is the Third Sunday of Advent, sometimes known as "Rejoice Sunday." On this day we are reminded that Jesus' birth brought joy to people's lives. We are invited to rejoice and be glad. Invite the children to discuss what makes them happy and excited as they get ready to celebrate Jesus' birthday. How do they show that joy? Comment that in

the Bible reading today the apostle Paul encourages us to rejoice in God's love every single day of the year, not just at Christmas.

Distribute bells and encourage the children to ring their bells and move in a joyful way. If you have time, finish by singing "Joy to the World." Invite children to ring their bells and dance to the music.

Pray with the children, giving thanks for the gift of joy at Christmas.

The Sermon: The Nearness of God
Scripture: Philippians 4:4-7

I once taught a course for freshmen at Duke called "The Search for Meaning in Life." The students flocked to the course, which was mostly designed and taught by a friend of mine, an economist of all things. In the course, we looked at the ways in which people find meaning in their life by studying fiction, philosophy, and art.

During the first class we put students through an exercise that became emblematic of the course: "The Fable of the Deserted Island." We told them: You are on a voyage of discovery in the 18th century. There is a storm. Your ship is wrecked; all are lost except for you. You wash up on an utterly deserted island. Though no other humans live on the island, there is plenty of food and water. But you are stuck alone on the island. Question: What would you do for the rest of your life?

You know where we were going with this: You are alone in the world, isolated, left to your own resources. What will you make of your life? How will you put things together in such a way that you have a reason to get out of bed in the morning?

Some of the students said they would get to work building a boat. We ridiculed them. Others said that they would try to adapt to their circumstances: take up shell collecting and classification, write poetry on the back of a palm leaf, sit quietly and watch the sun set. Some said they would simply kill themselves, so horrible was the prospect of being alone for the rest of their lives with nowhere to go and nothing to do.

"The Fable of the Deserted Island" was meant to prime them for the course. Get real. You are alone in this world. Now, what are you going to do about it? We'll give you some books to read that will give you something to think about for the rest of your life. True, you are alone, and no one gets off this island alive, but here are some things that Aristotle thought about that will give you something to think about as you sit alone and watch the sun set.

Rather grim view of our situation, isn't it? Yet, it does ring true. I had another friend who fancied that view of the earth, that famous photo taken from some rocket of our spaceship earth, spinning blue and white, alone in the universe. He framed it and put it in his office.

A visiting student, gazing at that image of the earth, blue ball set in a dark, empty space, said to himself, "That's the saddest thing I've ever seen."

When, after the last space shuttle tragedy, some talked of ending our space exploration, more than one person defended its continuance by saying, "We are inherently exploring, investigating, probing creatures. We must keep moving out into the universe."

If someone were to ask, "But where? What's the grand point of simply thrusting ourselves out into the darkness?" What would be the answer? Boat builders, we are.

More, many more Americans commit suicide than are victims of homicide. Every two weeks, on average, someone jumps from the Golden Gate Bridge, the world's leading suicide location. ("Jumpers: The Fatal Grandeur of the Golden Gate Bridge," *The New Yorker,* Oct. 13, 2003, p. 48.)

Few of us react to our situation by jumping off the Golden Gate Bridge. Most of us, isolated and desolate on our island home, are more the shell collectors, boat builders, sunset gazers than the bridge jumpers.

Now, you may have noted a theme in all of today's scripture for this Sunday in Advent. The prophet Zephaniah, speaking into the darkness of Israel's exile, brings to Israel words of hope. "You will be brought back home," he says. St. Paul says to an early congregation, "Your God is coming. The Lord is near." And John the Baptizer intrudes into the wilderness, speaking of the advent of a Messiah who shall deliver.

Wherein is our hope? Ask those who are stuck on the deserted island. A typically biblical answer is: your hope is neither within nor here on the island. Your hope is in the possibility of something, someone coming to you from without. We need a bridge built from Creator to creation, a bridge we cannot build ourselves. We need a light into our darkenss, a reason to go on, not devised by our own limited reasoning.

This is the great, grand majestic claim of the Christian faith. God Almighty reached out to us, came to us, dared even to become one of us, one with us. Incarnation, we call it; Bethlehem, we name it.

We look forth from the isolated, desolate island we have made of our lives and, behold, there is something visible on the horizon. Coming toward us, a sign, a promise of deliverance. Call out to the rescuer. Shout aloud with appropriate song, "Come, Thou Long Expected!" "Come, O Come! God With Us!"

All of today's scriptures, all of the church's great expectations, all of our desperate hope can be met in the words of the last prophet of the Old Testament. (Read aloud Zephaniah 3:14-20.)

– William H. Willimon

Hymns
Opening: Rejoice, Ye Pure in Heart
Sermon: Put Peace into Each Other's Hands
Closing: He Comes to Us as One Unknown

December 23, 2012

4th Sunday of Advent

Lessons

Semi-continuous (SC)	Roman Catholic (RC)
Mic 5:2-5a	Mic 5:1-4
Lk. 1:47-55 or Ps 80:1-7	Ps 80:2-3, 15-16, 18-19
Heb 10:5-10	Heb 10:5-10
Lk 1:39-45 (46-55)	Lk 1:39-45

Speaker's Introduction for the Lessons

Lesson 1
Micah 5:2-5a (SC); Micah 5:1-4 (RC)

The book of Micah is an oscillating mix of judgment and salvation. Salvation comes into a situation of dire need as the people of God are surrounded by their enemies and walled in by their foes.

Lesson 2
Luke 1:47-55 (SC)

The Magnificat of Mary praises God who not only has shown favor to her but who brings justice and equity in a stark reversal of this world's usual values.

Psalm 80:1-7 (SC); Psalm 80:2-3, 15-16, 18-19 (RC)

The community raises a lament, calling upon God to intervene as shepherd and bring restoration and salvation.

Lesson 3
Hebrews 10:5-10 (SC/RC)

The book of Hebrews is an extended discourse on the person and work of Jesus. Today's reading urges the superiority of Jesus' death as a "once for all" sacrifice trumping other competing claims.

Gospel
Luke 1:39-45 (46-55) (SC); Luke 1:39-45 (RC)

Advent began with readings of Jesus' teachings about the future, then worked backward through John's preaching and Jesus' baptism to

175

today's story within a story. This narrative of Mary and Elizabeth is set within a larger story of God sending the promised Messiah.

Theme

If ever we flee from God, God will go before us and meet us.

Thought for the Day

Bring up a picture in your mind's eye of those who have known you to the core, yet still welcomed you. Imitate their embrace.

Sermon Summary

Perhaps Mary's visit to her cousin Elizabeth's originated in some doubts about her own "Yes" to God. If this is true, her doubts and journey render her more human – more like us. In Elizabeth, God meets Mary and welcomes her. God meets and welcomes us, doubts and all.

Call to Worship

> One: Give ear, O Shepherd of Israel,
> **All: You who lead Joseph like a flock!**
> One: Stir up your might,
> **All: And come to save us!**
> One: Restore us, O God;
> **All: Let your face shine, that we may be saved.**

Pastoral Prayer

Blessed are you, O God, Father, Son, and Holy Spirit. From you springs all creation, by you alone is there any mercy, and only in you have we any strength.

Blessed are you, Name above all Names, Immanuel, Comforter. Only by your imagination are we alive. Only by your death do we live again. Only by your eternal upholding have we any hope of living eternally with you.

Blessed are you, God of Abraham, Isaac, and Jacob, for by our mothers' wombs we are born and by the fruit of Mary's womb are we born again. You see through our eyes into our very souls, yet welcome us home. You know our darkest thoughts this very morning, yet embrace us. Before

we arrived, you were here preparing to meet us, to greet us, to love us in
Jesus Christ. To you be all majesty, honor, and praise forever. Amen.

Prayer of Confession

Shame on us, God, for squandering your creation. Shame on us, Lord of
the universe and Lord of our bodies, for our philandering and our carous-
ing. Shame on us, Alpha and Omega, for stonewalling your plans and
prophets for the sake of pursuing our own purposes apart from you and
neighbor. Of you and your goodness, we are not worthy. But, in Christ,
we are received and presented anew before your throne. Blessed are you
that in Christ, our shame is no more. Blessed are you that in Jesus' death,
our "No" is canceled. Blessed are you that in Jesus' resurrection we hear
and receive your final "Yes." Amen.

Prayer of Dedication of Gifts and Self

Dear God, receive these offerings we bring this morning, even if we are
slow to part with them. As you stretch them to use in your good purposes,
so stretch our hearts and spirits in that same service of Christ, who came as
servant to all, and who commissions us to go and do likewise. Amen.

Hymn of the Day
Away in a Manger

What simpler, more familiar, or more beautiful hymn could we want?
Although Martin Luther has sometimes been attributed as the author, evidence suggests that it is of anonymous, American origin. The first known
printing was in 1885. Two tunes are associated with the text: AWAY IN A
MANGER, written by James R. Murray in 1887, and CRADLE SONG, written
by William J. Kirkpatrick around 1895. The hymn provides an opportunity for children to sing by themselves, or for an appreciative intergenera-
tional congregational expression. Each one may sing to Jesus, "I ask thee to
stay close by me forever, and love me, I pray."

Children's Time: Special Babies

(Bring a manger (box), a bag of clean straw or shredded paper, and some baby items.)

Show the baby items and comment that people often get very excited when they find out they're going to have a baby. Talk about the kinds of preparations people make as they get ready to welcome a new baby.

The Bible story today is about two special mothers. Mary was going to be the mother of Jesus. Mary was so excited when she found out that she was going to have a baby that she went to visit her cousin Elizabeth to share the good news. Elizabeth was also getting ready to welcome a special baby. Elizabeth was going to be the mother of John the Baptizer.

Mary and Elizabeth would have done many things to get ready to welcome their special babies. They probably prepared special beds for them. Gather around the manger and remind the children that Jesus' first bed was a manger. Invite the children to help prepare a bed for the baby Jesus. Have each child take a handful of hay and place it into the manger.

Pray, giving thanks for the birth of Jesus and John.

The Sermon: For All Who Sometimes Run
Scripture: Luke 1:39-45

There is a Native American saying about the value and worth of a story, which suggests that the first business for listeners is to make room in themselves for the story to stay. "So now the story has made camp in you," the proverb reads. "If you let it, it will hunt meat for you, and at night its campfires will keep you warm."

We are deep into the most storied season of the Christian year. By this Fourth Sunday of Advent, we have sung or heard dozens of Christmas hymns and carols. When we listen to Christmas carols straight from Thanksgiving to Baptism of Jesus Sunday, the music makes camp in us. The melodies get inside our heads, settle down into our bones, build themselves a home in our memories. They warm us; their lyrics feed us. Quite often we will hear a stanza differently than before – then the story is hunting meat.

If you lean in closely, soon the lyrics will have a meal for you. I am fed yearly by verse two of "In the Bleak Midwinter": "Heaven cannot hold him, nor the earth sustain; heaven and earth shall flee away when he comes to reign." As I chew on this, I reflect on the obvious truth that nothing I say, write, sing, or even believe wholly contains God. God may condescend to use my words, but God will not be contained by my words. Heaven cannot hold the triune God. Neither will our prayers, passions, and petty offerings sustain Immanuel – God with us – here on this earth. God is bigger than you, me, this church, our denomination, this country, planet, solar system, galaxy, and universe. Nothing contains God, yet God contains all.

Now, while talking about music I am talking about scripture, too. Take the familiar story before us today. It sings. Once inside us, this story feeds us. Pregnant, unwed Mary bolts for the hills. Dazed or dazzled by the startling message that she was carrying a child by a Father not of this earth, Mary gets out of town. If heaven cannot hold God, Nazareth cannot hold Mary. She makes "haste," Luke says. With burning zeal, she beat a path for the Judean hills.

Where cousin Elizabeth lived remains a mystery. Luke is silent on this subject. Do we need to know exactly where Mary was headed to know that Mary was intently headed somewhere far away from where she had heard the word of the Lord? In this regard, Virgin Mary reminds me of Jonah. Jonah heard the word of the Lord in Gath-Hepher, which is just three miles to the northeast of Nazareth – the little town where God "shocked and awed" Mary into giving the Word room in her womb. God also "shocked and awed" Jonah who promptly fled for Tarshish – the exact location of which is also unknown.

Mary and Jonah: who would think them neighbors or alike in any significant way except that both were visited by God? Yet, I think Jonah and Mary are alike. God chose each to give birth: Jonah to the word of the Lord; Mary to God's Word incarnate. Before each, the heavens split wide, and each – having heard God's will for them – leaves town.

It is not until the end of Jonah's story that we learn why Jonah fled. As it turns out, Jonah was displeased that God showed mercy to the Ninevites. But why Mary fled is still a mystery, though the church has made plenty of assumptions. After Mary settles into Elizabeth's house she speaks such beautiful words, the Magnificat, that we've all assumed she went there to ponder the glory of God. Yet, what if she were fleeing? What if she is like those of us who put our hand to the plow and then turn back? What if Mary says, "Yes, here I am Lord," and then has second thoughts?

We modern folks have over-romanticized desert retreats. We fashion our retreat weekends around prayer, solitude, and silence. We then assume Mary went out into the wilderness for the same reason – namely to get closer to God. Only in Mary's case, God was, I think, already a bit too close. After all, the angel had said God would "overshadow" her. Perhaps all she wanted was to get away from God.

Mary was human. We also. We all have our moments. No matter how confident we are when first we hear God speak to us and no matter the sincerity of the baptismal vows we make, we all have doubts, moments of failing, fears. When fear strikes, when doubts grow, when our promises exceed our resolve, we run for places not easily found. When God gets just a bit too close, we decide it is time to get away.

So, hear the good news. Wherever we flee, God has gone there before us and will be waiting. Mary was overshadowed by the Most High and when the angel left her, perhaps her courage went also and she ran. Do not hold this against her. We would probably do the same. Like the prophet Elijah, Mary ran to the wilderness. But God was already there before her – not in wind, earthquake, or fire but in gentleness. She met one who looked deep into her eyes, knew her soul, took her in, blessed her, and loved her.

Jonah booked fare for Tarshish and met God in a pitched storm and the stinky stomach of a giant sea creature. Elijah stood up to 400 prophets of Baal and 450 prophets of Asherah, then wilted in fear before one woman, turned, and ran. Yet, God embraced Elijah at the mouth of a cave. God blessed Mary in the welcome of her cousin. God met Elijah in a cave, Jonah in a fish, and Mary in the arms of Elizabeth.

Wherever we run, God is there. God asks for our hearts. This is so, so much harder than just giving money. Even when we say yes and then flee, God will go before us. In the voice of those who look through our eyes and see our soul, then welcome us, bless us, and give us lodging – in them we meet God.

– William L. Mangrum

Hymns
Opening: Come, Thou Long-Expected Jesus
Sermon: My Soul Proclaims with Wonder
Closing: In the Bleak Midwinter

December 24, 2012

Christmas Eve

Lessons

Semi-continuous (SC)
Isa 9:2-7
Ps 96
Titus 2:11-14
Lk 2:1-14 (15-20)

Roman Catholic (RC)
Isa 9:1-6
Ps 96:1-3, 11-13
Titus 2:11-14
Lk 2:1-14

Speaker's Introduction for the Lessons
Lesson 1
Isaiah 9:2-7 (SC); Isaiah 9:1-6 (RC)
The prophet foretells an heir to the throne who will break the rule of
military, political, and economic oppression. The resulting new age
will be characterized by joy, light, peace, celebration, and justice.

Lesson 2
Psalm 96 (SC); Psalm 96:1-3, 11-13 (RC)
The psalmist invites all peoples and creation itself to raise a new song
to God who is sovereign over all and whose justice will come to pass.

Lesson 3
Titus 2:11-14 (SC/RC)
This epistle traditionally attributed to Paul celebrates in these verses
the grace of God bringing salvation to all that bids us to wait and live
with hope.

Gospel
Luke 2:1-14 (15-20) (SC); Luke 2:1-14 (RC)
The Gospel of Luke witnesses to the birth of Jesus in Bethlehem, a
birth sung by angels, celebrated by shepherds, and pondered by Mary.

Theme
Because we are reticent to be quiet, we often miss the voice of God.

Thought for the Day

Go for a walk, and notice something ordinary and common. Then find a quiet place and hold your observation quietly for 15 minutes in your mind. Ponder it; let God speak to you.

Sermon Summary

God wishes to speak with us, too! The problem in hearing God is not on God's side, but on ours. We are chatty and gossip about every event of our day. To hear God, we must practice reticence, silence, and the lost art of pondering.

Call to Worship

> One: Ascribe to God, O families of the peoples,
>
> **All: Ascribe to God glory and strength.**
>
> One: Ascribe to God the glory due God's name; bring an offering and come into the courts of God.
>
> **All: Worship God in holy splendor; tremble before God, all the earth.**

Pastoral Prayer

We are gathered to hear, see, and feel you move among us, O Most High and Holy God. On this night, we long for another miracle. We marvel again at the simple story of your Son's coming: of Mary's yes, of Joseph's trust, of the shepherd's visit, of angels crying out, " Glory to God in the highest!" This story carries all of our hopes and dreams, and we long for it to transform us. Though we are not completely convinced it will, we open ourselves with hope. Though we are not fully certain about Jesus' mission, we open ourselves to your call. Though we do not always recognize you, in Jesus we realize that you come to us. So, come Lord Jesus, come tonight. Meet us, in this place. Amen.

Prayer of Confession

We confess to you, O God, that we have not always kept well the treasure
you have entrusted to us on this sacred night. Sometimes we have locked
this story in our hearts of stone so that it is not heard. Often we have
squandered Jesus on our own frivolous nationalistic agendas and frittered
away his majesty on petty church politics. We have tried to master the
story of Jesus, rather than being its servants. Forgive us. Take us up into
the holy community of those who have been faithful and have obeyed.
Holy God, let the story of Jesus take hold of us so that we might belong
not to ourselves but to you. Amen.

Prayer of Dedication of Gifts and Self

Hear now, O God, our prayers of dedication. We are moved by candle
and song, procession and decoration, story and silence to renew again
our vows of allegiance. We belong not to ourselves but to you. We belong
not to our jobs but to you. We belong not to our country but to you. We
belong not to our dreams but to you. We belong not to our institutions
and endowments and investments but to you. Accept now these gifts we
offer, through your Son, our Lord Jesus Christ. Amen.

Hymn of the Day
On Christmas Night

What a delightful, bright, and uplifting Nativity carol! The authorship of
the text and tune is unknown. They are of "traditional English" origin,
probably of the early 1930s. This makes an excellent carol for antiphonal
singing. Either a soloist or choir may sing the first two lines of each stanza,
with the congregation responding with the singing of lines three through
six. Perhaps the Christmas Eve service could start with a soloist or choir
singing the first two lines from the back of the sanctuary and another
soloist or choral group responding from the front. The entire congregation
could join on the final stanza.

Children's Time: Jesus Is Born

(Bring a flashlight and a variety of Christmas cards with scenes from the Christmas story. If you are expecting a lot of children you may want to bring extra cards. Don't worry if some scenes are duplicated. Recruit some volunteers to help – older children or youth might enjoy being your helpers.)
Invite the children to choose one card to hold. Explain that you will use the pictures to tell the story of Jesus' birth.

Ask the children to listen carefully to the story and decide if the picture on their card shows what you are describing. When it does, they can hold the card up for everyone to see. Explain that there will probably be more than one card held up at any given time, and some cards may be held up more than once.

Slowly retell the story of Jesus' birth, pausing between each scene. Direct your volunteers to help cue the younger children when it is time to hold up their cards. Give the flashlight to another volunteer and ask her or him to shine it on each card as it is held up.

Pray with the children, giving thanks for the wonderful story of the birth of Jesus.

The Sermon: Ponder This . . .
Scripture: Luke 2:1-14 (15-20)

I was unemployed and living in a strange town. My wife held a good job and my daughter was in school – both of them were thriving in this new place. I, however, was sinking into a deep, dark well of doubt and self-pity. I had no friends and little to occupy my energies during the day. I sought work with a theological institution but did not have sufficient credentials. I sought work with area churches but had too many credentials for entry-level positions. I finally found work – waiting tables for private dinners held at a local seminary.

One day I served lunch at a gathering of 25 denominational leaders. These were the movers and shakers of several regional districts. Many of them had reviewed my resume for possible placement within their boundaries. A couple of them recognized me; most never noticed those who waited upon their needs. After they departed, the other waiters and I cleared away the cups and plates, gathered up the dirty linens, and tossed out the table scraps. As was permitted, I then prepared a parcel of leftovers for my family's evening meal.

It was drizzling as I walked the two miles across the campus and through town to our apartment. Along the path home I tried calling my wife, but she was away from her desk. I looked in vain at my cell phone directory and realized I had no one else to call. I was alone with my thoughts and my fears. I was afraid of the future – walking alone in a midday mist with a bag of pan-seared salmon and two pieces of chocolate cake. I was troubled. Yet, I had no one with whom I could immediately share either my worries or the good news of supper secured. It was just me – with my underemployment, my sense of being an outsider, my desire to serve, and my banquet leftovers.

Somehow, as I walked I thought of Mary: Mary in her singleness, with her chastity; Mary – still childlike and yet now herself with child; Mary with her surprise visit from an angel and her questions about her future; Mary pondering. Scripture tells us that Mary pondered. She stored up all that happened and set to thinking about her life and God's claim on her body. Mary had no cell phone, instant messaging, or blogging. Mary was alone with her cascading thoughts, angelic voices, and celestial visions. Mary was without peers, for who could comprehend her story?

In that lonely moment on that drizzling afternoon, I knew what kept Mary sane. I saw the pathetic state of my own soul cowering alongside the radiant brilliance of her strength. I grasped the difference between us and understood why, as of yet, God had not yet been born through me. In her heart, Mary pondered and thus cleared the land for God to plant. The reason we are so unable to approximate Mary's virtue in our own lives is because we have accepted it as impossible to live with a thought unexpressed, a sorrow unshared, a vision of God unheralded to a vast network of friends and acquaintances. We moderns barely taste the newly poured wine before we begin pronouncing on its body and color. Everything that happens to us is turned into news. We lack reticence. So little is held in reserve. So little is deeply pondered.

What are you pondering this evening? What mysterious unveilings of God are you hiding away in your soul? What visitations of beauty capture your eye, holding your gaze in reverential awe? What "word of the Lord" has settled into your heart, taken root, and grown to harvest? What message are you pondering? Or do you ponder?

The secret to pondering is secrecy. Mary was good at keeping her thoughts to herself and so she was good at pondering. Too often pastors, ministers, social workers, therapists, counselors, and teachers espouse a different way to mental health. "Talk about it," we say. "Get your feelings out. Share your frustration or your anger or your doubts." Now, maybe that "let it all out" approach is good for us. Or maybe not.

Perhaps we should ponder pondering. Pondering is a little-advocated spiritual discipline and I, for one, would like to commend the renewal of pondering as a regular practice. I should like to suggest that the next time we find ourselves pregnant with God that we shut up. I should like to suggest that the next time the pizza delivery man comes knocking at our door in the middle of the night, saying, "God sent me here with this pizza 'cuz you're going to have a divine birthing real soon," that we take the pizza, latch the door, and be still. I should like to suggest that the next time we are afraid and can't "reach out and touch someone" by phone, that we accept the moment as God's ringing call for us to ponder.

You see, I believe God still speaks, though what God says is often difficult to discern. However, the most obvious difficulty with divine-human communication is not God's silence, it's our steady muttering of our hurts, feelings, and opinions. I should like to suggest that the difference between Mary and all the others who marched to their hometowns that same month according to the dictates of the Emperor's Office of Imperial Tax Assessments is that Mary "pondered" all. She didn't chat up her anger; she kept silence. She didn't gossip round her visitation; she held it in reverence. While others were complaining and arguing, Mary pondered deeply all that she heard, and saw, and knew of God.

I believe there are many Christmas Evenings still to come and many Christs waiting to born if only we would ponder his coming and prepare him room. This is what Mary did. She pondered his coming and prepared him room. We are called to do no less. Perhaps this strikes you has a dangerous thought, but it is not such a heretical notion. "O holy Child of Bethlehem, descend to us, we pray; cast out our sin, and enter in; be born in us today."

Ponder this . . . and may you find Christ being born in you tonight.

– William L. Mangrum

Hymns
Opening: People Look East
Sermon: Savior of the Nations, Come
Closing: Sing We Now of Christmas

December 25, 2012

Christmas Day

Lessons

Semi-continuous (SC)	Roman Catholic (RC)
Isa 52:7-10	Isa 52:7-10
Ps 98	Ps 98:1-6
Heb 1:1-4 (5-12)	Heb 1:1-6
Jn 1:1-14	Jn 1:1-18 or Jn 1:1-5, 9-14

Speaker's Introduction for the Lessons

Lesson 1

Isaiah 52:7-10 (SC/RC)

All seems well as the promised ruler approaches Zion. All are ready for a show of power befitting a King of eternal majesty.

Lesson 2

Psalm 98 (SC); Psalm 98:1-6 (RC)

The psalmist's praise of God as sovereign inspired Isaac Watts to pen a many-stanzaed poem we know more popularly as "Joy to the World."

Lesson 3

Hebrews 1:1-4 (5-12) (SC); Hebrews 1:1-6 (RC)

This sermon was written to sustain a young Christian community facing difficult, even hostile challenges. Christ can be trusted as the true Word of God. In fact, Christ is superior to both prophets and angels.

Gospel

John 1:1-14 (SC); John 1:1-18 (RC)

This prologue to the Gospel of John opens with the Word ever-present from the beginning with God who now comes among us, fully human, whose light cannot be overcome.

Theme

In Christ, God comes to dwell among us.

188

Thought for the Day

Imagine hands that spun stars and fashioned DNA strings now wriggling to wrap around one of Mary's fingers. Welcome to the metaphor and mystery of incarnation.

Sermon Summary

Popular images of God often depict an absent, benevolent, and somewhat uninvolved figure who watches us from a distance. In the Gospel we we encounter a God not distant but who in Christ comes to us as a sovereign intending to live – up close and in person – with the people.

Call to Worship

One: O sing to the Lord a new song, for God has done marvelous things.

All: God has remembered, with steadfast love and faithfulness, the house of Israel.

One: All the ends of the earth have seen the victory of God.

All: Let the sea roar, and all that fills it; the world and those who live in it.

One: Let the floods clap their hands; let the hills sing together for joy at the presence of the Lord.

All: God is coming to judge the world with righteousness and the peoples with equity.

Pastoral Prayer

The noise of the morning is now fading, O God. We bless you for calling us together and for all your many gifts to us this Advent season. Some of us have come here to give thanks for family who are still slumbering at home. Some of us have come to give thanks for friends and loved ones still en route or unable to meet us this Christmas. Some of us have come to see a friendly face on what will be a very lonely day. Some of us have come simply for your love, mercy, and forgiveness. We know you will not be stingy. May your plan for the salvation of the world – already set loose in Jesus Christ – find home and voice in us. May the hope we feel grow and burst forth in new songs of praise, new words of encouragement, new eyes to see you already before us and at work in the world. Take us and make us whole and holy servants of your Word. Amen.

Prayer of Confession

O God who rules all creation, hear now our confession. We do not always bring joy to this world: in words spoken in anger, or words silenced by fear. We do not always go and tell it on the mountain, lest someone expect us to practice what we preach. We do not always let your light shine through us, lest it reveal places in our lives we prefer to keep in shadows. So forgive us, O God: for not being your children, which is to say for not being ourselves. And we give you thanks on this good and glad day of Christmas that you come not to run us into the ground but to raise us up to new life. And let the people of God say: Amen.

Prayer of Dedication of Gifts and Self

Blessed are you, O Lord of Hosts and, through the birth of Jesus Christ, our Friend. We dedicate ourselves and these gifts to Jesus. Through them: change this world and change us, renew this world and renew us, and restore all to yourself. In Jesus Christ we pray. Amen.

Hymn of the Day
Joy to the World

This hymn provides a grand musical announcement for the opening of Christmas Day worship. The text by Isaac Watts is a paraphrase of Psalm 98:4-9. It first appeared in his book, *The Psalms of David, Imitated in the Language of the New Testament,* of 1719. The hymn helps us join with heaven and earth in rejoicing in the coming of Christ. Of course the hymn can be effective when sung at times other than Christmas. An explanation of its Psalm 98 origin would be especially helpful at such times. The fourth stanza also can be a reference to Philippians 2:10: "At the name of Jesus every knee should bend."

Children's Time: God's Amazing Gift

(Bring a nativity creche. Place the baby Jesus figure into a gift box. Print the words "To the world, with love from God" on a gift tag and attach it to the box.)

Invite the children to gather around the Nativity creche. Have a brief discussion about Christmas gifts: What was your favorite gift this year? What kinds of gifts did you give to others? Comment that giving and receiving gifts is a wonderful Christmas tradition.

Mention that the Bible passage today tells about a wonderful gift God gave to the world on the very first Christmas. Show the gift box and read the tag. Ask the children what they think might be inside. Invite a volunteer to unwrap the package and carefully place the baby Jesus figure in the manger.

Explain that God's special gift to the world was Jesus. Jesus came to tell us that we are all God's children and that God loves us very much. Express excitement for God's amazing gift.

Pray with the children, giving thanks for Jesus, who came to tell us about God's love.

The Sermon: Up Close and In Person
Scripture: John 1:1-14

A few years ago a popular song proclaimed, "God is watching us." Well-known singers such as Bette Midler, Nanci Griffith, and Kathy Mattea have offered moving renditions of this song, "From a Distance." Perhaps you will recall that the lyrics speak of beautiful snowcapped mountains, lush green forests, and deep blue waters encircling the globe. This view, the songwriter tells us, is of our planet from space – "from a distance." Such is God's perspective of this terrestrial ball because God lives at an immense distance from us.

Up close to the action, down here on earth, it is in fact quite a different story. The snowcaps are melting because of global warming. The forests are decimated as are hundreds of mammal, reptile, and insect species. The streams, rivers, and seas are polluted. And we humans reserve our greatest powers of ingenuity and creativity for humiliating and destroying other human beings. When viewed up close and in person, our world is messy.

191

The song appeals to God's view of us, and asks us to become who we are when viewed "from a distance." From a distance we are one, no one is in need, harmony echoes through the land, and hope dwells abundantly in every home. If only we could see ourselves the way God sees us, all wars would immediately cease, enemies would fast become friends, and the noble character of humanity would shine undimmed in every endeavor henceforth and forevermore. If only we could see ourselves as God sees us, we would desire to be different.

Now, "From a Distance" is a great song. In fact, it reminds me a bit of the apostle Paul who, when addressing the Philippian congregation, urges them on to repentance, change, and holy living by intoning, "The Lord is near" (Phil 4:5b). Obviously, both the apostle Paul and Julie Gold, the songwriter, hold that belief in God is a powerful motivator of human transformation.

However, for the songwriter, we must climb up and out of the hole we are in. God is "up there" and "looking down." The song suggests that God cannot save us; only we can save ourselves. The changing, the peace-making, the forgiving, the healing, and the saving is our work. Paul is also concerned about the gap between humans and God. However, unlike the song, the unified thrust of the biblical writers is this: the gap is closing, and from God's side. God is coming closer. For example, Paul motivates real, substantive change among his parishioners in Philippi by announcing, "The Lord is near." God's increasing nearness is not because we have climbed up but because God has climbed down.

John the Baptist, in the tradition of the prophet Isaiah, appealed to God's proximity to humankind – to God's eventual and certain coming – as a way of urging humans to live justly and mercifully with each other. "Prepare the way of the Lord," John shouted. "Make his paths straight." God will come, John announced, and in that day "all flesh shall see the salvation of God" (Lk 3:6).

In fact, in today' lesson from the Gospel of John we are told that God is not content to watch from a distance as we go on bungling creation and mangling each other. Rather, God is coming; the gap is closing.

There is, to be sure, a very real distance between God and us, as there must always be between creator and creature. We are the work of God's hands; we are not now and will never be God. There is a very certain divide between God and us. The "stuff" of God is different than the "stuff" of humankind. Now, this distinction between God and us is so grand and infinite that many assume it is insurmountable, unbridgeable. This Christmas morning, however, I proclaim to you the good news that this gap has been breached. Last night, God rushed into the world to meet us. Last night, soaked in sweat and covered in straw, Mary birthed God for us. Last night, God traversed a great distance and came home. Last night, God arrived up close and in person – Infinite, Almighty Creator squeezed into a human child. Last night, God took flesh and entered this messy world. Last night, "the Word became a human being and lived here with us" (Jn 1:14 CEV).

In the light of Christmas morning we can tell the truth. And this is the truth: Once our King lived in a land far away. Darkness fell upon the land. Though from a distance, our King watched over us, others ruled, and often despotically. But from the beginning our King always intended to return. As time passed, our King sent messengers to announce his impending arrival. Some of us mocked the King's agents, some of us even threw stones, and most all of us ignored the announcements of the King's approach. Yet still our King approached and would not relent in his plans to rule, to restore the glories of his kingdom.

Last night, our King returned. Now our King is no longer out there, but here – next to you, and you, and you, and me. Our King no longer watches over us from a distance but has come to live with us. This is not merely a visit. Our King has returned. In Jesus Christ, God lives – up close and in person. Amen.

– William L. Mangrum

Hymns
Opening: New Songs of Celebration
Sermon: Long Ago, Prophets Knew
Closing: Break Forth, O Beauteous Heavenly Light

December 30, 2012

1st Sunday after Christmas

Lessons

Semi-continuous (SC)	Roman Catholic (RC)
1 Sam 2:18-20, 26	Sir 3:2-6, 12-14
Ps 148	Ps 128:1-5
Col 3:12-17	Col 3:12-21
Lk 2:41-52	Lk 2:41-52

Speaker's Introduction for the Lessons

Lesson 1

1 Samuel 2:18-20, 26 (SC)

> The boy Samuel, an offering to God from his mother Hannah, is serving God by helping Eli, the priest. Love, gratitude, the grace of God, and the fruits of obedience are seen here.

Sirach 3:2-6, 12-14 (RC)

> These verses from this apocryphal book detail right relationships of children toward parents.

Lesson 2

Psalm 148 (SC)

> The psalmist invites diverse elements of creation, natural and human, to praise God.

Psalm 128:1-5 (RC)

> This song associated with pilgrimage made to Jerusalem uses imagery of family to speak of God's blessings.

Lesson 3

Colossians 3:12-17 (SC); Colossians 3:12-21 (RC)

> How should Christians think about the qualities they are to embody in daily life? Paul uses the concept of clothing oneself as a metaphor for how Christians should behave. His persuasive words are great reminders to us all.

Gospel
Luke 2:41-52 (SC/RC)

Mary and Joseph are in Jerusalem to celebrate the Passover. Jesus, on this trip, does something surprising that signals a new phase of his growth and human ability to take on the mission for which he has been born.

Theme

Do you know where Christ is?

Thought for the Day

We do not need to search for Christ. He says, "Listen! I am standing at the door, knocking . . ."

Sermon Summary

Losing track of a child can be a heart-wrenching experience. To find that loved one again brings great joy. When we lose track of our true source of joy and happiness, we can look for it in the wrong places; but when we look to Christ our happiness is fulfilled.

Call to Worship

One: The Holy One is present in this sanctuary.
All: We open ourselves to God's presence.
One: The Holy One will search for those who are lost, who strayed away.
All: God will bring them safely home again, and will bind up the injured.
One: The Holy One will strengthen the weak and feed them.
All: God is present in this sanctuary – let us open to Holy Presence.

Pastoral Prayer

We come to you, O Lord, as humbly as we know how, thanking you for your constancy and presence without fail. You know where we are at all times and never lose track of us or what we are going through. We thank you for the grace of your Holy Spirit that ministers to us in difficulties, your unconditional love that holds us up, and your power that carries us through. We pray for those who do not know you, O God, who are lost in the dark and are looking for peace where it will not be found. Use us, O Lord. May our light shine as a beacon, that we may lead people into the light of your holy presence, so they may know the great joy of truly being found. In the name of Jesus the Christ, who keeps us and saves us. Amen.

Prayer of Confession

God, we confess our weakness before you. In this world that brings so much pain to so many, we seek an easy way out. We seek to protect ourselves by surrounding ourselves with things that can take us away from the hard work of faith. We hoard items of comfort, live vicariously through others as we watch television or movies. We look for our share of the pie, instead of looking to give to others from the blessing of your goodness to us. Help us to remember that true joy is found in you. Open our hearts, that we may not hold on so tightly to temporal things, but to the treasures that are everlasting. Help us to enrich the lives of others, knowing that richness of spirit is far more valuable than earthly possessions. In the name of Jesus Christ, we pray. Amen.

Prayer of Dedication of Gifts and Self

We dedicate these tithes and offerings to the work of your sovereign realm. May they be used to feed the hungry in body and spirit, and to find the lost, that they may come to know you, Lord. Amen.

Hymn of the Day
Once in Royal David's City

The hymn text was written by Cecil Frances Alexander and published in her *Hymns for Little Children* in 1848. Alexander, married to an Irish pastor, wrote this hymn and others as a way of teaching children the meaning of the Apostles' Creed. This hymn is centered on the phrase "who was conceived by the Holy Spirit, born of the Virgin Mary." The stately tune IRBY, written for this text, lends itself well for using this hymn as a processional hymn. Perhaps a single child's voice or a children's choir could sing the first stanza, followed with the congregation singing the remaining stanzas as the processional.

Children's Time: Learning and Growing

(Bring photographs that show you or a family member at different ages.)
Show the photographs. Enjoy noticing all the changes. Invite the children to share stories they have of growing, changing, and learning. Marvel at all the ways you have grown since you were born.

Observe that, just like us, Jesus didn't stay a baby. He learned and grew, just like any other child. Today's Bible story is about something that happened to Jesus when he was 12. Tell the story of Jesus in the temple.

Comment that in this story Jesus was both a learner and a teacher. Ask: What questions might Jesus have asked the Jewish teachers about God? What kinds of questions do you have about God? What do you think Jesus may have taught the leaders about God? Affirm that asking questions is a great way to learn.

Comment that, just like Jesus, we are all learners and teachers. There are so many wonderful things to discover about God and we can work together at learning them.

Pray with the children, giving thanks for the marvelous ways in which we all learn and grow.

The Sermon: Do You Know Where Christ Is?
Scripture: Luke 2:41-52

The festival of the Passover was the most important of the three great Jewish celebrations that also include Pentecost and Tabernacles. Passover commemorates the night the angel of death killed the Egyptian firstborn while passing over the homes of the Jews. Along with the great throng of pilgrims making the sojourn to Jerusalem, the backdrop to this Passover's celebration included entrepreneurs and merchants who offered their wares of all kinds and lodgings to the travelers. There would have been a great deal of hustle and bustle with many things to see and do. The sights, sounds, colors, smells, and tastes would have filled those present with an excitement one did not experience daily in humdrum hometown life.

There must have been a throng of young people present. Jesus, a very human boy, no doubt would have been as outgoing as anyone there. You can imagine that he wanted to meet others and explore his surroundings with them. Perhaps checking in with mom and dad from time to time, he was allowed to venture away, as long as they knew his general whereabouts. It must also be acknowledged that in Jesus' day a twelve-year-old boy was considered almost an adult and would not be expected to tag along everywhere with his parents. It would be the next year that he would be presented as one ready to take his place in the religious community.

In addition, on the trip to and from Jerusalem, it was customary for the women and children to travel in the front of a caravan with the men bringing up the rear for protection. It would have been acceptable for Jesus to be in either place. It is, as you see, quite understandable that his whereabouts were easily assumed, given the social norms. It was in this delicate dance of freedom and security that Jesus turned up missing.

Those who have been through the experience of temporarily losing track of a child in the grocery store, or at a baseball game, or at some other event with crowds of people know the feeling that sits in the pit of your stomach, marking the terror and fear you experience in that moment of realization. It is a parent's worst nightmare to lose a child. The news reports of a missing child are heartbreaking to hear no matter whose child has been lost. I would imagine this human response was the same in Jesus' day, even if the community was somewhat safer than our own times.

The Bible says they found Jesus after the third day. It is not absolutely clear whether the scenario includes the days of travel to get back to Jerusalem. If so, then Joseph and Mary looked first among the extended family and friends. They had already traveled a day's distance and so took a second day to get back to Jerusalem. The third day was spent looking for their son. However, the biblical account could also mean that it took three days from the time they arrived back in Jerusalem. In either case their concern is not mitigated by length of time.

Now, Mary and Joseph knew their son was unique, that God had given him to them for a special purpose. That did not prevent them from fearing for his safety, for they did not know how or when his unique mission would actually take effect and make itself known.

Where do you think they looked for Jesus? They probably checked the marketplace with its many shops and the homes of friends and/or acquaintances. After agonizing hours passed they finally looked in the right place. They found him in the temple! And they were amazed. Upon questioning him, no doubt relieved and upset, they were even more amazed at Jesus' response to them. He reminded them of his life's mission and pointed to the temple as the logical place he would be. It seemed Mary and Joseph looked many other places before trying the temple. Jesus seems to be saying it should have been the first place.

Mary and Joseph had lost something precious to them. It was Jesus. This story becomes a powerful analogy when we connect it to our own losses in life. When we lose something important in our lives – love, wealth, happiness, beauty, security, or peace of mind – we can be tempted to search for them in all the wrong places. Many people look for their salvation in the wrong places. Some look in the marketplace, in the world of things, in money and possessions. The market advertises itself as a place where you can purchase that which will make you happy and perfect. It says, "Buy this toothpaste to get the perfect smile." Or, "Buy these clothes to attract the woman and man of your dreams." Or, "Live here for the best life." Furthermore, people pay expensive fees for cosmetic surgeries, looking for salvation in youthful appearance.

Just as Mary and Joseph may have looked in homes to find what they were looking for, we too can think, when we look in others' homes, that if we had what someone else has, our lives would be better and happier. Some even go as far as to covet another man's wife or another woman's husband, thinking it to be a solution to make up for the lack one may be experiencing in his or her own marriage. Solomon's wisdom, however, warns against this folly in Proverbs 5:15-23.

Jesus' response to his parents is also his response to those looking for Christ today. He says, in essence, that he is not difficult to find. He is in the temple of the heart. For those who have already taken Christ into their hearts, we sometimes forget that Christ is in us, close by. We must remember the words of 1 John 4:4 and claim them for ourselves: "For the one who is in you is greater than the one who is in the world."

The outside world can take away our peace, joy, and sense of stability; and we can respond without first looking in the right place for sustenance and spiritual renewal. When life tosses us around and we lose sight of our happiness and joy, we must remember that Jesus says, "I have said this to you, so that in me you may have peace. In the world you face persecution. But take courage; I have conquered the world" (Jn 16:33).

As a new year dawns, whatever challenges, doubts, or fears you may have about the future, know that Christ is in the temple of your own soul. Christ is always there – never lost – and ready to give you the resources of wisdom, unconditional love, grace, mercy, peace, joy, and power for life. Amen.

– David P. Sharp

Hymns
Opening: When Morning Lights the Eastern Skies
Sermon: I Want Jesus to Walk with Me
Closing: Go with Us, Lord

January 6, 2013

Epiphany

Lessons

Semi-continuous (SC)	Roman Catholic (RC)
Isa 60:1-6	Isa 60:1-6
Ps 72:1-7, 10-14	Ps 72:1-2, 7-8, 10-13
Eph 3:1-12	Eph 3:2-3, 5-6
Mt 2:1-12	Mt 2:1-12

Speaker's Introduction for the Lessons
Isaiah 60:1-6 (SC/RC)

Isaiah, a prophet in the eighth century before Christ, encouraged the people of Judah in exile in Babylon. In times of hardship, an encouraging word is welcome. Isaiah speaks words of promise and hope as he seeks to inspire faith.

Lesson 2
Psalm 72:1-7, 10-14 (SC/RC)

This psalm is a prayer for guidance and support for the king and those in positions of power.

Lesson 3
Ephesians 3:1-12 (SC); Ephesians 3:2-3, 5-6 (RC)

Written in the final decade of the first century after Christ, this epistle is a manual of Christian living. This passage speaks of the mystery of God's plan to unite all in Christ.

Gospel
Matthew 2:1-12 (SC/RC)

All did not welcome Jesus' birth. As the star shone, darkness filled the hearts of some. Deceit and intrigue are in play here. Will wisdom rule or will treachery win in the battle over the baby Jesus' life?

Theme

Wise people listen to God.

Thought for the Day

Rebellion to tyrants is obedience to God.

> – Thomas Jefferson (this is the motto on his seal)

Sermon Summary

The magi came to Jesus, honored and worshiped him. Obeying God's direction, they did not go back the same way; they returned in a different direction. Likewise, when people go to church, they should not go out the same way they came in. Christ changes us.

Call to Worship

One: God is the king of justice.
All: And Jesus the prince of peace.
One: God judges with righteousness.
All: God defends the poor, delivers the needy, and is against oppression.
One: May God be to you like soft rain falling on grass, and like showers that water the earth.
All: And may righteousness and peace flourish in our lives and in the world.

Pastoral Prayer

We thank you, O God, for the privilege of coming to you in prayer. We honor and praise you for your love and power and mercy. Bless us with wisdom for the days ahead and the years to come, that we might move in the direction you would have us move. Help us to meet the challenges of each moment with grace and compassion. Open the ears of our hearts, that we might hear your voice clearly, listen with eagerness, and respond with complete trust. May we create the spaces in our day to pray, to meditate on your word, and to seek your presence, lest we lose our way. We ask these things in the name of Jesus, the Christ and Savior of all. Amen.

Prayer of Confession

We confess, O God, that we want to go our own way. We prefer to listen to our own voices instead of yours. We confess our need for power and our unwillingness to submit ourselves to you. It feels good to do things our way – to think we cause our own success and to believe our power is an end unto itself. Forgive us, and help us to have a more humble spirit. We know that your wisdom is better than our own, and your direction for us will lead to a better destiny. Help us to have more desire and commitment to receiving the grace and wisdom of your Holy Spirit. In the name of Jesus Christ, the One whose path we follow. Amen.

Prayer of Dedication of Gifts and Self

We bring these gifts to you, O God, as an ongoing sign of our knowing that all blessing comes from you. As you have given us the priceless treasure of life, we return a portion to give life to the work of church. We thank you for the means to provide for our family and loved ones, and to respond to the needs of this world. So we pray, even as we give, in the name of Christ. Amen.

Hymn of the Day
As with Gladness Men of Old

This hymn celebrating the coming of the wise men was written around 1858 by Scottish insurance executive William Chatterton Dix. The first three stanzas of the hymn detail the Epiphany story. Stanzas four and five serve as a prayer that we will be kept in the narrow way and admitted to heaven where we will "ever sing alleluias to our King." The popularity of the hymn began with its inclusion in the first edition of the esteemed British hymn collection, *Hymns Ancient and Modern,* published in 1861. The tune Dix has been associated with the text since 1861.

Children's Time: Special Gifts for Jesus

(Bring a baby doll and a basket containing a few baby items. Bring some sticky notes.)
Show the doll and invite the children to take turns holding it if they wish. Comment that people often celebrate the birth of a baby with special gifts.

Show the basket of baby items. Have the children take each item out of the basket and say how the parents of a young child might use it.

Mention that the Bible story today is about a time when some wise people gave gifts to Jesus. Relate the story and ask the children what they think about the gifts Jesus received. You may have to explain what myrrh and frankincense are, and how they might be used.

Explain that the magi brought very special gifts for Jesus. They gave the best they could. We can also give special gifts to Jesus. Recall that when we show love to others, we are showing love to Jesus. What kinds of gifts might we bring to Jesus this year? Write the children's suggestions on sticky notes and place them on the worship table.

Pray with the children, giving thanks for the coming of Jesus and offering the children's special gifts.

The Sermon: Another Way
Scripture: Matthew 2:1-12

When I was in high school, most everyone knew I was a preacher's son. I remember times when guys (mostly bigger) would cunningly try to coerce money from me by forcefully asking me for, say, a quarter. Since I rarely had extra money, I would say, "I don't have an extra quarter." The request would then drop to a dime, still prompting a polite, "I don't have an extra dime" from me. At this point I would immediately hear a diatribe concerning of unwillingness to give, and on top of that came a veiled threat of something terrible happening to me in the future because of it – "What? You're not going to give me even a dime? Okay, I'm gonna remember that!" This was, of course, done in the presence of that person's friends, and done in an intimidating manner, with the strategy being that next time they asked, I would be more likely to give than to receive another guilt-intended word lashing. Ultimately, it just made me avoid them and go another way.

These street-smart young men were attempting to use my kindness against me – their cunning versus my honest spirit. I have seen this contest played out many times with others; sadly, cunning wins most times. The Christian call and character trait of giving of ourselves is taken advantage of by those who know how we are suppose to respond. As an adult the same is true. There are people of great cunning who attempt to use our kindness and desire to do good against us for their own selfish profit and motives.

King Herod the Great tried to use the kindness of the wise men against them – to get to Jesus that he might kill him. He heard the news that magi had come from the east to see the One who had been born King of the Jews. This news was greatly disturbing to King Herod. He called all the chief priests and scribes of the people and asked where this child was to be born. When they said Bethlehem, he then met secretly with the wise men, who were Zoroastrian priests. Herod, inquiring of the exact time the star appeared, asked them to go to Bethlehem and make a careful search, and then to come back to tell him where the child could be found so that he could go and pay homage to him.

Now, you might imagine the kindness and sweetness of voice with which Herod made this request. In his eyes may have been the affect of sincerity. Evil is a great actor and this Herod was cunning indeed, and cruel. He was ruthless in his need for power and control and destroyed any perceived threat to his rule. He murdered his wife, three of his six sons, mother-in-law, brother-in-law, uncle, and many others. He was set on protecting his throne for himself and his surviving sons (all three becoming rulers).

After the wise men visited Jesus, they were warned in a dream not to go back to Herod. And they went back to their country another way. It is interesting that the Bible says, "and having been warned in a dream." It seems these men were given a shared vision, which powerfully demonstrates God's ability to get through to us. There was agreement, and instead of going back to Herod, they went back to their country another way.

After Herod realized he had been outwitted, he became furious and had all the boys in Bethlehem and surrounding areas who were two-years-old or younger killed. But Jesus was unharmed because Joseph obeyed directions to escape to Egypt, given to him in a dream. So, because of two dreams – and obedience to the God who gave the dreams – we are here today. Because Joseph followed his dream, and because the wise men obeyed and followed the shared dream God had given them, Jesus survived. It must be remembered that Jesus was a human being and could have been killed along with the other children.

When we follow the leading of the Spirit, our dreams truly can come true. In addition, God's dreams for us benefit not only ourselves but also others. We do not always get to know who or how, but we can have a feeling of peace trusting that God is in control.

Have you ever felt the leading of the Spirit and didn't follow it – only to find out later you had missed out on a blessing or could have prevented someone from doing harm to themselves or someone else? Has anyone ever told you, "Don't go down that road, go another way"?

Whatever brought you to Jesus probably sent you out in a different direction. You did not go back to your life the same way but were sent on a different path. You didn't go back to the Herod that wanted to kill the Christ in you. When we come to Christ, God will direct our path. We are pointed in the direction of life and are steered away from that which seeks to destroy us along with the God in us.

There are Herods among us today – would-be tyrants that seek power and reign in our lives. These cruel and dangerous rulers range from life-draining addictions to joy-stealing-isms (workaholism, racism, consumerism, etc.). But when we make the long journey to Christ and worship him, as the wise men did – and when we open ourselves and give Jesus the treasures of our hearts, whether it be our most precious pains, heartaches, worries, fears, or hopes and dreams – he will send us away in a new direction. Christ will impart a new dream for our life and give us wisdom for the road ahead, that we might safely travel in the direction of his leading. There is no better road.

– David P. Sharp

Hymns
Opening: Bring We the Frankincense of Our Love
Sermon: Rise Up, Shepherd, and Follow
Closing: Hail to the Lord's Anointed (based on Psalm 72)

January 13, 2013

1st Sunday after Epiphany
The Baptism of Our Lord

Lessons

Semi-continuous (SC)	Roman Catholic (RC)
Isa 43:1-7	Isa 42:1-4, 6-7
Ps 29	Ps 29:1-4, 9-10
Acts 8:14-17	Acts 10:34-48
Lk 3:15-17, 21-22	Lk 3:15-16, 21-22

Speaker's Introduction for the Lessons

Lesson 1

Isaiah 43:1-7 (SC)

In language reminiscent of both the creation and the exodus, God promises to "pass through the waters" and "walk through fire" with Israel, whom God has called by name. The children of Israel will be gathered again.

Isaiah 42:1-4, 6-7 (RC)

The first of Isaiah's "Servant Songs" identifies this messianic figure as the chosen one upon whom God's Spirit rests and whose covenant calling is to bring light and freedom as part.

Lesson 2

Psalm 29 (SC); Psalm 29:1-4, 9-10 (RC)

The imagery of a thunderstorm forms the backdrop of praise for the God whose voice thunders over the waters.

Lesson 3

Acts 8:14-17 (SC)

Peter and John pray with Samaritan believers. The Spirit is given to those long considered outsiders, and they become with the rest of the Christian community children of the Spirit.

Acts 10:34-48 (RC)

Peter preaching to Cornelius and his household opens with references to the "baptism that John announced" and "how God anointed Jesus of Nazareth with the Holy Spirit."

Gospel
Luke 3:15-17, 21-22 (SC); Luke 3:15-16, 21-22 (RC)

The people look expectantly toward John the Baptist, wondering if he is the Messiah. John points away from himself and toward the One who will baptize with the Holy Spirit.

Theme
Seeing by assumption or by hope.

Thought for the Day
What do you expect of God – and from that, what do you expect of yourself?

Sermon Summary
In the midst of the people's spiritual hungering and messianic expectations, John the Baptizer points to one who will baptize, not with water but with the Holy Spirit. When Jesus is baptized and is praying, a heavenly voice declares him to be "the Beloved Son," the one for whom John prepares and the people hunger.

Call to Worship
One: The voice of the Almighty is powerful;
All: The voice of the Sovereign One is full of majesty.
One: The Holy One is in this place.
All: Praise be to God.
One: Draw your strength from God.
All: And may God bless creation with the gift of shalom.

Pastoral Prayer
Holy God, John the Baptist promised that you would bring fire, and it is with fire that we ask you now to come. Come with fire to enliven our weakened spirits and our dimmed hopes. Come with fire to light the path to your truth. Come with fire to burn away all in our world and in us that stands in the way of your Word. Come with fire to warm hearts grown cold and to comfort those against whom the stormy winds have blown. Come with fire to draw us into the holiness of your life, to empower us

with your Spirit, and to send us with zeal into the world you love. We ask this in the name of your Beloved Son, even Jesus Christ our Lord. Amen.

Prayer of Confession

God, we come in confession. We see people in pain and ignore the opportunity to help; we walk by the homeless on the street pretending we don't see them. We hear people speaking in ways that degrade other races and cultures, and we laugh unashamed or maintain an apathetic silence. We hear troubling news and switch to shows that dwell on gossip. We prefer easy lives. This we confess, Lord, and ask for your forgiveness and renewal. For we also confess this day your grace to transform and empower us for new ways. And we confess our hope in Jesus Christ, in whose name we pray. Amen.

Prayer of Dedication of Gifts and Self

We return to you, O God, a portion of what you have given us. We dedicate these offerings to the ongoing mission of the church in the cause of Jesus Christ. Keep us humble of spirit, so that we might not only remember those less fortunate but walk and serve with them – as you walked and served with us. In Jesus Christ. Amen.

Hymn of the Day
When Jesus Came to Jordan

This hymn was written by British minister Fred Pratt Green in 1973 to meet the specific need for hymns celebrating the baptism of Jesus. Although not found in some hymnals, the hymn is worth locating and singing. A variety of tunes have come to be associated with this text. The tune COMPLAINER, unlike its name, provides a bright, major key setting. In contrast, the tune DE EERSTEN SUN DE LAATSTEN gives a more somber, minor key setting. Or, choose a 7.6.7.6.D. tune that's already known by the congregation as the setting for this important text.

Children's Time: Jesus Is Baptized

(Bring a jug of water and some cups, a sheet of drawing paper, and powdered paint.)
Invite the children to join you for a drink of water. As you pour and distribute the water have a brief conversation about the wonder of water and all that it does.

Sprinkle a little paint powder on the paper. Lightly drizzle some water from your cup on the powder. What happens when the water touches the powder? Tip the paper up so that the paint runs down. Observe that the water has made it possible for the paint to leave a mark on the paper. Comment that in our Bible story today water is used to help get Jesus ready to leave his mark on the world.

Tell the story of Jesus' baptism. Explain that Jesus' baptism marks the time when Jesus started teaching about God's love.

Comment that people are still baptized today to show that they are Jesus' followers. Encourage the children to share stories of their own baptism or the baptism of other people, being sensitive to those who have not been baptized.

Pray with the children, giving thanks for the story of Jesus' baptism.

The Sermon: What We Expect to See
Scripture: Luke 3:15-17, 21-22

Perhaps it is just a legend; I don't know for sure. But even if it is just a legend, it is still true to human nature: we see what we expect to see. Near where I once lived is the little town of Grover's Mill, New Jersey. There is not much there now: a farm supply store, a bend in the road, an old wooden water tank, and acres of sod fields. Locals report that if you look carefully at that old water tower you can still see the buckshot markings from over a half-century ago.

What happened was this: In the late 1930s on his radio show, *The Mercury Theater of the Air,* Orson Welles broadcast an updated version of H. G. Wells's *War of the Worlds,* a story about Martians who invade the earth. The writers had picked, of all places, little Grover's Mill as the site of the Martians' landing, and when the show was broadcast, it was so realistic that people believed it was real news, not fiction. Frightened farmers in the area grabbed their shotguns and headed into town, looking for the

Martians and their spacecraft. There in the moonlit October night, they looked up into the sky and spied the water tower. Seeing the spaceship they expected to see, they opened fire.

Expectation is a powerful force, shaping our experience. When the people came out to hear John the Baptist, what attracted them was not simply that he preached powerfully or that he offered baptism for the forgiveness of sins. It was that John matched their expectations of what a prophet should be and should say. In fact, John so perfectly matched the religious expectations of the people, the rumor was floating around that he was the long-expected Messiah. In the same way that the farmers of Grover's Mill saw what they expected, the people standing on the banks of the Jordan looked at John and saw the figure for whom their hearts hungered. John looked like a religious-supply-house catalog Messiah; that's what was expected and that's what they saw.

Expectations can make us see something that isn't there, but they can also blind us to something that is there, too. In one of her exquisite sermons, Barbara Brown Taylor describes an experiment in perception that shows how expectations can keep us from seeing:

> *Here's how it goes. [The experimenters] sit you down at a table in front of an ordinary deck of cards and they flash six of them at you, asking you to identify them as fast as you can — nine of diamonds, three of hearts, jack of clubs — whoops! What was that one? Then they repeat the exercise, slowing it down a little so you can get the ones they missed the first time.*
>
> *The third time is so slow that you think you must be an idiot because there is one card you simply cannot identify. You think you know what it is, but you are not sure, and it is not until the cards are laid on the table in front of you that you can see what the problem is. The mystery card is a six of spades, only it is red, not black. The deck has been fixed. Someone has changed the rules, rules that prevented you from seeing what was there. You could not see a red spade because spades are supposed to be black.*
>
> *Our expectations, however faithful, may prevent us from seeing what is there.* (Barbara Brown Taylor, *Bread of Angels* [Boston, MA: Cowley Publications, 1997], p. 157.)

Because the people expected a Messiah that looked like a Messiah should look, they overlooked Jesus. They were looking for a prophet, something like a Jeremiah or an Elijah perhaps, and what they got was an itinerant preacher who said things like "Blessed are the poor." They expected a great judge who would shovel a pitchfork under the mixed stubble and stalk of history and burn away the enemies of the faithful. What they got was a roving preacher whose ministry was financed by women and who healed people on the Sabbath day. They expected a hero king like David who would restore the fortunes of the nation. What they got instead was a teacher who wept over Jerusalem before riding into town on a mule, only to have himself nailed to a cross. He was the red six of spades, and people couldn't see him because they expected something else.

"Don't look at me," John said. "Despite your expectations, I am not the Messiah. I am not worthy to untie the thongs of his sandals." But John himself had his problems with expectations. Only a few chapters later in Luke, John is not so sure that Jesus is the hoped-for one. "Are you the one who is to come," he wondered, "or are we to wait for another?" Jesus was the red six of spades, violating John's own messianic expectations.

In her book *Operating Instructions,* Anne Lamott tells the story of a family being interviewed on *60 Minutes.* The family was a religiously devout mother in her 30s, a somewhat older and painfully shy father, and their ten-year-old daughter bound to a wheelchair by spina bifida. Every year this family made a pilgrimage to Lourdes, where healing is reputed to occur.

According to Lamott, the interviewer, Ed Bradley, was giving the family a hard time for being so gullible. At one point he turned to the little girl and asked, "When you pray, what do you pray for?" She replied, "I pray that my father won't be so shy. It makes him terribly lonely."

That stopped Bradley for a few seconds, but then he pressed ahead, questioning the family's wisdom, saying to the mother that they spend thousands of dollars every year going to Lourdes and that still they have no miracle. Looking at her loving daughter, the mother answered, "Oh, Mr. Bradley, you don't get it. We have our miracle."

Bradley had his expectations, and the only miracle worth noticing, the only miracle that would count, was the one that fit his definition: the little girl would get up out of the chair and walk. But he missed the miracle of a daughter's growing love, the miracle of a family held together in faith. He missed the miracle of joy growing in soil that should not, by all rights, sustain it. God does not work in the world in the ways we expect, because God's mercy breaks the bounds of our narrow imaginations.

To tell the truth, Ed Bradley is probably like most of us: he really didn't expect any miracles. We live in a world that has stopped expecting them. Jesus, the Messiah, has promised, however, that one day the deaf will hear, the blind will see, and the lame will walk. One day, in ways that we least expect, that little girl and all like her will get up healed in the power of God. And those of us who have expected far too little will be genuinely surprised.

– Thomas G. Long

Hymns
Opening: O, Christ, the Great Foundation
Sermon: What Ruler Wades through Murky Streams
Closing: Fill My Cup

January 20, 2013

2nd Sunday after Epiphany
RC/Pres: 2nd Sunday in Ordinary Time

Lessons

Semi-continuous (SC)	Roman Catholic (RC)
Isa 62:1-5	Isa 62:1-5
Ps 36:5-10	Ps 96:1-3, 7-10
1 Cor 12:1-11	1 Cor 12:4-11
Jn 2:1-11	Jn 2:1-11

Speaker's Introduction for the Lessons
Lesson 1
Isaiah 62:1-5 (SC/RC)

> Isaiah the prophet sings of the delight that the Lord has in the people of Israel. "God shall rejoice over you."

Lesson 2
Psalm 36:5-10 (SC)

> The psalmist reflects on the vast scope of God's steadfast love.

Psalm 96:1-3, 7-10 (RC)

> This psalm of enthronement invites new songs to be sung to God the just sovereign of all creation.

Lesson 3
1 Corinthians 12:1-11 (SC); 1 Corinthians 12:4-11 (RC)

> Paul writes to the church at Corinth concerning "spiritual gifts," noting the way that all of these gifts are given to build up the body of Christ.

Gospel
John 2:1-11 (SC/RC)

On the third day Jesus attends a party after a wedding in Cana of Galilee. There, he manifests his glory.

Theme

When Jesus is present, miracles are possible.

Thought for the Day

A man can't always be defending the truth. There must be a time to feed on it.

– C. S. Lewis

Sermon Summary

God in Christ is a sign of God's effusive love for us. Christ brings us an overabundance of love, enables us not only to express God's love but also to give love away to others.

Call to Worship

> One: O sing to the Lord a new song.
> **All: Sing to the Lord, all the earth.**
> One: Sing to the Lord, bless God's name.
> **All: Tell of God's salvation from day to day.**
> One: Declare the glory of the Lord among the nations,
> **All: God's marvelous works among all the peoples.**
> One: For great is the Lord,
> **All: And greatly to be praised.**

Pastoral Prayer

We thank you, O God, for the blessing of life, the celebration of worship, and the hope for salvation that we have in you. We pray for those who do not know you, that they may receive the good news of Christ Jesus. We pray for those in leadership, that they may plan with insight along with a willingness to shift gears as need be. We pray for those who are making important commitments, that they will receive power to see them through. We pray for those who need renewal, that they may receive the newness of spirit available in Christ. We pray for those who need faith, that they may find you in their seeking. Amen.

Prayer of Confession

God, we confess that we wrestle with our the contradictions in our lives. We want to be humble, yet pride invades. We want to look good in the eyes of the world. We want what others have. And we want more when we have enough. We become envious when others acquire what we want. We admit frustration when we don't make as much money as our acquaintances. We question your love for us when we see those we consider equal in position or rank gaining material possessions as we struggle. We pray, O God, for a renewal of mind. Restore a right perspective, that we may be more like Christ. Help us to trust that you know what we need; and that you have the power to provide for us at all times. We ask these things in the name of Jesus Christ. Amen.

Prayer of Dedication of Gifts and Self

We present these tithes and offerings, generous God, thanking you for the blessings you have bestowed upon us. We ask your blessings on them, that they may truly serve the needs of the congregation and the community. As you have provided for us, may we provide for the needs we encounter near and far. Increase our desire to be a blessing in the world, that we may ever seek to do all we can for your promised and present realm. Amen.

Hymn of the Day
Blessed Jesus, at Your Word

We owe Catherine Winkworth our gratitude for this translation of the original German hymn, "*Leibster Jesu, wir sind hier.*" The German hymn was written in 1663 by Tobias Clausnitzer and appeared in Winkworth's second series of Lyra Germanica in 1858. Clausnitzer, a pastor in Weiden, Saxony, intended the hymn to be sung just prior to the sermon. The text applies to the 21st-century church as well, as we acknowledge that "all our knowledge, sense, and sight lie in deepest darkness shrouded, till thy spirit breaks our night . . . " The German tune LEIBSTER JESU, written in 1664, has long been associated with this text.

Children's Time: Jesus Goes to a Wedding Party

(Bring a party hat and a noisemaker.)

Get the children's attention by putting on the party hat and blowing the noisemaker. Ask the children about times they have gone to a party. What was being celebrated? Who was invited? Was there special food to eat? Observe that today's story is about a time when Jesus went to a wedding party.

Invite the children to help you retell the story. Ask for volunteers to play the different parts in the story – Mary, Jesus, the steward, the disciples, the servants. If you have a large group others can be guests. Explain that each time a new character is mentioned, the person playing that character can step forward and mime the actions. Retell the story of Jesus at the wedding in Cana. Tell the story slowly, pausing where necessary, to allow the children to play their parts.

Mention that the stories during Epiphany show us how the light of God's love shone out into the world through Jesus and Jesus' followers. Today we saw God's love in action at a wedding party.

Pray with the children, giving thanks for stories that show us God's love in action.

– Sandra Anderson

The Sermon: Abundance
Scripture: John 2:1-11

You and I are apt to have some difficulty with today's Gospel, Jesus at the wedding at Cana miraculously turning water to wine. John says that this was the first of Jesus' signs. Signs of what?

We may have difficulty because we are modern, North American people. That means that we are people who live in a considerably reduced world. Yet in this story, Jesus beckons us into a renewed, expanded, more abundant world.

"Let's ask Jane to take on this job," said one of the members of the planning committee. "Jane always does such a good job on anything she undertakes." There was widespread agreement in the group.

His pastor said, "You really think that is fair to Jane? She already has two or three jobs in the church. She is one of our busiest members, one of our hardest workers."

"That is just my point," said the chairperson. "Everybody knows, if you want a job done right, always ask the busiest person to do the job. Busy people always seem to be the people who are able to find time somehow to do more."

Next week, different church committee meeting:

"Pastor, we have decided to adopt the foster child that we have been keeping, such a dear little thing. The parents have given him up for adoption, and we think that we ought to do it," she said.

And I as a pastor asked, "Do you really think that is wise? You already have three children. You are a great mother, but don't you think there are limits? Aren't there limits to how much love you can give?"

"When it comes to love," she said, "I have not yet found the limits. From my experience, love is a renewable resource. The more love you give, the more love you seem to have. That's how it's been in my experience."

Well, we're in the season of Epiphany, that time when the church celebrates the wonder of God with us as Jesus the Christ. The moment that Jesus stepped on earth, according to John, things broke forth, broke out, and overflowed. Our story has more than a hint of Easter. It occurred on the third day (Jesus rose on the third day after his death), the jars are filled up to the brim. There is no cautious, careful restraint in this story. Jesus just shows up at the party after the wedding and there is this miraculous effervescence of glory.

I think we are apt to have trouble with this story, not because we are so modern and sophisticated and scientific but because we are so careful, cautious, and restrained. We don't make big moves in life. We don't ask big things of God. We keep our faith to ourselves, safely tucked away in the confines of our church. We keep our prayers chastened, cautious, and careful.

Perhaps it's because we think of our relationship with God as a matter of what we feel, what we believe, or what we do. And we all know how limited, how frail and finite are our resources. We have our limits.

How many times has someone come to me and confessed, "I fear I'm losing my faith." Perhaps they are going through a tough time in their lives, their faith is being tested by present circumstances, and they fear that they are about to lose the little faith they have. What can I do to hold on to my faith? they wonder.

But what if our faith, our belief, our love for God is a gift of God and not our achievement? What if God is there, wanting to give us even more faith, more love, more energy to meet the demands of discipleship?

In short, what if this Sunday's Gospel is true? Jesus comes to a party in Cana, out in Galilee. When the wine gives out, he tells them to fill up the large stone jars with water. When they do, the water is turned to wine, lots and lots of wine, more wine than anybody could possibly need to have a good party!

I want you to ponder this story from John's Gospel as a sort of parable of abundance, a promise that God will give you what you need to be a faithful, resourceful disciple.

– William H. Willimon

Hymns
Opening: Great Is Thy Faithfulness
Sermon: Trust and Obey
Closing: God of Our Life

January 27, 2013

3rd Sunday after Epiphany
RC/Pres: 3rd Sunday in Ordinary Time

Lessons

Semi-continuous (SC)	Roman Catholic (RC)
Neh 8:1-3, 5-6, 8-10	Neh 8:2-4, 5-6, 8-10
Ps 19	Ps 19:8-10, 15
1 Cor 12:12-31a	1 Cor 12:12-30 or 12:12-14, 27
Lk 4:14-21	Lk 1:1-4; 4:14-21

Speaker's Introduction for the Lessons

Lesson 1
Nehemiah 8:1-3, 5-6, 8-10 (SC); Nehemiah 8:2-4, 5-6, 8-10 (RC)

What a joy it must have been for the returning exiles to rediscover the Law and their special covenant with God. In this reading we hear about that rediscovery.

Lesson 2
Psalm 19 (SC); Psalm 19:8-10, 15 (RC)

The psalmist meditates upon the glory of God revealed in creation and in the gift of Torah.

Lesson 3
1 Corinthians 12:12-31a (SC); 1 Corinthians 12:12-30 or 12:12-14, 27 (RC)

This passage clearly points out that our personal relationship with God is incomplete. We need other members of the body of Christ if the work of God is to be accomplished.

Gospel
Luke 4:14-21 (SC);

Jesus spoke openly to the people of Nazareth about who he was. Here he clearly implies that he is the Messiah, the Christ.

Luke 1:1-4; 4:14-21 (RC)

In addition to the Nazareth episode described above, the opening verses of chapter 1 relate how Luke intends to provide an "orderly account" in addition to others of Jesus' life and ministry.

Theme

Community is essential to bring to fruition our relationship with God.

Thought for the Day

Is community just a forum for expressing my personal faith or a gift through which my faith can grow?

Sermon Summary

Christianity is not a do-it-yourself religion. Our faith may begin as a personal relationship with God, but it is supported, strengthened, and increased by our relationship with a Christian community. God gave us the church as a gift to enable us to grow spiritually.

Call to Worship

One: Look around. We are surrounded by a great cloud of witnesses.

All: Some we can see. Some are invisible to our earthly eyes.

One: We recognize, too, the presence of Jesus Christ among us be-cause we are gathered in his name.

All   We recognize Christ in one another because we are members of his body.

One: Let us come together and rejoice in the gift that God has given us in Christ,

All: Let us rejoice in the gift God has given us in one another and in the entire church, that great mystery that is the body of Christ.

Pastoral Prayer

O God, let us recognize Christ present in this place. Let us recognize Christ in one another. Let us recognize Christ in those not present here. We are the members of your body and you have called us to do your work in the world, to show forth your love and your mercy until you come again. Let that work begin with those present here today. Enable us to carry your work into our community, and even throughout the world. Open our eyes of faith to see you, Lord, in all the peoples of the earth. In the power of the Spirit, enable us to be your instruments of peace, of grace, of redemption. Amen.

Prayer of Confession

All too often, merciful God, we have not recognized your presence among us. All too often, we have not seen you in one another, particularly in those we consider different from ourselves. All too often we have failed in proclaiming you to others through the way we live and act. Forgive us and open our eyes of faith that we may see you more clearly in the many ways you come to us. Help us ever to act toward our brothers and sisters as we would act toward you. Forgive us when we fail. May we, by your wisdom, recognize and learn from our failures that we may serve ever more faithfully day to day. Amen.

Prayer of Dedication of Gifts and Self

These gifts, Lord, represent our lives, our possessions, all that we are and have. We offer them now to you as symbols of ourselves, so that you may take us and bless us and, through the power of your Spirit, shape us into the hands and feet and voices that embody Christ today. Amen.

Hymn of the Day
God of Change and Glory

For those looking for a fresh, contemporary hymn text and tune that celebrate the diversity of gifts as highlighted in 1 Corinthians 12, this is a match. The hymn was written in 1973 and is one of the earliest to acknowledge diversity as a gift from God. Its author, Al Carmines, in addition to serving as a United Church of Christ pastor in New York City, is a composer, playwright, performer, and teacher. He is a fellow of the Society for the Arts in Religion and Contemporary Culture. The hymn can be found in *The New Century Hymnal,* number 177.

Children's Time: Can You Spot Jesus?

Play a couple of rounds of "Can you spot?" Start the game by saying, "I'm thinking of a person in the church. She has blond hair and works in the church office." (Adapt as needed.) The children work together to spot that person in the church. Comment that in order for the game to work you need a good description of the mystery person so others can recognize her or him.

Explain that many years before Jesus was born, the prophet Isaiah described a very special person called the "chosen one." Isaiah wanted the people to be able to recognize God's chosen one. This person would be filled with God's Spirit, bring good news to the poor, help the blind people see, and bring hope to those who had no hope. Ask the children if this description reminds them of anyone in particular.

Comment that in our Bible reading today, Jesus reads Isaiah's words in front of all the people. Then Jesus told the people that he was the one whom Isaiah had described. It was a very unexpected announcement.

Pray with the children, giving thanks for Jesus who came to bring good news, healing, and hope to the world.

– Dick Underdahl-Peirce

The Sermon: Can We Be One with Christ?
Scripture: Luke 4:14-21

In case you had not noticed, there is an ambiguity in the title of today's sermon. Most of you will take the title to ask whether we can be united with Christ. Can we be so identified with our Savior that we might be said to be one with him?

But the way I want to read the question of the sermon title is this: Can we be alone with Christ? Can we be solitary Christians, having a personal relationship with Jesus but disregarding the community of the local church and the community of the broader church – the entire body of Christ? In other words, can we, in the company of Christ, be "do-it-yourself" Christians?

To ask the question in this form is essentially to answer it. We are part of a larger company of members of Christ's body. Paul tells us that each of us has a role to play within that body, just as each of our organs has a role to play within our physical bodies. There are many more passages in scripture that underline our essential unity in Christ, a unity that is more than a number of humans who share the same beliefs or are members of the same organization. We are, as Christ taught, branches of the same vine. We are one as the Father and Christ are one. We are one in that we are all temples of the same Holy Spirit. We cannot ignore this unity and claim that our personal relationship with Christ is all that really matters. We need each other in a fundamental way to grow spiritually and to become all that Christ calls us to become.

Too many Christians, and one is too many, think they can grow spiritually by praying alone, studying the scripture in the privacy of their homes, and never attending church. And, no doubt, by the grace of God, some Christians have achieved significant spiritual growth in this way. But we can use all the help we can get in our spiritual journeys. Perhaps we think we come to church to worship God; thus, our attendance at services is our gift to God. But the reality is that the church is God's gift to us. We come to church not for God's sake but for our sake. It is through our presence at worship that we can and should receive many spiritual benefits we would miss otherwise.

First, there is increased power in prayer when many Christians are gathered in prayer. Prayer generates spiritual power. If you have one lamp turned on in a room, the room is not as bright as if there are twenty lamps shining in that same room. When we pray together as the church, our prayer is more powerful than when we pray alone because we are praying as the church, not just as individuals.

Second, gathered as the people of God, we can learn from listening to the words we pray, listening to the sermon, listening to scripture read at the service. We can ask others to pray for us and we can exercise one of our great privileges as Christians to pray for the world and for the church. We can listen for the voice of God in others we meet. We do not know what words that others speak might touch our hearts, but we will not hear them if we are alone and not in church.

And, of course, it is at church and in community that we receive the sacraments. The sacraments are channels of grace given by God to help us. There is the Eucharist, for one, that is essential to a healthy spiritual life. The Eucharist is a reason to come to church if you can find no other reason convincing.

But I am sure at least a few of you are thinking that coming to church has disadvantages as well as advantages. We may have to put up with people we don't like. The sermon may be dull and uninspiring; it might even be a spiritual turnoff. We might be asked to become involved in activities that do not interest us and for which we do not have the time. We might indeed feel more comfortable curled up in our favorite easy chair at home reading the Bible than getting dressed up, driving to church, and sitting in a hard pew listening to babies squealing throughout the service.

All of these reasons given for not coming to church, however, can be turned around and made reasons why we ought to come to church. We need to recognize Christ in others, even those we do not like. We need to realize that Christ can talk to us even in the dullest of sermons if we are open to hear him. We should rejoice that there are infants in worship because if there were not, the future of the church would be dismal indeed. We should realize that the church is a gift. And I shall state frankly, if you do not find this particular church to be a place of comfort and healing, then find a church in which you will find what you think you need.

What we need most is God. And in church, God comes to us in a special way through the prayer of the body of Christ and the sacraments. Humans are weak and not always to our liking, but we are all in this together. We can separate ourselves from the church only by separating ourselves from Christ. We can ignore our membership in the body of Christ and the responsibilities that flow from that membership only at our spiritual peril.

Think carefully about the gift that Christ has given you through the church, the visible manifestation of his grace and his presence on earth. Take seriously your responsibilities as members of Christ's body and your essential bonds with all Christians everywhere. Come to church for your sake, not God's.

– Michael Gemignani

Hymns
Opening: O God of Every Nation
Sermon: We Are One in the Spirit
Closing: Faith of Our Fathers

February 3, 2013

4th Sunday after Epiphany
RC/Pres: 4th Sunday in Ordinary Time

Lessons

Semi-continuous (SC)	Roman Catholic (RC)
Jer 1:4-10	Jer 1:4-5, 17-19
Ps 71:1-6	Ps 71:1-6, 15-17
1 Cor 13:1-13	1 Cor 12:31—13:13 or 13:4-13
Lk 4:21-30	Lk 4:21-30

Speaker's Introduction for the Lessons

Lesson 1

Jeremiah 1:4-10 (SC); Jeremiah 1:4-5, 17-19 (RC)

Jeremiah recognizes his ignorance of the Lord's ways, so God gives him words and visions to teach him what he must say to the people of Israel who have forsaken the Law.

Lesson 2

Psalm 71:1-6 (SC); Psalm 71:1-6, 15-17 (RC)

The psalmist prays for deliverance from enemies to the God who has been the psalmist's rock and refuge since birth.

Lesson 3

1 Corinthians 13:1-13 (SC); 1 Corinthians 12:31—13:13 or 13:4-13 (RC)

The famous love hymn of 1 Corinthians is actually written to parties in a nasty church fight. Paul says that no matter how faithful, spiritual, knowledgeable, or charitable one is, if there is no love, it amounts to nothing.

ing the hymn, he gave it to composer Lowell Mason who wrote the tune OLIVET for it. The hymn helps us to acknowledge our divine Savior and to express the desire for our love of the Savior to be "pure, warm, and changeless . . . a living fire!"

Children's Time: Some Didn't Follow

(Bring a box of toy figures of people. Place the toy figures on the floor.)
Invite the children to pick one to represent Jesus. Explain that when Jesus was on earth he traveled around teaching about God's love and God's way for our lives. *(Place Jesus in front of the toy figures.)* Some of the people who heard Jesus' message followed Jesus. *(Invite the children to place some of the toy figures in a group around Jesus.)* And some of the people did not. *(Have the children move the other figures away from Jesus.)*

Mention that in the Bible story today we hear about a whole town of people who decided not to follow Jesus. *(Move all the figures away from Jesus.)* In fact some people got so angry at what Jesus had to say that they tried to hurt him. Jesus had to slip away quietly. Comment that Jesus must have been sad about this, but nothing would keep him from talking about God's love.

Comment that eventually some of the people from that town changed their minds and did follow Jesus. *(Place some of the toy figures in a group around Jesus.)*

Pray with the children, giving thanks for Jesus, who never stops telling people about God.

The Sermon: To the Outsiders
Scripture: Luke 4:21-30

There was once a small, church-related college that had an annual event called Christian Emphasis Week. The student Christian group would invite a speaker to campus, who would preach several times and have discussions with the students – all aimed at deepening faith and creating a mood of religious revival.

One year, however, the students at this college got more than they bargained for. They invited a speaker whom none of them had heard before, but he had the reputation for being dynamic and exciting. Indeed, he was. On the first night of the special week, the campus chapel was filled with the faithful. Of course, the "Animal House" types and other impious students stayed away; this was, after all, an occasion for religious insiders, for the truly Christian.

The speaker began by opening the Bible and reading a passage of scripture. When he had finished, he closed the Bible and then suddenly flung it across the stage and out an open window. The congregation sat in stunned silence. Were their eyes playing tricks on them? Did the preacher really throw the Bible out a window? The preacher looked at them and said, "There goes your God," and proceeded to preach a challenging sermon on the difference between worshiping the Bible and worshiping the God who comes to us through the scriptures.

In a way, Jesus performed something similarly shocking in his hometown synagogue at Nazareth. At the outset, it seemed like a normal service. Jesus opened up the scriptures and read from the familiar text: the word from the prophet Isaiah about good news being preached to the poor and release being given to the captives. Then he preached. Luke does not preserve the whole sermon, just the main point: "Today this scripture has been fulfilled in your hearing" (v. 21).

At first, the congregation responded warmly, enthusiastically. "Good sermon!" "Beautiful words!" Heads nodded, people murmured their assent and pride in this hometown boy who was so eloquent. But then a question began to stir among them. If Isaiah's prophecy has really been fulfilled today, how come nothing happened? How come Jesus didn't perform any of those mighty deeds we have heard he did in Capernaum? What does he mean, "Today this scripture has been fulfilled in your hearing"?

It was then that Jesus threw the Bible out the window – or at least their understanding of the scripture. They thought that Isaiah's words were only for them, for Israel, for Nazareth, for the local folk. Jesus proceeded to throw that understanding of the Bible out the window by saying that God's care for the poor and the oppressed has always been for the outsiders as much as for the insiders. Indeed, when insiders try to restrict God's grace to themselves, they cut themselves off from that very grace.

What happened at that little college? The congregation that night steamed in outrage and left the service muttering blasphemy. Word spread around campus about what had happened, and the next night the religious regulars stayed away, but the "tax collectors and sinners" drew near. The place was packed with fraternity types, those who would never think of themselves as religious, and the curious.

The preacher chose to preach that night on forgiveness, and when it was done, he engaged the congregation in dialog. One in the audience, intrigued but skeptical, said, "I heard what you said tonight, but how can a person know – really know – they are forgiven?"

The speaker looked directly at the questioner and said firmly, "I tell you, in the name of Jesus, you are forgiven."

"Right, right," responded the student. "I heard you say that. But my question is, How can you really know that for a fact?"

"I tell you," repeated the speaker in an even more forceful voice, "in the name of Jesus, you are forgiven."

"I don't think you catch my question," protested the student. "I want to know how you can really know, I mean know for sure, that you're forgiven."

Now a third time the speaker looked him in the eye and said, "I tell you, in the name of Jesus, you are forgiven." It was then that something electric happened in the room. The word took hold in a way beyond understanding, and this student, this outsider, this one who would never have darkened the door of a church, sat down knowing in his heart that "in the name of Jesus" he was forgiven.

– Thomas G. Long

Hymns
Opening: God Has Spoken to His People
Sermon: The King of Love My Shepherd Is
Closing: Lead Us, Heavenly Father, Lead Us

February 10, 2013

Transfiguration/Last Sunday after Epiphany
RC/Pres: 5th Sunday in Ordinary Time

Lessons

Semi-continuous (SC)	Roman Catholic (RC)
Ex 34:29-35	Jer 17:5-8
Ps 99	Ps 1:1, 4-6
2 Cor 3:12—4:2	1 Cor 15:12, 16-20
Lk 9:28-36 (37-43)	Lk 6:17, 20-26

Speaker's Introduction for the Lessons
Lesson 1
Exodus 34:29-35 (SC)

Moses' encounter with God on Mt. Sinai leaves his face radiant and signifies Moses, special status as messenger of God's glory and a vision of the face of God for the community of faith.

Jeremiah 17:5-8 (RC)

Jeremiah uses theme and imagery from the natural world that parallels Psalm 1, contrasting what becomes of those who trust God and those who do not.

Lesson 2
Psalm 99 (SC)

The psalmist bids the people to praise God, the lover of justice, and worship at God's holy mountain.

Psalm 1:1, 4-6 (RC)

This wisdom psalm contrasts the paths and destinies of the wicked and the righteous.

Lesson 3
2 Corinthians 3:12—4:2 (SC)

The apostle Paul is confident that God's promises will be made good in God's own time, and that in Christ we can know the freedom and glory of a new relationship with God.

1 Corinthians 15:12, 16-20 (RC)

Paul asserts the centrality of resurrection to Christian faith: Christian faith, without resurrection, is futile and ineffective.

Gospel
Luke 9:28-36 (37-43) (SC)

Jesus has been teaching about his coming death and resurrection, but the disciples do not understand. God transfigures Jesus on the mountaintop to confirm Jesus as the chosen one.

Luke 6:17, 20-26 (RC)

This passage encompasses the first part of Luke's so-called sermon on the plain, relating both the blessings (beatitudes) and woes that Jesus pronounces, with slight but significant differences from Matthew 5's account.

Theme
A vision of Christ's suffering and glory sustains us.

Thought for the Day
Our ministries today are held in the context of God's eternal saving plan.

Sermon Summary
In the transfiguration, God confirms Jesus' ministry of healing and his call to suffer and die. We can take heart from this as we face hardships and challenges in our own daily ministries.

Call to Worship
One: The Lord our God is holy and brings justice and salvation.

All: Bless the Lord, O my soul.

One: God is merciful and gracious, abounding in steadfast love.

All: Bless the Lord, O my soul.

One: Cry out and the Holy One of all creation will answer.

All: We give thanks and praise to the Lord our God.

Pastoral Prayer

We give thanks to you, Holy God, for your saving purpose for the world, especially as it is revealed to us in the death and resurrection of Jesus Christ. Help us to keep our hearts and minds fixed on Christ as we follow him in our daily lives. Through him, strengthen us to do your loving will, and give us the courage to follow even when our work is difficult and the way unclear. Bless the whole church with your Spirit of wisdom and strength, so that it may continue to be a faithful witness to the grace received through Jesus Christ and a beacon of hope in our troubled world. Amen.

Prayer of Confession

Gracious God, we confess to you that we grow weary in following Christ and doing your good will. We become lost in our own agendas and priorities; we often desire only glory and victory for ourselves and our families. We prefer to stay on the mountaintop rather than serve in the valley. We can be discouraged easily by opposition and disappointments, fearing the criticism of others and, then, giving up quickly. Forgive our fainthearted efforts and lukewarm devotion in our attempts to follow. Open our hearts and minds to the good news that Christ is with us in our suffering and struggle, and that he will never abandon us. Give us the faith to live for Christ and to trust in the gift of his presence with us and the promise of the kingdom for all eternity. In Jesus' name. Amen.

Prayer of Dedication of Gifts and Self

You have richly blessed us, O God, and we give you thanks with our offerings here today and with our lives of service each day. Reveal to us your loving will for our lives and give us the faith to go where you call us. Draw us together in your name that we may strengthen one another in all our ministries. Give us joy in the talents and abilities you have given to us, so that we may delight in doing your will. Amen.

Hymn of the Day
O Wondrous Sight, O Vision Fair

This hymn helps paint a picture of Christ's brilliant glory in his transfiguration. It also provides encouragement that those who "joy in God" will one day share in a similar glory. The text is an anonymous Latin hymn written for the Feast of the Transfiguration in the 15th century. It first appeared in Sarum Breviary of 1495. The English translation first appeared in the 1868 edition of the *British Hymns Ancient and Modern*. The tune WAREHAM, first published in 1738, provides a strong musical setting for a triumphant and somewhat mystical expression of the text. A broad and majestic tempo is suggested.

Children's Time: God's Glory

(Bring a bright flashlight, something that sparkles in the light such as a cut crystal ornament, and some sparkling stickers.)

Shine the light on the glittering object, admire it together, and enjoy the sparkles. Explain that the object looks so pretty because it reflects the beauty of the light. Tell that the Bible story today is about a time when Peter, John, and James saw God's beauty reflected in the face of Jesus. Tell the story of the transfiguration. Discuss what it might have been like on the mountaintop with Jesus, Peter, James, and John. What words might the disciples have used to describe what happened to them?

Gather the children in a circle around you and one by one shine the flashlight on their faces. Comment on how beautiful they look as the light reflects off their faces. Explain that as God's children, they show the beauty of God's love in their faces, in their smiles, in their eyes, and in the way they care for others. Place a sparkling sticker on each child's hand as a reminder that they reflect the beauty of God's love.

Pray with the children, giving thanks for the exciting story of Jesus on the mountaintop.

The Sermon: On the Right Track
Scripture: Luke 9:28-36 (37-43)

Long ago my husband was working to persuade me to take my first backpacking trip in the mountains of the Pacific Northwest. I had hiked before, but not in a place that involved gaining and losing thousands of feet in altitude, and not with a 50-pound pack on my back. As you can imagine, it wasn't easy to convince me that this would be worth the effort.

It was the pictures that finally won me over. My husband brought out pictures of the trail he hoped we would hike and dazzled me with views of cascading waterfalls; deep, green, lush forests; and breathtaking panoramic views of mountain valleys and distant peaks. These pictures inspired me to attempt that backpacking trip, and they helped to energize me when we were struggling up those steep trails and enduring the weight of our heavy packs.

Whether it is a backpacking trip or some other journey, it helps to be able to picture what the journey will entail and what the end will be like. In our journey of faith, the story of Jesus' transfiguration is something like the pictures I viewed before attempting my first mountain hike.

Jesus' transfiguration happens just after Peter has confessed that Jesus is the Messiah and Jesus announces that he must suffer, die, and on the third day rise. Jesus' coming death looms large on the landscape of his ministry. Peter and the disciples can hardly believe it, let alone begin to accept such a tragic fate for their beloved Savior.

But then comes the transfiguration. Jesus glows with the light of God. Moses, the bearer of law, and Elijah, representing all the prophets, are right beside him there. It is as if God is saying through them, "Jesus, you are on the right track." Then the words from the cloud – "This is my Son, my Chosen; listen to him!" (9:35) – further confirm that Jesus' work, even if it means suffering and death, is exactly what God has in mind.

Not only is Jesus' ministry confirmed but the disciples also are encouraged. They will need such a sign – a glimpse of glory – to steady them in the future. The transfiguration is glimpse of the resurrection, of the crown beyond the cross, and of the victory beyond the humiliation of crucifixion. These disciples have hard days and years ahead of them. They will need the memory of this day to strengthen them.

We know, in our own journeys of faith, that following Jesus is not one long march from victory to victory. When we are faithful to our Lord, we sometimes find ourselves in difficult situations: helping people who seem to be beyond help, struggling to forgive what seems unforgivable, giving one more ounce of care and concern when we think we're running on empty, and continuing to share our gifts and financial resources even when there is no immediate return.

Jesus' transfiguration is our signpost, telling us that this is the right way to go. Sacrifice, love, and generosity may not pay off immediately, but they are all a part of God's glorious plan. We are on the right track. One day, all that is good will be illuminated by the dazzling light of God. For now, the transfiguration is a signpost telling us that God is present in each and every day.

Consider the event that immediately follows the transfiguration on the mountain that day. A dad brings his son with seizures to Jesus and begs for Jesus to heal him. Down from the mountain, down from glorification, Jesus is called to get right to work again. The boy is healed, restored to his father, and all are astounded at the greatness of God. The cross awaits Jesus in Jerusalem, but God is determined to accomplish good things through him every day along the way. The entire ministry of Jesus makes this clear.

God's glory and God's good will are a part of each day in our lives, too. Even though the journey may be long and difficult, God is at work to accomplish good through our words and deeds. What good news for our daily walk of faith! This week none of us will probably have anything close to a transfiguration experience, but this doesn't mean that God isn't working through us and around us. God is at work every time you and I forgive a wrong and help restore a friendship; every time we are generous to someone in need, whether it be through a food pantry or a check to support cancer research; every time we stop to listen to someone's grief or teach a child about the faith; every time and any time we seek to bring hope and healing to a hurting world.

In our journeys of faith, remember the transfiguration. It is just one more sign that in Jesus Christ, crucified and raised, God is at work – bringing light and hope to the world God loves. Like the disciples, we also bear this light. It is a long journey, but with a promised and glorious ending.

– Jeanette B. Strandjord

Hymns
Opening: Jesus on the Mountain Peak
Sermon: Arise, Your Light Has Come
Closing: Love Divine, All Loves Excelling

February 13, 2013

Ash Wednesday

Lessons

Semi-continuous (SC)	Roman Catholic (RC)
Joel 2:1-2, 12-17 or Isa 58:1-12	Joel 2:12-18
Ps 51:1-17	Ps 51:3-4, 5-6, 12-13, 14, 17
2 Cor 5:20b—6:10	2 Cor 5:20—6:2
Mt 6:1-6, 16-21	Mt 6:1-6, 16-18

Speaker's Introduction for the Lessons
Lesson 1
Joel 2:1-2, 12-17 (SC); Joel 2:12-18 (RC)

The prophet Joel, seeing the devastation of the land caused by a locust plague, calls God's people to repent and speaks God's gracious invitation for the people to return to God.

Lesson 2
Psalm 51:1-17 (SC); Psalm 51:3-4, 5-6, 12-13, 14, 17 (RC)

This prayer, traditionally attributed to David after the prophet Nathan confronted the king over his adultery with Bathsheba and treachery in her husband's death, cries out for mercy, forgiveness, and renewal.

Lesson 3
2 Corinthians 5:20b—6:10 (SC); 2 Corinthians 5:20—6:2 (RC)

The Lord has gone to extreme lengths to reconcile us to God. In sending Christ, God invites us not only to have our sins forgiven but also to live in a new relationship with God.

Gospel
Matthew 6:1-6, 16-21 (SC); Matthew 6:1-6, 16-18 (RC)

Jesus teaches about our sincere response to God in our almsgiving, prayer, and fasting. He counsels us to practice these privately and not as displays of our own righteousness.

Theme

Faith is its own reward apart from public recognition.

Thought for the Day

We repent because of the cross, which stands at the end of the Lenten pilgrimage.

— Herman G. Stuempfle Jr.

Sermon Summary

Jesus counsels us to practice our faith without calling attention to our own piety and good works. This is the way to journey faithfully in relationship to God. We keep our eyes on Jesus and his cross in our Lenten walk.

Call to Worship

One: Create in me a clean heart, O God.
All: Keep our eyes on Jesus, our crucified Lord.
One: Put a new and a right spirit within me, O God.
All: Keep our hearts in Jesus, our crucified Lord.
One: My footsteps falter and I lose my way.
All: Restore us to the joy of your salvation.
One: Turn me toward you, O God.
All: Open our lips, that we may declare your praise.

Pastoral Prayer

We give you thanks, O God, that in every age and time you call us to you. Open our hearts and minds to those, like the prophet Joel, who warn us of our sin and bid us to repent. In our repentance restore us in body and spirit, so that we may live with generous hearts toward all and seek your peace in world. During our Lenten journey keep our eyes on our crucified Lord Jesus, so that we may live faithfully, trusting only in Christ as Lord over life and death. Let our mission together as God's people be centered on you and your saving purpose for our world, that we may journey with unity and clear purpose. Amen.

Prayer of Confession

Mighty Lord, we confess that we are lost without you. Gather us, so that we may join our hearts and voices together in seeking your forgiveness and direction. So often we would go our own way, desiring only our personal success and public glory. Forgive us. In our practice of the faith, may our right hand not be concerned with what the left is doing. So often we forget that without you we are but dust and ashes with no hope beyond this life. Forgive us. In our assembly and in our daily lives keep our hearts and minds fixed on the cross of Christ; remembering that our hope rests in his death and resurrection. May our journey be one of faith in you and generous service to your world. Amen.

Prayer of Dedication of Gifts and Self

Great God, who created us and continues to sustain us in this world, we give you thanks and praise for the blessings we have received through your bountiful grace. Use our lives and the resources you have given us, so that we may glorify you in all we say and do as we minister to all in need in this world. Unite us in our journey of faith, that we may strengthen and support one another in our walk of faith and our mutual ministry, all to your glory. Amen.

Hymn of the Day
Jesus, Priceless Treasure

This hymn is most often heard as a choral selection or organ composition and is not easily sung by a congregation. In the proper setting, however, this text and tune make a meaningful congregational statement. Perhaps a choir or soloist could sing the first stanza, setting the desired mood and providing a secure introduction to the hymn. The original German text was first published in 1653 and translated by Catherine Winkworth in 1864. The tune JESU, MEINE FREUDE appeared with the hymn in the 1653 publication *Praxis Pietatis Melica* and is attributed to German composer Johann Cruger.

Children's Time: Ash Wednesday

(Bring a container of ashes and a damp cloth.)

Ask the children to look around the church and notice the changes in the worship area. Explain that today is Ash Wednesday, the first day of Lent. Describe Lent as a special season of the church year when we think about being God's children and the things that Jesus did while he lived on the earth.

Tell how many people put ashes on their foreheads or hands this day. Invite the children to look at the ashes and touch them if they wish. (Have the cloth ready to wipe the children's hands afterwards.) Explain that ashes are used as a sign of sadness. Ash Wednesday is a time to think about how we could do a better job of being God's children. It is a day to say "sorry" to God. What kinds of things might we say sorry for? Wearing the ashes is also a sign that we want to change. What might we want to change? Conclude your time together with the simple reminder that God loves us very much and will forgive us when we say sorry.

Pray with the children, giving thanks for the gift of God's forgiveness.

The Sermon: Journeying with Our Eyes on Jesus
Scripture: Matthew 6:1-6, 16-21

We could think of the season of Lent as a long road that stretches out before us. We walk along this road during the weeks of Lent, not concentrating on the tiny steps we take but focusing on our destination: the cross of Jesus. The cross of Jesus Christ casts a long shadow over this Lenten road and this shadow reaches all the way back to the beginning, to Ash Wednesday. So tonight we lift our eyes to the cross as we begin our Lenten journey with confession, then ashes on our foreheads as a sign of repentance, and then, finally, the gift of Holy Communion.

The shadow of the cross is before us, not to make us feel bad and certainly not to make us feel so guilty that we will punish ourselves by giving up something for Lent. The cross, instead, comes to once again make real God's deep love and mercy for us and for our world. When we walk the road of Lent, we walk toward the love and mercy of God, given to us in Jesus Christ.

One simple meaning of the word repentance is "to turn around." Lent calls us to turn around toward God – toward our crucified Lord Jesus Christ. Once turned, we walk toward him. He is our focus this season. The focus of Lent is not ourselves and not the opinions of others.

Jesus talks about this in our Gospel reading from Matthew 6. Here Jesus warns you, me, and the whole Christian community not to lose our direction and our focus on God. As we walk our journey of faith, we are in danger of doing just this; it's too easy to start to concentrate on the little steps that we take – the good deeds that we do. When we do this, the opinions and approval of others begin to matter much more than they should. In Matthew's Gospel, Jesus tells us that when we practice giving alms, when we pray, and when we fast, we must not do these things for public approval. This is like watching the little footsteps we take along our faith journey and waiting for the applause of others for our meager progress. When we live this way, it is all about the approval of others and not about our relationship with God.

This is how our society likes to work, and we must be careful not to be entrapped by it in our walk of faith. Today we have society sections in our newspapers picturing who has attended the latest charity function and how much was raised. Very worthy charitable or nonprofit groups are careful to publish donor lists on their programs or in their newsletters, bending over backwards to recognize all who contribute and to publicize how much was given. They've developed the "Gold Givers," the "Silver Givers," and the "Bronze Givers" categories. This is not necessarily bad, until we transfer this approach to our practice of our life of faith. Jesus tells us that, for our own spiritual health, we need to practice our almsgiving, prayer, and fasting in private, and not seek any honor or earthly reward because of it. God does not have "Gold," "Silver," and "Bronze" categories for us.

On this Ash Wednesday, we lift our eyes and our hearts to the cross of Christ. Yes, we will pray; yes, we will give offerings; yes, some of us may even fast. But may all these things be because of Christ and not because of any hope for approval and recognition. Many of us will come forward to receive the sign of the cross in ashes on our foreheads as a sign of our true repentance. This can be very meaningful for us as individuals and as a worshiping community – we are all marked by sin and the power of death. Ashes, especially on the forehead of a baby, are a startling reminder of the harsh reality of sin and death, and our need for forgiveness and salvation.

This harsh reality comes home to us even more strongly when we stand at the open grave of a loved one. At the grave we have run out of things to do. Our hands are empty. Most likely everything has been tried: doctors, hospitals, prayers, positive thinking, good deeds, special diets, and whatever remedies are at hand. We are mortals, flesh and blood. We may be able to put death off sometimes, but we cannot stop it, and we certainly cannot raise ourselves from the grave.

Our hands are empty, but God's are not. Because God loves us and we are God's children through Jesus Christ, we have the gift – the absolute gift – of new life beyond the grave. This is the promise and the relationship that hold us in life and in death. This is a promise worthy of our attention, worthy of the commitment of our whole selves. This is why we walk the road of Lent with our eyes on our crucified Lord and Savior.

In this season of Lent, listen to Christ. Let's all stop looking at our own little footsteps and waiting for the approval of the crowd. As we live in relationship with Christ, our prayers don't have to be impressive and long; our giving should be generous, but done in secret; and our fasting or devotional reading or self-denial should never be flaunted for public consumption. God hears and sees us and, as Jesus promises in our Gospel reading, we will be blessed by God.

You and I are on the road to the cross of Christ. Keep your eyes on Jesus and his saving death and resurrection for you. Do pray. Do help others. Do discipline yourselves with faithful practices. But do them all in thanksgiving and to the glory of the God who saves you.

– Jeanette B. Strandjord

Hymns
Opening: O Lord, throughout These Forty Days
Sermon: In the Cross of Christ I Glory
Closing: I Want Jesus to Walk with Me

February 17, 2013

1st Sunday in Lent

Lessons

Semi-continuous (SC)	Roman Catholic (RC)
Deut 26:1-11	Deut 26:4-10
Ps 91:1-2, 9-16	Ps 91:1-2, 10-15
Rom 10:8b-13	Rom 10:8-13
Lk 4:1-13	Lk 4:1-13

Speaker's Introduction for the Lessons
Lesson 1
Deuteronomy 26:1-11 (SC); Deuteronomy 26:4-10 (RC)

The Israelites are settled in their new land, and God commands them to offer the first fruits of their harvest as a sign of their dependence on God and their gratitude for the land.

Lesson 2
Psalm 91:1-2, 9-16 (SC); Psalm 91:1-2, 10-15 (RC)

The psalmist confesses trust in God's protection and care, including one image that is clearly in the background of the Gospel's story of temptation to make a spectacle by jumping off the temple wall to test God's promise.

Lesson 3
Romans 10:8b-13 (SC); Romans 10:8-13 (RC)

Paul writes that the goal of the law is Christ. Christ fulfills the law, bestowing righteousness on all who confess him as Lord and giving them salvation.

Gospel
Luke 4:1-13 (SC/RC)

After Jesus is confirmed as God's beloved Son in his baptism, God then sends Jesus into the wilderness to face temptation. Jesus refuses the devil's offers and remains faithful to his mission as God's Son.

Theme

Our identity is God-given.

Thought for the Day

It's a mind-blowing concept that the God who created the universe might be looking for company . . . Love interrupts, if you like, the consequences of your actions.

> – Bono, lead singer of the rock group U2, *The Christian Century,* September 6, 2005, p. 7

Sermon Summary

When we remember the history of God's gracious dealings with us and the world, we gain a faithful perspective on our lives. God's grace shapes us and shapes the world. In giving thanks for this great gift, we also rededicate our lives to God.

Call to Worship

One: Come to the Lord, our strong fortress and deliverer.
All: Let us find refuge in God's shadow.
One: God will protect you; under the Lord's wings you will find refuge
All: From snares, terror, and destruction.
One: Seek the Lord and the Lord's dwelling place,
All: That we may hear and follow.
One: Call on the name of the Lord in trust and worship.
All: All praise to our Refuge and Strength!

Pastoral Prayer

We give thanks to you, O God, for the gift of your creation that continues to sustain us, and for all of your servants and witnesses in every generation. Help us to remember all that you have done for us since the beginning of time, that we may be inspired to serve you faithfully now. Give us thankful hearts, that we may share the gifts we have been given with those who are in need. Help us share our resources and talents in our congregations, to carry on ministry in your name and to your glory. Keep our eyes on Jesus Christ, in whom our lives – past, present, and future – are grounded. Amen.

Prayer of Dedication of Gifts and Self

Most gracious God, we thank you for the gifts of all creation and especially for the gift of your own dear Son, Jesus Christ. We thank you for your saving faithfulness from generation to generation. Receive these gifts we offer in thanksgiving for all your mercies, and use them to your good purpose. Renew us by the power of your Holy Spirit, that we may live in faith in you and gladly share your gifts in service to your world. In Jesus' name we pray. Amen.

Hymn of the Day
Lord, Who throughout These Forty Days

This hymn focuses on the fullest meaning of the Lenten season. Antiphonal singing between a soloist or choir and the congregation can be a meaningful way of singing the hymn. In a four-stanza setting, the soloist or choir would sing the first and third stanzas and the congregation the second and fourth. The text was written in 1873 by British hymn writer, Claudia F. Hernaman. Although the tune St. FLAVIAN is most generally associated with the hymn, the tune LAND OF REST gives a poignant interpretation of the text.

Children's Time: Giving Thanks

(Bring some loose change, a bag of groceries, and a calendar.)

Comment that we enjoy many good things in our lives. Have the children list some of the things that fill their lives with happiness – things for which they are thankful. Comment that there are many ways to say thank you to God. The Bible tells us that one way is to give back some of what we have to God, and it should be the first thing we do.

Show the loose change. How might we give some back to God? Accept all ideas, and if no one else says it, suggest you might put some of the money in the offering plate where it will get used for God's work.

Show the groceries and ask how we might give some groceries back to God. Invite the children to help you choose a few items and put them in the collection box for the food bank.

Open the calendar and observe that every day is a gift from God. How might we give some of our day back to God? Perhaps we could spend some time each day helping others.

Pray with the children, giving thanks for all God's blessings.

The Sermon: Remember, Rejoice, Rededicate
Scripture: Deuteronomy 26:1-11

"Oh, no! Not more heritage!" my youngest daughter protested one Sunday afternoon as we planned to visit yet another historical site in my home state of Wisconsin. Why was it, she wondered, that we had to talk about all this old stuff, walk through old buildings, and listen to tour guides. "It's history, your history!" I tried to encourage her, but with little success.

Those days were long ago, but the reason for "more heritage," as my young daughter put it, remains. It was so that she would better understand where she had come from and who she is meant to be. I think many parents share this goal for their children. Sometimes it is the parent, and if we're fortunate, the grandparent, who takes the child on his knee and tells her about the old days. Suddenly the child's life is held in a much larger frame than before. She is here because someone before her took an ocean voyage from Norway to New York or endured a difficult resettlement from Vietnam to the United States.

Our reading from Deuteronomy 26:1-11 puts everything into larger perspective, too. One important part of this passage is full of remembering. The response God calls for begins this way: "A wandering Aramean was my ancestor . . ." Before God brought the Israelites into the promised land, they were wandering in the desert with no home and no clear idea of where they were or who they were to be as a people. These newly freed slaves were totally dependent on God for their present and their future. This liturgy of the presentation of the first fruits of the harvest calls for God's people to remember this heritage. And even more important for them to remember was that it was God alone who freed them from slavery and brought them to this land "flowing with milk and honey."

If God's people did not remember this history, then they might begin to think that it was because of their own virtue or perhaps even blind luck that they were finally settled in their own land. They might begin to think that their harvest and whatever else they owned belonged solely to them and was for their use and pleasure. They might begin to think that they were the captains of their own future and not indebted to anyone else.

One of the reasons I took my children to see not only state historical sites but also the homesteads of their grandparents was because I wanted them to understand the larger picture of their personal history and the history of the state and country. Great sacrifices had been made and daring moves taken so that they could be where they were and have what they had. What they saw and learned gave them a greater appreciation for their current place in the world.

As Christians we have a long history. A "wandering Aramean" was our father, too. God has been at work in our world since the beginning of time to draw us close to God and save us from the sin and evil in ourselves and in our broken creation. God is at the center of our history, especially through Jesus Christ who lived and died for us. Every time we confess our creeds together, we are celebrating that history. Every time we remember our baptisms, we are reclaiming our identity as God's forgiven and beloved children. This is our central story.

In this season of Lent, we would do well to remember our identity and celebrate it. Lent helps us focus on what God has done for us, and on our absolute need for the grace of God. We need to do this so that some false story does not obscure who we really are and who we are meant to be. There are plenty of false stories around: rugged individualism (I don't need anybody), consumerism (I am what I own), nationalism (my country is everything), hedonism (whatever feels good is my soul purpose), and whatever else gives us the idea that we are the center of the universe.

The writer of Deuteronomy calls the people to celebrate the true story of who they are: God's chosen and redeemed people. This remembering and rejoicing leads to renewed dedication and the humble offering of the first fruits of the ground. In this season of Lent, it is good for us to focus on this call for renewed dedication and the offering of what we have been given. When God rescued the Hebrew people from Egypt, when God sent Jesus to the world, when God baptized you and claimed you in Christ, it was to bring you into close, saving relationship. God loves you. God loves the world in which you live. Let's take time to see this grand picture of salvation and grace. It frames us, our whole life, and all of creation. And then we can respond in thanks and praise.

My youngest daughter is now an adult. She even has thanked me for making her spend time on her heritage. She says that it put things in perspective for her, helped her make decisions about what to do and what not to do. It still gives her determination to use her life as she believes God intends and as God has made possible. It's good to know one's history.

Your history – our history – is in relationship with God; the One who sent God's own Son to die and rise for us. This is our story, a true story. In this season of Lent, may we be reenergized to give God thanks and to offer our whole selves to God's good purposes.

– Jeanette B. Strandjord

Hymns
Opening: O God, Our Help in Ages Past
Sermon: Be Thou My Vision
Closing: The Church of Christ, in Every Age

February 24, 2013

2nd Sunday in Lent

Lessons

Semi-continuous (SC)	Roman Catholic (RC)
Gen 15:1-12, 17-18	Gen 15:5-12, 17-18
Ps 27	Ps 27:1, 7-9, 13-14
Phil 3:17—4:1	Phil 3:17—4:1 or Phil. 3:20—4:1
Lk 13:31-35 or Lk 9:28-36	Lk 9:28-36

Speaker's Introduction for the Lessons

Lesson 1
Genesis 15:1-12, 17-18 (SC); Genesis 15:5-12, 17-18 (RC)

God had promised Abram land and descendants, but Abram remains childless. In our passage God comes with the covenant promise once more to steady Abram in his uncertainty.

Lesson 2
Psalm 27 (SC); Psalm 27:1, 7-9, 13-14 (RC)

The psalmist affirms trust in God as light and salvation, and because of whom the psalmist need not fear.

Lesson 3
Philippians 3:17—4:1 (SC); Philippians 3:17—4:1 or 3:20—4:1 (RC)

Paul affectionately exhorts the Philippians to remember that their true home is in heaven and to resist hedonistic ways. Their conduct should be in keeping with their God-given, eternal identity.

Gospel
Luke 13:31-35 (SC)

On the road to Jerusalem, Jesus warns of coming judgment and anticipates his rejection in that city. Still, not even warnings about Herod's plan to kill him deter Jesus from faithfully completing his God-given mission.

Luke 9:28-36 (RC)

Jesus' transfiguration is God's confirmation that this chosen one who will die in Jerusalem is indeed the Son of God. Suffering and defeat will not have the last word over Jesus or his church.

Theme

Do not fear, God has the last word.

Thought for the Day

Do not be afraid, little flock, for it is your Father's good pleasure to give you the kingdom.

– Luke 12:32

Sermon Summary

"That fox" Herod seeks the life of Jesus. But Jesus is not deterred from his God-given mission to go to Jerusalem. Many things in life threaten us and make us afraid. Still, we can live confident of God's saving love and continue our mission in the name of Jesus Christ.

Call to Worship

One: The Lord is my light and my salvation,

All: We will not be afraid.

One: The Lord is the stronghold of my life,

All: We will not be afraid.

One: Even when our adversaries and foes seek to destroy us,

All: We will not be afraid.

One: Come to the house of the Lord and behold God's beauty.

All: We will sing to the Lord and trust in God!

One: We will see the goodness of the Lord.

All: We will be strong and place our trust in God!

Pastoral Prayer

Gracious God, our rock and defender, we give you thanks for your faithful lovingkindness to your people of every age and time. Especially we praise you for Jesus Christ, and his death and resurrection for us and your world. May Christ's courage and faithfulness empower us to follow Jesus with such faith and courage of our own. Make us bold in facing the foxes of our day, that we may not be undone. Help us to remember your love for us and to entrust our present and our future to you, so we may live unafraid as we seek to do your work in our world. Unite us in our mission with your universal church, that we may serve together in gladness. Amen.

Prayer of Confession

We confess to you, O God, our fears that stem from varied sources: the criticism of others, the uncertainty of our own time, the hardships that veil our eyes from your loving purpose, our own sin and failure, and the evils of terror and war threaten to undo us. Too often we give in to fear, despairing and acting as if you have abandoned us. Forgive us, God. May your Spirit renew our faith and courage, that we may faithfully and not fearfully face each challenge in our lives. This we ask in the name of Christ, who is our hope now and for all time to come. Amen.

Prayer of Dedication of Gifts and Self

For the blessings of this beautiful creation, of health, of work, of community, and of family, we give you thanks, O Lord. Receive these gifts we offer and use them and us to continue to bring your blessing to the whole world. Empower us to be peacemakers in your name and to work for your justice and the welfare of all. When our courage falters, lift us up in our God-given mission, that we might persevere in confidence and joy. Make your way our way, and strengthen us for the journey. Amen.

Hymn of the Day
O Jesus Christ, May Grateful Hymns Be Rising

Based on Matthew 23:37-39 and Luke 13:34-35, this hymn enables us to reflect through a poetic prayer on our desire to minister by Christ's example. It is especially suited to a focus upon urban ministry. It was written by American Methodist minister Bradford Gray Webster in 1954 and chosen the same year by The Hymn Society of the United States and Canada for inclusion in its publication, *Five New Hymns on the City.* Various tunes have been associated with the hymn, including CHARTERHOUSE, WELWYN, and CITY OF GOD, each lending special meaning to the request for "new courage . . . to venture and to dare."

Children's Time: Mother Hen

(Bring some pictures of mother animals with their young, some feathers, and a large blanket.)
Show the children the pictures. Talk about some of the ways in which mother animals clean, feed, and protect their babies. Comment that the Gospel story today is about a mother hen and her baby chicks. Explain that mother birds often cover their young with their wings to protect and shelter them. Comment that the chicks must feel very safe and warm. One day Jesus was talking to some people and said that he wanted to gather the people of Jerusalem like a mother hen gathers her chicks under her wings.

Ask the children to imagine what it would be like to be enfolded in Jesus' arms.

Unfold the blanket and place it over your shoulders, hold the corners, and spread out your arms like wings. Invite the children to become chicks resting safely under the mother's wings. Encircle and cover the children as you remind them that Jesus' love will enfold them like the wings of a bird.

Finish your time together by giving each child a feather as a reminder of Jesus' love.

Pray with the children, giving thanks that we are enfolded in Jesus' love.

The Sermon: Take Heart – The Foxes Will Fail
Scripture: Luke 13:31-35

A fox is a wild animal. A chicken is a domestic animal. Foxes slink about under the cover of darkness ready to strike quickly and tear animal flesh apart with sharp teeth. A chicken roosts at night, doesn't even have teeth, and feeds on insects and grain. These are two very different animals and yet here they appear almost side by side in our reading from Luke.

I grew up on a farm with a henhouse and have seen how defenseless chickens are against a predatory fox. A single fox can wipe out a small flock of chickens in just one night of havoc in the chicken coop. Once the fox is inside the coop and attacks, there's really no hope for hens or baby chicks.

The fox in our Gospel reading is King Herod. He is a ruthless man. It is thought that he even had two of his own sons murdered because he feared their growing political power. Now Herod is out to kill Jesus. The Pharisees, pretending concern, come to warn Jesus of this. Maybe they hope to intimidate and frighten Jesus, for they are certainly no allies of his. But Jesus is not intimidated by either the Pharisees' scare tactic or Herod's threats.

Jesus declares that he must be "on his way" and that he will reach Jerusalem. There is something much larger than Herod the fox working in this world and in this ministry of Jesus. Often we hear in Luke's Gospel that Jesus is on his way. Especially memorable is the time when the crowd outside of Nazareth sought to throw Jesus over the brow of the hill, but Jesus "passed through the midst of them and went on his way" (Lk 4:30). Jesus has a mission, and God is with him to complete it. No one but God is truly in control of Jesus' life and mission – not the crowd in the temple that day in Nazareth and certainly not Herod.

In our own Lenten journey and walk of faith, there are plenty of foxes – foxes that seem out to get us. Sometimes the fox is our own illness or despair, sometimes our own weakness and sin. Or we might face the situation of someone in the workplace, someone we know socially, or even someone in our family who deliberately hurts us. Such foxes can be untruthful, false friends, sneaky, and deceptive. Worse is when we fear for our lives in a situation of domestic violence. We've also seen foxes in the public arena. Smear campaigns still take place in public elections, using the power of innuendo and scare tactics to intimidate and defeat many a good person.

Some years ago I visited the new Abraham Lincoln Presidential Library and Museum in Springfield, Illinois. One of the most memorable parts of that museum is the whispering gallery. Abraham Lincoln and his wife, Mary, endured a great deal of criticism, ridicule, and gossip when they lived in Washington, D.C., during Lincoln's presidency. In the museum, the whispering gallery contains all of the foul, unkind, and untrue words being whispered about them by others in their community. When you walk through this gallery it is as if the whispers are coming at you from all directions. They seem to inhabit your own head. It's very powerful; it's also frightening.

There are a lot of foxes in our world. Jesus shows us how to deal with them. Jesus is clear about who holds his life and his future. God does. Jesus does not let Herod's threats stop him from doing what he knows is God's will for him and the world. Jesus will go to Jerusalem; Herod can't stop him. Jesus will be killed, but it won't be Herod's doing. And his death will not be God's final word either. The final victory belongs to God and the risen Christ.

The foxes of this world don't have the last word over us either. Lent is a journey. Life is a journey. As we seek to live faithfully, it is important for you and me to remember who holds us, and who has the final word over us. God does. So we face the foxes with courage and determination, refusing to be drawn into their hurtful and evil ways. Their way is finally doomed. Instead, the way of love – God's way – will triumph.

Jesus uses the illustration of a hen gathering her chicks to describe what God is about. God desires to gather us all into a place of protection and safety. Seems hopeless, though – after all, what chance does a hen and her chicks stand against the wily fox? But we who know the whole story know that it is not hopeless. God will have the victory. God raised Jesus Christ from the dead and God will save us, too. The journey ends with the powerful grace of God.

The whispering gallery in the Lincoln museum was oppressive and made me claustrophobic. My walking pace quickened almost unconsciously and my shoulders shivered at the sound of so much meanness. How telling, though, that this little whispering gallery is held within a much larger building that honors the very man those "foxes" sought to bring down. The truth, honor, and good that Lincoln strove to do far outshine any foxiness aimed against him.

Jesus followed God with courage and determination, sacrificing even his own life for us and the whole world. As his disciples, we are called to follow with courage and determination. God is with us, full of love and grace, seeking always to gather us as a hen gathers her brood under her wings. We need not let the foxes of this world frighten us and derail our mission.

– Jeanette B. Strandjord

Hymns
Opening: We Are Marching in the Light of God
Sermon: My Song Is Love Unknown
Closing: Thy Holy Wings

March 3, 2013

3rd Sunday in Lent

Lessons

Semi-continuous (SC)	Roman Catholic (RC)
Isa 55:1-9	Ex 3:1-8, 13-15
Ps 63:1-8	Ps 103:1-4, 6-11
1 Cor 10:1-13	1 Cor 10:1-6, 10-12
Lk 13:1-9	Lk 13:1-9

Speaker's Introduction for the Lessons
Lesson 1
Isaiah 55:1-9 (SC)

This chapter concludes a section of the book called "Second Isaiah" by many scholars. The meal symbolizes God's love and abundance for all peoples.

Exodus 3:1-8, 13-15 (RC)

"I am," or YHWH, is a tetragrammaton – a four-letter word – used most often for God in Hebrew Scriptures. In Judaism it is not read aloud but replaced with Adonai ("my Lord") and sometimes Hashem ("the Name").

Lesson 2
Psalm 63:1-8 (SC)

The psalmist offers a prayer of trust in the God whose providential care has sustained through experiences of wilderness and darkness.

Psalm 103:1-4, 6-11 (RC)

The psalmist offers words of blessing for God whose redemptive work is confessed in healing and forgiveness, and in the gift of God's steadfast love and mercy.

Lesson 3
1 Corinthians 10:1-13 (SC); 1 Corinthians 10:1-6, 10-12 (RC)
The population of Corinth, a center for industry and shipbuilding, as well as the arts, came from many places. Paul here responds to two letters concerning lack of harmony and internal strife in the Corinthian church.

Gospel
Luke 13:1-9 (SC/RC)
While the slaughter of Galileans as they brought sacrifices to the temple cannot be confirmed, it is plausible given Pilate's reputation. The idea that a person's sin causes such brutal treatment is a long-standing belief.

Theme
There's no chance like the second chance.

Thought for the Day
People changed other people's lives every day of the year. There was no call to make such a fuss about it.
— Anne Tyler *(Saint Maybe,* Random House, 1991, p. 373)

Sermon Summary
God has given us second chances in Jesus Christ. Our choice is what to do with them.

Call to Worship
One: O God, you are my God, I seek you, my soul thirsts for you; my flesh faints for you, as in a dry and weary land where there is no water.

All: So I have looked upon you in the sanctuary, beholding your power and glory.

One: Your steadfast love is better than life, my lips will praise you.

All: I will bless you as long as I live; I will lift up my hands and call on your name.

Pastoral Prayer

We pause to think about the fig trees of the world, O God – people and places where lives and ways of living do not bear good fruit. We pray for our brothers and sisters in places where war is real and waging war is a way of life. Turn our hearts, that we might use our money, creativity, and passion to wage justice, love, and peace. We remember those who suffer in body, mind, and spirit. We pray that, through our compassion and actions, loneliness, pain, and sorrow may be replaced by the comfort and healing of Christ's spirit. But miracle of miracles, in the dailyness of all that is broken, the light and power of your goodness, grace, and joy flow steady. For all the blessings of this day – the people, moments, activities, and things that make our hearts sing – we give you thanks. Amen.

Prayer of Confession

God, you call us to honesty about who we are and all that we do. In these moments, make us honest with ourselves. We remember now those things we have done or left undone that have hurt others, that have caused suffering and pain to our world, that have betrayed our love for ourselves. *(Pause for silent reflection.)* Give us now the courage and the wisdom to do things differently, to change our behavior so that in asking for forgiveness we might lead forgiven lives. In the spirit of Jesus Christ who befriended and loved all sinners, we now pray. Amen.

Prayer of Dedication of Gifts and Self

Bountiful God, bless now these gifts, our giving, and the fruits of our actions, that in all of it your glory and work might shine in and through the opportunities and second chances they enable and empower. In Jesus' name, make this so. Amen.

Hymn of the Day
There's a Wideness in God's Mercy

Frederick William Faber wrote this hymn in 1854, 19 years after leaving the Anglican priesthood for membership in the Roman Catholic priesthood. The hymn helps us focus on the reality of the true expanse of God's greatness. The hymn offers illustrative comparisons between God's mercy and the expanse of the sea, God's justice and liberty, and God's love and the limits of our mind. Two tunes are most generally associated with the hymn: WELLESLEY, with its four stanza text arrangement; and IN BABILONE, with a two stanza text arrangement. Or, you may wish to use another 8.7.8.7.D. tune.

Children's Time: Growing and Blooming
(Bring some seeds.)

Show the seeds and invite the children to choose a seed to examine. What will happen if the seeds are planted? What kinds of plants might grow? What might they look like? Ask the children to share experiences of planting seeds and caring for the seedlings. What do plants need in order to grow well?

Comment that the Bible story today is about a fig tree that wasn't growing very well. Tell the parable of the fig tree (13:6-8). Comment that Jesus didn't say what happened to the fig tree, he just left it to our imaginations. Invite the children to help you finish the story.

Observe that seeds given proper care will grow well. In the same way, through gentle care we can encourage and help others to grow to be healthy and strong. What kinds of things can we do to help others grow?

Pray with the children, giving thanks for Jesus whose love and care helped many people to grow.

The Sermon: Church of the Second Chance
Scripture: Luke 13:1-9

Ian Bedloe walked past the Church of the Second Chance. It might have been the sign at the intersection that said "DON'T WALK" that made him give it a second thought. Inside, it was ordinary, an abandoned store with about twenty people standing, singing, and turning to look at him and smile when the bell clanged on the door as he entered. It was a Wednesday evening prayer service and Ian found a seat. Each time a member brought a concern to the congregation, the preacher led them in silent prayer, ending with a resounding "Amen."

Ian found himself standing when the preacher asked for the third time, "Any other prayers?"

"I used to be good," he told them. "Or I used to be not bad, at least. I don't know what happened. Everything I touch goes wrong . . . Pray for me to be good again . . . Pray for me to be forgiven" (Anne Tyler, *Saint Maybe,* Random House Publishing Group, 1991, p. 129). Ian felt washed in their silent prayers that were just for his forgiveness. "How could God not listen?" he wondered (p. 129).

After the service, Ian was shocked when Rev. Emmett asked him what he'd done that needed forgiveness. Resisting the urge to run, Ian said he'd caused his brother's suicide by telling him that his wife had been unfaithful. His brother's wife had, in turn, killed herself. It looked like Ian's parents would be raising three more children. Ian asked Rev. Emmett if he was forgiven.

"Goodness no," Rev. Emmett said. Unfair! Ian thought God forgave everything. Yes, Rev. Emmett told him, "But you can't just say, 'I'm sorry, God.' Why, anyone could do that much! You have to offer reparation – concrete, practical reparation, according to the rules of our church" (p. 133).

That's how Ian ended up dropping out of school and helping his parents raise his brother's children.

Second chance. The fig tree got one because of a caring gardener – one last, important second chance.

This story is a paradigm for Jesus, bringer of second chances. At least twice in the Hebrew Scriptures, other religious leaders negotiate with God for second chances. In Genesis 18, Abraham gets God to agree to spare Sodom and Gomorrah if there are ten righteous men in the towns. When Moses was delayed on Mt. Sinai and the people made idols of gold and worshiped them, God's anger was so fierce that it threatened to "consume them" (Ex 32:10). But Moses begged God not to do it, reminding God of the covenant made with the Israelites. "And the Lord changed his mind about the disaster that he planned to bring on his people" (32:14).

Second chances. The fig tree got it, but it had to change. No fruit next season – no tree next season. In human terms it's called reparation.

Often, we in the liberal Protestant church settle for what Bonhoeffer called "cheap grace" – forgiveness not only without reparation but also without repentance. As we sit in the security of our pews on Sunday mornings, confessing sins through a prayer that someone else wrote, there's no Rev. Emmett to remind us that, in the realm of God, saying, "I'm sorry" is only the first step. It's too easy, even for pastors, to practice "cheap grace."

I know firsthand. I've had too many women tell me about abusive fathers or husbands, only to stand around talking with these men after worship as if their horrific sins had not been committed. While nothing might be the right thing to say in those moments, it seems like, "Good to meet you," and, "How are you" are ingenuous.

Twice in today's Gospel reading Jesus says, "Unless you repent, you will all perish" (13:3, 5). We tend to think of this perishing as happening at the end of time. In part, that is what Jesus means. But Jesus was also talking about present time. What we do or don't do always matters. Consider how very hard it is for most of us to even tell someone we've offended that we're sorry. Every time we fail to make things right, we erect barriers in our relationships, and behind those barriers we perish a little in the here and now.

Second chances. Usually, when Jesus forgives sinners, he tells them to go and sin no more. In other words, do something about your situation. That's what reparation is about. It's doing something not only to acknowledge that what we did was wrong, but also that what we will now do is, if not right, then on the right track.

Ian's parents were shocked and resistant when he told them his plan. When they asked him who would help, he told them about the church "that believes you have to really do something practical to atone for your, shall we call them, sins. And if you agree to that, they'll pitch in" (p. 138). His parents were shocked, "Have you fallen into the hands of some sect?"

His mother reminds him that her church doesn't ask them to "abandon our entire way of life." "Well maybe it should have." Ian responds (p. 138). Then, following Rev. Emmett's instructions, he tells his parents what he had said to his brother before his car hit the wall. In their silence, he left to check on the children. That night, in a dream, his brother came to him, smiling (p. 140).

"People changed other people's lives every day of the year. There was no call to make such a fuss about it" (p. 373). That's how Anne Tyler ends *Saint Maybe,* her story of Ian Bedloe.

Second chances. If we think hard enough, we see she's right. Each moment and every day is a second chance. Every church on every street is the Church of the Second Chance. We are each other's Rev. Emmett. The challenge for each one of us is the same as for that fig tree in the garden and Ian Bedloe waiting at the stop light – what are we to do?

– Rosemary A. Rocha

Hymns
Opening: Come, O Fount of Every Blessing
Sermon: Amazing Grace
Closing: Take My Life, God, Let It Be

March 10, 2013

4th Sunday in Lent

Lessons

Semi-continuous (SC)	Roman Catholic (RC)
Josh 5:9-12	Josh 5:9-12
Ps 32	Ps 34:2-7
2 Cor 5:16-21	2 Cor 5:17-21
Lk 15:1-3, 11b-32	Lk 15:1-3, 11b-32

Speaker's Introduction for the Lessons
Lesson 1
Joshua 5:9-12 (SC/RC)

> Under God's directive, Joshua has circumcised all males in prepara-
> tion for their second Passover on the eve of entering the promised
> land.

Lesson 2
Psalm 32 (SC)

> This psalm of confidence and hope in God our creator and redeemer
> reminds us that the universe is full of God's steadfast love and that we
> can trust in that love.

Psalm 34:2-7 (RC)

> The psalmist blesses God for an act of personal deliverance.

Lesson 3
2 Corinthians 5:16-21 (SC); 2 Corinthians 5:17-21 (RC)

> Writing from Macedonia, stung by criticism, Paul plays with the
> noun and verb for reconciliation. In Greek these words can signify a
> change in relationship with financial overtones. The cost of faithful-
> ness? A life lived differently.

Gospel
Luke 15:1-3, 11b-32 (SC/RC)

Today's Gospel is about lost and found – animals, money, people. All are so important in God's realm that losing even one among many is reason enough to go looking for the one that got away.

Theme

With Christ, what is separated, lost, or broken is reconnected.

Thought for the Day

I am part and parcel of the whole and cannot find God apart from the rest of humanity.

– Gandhi

Sermon Summary

Faith seems to be a dance of brokenness and reconciliation within ourselves, with one another, with our world, and – most important – with God. When it comes to God, the ledger sheet is never balanced, at least not in this life. Always, it is open to the possibility of reconciliation.

Call to Worship

One: Praise God, for God has set us free.
All: The past is behind us. Let us be renewed in God's Spirit.
One: Come, let us join the circle of Jesus.
All: We are children of God's household.

Pastoral Prayer

In this moment of thoughtfulness, we thank you, Creator and Sustainer and Hope. For bodies that run and walk, hearts that beat, and lungs that pump; for days that turn to nights and suns that follow moons; for mountains, valleys, rivers, oceans, and puddles; for glimpses of holy and breathtaking opportunities for loving; for all of this and so much more, thank you. In the stillness of this moment, we bring our concerns, anxieties, fears – for ourselves, for families and friends, and for our world. We give thanks for all the nameless ones who work faithfully and selflessly in big and little ways to turn us away from violence and estrangement toward your way of peace and unity. We pray that your reconciling love will infiltrate the places of resistance in our hearts and in the hearts of our world communities, so that soon we might live united, supportive, and loving of one another. Amen.

Prayer of Confession

Gracious God, sometimes we ignore the one who is lost in favor of the many who are available. But then, in the midst of a hundred good thoughts and ideas, we focus on that one remark or look that leads us down the path of self-doubt and fear. Help us understand which to seek after and which to leave behind. In the spirit of Christ, who promises to walk beside us on the path. Amen.

Prayer of Dedication of Gifts and Self

Can what we bring to this time of offering really heal a broken world? Can our hour of prayer and song transform our hearts and minds to doing your work in the world? In faith, we trust that we can and we will. Bless now our intentions and our offerings, Holy God. Bless now our lives and our commitments. By your Spirit, reform our lives into ones worthy of the task you place before us. In the spirit of Jesus our Christ, we pray. Amen.

Hymn of the Day
Beneath the Cross of Jesus

This hymn enables us to consider the implications that the cross of Christ provides for Christian discipleship. Even with the challenges of 21st-century Christian life, here we have the assurance that the cross of Christ is indeed "the shadow of a mighty Rock," and that we can be "content to let the world go by." The text was written in 1872 by Elizabeth Cecilia Clephane, Scottish humanitarian, poet, and member of the Free Church of Scotland. The tune St. Christopher was written by Frederick C. Maker for this text and was first printed in the 1881 *Bristol Tune Book*.

Children's Time: Lost and Found

(Bring a simple puzzle with large pieces. Place one of the pieces on the floor somewhere in your worship space.) Invite the children to put together the puzzle. When it is discovered that one piece is missing, ask everyone to search around for it. Express joy when the piece is found. Invite the children to share stories of a time when they were lost or something important

to them was lost. Comment that today we hear a story that Jesus told about being lost and found.

Relate the story of the prodigal son. Talk about the different people in the story. How do you think the son, the servants, the father, and the brother felt after the son came home? Explain that Jesus told this story to remind everyone that God loves us as much as the father loved his son in the story. Comment that this is something to celebrate.

Play some lively worship music, and invite the children to join you in a dance of celebration. God really loves us.

Pray with the children, giving thanks for God's amazing forgiveness and love.

The Sermon: Prodigal Reconciliation
Scripture: Luke 15:1-3, 11b-32

There would be no need for reconciliation if there were not the reality of brokenness. Whether it's the story of the prodigal son, our families, or the global political scene, we know that brokenness is real. God's call to us, then, is all the more clear. As a community of faith we are, in Paul's words, ambassadors of Christ – called to live out a ministry of reconciliation in whatever context we find ourselves.

Reconciliation is an interesting word. In high school I worked for a man who was the secretary-treasurer of a union. Among other things, it was my job to record dues and each month to reconcile the accounts.

There was one problem. I had never seen a checkbook and hadn't a clue about what to do with a ledger sheet! That first month was not pretty. Again and again, and again, my boss sat down with me and made me reconcile the accounts. Years later his daughter told me that her dad thought I had been the best secretary he'd ever had. He could have fooled me in those first weeks!

In the realm of finances, reconciliation is making peace with the numbers. In the realm of human endeavors, reconciliation is making peace with or within people; bringing conflicting and divergent things together so that they balance. Sometimes reconciliation is internal. In my 30s I had to reconcile myself to the fact that I would never be a biological mother before I could be a mother of children I adopted. Reconciliation can be personal, as when we restore a friendship and bring harmony to a relationship – like what happened between father and son in our story. Reconciliation can be communal as when countries, congregations, or communities work out differences.

Luke's story of the prodigal son is an all-too-familiar story of family estrangement. The reconciliation that takes place as the story progresses moves through several characters and scenarios, attempting to balance values and life choices.

The youngest son, intent on getting on with living his life, takes what would be due him at his father's death and moves out into the world. In the midst of his enjoyment and extravagance, he soon must reconcile himself with the fact that he is unable to make it on his own. His moment of internal reconciliation becomes the catalyst of interpersonal reconciliation with his father.

Janice is a methamphetamine addict. She is also a single mother of two children, both under the age of six. Most of the time she is high, getting high, or trying to figure out how to get high. When she isn't, she is angry, impatient, and on the brink of violence. One day she found her children eating cookies on the kitchen floor, happily sitting amidst the wrinkled wrappings and crumbs. She hadn't yet figured out how to get her meth needs satisfied, and the sight of her children enraged her. Screaming at them, she picked them up, put them in her car, and drove into the desert. She opened the door and made them get out. As she drove away and watched her children standing there, growing smaller in her rear view mirror, a voice filtered through her muddled mind. "What kind of parent does this?" Horrified, she turned around, picked up her children, and drove home. Janice entered a treatment center. She lost custody of her children when her parents reported her to authorities. She has come to know – at least in theory – that the path to reconciliation with her children and her parents comes only through reconciliation with herself.

We are never really sure about the internal workings of biblical characters, but the fact that the father excitedly and graciously welcomed his wayward son back makes me think that he'd never reconciled himself to the idea that his son was truly gone. In his mind, the balance sheet was open. When he sees his youngest coming up the road, he doesn't wonder if it's a trick or a manipulative act to get more money. No, he assumes that things are coming into balance and throws a celebration to that end.

I finished college at a time when most women got married right after graduation. Instead, I left home the next day. I lived with a cousin and worked temporary jobs until a teaching position opened up. Eventually I got my own apartment. It was not what my parents wanted for their only daughter. For months we hardly spoke to each other. One day, I went home for a visit and my mother handed me a bag – nothing fancy, no ribbons or cards – just a bag from a discount department store. In it was a set of bed sheets. Acts of reconciliation happen often in very simple ways, yet the effect of such connections can change lives.

The one character in our story that doesn't seem to be reconciled is the oldest son. Perhaps he had been reconciled to the foolishness of his brother and to his own importance as his father's only responsible child. But his brother's return changed any emotional balance he might have had. For him, everything was turned upside down – his relationship with his father, with his brother, with himself. For him, the work of reconciliation had just begun.

The life of faith seems to be a dance of brokenness and reconciliation within ourselves, with one another, with our world, and – most important – to and with our God. Our story today tells us that when it comes to God, the ledger sheet is never balanced – at least not in this life. Always, it is open to the possibility of reconciliation. It seems to be left in our court as to whether or not we have the courage or the humility to move into that realm of hospitality and grace that is God's gift of reconciliation.

– Rosemary A. Rocha

Hymns
Opening: Called as Partners in Christ's Service
Sermon: If I Have Been the Source of Pain, O God
Closing: What a Covenant

March 17, 2013

5th Sunday in Lent

Lessons

Semi-continuous (SC)	Roman Catholic (RC)
Isa 43:16-21	Isa 43:16-21
Ps 126	Ps 126:1-6
Phil 3:4b-14	Phil 3:8-14
Jn 12:1-8	Jn 8:1-11

Speaker's Introduction for the Lessons

Lesson 1
Isaiah 43:16-21 (SC/RC)

God's past redemptive activity in the exodus from Egypt becomes both reason to trust and invitation to open to the "new things" that God is about to do for the sake of the people's redemption.

Lesson 2
Psalm 126 (SC); Psalm 126:1-6 (RC)

This brief song celebrates God's past restoration from exile even as it prays for such action on God's part once more.

Lesson 3
Philippians 3:4b-14 (SC); Philippians 3:8-14 (RC)

Paul's former boasting about his religious heritage now takes shape in humility that seeks only to "know Christ and the power of his resurrection."

Gospel
John 12:1-8 (SC)

In her anointing of Jesus, Mary discerns and marks the extraordinary character of this moment in Jesus' life: he is now moving toward his own sacrificial death.

John 8:1-11 (RC)

A woman caught in adultery is used as a trap to ensnare Jesus in pians 3:12-14 and was written to cap a sermon based on this passage. The hymn makes use of the imagery of the Greek games, with which the apostle Paul was quite familiar. The text uses the race as a symbol of the strong Christian life in which heaven is the prize. Many authorities believe this is the best hymn written by Doddridge. Some even call it "immortal."

Children's Time: A Special Gift

(Bring a bottle of lightly scented nonallergenic oil such as baby oil).
Open the bottle of oil and let the children smell the contents. Ask if anyone would like to have a drop of oil placed on her or his hands. Encourage the children to rub it into their skin. Mention that oil can be very soothing when rubbed into dry skin.

Explain that in Jesus' time, people walked a lot wearing sandals and that their feet often got tired and dry. Sometimes when they stopped to rest, they would wash their feet and rub them with perfumed oil to keep their skin soft. The perfumed oil was very expensive, so people would only use a few drops. Comment that in our Bible story today someone gave some perfumed oil to Jesus as a special gift.

Relate the Gospel story, emphasizing the extravagance of Mary's loving gift. Comment that Mary gave Jesus a special gift of love. Ask: How do you think Mary's gift helped Jesus? Invite the children to name some ways that they might show their love to Jesus.

Pray with the children, giving thanks for the story of Mary and her special gift of caring for Jesus.

cerns.

All: Anoint our hands with your Spirit, that what we touch, we touch with love.

One: O God, we stand at this place of comfort and stability.

All: Anoint our feet with your Spirit, that wherever we walk, we walk your walk.

One: O God, we stand in love and affirmation of you and your world.

All: Anoint our bodies, minds, and hearts with your Spirit, that our worship will be filled with signs of your presence.

being asked for money evoked from people their true feelings about the church and their faith: the joyful rejoiced, the self-centered resisted, and the unhappy complained.

I never will forget two visits I made back-to-back. One was to a man who served as the chief development officer for a major charity. "This will be a piece of cake," I remember thinking. "This guy knows the meaning of charitable giving, and he will respond with the same generosity he counts on in his own work." To my astonishment, though, he would not even let me in the house. He opened the front door an inch, begrudgingly took the pledge card through the crack, scribbled a pittance on it as I stood and waited, and shoved it back, pulling the door closed with a crisp and final snap.

The next visit was to an elderly widow on a fixed income. She and her striped cat lived in a modestly furnished apartment. When I told her I was there from the church, she said she was pleased to see me, and invited me in for a chat, during which she indicated her appreciation for all the church had meant to her. When the time came to pass over the pledge card, she took it from my hand with joy and increased her pledge, which I knew would mean sacrifice for her.

How to account for generosity and devotion? When Jesus was at dinner with his disciples and some of his friends that night in Bethany, there was a dramatic and profound act of devotion. But, just as was the case for me on those stewardship visits, it came from an unexpected source. It did not come from Peter, or James, or John, and it certainly did not come from Judas, who loudly protested its extravagance when it occurred. It did not even come from Lazarus, whose presence at the dinner party was possible only because Jesus had raised him from the dead. It came instead from Mary, who took a bottle of very expensive perfume and poured it on Jesus' feet, then wiped his feet with her hair. How to account for generosity and devotion?

Part of the secret of generosity and devotion is discernment. Those who pour out adoration toward God are those who have a discerning sense of what is truly at stake, what is really happening in life. Check the lobby of any hospital in the morning, and you will hear the voices of the patients being discharged. Some cry out in rage ("I'm going to be on crutches for a blankety-blank month, and I have to take six of these stupid pills every day!"), while others are full of gratitude and praise ("Thank God for the blessings of health"). All of these patients are going home, but only some of them have the discernment to be thankful. In our story from John, the room was full of people, but only Mary discerned the presence of Jesus in a way that prompted gratitude.

But the issue is more than just discernment. Mary was not blowing up helium balloons to celebrate her discernment of Jesus' presence. She wasn't lighting candles on a cake out of gratitude for her discernment of what Jesus meant to her. By pouring on him the costly ointment, she was anointing Jesus for death. "Leave her alone," Jesus said in defense of her actions. "She bought it so that she might keep it for the day of my burial." Mary's costly gift of gratitude grew out of an awareness of the cost of Jesus' gift of sacrifice – his own life. As New Testament scholar Gail O'Day has observed,

> She gives boldly of herself in love to Jesus at his hour, just as Jesus will give boldly of himself in love at his hour . . . [The vision] of a community shaped by love and grounded in relationship to Jesus is first enacted by a female disciple who has no claim to that position. *(New Interpreter's Bible, Vol. IX,* Abingdon, p. 703.)

Maybe that's the key – those who recognize the cost of kindness and redemption are those who love most freely and most generously. It should come as no surprise, then, that self-sufficient executives shove pledge cards through doorjambs like tips to bellhops while widows who can barely afford to feed themselves and their cats joyously pour out the costly ointment.

My wife is a pastor, and we live in a parsonage near the church. Periodically, there is a knock on the parsonage door on Thursday night. A local chapter of AA meets at the church on Thursdays, and they pay a small monthly rental for the use of the room. When the rent is due, one of the members will come over to our house on the meeting night carrying an envelope with the rental money collected from the group. Many of the members of this AA group have had very difficult lives. Some have lost jobs, some have lost their families, all have struggled with addiction. None of the members is wealthy, and they pass the hat for the rent, tossing in ones and fives and change until they scrape up enough.

One Thursday night, a week before Thanksgiving, there was the usual knock, and when I went to the door, indeed, there was a member of AA holding an envelope. The man handed it to me and said, "There's a little extra in there this time." Sure enough, the envelope was crammed with wrinkled bills and an assortment of coins, almost double the usual amount. A note was found with the money, "With thanksgiving to God and to the church for all the blessings we have received."

Some said the envelope was fragrant with costly perfume.

– Thomas G. Long

Hymns
Opening: Jesu, Jesu, Fill Us with Your Love
Sermon: Said Judas to Mary
Closing: A Woman Came Who Did Not Count the Cost

March 24, 2013

Passion/Palm Sunday

Lessons

Semi-continuous (SC)	Roman Catholic (RC)
Isa 50:4-9a	Isa 50:4-7
Ps 31:9-16	Ps 22:8-9, 17-18, 19-20, 23-24
Phil 2:5-11	Phil 2:6-11
Lk 22:14—23:56 or Lk 23:1-49	Lk 22:14—23:56 or Lk 23:1-49

Speaker's Introduction for the Lessons
Lesson 1
Isaiah 50:4-9a (SC); Isaiah 50:4-7 (RC)
Part of a longer poem portraying the exile as the result of the nation's sin against God, this passage is seen by the early Christian church as a prophecy of Jesus' unjust trial and conviction.

Lesson 2
Psalm 31:9-16 (SC)
The psalmist confesses trust in God as well as lament over circumstances that evoke distress and terror in the face of those who plot the psalmist's death.
Psalm 22:8-9, 17-18, 19-20, 23-24 (RC)
The psalmist cries out in anguish and lament at the point of death, yet confesses God's dominion even in the face of death.

Lesson 3
Philippians 2:5-11 (SC); Philippians 2:6-11 (RC)
Paul uses this early Christian hymn to make a point about choosing a lowly position in life in the service of others. Then, as now, the message was counter to the prevailing culture.

Gospel
Luke 22:14—23:56 (SC/RC)
Luke's passion story moves through Jesus' interactions with many

people; yet, in the final scene, he is alone before the God he has lived and died to serve.

Theme
Imitation is a way to faithfulness.

Thought for the Day
The point here is that our way of being with and for one another flows from Christ's way of being with and for us.

– Tony Robinson (www.anthonybrobinson.com)

Sermon Summary
Imitating Christ is the call of the gospel. It is a difficult and sometimes life-threatening challenge.

Call to Worship
One: Cry "Hosanna" to the Christ who comes!
All: But wait: is this the One we were expecting?
One: Shout "God saves" for the Christ who comes!
All: But why does he not take power right now?
     Why does he end up judged, not judging?
One: Come and see the Christ we would follow!

Pastoral Prayer
God, you move in the very fiber of our beings, pulsing through every cell, every heartbeat. So often we are unmindful of our intimate connection with you. In these moments help us to live in that connection, that we might be your voice and hands and heart. We remember friends, family, and loved ones who live with terminal illness, who endure chronic pain as their constant companion, who bear in their hearts and minds the reminders of past hurts, betrayals, and wrongs. In your love and grace heal them, comfort them, strengthen them. We remember people who live in war zones, who scavenge for food, shelter, and peace. Empower our commitments to them; show us in small and large ways how to work for their

release from the results of human greed and vengeance, natural disaster, political negligence, and personal weakness. Amen.

Prayer of Confession

Gracious God, on this most holy day, when anticipation of what could be and foreboding of what will be meet, we pause to remember. We recall times when we have been faithful to dreams and loyal to people and commitments, and times of difficulty when we have abandoned them. We remember fear that grows within and keeps us from standing by our ideals, our friends, our God. We remember despair that leads us to lose hope in ourselves, in you, in life itself. Gracious God, help us to walk the path of your Christ. Give us courage and strength to face our trials, our abandonment, even our death. Renew in us hope that in suffering there is wholeness, in pain there is healing, and in death there is life. In Jesus Christ. Amen.

Prayer of Dedication of Gifts and Self

We come before you, O God, asking for so much – time, possessions, our very lives. Forgive us for holding back when it is time to offer our gifts and ourselves to you. Shape our frame of mind and will so that giving to you becomes our privilege and our joy. Embolden us by your Spirit so that gladly we offer you everything. Amen.

Hymn of the Day
All Glory, Laud, and Honor

The most well-known English translation of the ninth-century Latin hymn "Gloria, laus et honor," was done by the Reverend John Mason Neale in 1854. Bishop Theodulph of Orleans wrote the original Latin hymn around 820 as a poetical rendering of the biblical story of the triumphal entry. Neale's translation offers us the opportunity to bring before Christ a triumphant song of praise, our modern day "Hosanna." It can set the stage for Palm Sunday and its transition to a focus upon the passion of Christ. St. Theodulph, written by Melchior Teschner in 1615, is the tune most often associated with the hymn text.

Children's Time: The Name of Jesus

(Bring a book that lists names and their meanings.)
Invite the children to share something about their names, asking: Do you know why your name was chosen? Do you know what your name means? Comment that names are intriguing because most of them have a meaning. Use your book to look up your own name and some of the children's names.

Comment that in the Bible reading today we hear a very important name. That name is Jesus. Ask the children if they know what *Jesus* means. *Jesus* means "God saves." Explain that the name of Jesus is often joined with the word *Christ,* which means, "chosen one." If you put both names together, it means, "chosen by God to save." Jesus was chosen by God to show us God's love and forgiveness.

Explain that this Sunday begins Holy Week. This is the time when we remember the events of the last few days of Jesus' life on earth. One of the things that happened during that week was that Jesus chose to die on the cross rather than stop telling people about God's love. Jesus really did live up to his name didn't he?

Pray with the children, offering thanks for Jesus who was chosen to show us God's love.

The Sermon: The Sincerest Form of Flattery
Scripture: Philippians 2:5-11

In his book *A Pretty Good Person,* Lewis Smedes tells of spending a hot day at the Los Angeles County Jail waiting for someone he was bailing out. Midafternoon, still waiting, he went out to get a cold drink and met a man in a black suit and clergy collar. Assuming he was a prison chaplain, Smedes asked the cleric to join him. The man was, Smede discovered, an insurance salesman. Once a week he visited prisoners and, he told Smede, the collar gave him entrance into the jail. (Lewis B. Smedes, *A Pretty Good Person: What It Takes to Live with Courage, Gratitude, and Integrity,* Harper & Row, 1990, pp. 137-38.)

"Let each of you look not to your own interests, but to the interests of others. Let the same mind be in you that was in Christ Jesus" (Phil 2:4-5).

What would it be like to walk around as someone else? Children do it, dressing up in mommy's shoes, daddy's shirt, or big brother's baggy jeans. Actors get paid for doing it. Watching the movie *Ray*, it's hard to remember that it's Jamie Foxx on screen and not Ray Charles. Identity fraud testifies to how lucrative it can be to walk around as someone else. The Federal Witness Protection Program offers government assistance to those who need to create new identities. If imitation is the sincerest form of flattery, then Paul's idea of letting "the same mind be in you that was in Christ Jesus" must be the ultimate act of honor.

In *The Imitation of Christ,* German mystic Thomas à Kempis (1379-1471) identifies ways in which a person can act more like Christ. The WWJD (What Would Jesus Do) movement underlines the idea that considering our behavior in light of Christ's is basic to our life together.

But United Church of Christ minister Tony Robinson, in his comments on this Philippians passage, asks an important question. "Is this way – Christ's way – practical? Can we live in this world and follow Christ in humility, in sacrifice, in placing the interests of others above our own?" (www.anthonybrobinson.com).

"Let the same mind be in you that was in Christ Jesus." This is, indeed, heavy stuff. We might have to get serious about life were we to take this passage to heart. Many do. A professor traveled with colleagues and students to help with recovery efforts after Hurricane Katrina. While there, a student stole a large amount of money from an abandoned home. Returning to the dorm that night, the student bragged about "finding" the money. The professor was neither in charge of the group nor directly responsible for the student's behavior. Yet the question of what to do plagued the professor, who confronted colleagues and the student both during and after the trip. In the end, the professor reported the situation to the school, the student was suspended, and the money returned.

The professor was living out the reality of having the mind of Christ. It's hard work. Too often we sanitize and "saccharin-ize" the Christian life. We make it about feeling good personally and being at peace within ourselves. But to have the same mind as Christ means that we are committed to living like the man who sacrificed and suffered in his faithfulness to God. Having the same mind of Christ means confronting the Pharisees of our world, challenging our version of Roman governors and political religious dictators, and refusing to live by laws that are not of the Spirit.

The movie *Hotel Rwanda* tells the true story of how Paul Rusesabagina, a Hutu, saved the lives of more than 1000 Tutsi refugees by sheltering them in the hotel he managed. In that nightmare of human depravity, many clergy participated in the slaughter either by killing people or by helping trap them so that rebels could do their nasty work. Having the mind of Christ means, in many situations, a death or life calling, as people like Oscar Romero, Martin Luther King Jr., and many anonymous martyrs have testified to.

The Imitation of Christ, written by Kempis, is a dialog between Christ and "the disciple." In chapter three we read "The Voice of Christ" saying, "Do not think, therefore, that you have found true peace . . . or that all is well because you suffer no opposition . . . For the true lover of virtue is not known by these things, nor do the progress and perfection of a man consist in them.

"The Disciple: In what do they consist, Lord?

"The Voice of Christ: They consist in offering yourself with all your heart to the divine will, not seeking what is yours either in small matters or great ones . . . so that you will preserve equanimity and give thanks in both prosperity and adversity, seeing all things in their proper light."

In 2000, fashion designers Tara Subkoff and Matt Damhave started a company called "Imitation of Christ" (newyorkmetro.com/fashion/fashionshows/05/spring/preview/brandhistory.htm). While they aim to "transform undesirables into desirables," a very Christly theme, I doubt that high-priced, hip clothing made from recycled designer cast-offs has much to do with imitating Christ. It just goes to show that there's a lot in life that is a bad imitation.

How do we know that we are imitating Christ or that we have the same mind that was in Jesus? The answer, I believe, is biblical, simple, and the hardest thing we will ever do: love. Love God and love our neighbor just as if we were loving ourselves. To live every day in the excitement and challenge of this way of life is, I believe, to have the same mind that was in Jesus Christ. My friends, it is a challenge hard to live with, but one we cannot live without.

– Rosemary A. Rocha

Hymns
Opening: All Glory, Laud, and Honor
Sermon: Open Mine Eyes that I Might See
Closing: Ride On! Ride On in Majesty

March 28, 2013

Maundy Thursday

Lessons

Semi-continuous (SC)	Roman Catholic (RC)
Ex 12:1-4 (5-10), 11-14	Ex 12:1-8, 11-14
Ps 116:1-2, 12-19	Ps 116:12-13, 15-16, 17-18
1 Cor 11:23-26	1 Cor 11:23-26
Jn 13:1-17, 31b-35	Jn 13:1-15

Speaker's Introduction for the Lessons

Lesson 1
Exodus 12:1-4 (5-10), 11-14 (SC); Exodus 12:1-8, 11-14 (RC)

This text follows the prediction of the final plague in Egypt and comes right before the people leave Egypt. These words became important for the celebration of the Passover meal.

Lesson 2
Psalm 116:1-2, 12-19 (SC); Psalm 116:12-13, 15-16, 17-18 (RC)

The psalmist offers a song of thanksgiving for God's deliverance. The main portion excerpted here also seems to have been part of a liturgy or prayer related to an offering.

Lesson 3
1 Corinthians 11:23-26 (SC/RC)

Paul describes proper observance of the Lord's supper for the church at Corinth in the face of some chaotic and exclusive practices. These words are key for the church in the practice of communion.

Gospel
John 13:1-17, 31b-35 (SC); John 13:1-15 (RC)

As Jesus moves closer to the cross in John's Gospel, this passage offers a key image of Jesus' example of serving others in love.

Theme

Let us remember God's power for possibility.

Thought for the Day

When you feel fear or doubt about the future, remember all that God has done in the past.

Sermon Summary

The story of the exodus shapes us as we remember that God can do the impossible. God can deliver people from slavery. God can bring resurrection to Jesus. Our own stories remind us of the impossible things God has done. We can look ahead, expecting impossible things to be possible.

Call to Worship

> One: What shall I return to the Lord for all God's bounty to me?
>
> **All: I will lift up the cup of salvation and call on the name of the Lord.**
>
> One: I will offer to you a thanksgiving sacrifice and call on the name of the Lord.
>
> **All: I will pay my vows to God in the presence of all God's people,**
>
> One: In the courts of the house of the Lord, in your midst, O Jerusalem.
>
> **All: Praise the Lord!**

Pastoral Prayer

Our God, we come before you tonight, remembering Jesus' last night with his disciples. We praise and thank you for his life, death, and resurrection, for the great and holy events we remember this week. We add our thanks for Jesus' ongoing presence with us and with the church around the world. We ask that you strengthen us through this service tonight and prepare us to be ever more faithful disciples. Renew our faith as we hear again the stories of your powerful work on behalf of your people. In the name of Jesus Christ we pray. Amen.

Prayer of Confession

Loving and gracious God, we need your grace. We ask your forgiveness for the times we have acted out of fear rather than faith. We are all too like Jesus' disciples, who fled in fear. Forgive our forgetfulness, our difficulty in remembering your never-failing love and power, our flight from responsibility and call. This night, tomorrow, and in the days ahead help us to leave our fears behind and live out of your strength and hope, for Christ's sake. Amen.

Prayer of Dedication of Gifts and Self

Generous God, we offer these our gifts, together with ourselves, to support your work in our midst and in the world. May the result of our giving be that we come closer to your purpose. Amen.

Hymn of the Day
It Was a Sad and Solemn Night

Also known as "It Happened on That Fateful Night," this is one of few hymns specifically based on the Maundy Thursday experience. This hymn provides opportunity for a poignant reflection upon what took place the night before Jesus' crucifixion. The hymn by Isaac Watts first appeared with the opening line, "'Twas on that dark and doleful night" and appeared in his 1709 publication *Hymns and Spiritual Songs*. The pentatonic tune BOURBON first appeared with this text in 1825 in the American tune book *Columbian Harmony*. The use of a soloist or choir may be most effective for this hymn.

Children's Time: A Meal to Remember

Talk about the kinds of things we do when we celebrate special events such as birthdays, Christmas, or Thanksgiving. Accept all suggestions and, if no one else says it, mention that a good way to celebrate is to eat together. We might even have a feast. Encourage the children to name times when they have enjoyed a special meal with their families.

Comment that in the Bible reading today we hear about a special meal that God told the Hebrew people to eat. Explain that this special meal is still eaten today and has become an important part of the celebration of Passover. This is the time when the Jewish people remember and celebrate their release from slavery into freedom.

Comment that in the church we also have a special meal that we share together. This meal helps us to remember and celebrate the life, death, and resurrection of Jesus. Talk with the children about communion and about how it is celebrated in your church.

Explain that when Jewish people share the Passover meal they are reminded of God's care for them. When we share communion, we also know that God cares for us.

Pray with the children, giving thanks for God's love and care.

The Sermon: Do This in Remembrance
Scripture: Exodus 12:1-4, 11-14

What is your earliest memory? I remember sitting on the arm of a rocking armchair while my mother sat in the chair holding my baby brother, giving him a bottle and reading me a book at the same time. This is a memory that has shaped me over the years, and all my life I have been a reader, a book person.

Our text this evening is a story that has shaped the Jewish people from the first, right up to this day. Exodus 12 includes the instructions for the very first Passover. The people were to take a lamb and kill it and roast it. They were to eat a meal – this was not to be a relaxed family meal. They were to eat it with their shoes and their coats on, ready to go, because liberation from slavery was about to happen. In addition, the text says, "This day shall be a day of remembrance for you" (12:14). They were to remember this story, to tell it again and again. This became a story that shaped them. This was a night when the impossible happened, when freedom came, and they were never to forget it.

This night, Maundy Thursday, we remember Jesus' last supper with his disciples. Paul tells us in his description in 1 Corinthians that Jesus said, "Do this in remembrance of me." Jesus' story also shapes us, and we tell it again and again. His story tells us something important about who we are.

We are a people who find the impossible possible. Who would have thought that the people of Israel could have received freedom from slavery in a night? This story tells us it is possible. Who would have thought that Jesus could die and receive new life again? The stories of Holy Week tell us it is possible.

Every church has stories of the impossible becoming possible, in big and small ways. What's this church's story? A few people banding together in hope and imagination to begin a new community. An individual coming to faith as an adult for the first time. A building being raised. A conflict faced and overcome. A new spirit of vitality in the congregation. Some of these stories are in the past, some are happening right now. When we remember these stories and tell them again and again, we are reminding ourselves of the God we have and serve.

Without these stories, big and small, it is easy for us to forget who God is and what God can do. Our thinking remains too small. I recently took a retreat at a Trappist monastery in Lafayette, Oregon. It was a mostly silent retreat, which is something of an impossibility for a Baptist minister! I did have one conversation with Brother Mark, who meets with guests in the monastery. He quoted to me this phrase: "God does not believe in our God." God does not believe in our God. Our God does not do impossible things – but God does impossible things. The stories help us believe in God, a God far bigger than "our God," that limited God we imagine and create in our own minds. The disciples gathered with Jesus on this night also had a hard time believing as the events of the next few days unfolded.

In Through the Looking Glass, the Red Queen says, "Why, sometimes I've believed as many as six impossible things before breakfast" (Lewis Carroll, *The Annotated Alice,* Clarkson N. Potter, 1960, p. 251). As Christians, if we get up early to pray, we can believe even more than six. We could go around the room tonight and tell six, eight, ten impossible stories of how God has worked in our lives and in our midst. The fact that we are still remembering and telling these stories of the Passover and the last supper is impossible, but it is happening. God's story has been told, continues to be told, will continue to be told, and we are a part of that unfolding story.

So as we gather tonight around the table of the Lord, let us look not only to the past but also to the future. Let us put on our coats and our shoes and be ready to go out the door in faith when God calls us. The events we remember tonight – the events of this week – are as much about what will happen as what has already happened. God wants us to be a presence in the world, on the journey as the people of Israel were, as the disciples came to be.

St. Francis put it this way: "Start by doing what is necessary, then do the possible, and suddenly you are doing the impossible." The necessary is the regular practice of communion, the yearly observance of Maundy Thursday and the other services of Holy Week. That practice prepares us to do the possible, to live as Christians as best we can each day and each week. Then suddenly we find ourselves doing the impossible things that God calls us to do, like working for peace in the world, sharing God's message of love with others, and being God's people.

– Margaret Marcuson

Hymns
Opening: When I Survey the Wondrous Cross
Sermon: In the Cross of Christ I Glory
Closing: For the Bread Which You Have Broken

March 29, 2013

Good Friday

Lessons

Semi-continuous (SC)	Roman Catholic (RC)
Isa 52:13—53:12	Isa 52:13—53:12
Ps 22	Ps 31:2, 6, 12-13, 15-16, 17, 24
Heb 10:16-25 or Heb 4:14-16; 5:7-9	Heb 4:14-16; 5:7-9
Jn 18:1—19:42	Jn 18:1—19:42

Speaker's Introduction for the Lessons

Lesson 1
Isaiah 52:13—53:12 (SC/RC)

The prophet Isaiah speaks of the suffering servant who redeems Israel by his suffering.

Lesson 2
Psalm 22 (SC)

The cry of God-forsakenness raised by Jesus from the cross opens this powerful psalm of lament, lament that eventuates in affirmation of God's dominion and deliverance.

Psalm 31:2, 6, 12-13, 15-16, 17, 24 (RC)

The psalm blends a plea to be heard by God, a cry of lament to God about the terror surrounding the psalmist, and a trustful assertion that the psalmist's "times are in your hand."

Lesson 3
Hebrews 10:16-25 (SC)

"I will remember their sins . . . no more." This is the promise of this Good Friday lesson from the letter to the Hebrews.

Hebrews 4:14-16, 5:7-9 (RC)

The writer of Hebrews presents Jesus as our high priest, who comes before God on our behalf. Jesus is the source of our salvation.

Gospel
John 18:1—19:42 (SC/RC)
John gives the somber account of the betrayal, arrest, and crucifixion of Jesus.

Theme
Jesus practices nonviolence in the face of enemies and execution.

Thought for the Day
Imagine yourself in Gethsemane. Jesus says to you "put your sword away." What sword would be hardest to set aside? Go to Golgotha and find out how and why.

Sermon Summary
On this day, Good Friday, in the cross of Jesus, we see starkly revealed the truth about who we are. We are, despite our best intentions, a violent bloody people who trust the sword and its power more than God. Yet Jesus commands us, in the strongest terms, to put away our swords and to rely upon God's grace to preserve us.

Call to Worship
One: We gather in worship this Good Friday, a somber day, a day of darkness.

All: We remember Jesus' suffering and death.

One: We grieve over our own failure and sin.

All: We remember Jesus' suffering and death.

One: Yet we do not grieve as those who have no hope

All: We remember Jesus' suffering and death.

One: Because we know that our loving God offers a powerful promise even in the darkness.

All: We remember Jesus' suffering and death – and we remember and trust the promises of God.

Pastoral Prayer

Jesus, on this day, this fateful Friday, you faced the rejection of the crowds, the betrayal of your followers, and the cruelty of the state and went down that narrow way of Calvary, dragging your cross on your back. For us and our salvation you suffered. By our sin, you keep suffering because of us and for us. On this day may we be given the grace to ponder how we have grieved your heart and betrayed your way. And then might we be given the gift of gratitude for your loving sacrifice and determination to obey your will for us and to respond to your deep love for us. Amen.

Prayer of Confession

Holy God, all we like sheep have gone astray; we have all turned to our own way. This Good Friday, we are mindful of this reality. But we know this does not have to be the end of our story. We ask that you would forgive us, and help us return to your loving care. May we walk more closely with you, as your servants and disciples of Jesus for whose sake we pray. Amen.

Prayer of Dedication of Gifts and Self

We give thanks for your many gifts to us, O God. This day we give thanks most of all for the gift of your Son, our Savior Jesus Christ. His loving sacrifice changed the world and changes us. In the same spirit of sacrifice, we offer our gifts to you – how can we do less? We owe our very lives to you, from birth to death and beyond. May our gifts be used to renew the lives of others, in the name of Christ. Amen.

Hymn of the Day
Go to Dark Gethsemane

This hymn gives us opportunity to reflect upon what happened in the final days before Christ's crucifixion and how we may relate to Gethsemane, the judgment hall, the climb to Calvary's mountain, and the crucifixion. The words invite us to "early hasten to the tomb" of the risen Christ. The hymn concludes with our prayer, "Savior, teach us so to rise." Written by English poet James Montgomery, the text first appeared in print in 1820. The tune REDHEAD first appeared with this text in 1853. The hymn makes an excellent parting hymn at the close of the Good

Friday service. It is also effective to sing only the first three stanzas and to leave the church building in silence.

Children's Time: Jesus Dies

(Bring a newspaper or magazine photo that shows someone crying. Bring an ordinary candle and a candle that cannot be blown out.)
Light the ordinary candle. Show the picture and ask the children what the person in the picture is feeling. What kinds of things might cause someone to feel this way? Comment that sometimes when we feel very sad it seems as if the light of goodness has been blown out. Invite the children to tell of times they have felt sad. As the children share their stories, light and then blow out the ordinary candle several times.

Light the candle that cannot be blown out as you tell that in our Bible story today Jesus' disciples were very sad. When Jesus died on the cross, the disciples thought that the light of God's love had been blown out. They thought it was the end of everything. Invite the children to blow out the candle.

Comment that Jesus' death was not the end of the story. Nothing could destroy the light of God's love. Something amazing was about to happen. Explain that we will have to wait for a few days to hear the next part of the story, but it is wonderful.

Pray with the children, giving thanks for God's amazing love.

The Sermon: Put Away the Swords
Scripture: John 18:1—19:42

The story of Jesus' Passion ends in high drama, and not just in the movies. At last the moment comes for the soldiers to arrest Jesus. "Cops" first-century style. Whatcha gonna do when they come for you?

And at that moment the disciples ask Jesus a curious question: "Lord, should we strike with the sword?" (Lk 22:49). It is curious, because, well, these are the disciples, the ones closest to Jesus. What did Jesus teach up to this point that would lead the disciples to think that now they should "strike with the sword"? In John's Gospel, Jesus says immediately put away the sword (Jn 18:11).

There is a somber irony here. When Jesus is arrested the soldiers have swords. (No irony in that, all soldiers have swords. This is the way governments keep themselves afloat, with swords. This is the way we attain national security, with swords. As you pay taxes this year, for the largest military budget in the world, you know all that "In God we trust" is a lie, in a pinch, give us a good sword.)

The irony is that Jesus' own disciples have swords. Matthew, Mark, and Luke don't name the disciple with the sword. John's says that the sword-swinging disciple was none other than Peter, the rock, the church, us.

All of that Jesus talk about turning the other cheek, about resisting evil was fine for sunnier days back on the road when Jesus was popular and spiritual. But when it's dark, as the soldiers come with their swords, it's time for the church to be responsible, to be realistic, to take matters in hand, to take up the sword. Church, let's roll!

Here the people who have heard every word Jesus spoke, seen all of his acts, still ask, "Lord, now shall we strike with the sword?"

Of course we know that violence is not the way of Jesus. Jesus had worthy goals like love, justice, righteousness, and other sweet spiritualities. But sometimes you have to forget all that and take matters in hand. I remember those armchair campus liberation theologians who, while not thinking that violence was a good idea, particularly violence worked by the state, thought that the violence worked by Sandinista righteous revolutionaries on behalf of the poor was okay. Violence is wrong – unless it is in the interest of justice, which makes it right.

At this, his final word to them, his last command, the disciples of Jesus run away into the dark. And Jesus is left alone, to go head-to-head with the powers. He is led like a lamb to the slaughter. And we, with swords in our hands, flee to the darkness. And the Christian faith claims that this is the way God wins God's victories!

A few years ago, during Islamic Awareness Week, we had a panel. There was an imam from Chicago, a local rabbi, and me (representing all Christians everywhere, even though you didn't vote for me). During the discussion, the Imam said, "Islam is a very tolerant faith. In the Holy Koran, if an unbeliever attacks a believer, I am under obligation to punish the unbeliever. If my brother here, the Jew, is attacked by an unbeliever, the Holy Prophet commands me to punish the attacker."

The rabbi seemed pleased by this. For my part, I said, "Gee, I wish Jesus had said that. I got people that I want to punish, folks who need killing. Unfortunately, even when we tried to defend Jesus, he cursed us!"

It may be possible to have a good debate over the virgin birth of Jesus – Mark, Paul never mentioned it. It may be possible for us to have a real fight over whether or not the Bible really condemns homosexuality, the texts are few and some are conflicted. Alas, there is no debate over whether or not Jesus condemned violence for any purpose, in any cause noble or not.

A couple of presidential elections ago, there was debate about Senator Lieberman. "He's a devout Jew," some said. "He keeps kosher. If we have a national crisis and need to go to war on a Saturday, could we count on Lieberman?"

Nobody said, "George Bush is a Methodist, Al Gore is a Baptist, don't these Christians have some funny ideas about violence? Can we count on them to kick butt when we need it?"

Nobody asked, because, well, when it comes to such issues, you can't tell the worshipers of Caesar from the devotees of Jesus. In the dark, they've all got swords.

I don't know what to do about this. America is built on, bathed in, blood. I and my family are the beneficiaries of blood, as are you. I took a palm branch, joined the happy troupe behind Jesus, parading into the city shouting "Hosanna!" But at this point, as we move toward an unjust, horribly suffering death and defeat on a cross, I begin to lag. Do you?

On Thursday, when the disciples gather with Jesus in the upper room at the table, Jesus makes a curious remark. He says, "Now, the hour of darkness. Now Satan has entered. Now let him who has no sword buy one." And the disciples reply, "No problem. We've got two swords right here."

Why would Jesus urge his disciples to have swords when, just a few moments later, when the soldiers come and they try to use the swords, he rebukes them, tells them to put them away?

I don't know. One of my teachers, Paul Minear, said that he thinks these two swords may relate to the requirement, back in the book of Deuteronomy, for two witnesses to convict someone of a capital crime. You couldn't be convicted of a serious crime without two witnesses. Two.

See? Jesus asks, "When I sent you out earlier I ordered you not to take a sword, or an extra pair of shoes, or fat wallet, so that you might rely only on God to preserve you. Did you disobey me?"

And we say, "Sure, and we have these two swords to prove our disobedience. The power of God is fine but just in case this Messiah thing didn't work out, we kept a couple of Smith and Wessons in the glove compartment."

And Jesus says, "It is enough. My betrayer is at hand." I'll say. His betrayer is right here at the table with him. Us. With our swords, our defense programs, our guns and vengeance and all, you don't have to look far to find the betrayers of Jesus.

On the cross, his crucifiers screamed, "He trusted God, let God deliver him." We can't. We may print on our money "In God we trust," but when push comes to shove, we ask, "Lord, is now the time to strike with the sword?"

This day, this Good Friday, we are going to see that when Jesus says, "In God I trust," he means it.

God only knows what God now does with us and our disobedient bloody, bloody mess. Only God knows.

— William H. Willimon

Hymns
Opening: O Sacred Head Now Wounded
Sermon: Beneath the Cross of Jesus
Closing: Were You There?

March 31, 2013

Easter Day

Lessons

Semi-continuous (SC)
Acts 10:34-43 or Isa 65:17-25
Ps 118:1-2, 14-24
1 Cor 15:19-26 or Acts 10:34-43
Jn 20:1-18 or Lk 24:1-12

Roman Catholic (RC)
Acts 10:34a, 37-43
Ps 118:1-2, 16-17, 22-23
Col 3:1-4 or 1 Cor 5:6b-8
Jn 20:1-9

Speaker's Introduction for the Lessons

Lesson 1
Acts 10:34-43 (SC); Acts 10:34a, 37-43 (RC)

Peter's words here in Acts follow the conversion of the first Gentile. Peter not only bears witness to the resurrection but also proclaims the opening of the gospel message beyond the Jewish people.

Lesson 2
Psalm 118:1-2, 14-24 (SC); Psalm 118:1-2, 16-17, 22-23 (RC)

This psalm of thanksgiving rejoices in God in the wake of some unidentified act of deliverance from the threat of death.

Lesson 3
1 Corinthians 15:19-26 (SC)

Paul devotes a whole chapter to a closely reasoned discussion of the resurrection. These verses are part of his ringing affirmation of the reality of God's victory over death.

Colossians 3:1-4 (RC)

The resurrection is not just about Jesus but also about us and how we are to live in the world as his followers.

Gospel
John 20:1-18 (SC); John 20:1-9 (RC)

The climax of the Gospel, and of our faith, is Easter, Jesus' followers discovering the empty tomb and meeting Jesus. Mary Magdalene plays a key role in John's version of the story that never grows old.

Theme

Christ is risen this day!

Thought for the Day

Because Christ is risen, we carry resurrection hope in our hearts.

Sermon Summary

Easter hope can permeate all of our lives, even in the middle of the sorrow and struggle, that is part of all our lives at times. Easter hope gives us a solid foundation for living.

Call to Worship

One: Christ is risen!
All: Alleluia!
One: Because Christ lives, we live now and for all time to come.
All: Alleluia! Christ is risen indeed!

Pastoral Prayer

God of new life, we come before you with hearts filled with gratitude and praise. We praise you for your power even over death. We thank you for the newness of spring that surrounds us, lifting our spirits. And above all we thank you for the new life in Jesus Christ, which we can experience today and every day. We pray for our world and the places where death seems to reign supreme. We pray that your power for life might be seen in big and small ways, and that hope might shine through. May the same be true in the hopeless places of our own hearts. Give us hope for new life and new beginnings as, indeed, we begin again each day with you. Show us how to live as Easter people, as disciples of Jesus Christ, sharing this good news with others. Amen.

Prayer of Confession

We come before you to confess how slow of heart we are to believe your promise of new life. We expect the worst of the world and of those around us. We are equally hard on ourselves. Forgive us. Help us to receive the grace and hope you offer, and to give these same gifts to those around us. In the name of Jesus Christ, we pray. Amen.

Prayer of Dedication of Gifts and Self

We thank you not only for the special gift of Easter, Holy God, but also for the daily gift of life – the sun that rises each day, the food on the table at breakfast, the smile across the room. We offer to you in return our gifts, both of money and of ourselves. Use us, we pray, to give gifts to others in your name. Amen.

Hymn of the Day
Christ Is Risen! Shout Hosanna!

This is a rather recent hymn for the celebration of the Resurrection. The hymn was written in 1984 by Brian Wren, British-born American minister, hymn writer, and educator. In 1989 Wren suggested the tune W ZLOBIE LEZY (best known as the Polish carol "Infant Holy, Infant Lowly") be used with his text. That request has been honored in most hymnbooks. The tune HYMN TO JOY is used in some collections. It's interesting to compare the settings. The hymn provides modern day encouragement to "see what love can do and dare" and to claim the reality that "God the First and Last is with us."

Children's Time: The Easter Story

(Bring in an Easter basket containing a stone, an empty plastic egg, a small white cloth, a small container of water, an eyedropper, and a garden trowel. Bring some brightly colored streamers.)

Wish the children a happy Easter and invite them to sit in a circle. Explain that today is Easter Sunday, the day we celebrate how God raised Jesus to new life. Show the basket and comment that many people give and receive special baskets on Easter Day. Explain that the things inside the basket will help you tell the Easter story.

Pass each object around the circle as you retell part of the story: stone – John 20:1; empty egg – John 20:2-3; white cloth – John 20:4-10; water and eyedropper – John 20:11-13 (Mary's tears: use the eye dropper to drip a "tear" onto the children's hands); garden trowel – John 20:14-18 (Mary thought she was talking to the gardener).

Distribute the streamers, play some joyful music, and invite the children to join you in a celebration dance; Jesus is risen!

Pray with the children, giving thanks for the new life of Easter.

The Sermon: Living Easter
Scripture: Scripture: John 20:1-18

Early on the first day of the week, Mary Magdalene comes to the tomb. Then she goes to tell two other disciples – Simon Peter and the "one Jesus loved"– who themselves come to the tomb. Mary, Peter, and the unnamed disciple are the ones closest to Jesus, but none of them yet understands the significance of what they are witnessing.

After Mary sees the angels in the tomb, she sees Jesus himself. She doesn't recognize him at first. Not until Jesus calls her by name does she know who he is. She thinks at first he has returned as he promised, and now he will stay with her and the others, resuming their former relationships. But Jesus says, "Do not hold on to me" (Jn 20:17). Instead, he commands Mary to go and prepare Jesus' disciples for that coming of Jesus when the Spirit will be given.

As they approach the tomb, the disciples – first Mary and then the other two – are in the darkness of fear and pain. They are grieving their crucified Lord, and they are afraid. Mary says, "They have taken the Lord out of the tomb, and we do not know where they have laid him" (20:2).

We, too, experience pain, grief, and death in this world. There is plenty of suffering. We can turn on the television to see it up close. Some of you sitting here have lost loved ones this very year – you know suffering. We all know pain in our lives; it is part of the human experience.

Yet the disciples saw something surprising, which broke into their suffering and pain. Mary Magdalene saw Jesus himself, the first apostolic witness of the resurrected Lord. She saw that Jesus had passed into a different reality; something new was taking place.

Suffering is real, whether it is caused by overt decision, cowardice, disease, or the power of nature. And death comes to us all. But God's power triumphs over the realities of human life and death. We don't stop with Good Friday; we live on to Easter Sunday.

This good news affects far more than our individual lives. The hope brought into the world by the resurrection touches our whole world, and the cosmos itself. God's power is the real power – power over evil and power for good.

So we can look at our lives, even at the struggle and pain of life, through Easter eyes. It's as if we were color-blind before and now can see the glorious colors brought into the world. The colors of Easter eggs and Easter baskets, Easter clothes and flowers remind us not only of spring but also of the new life Christ brings us.

We can live our lives with a new perspective. We can build on a new foundation, even when the buffeting in this life begins anew. We will be "rooted and grounded in love," as the apostle Paul says.

When we live our lives founded solidly on the hope provided by this Easter story, we will be prepared for even the hurricanes of life. And they will come, as assuredly as hurricanes will continue to come to the Atlantic Coast. Yet the storms of life cannot destroy us, because God's power is stronger than they are.

So what did the disciples do? First, we see Mary; she went and told the disciples, "I have seen the Lord." In the same way, we, too, can share the hope we receive in Jesus Christ. We can proclaim to other people that "I have seen the Lord" – no matter what we see in the newspaper or on television, no matter what our very real concerns are about our nation, our world, our community, our jobs, and our families.

Polly Berrien Berends wrote a little poem entitled "A Secret," which says, "God means good" (Polly Berrien Berends, *Gently Lead,* The Crossroad Publishing Company, 1998, p. 18). "God means good" says to us that God's power triumphs over evil and death. It means that none of the realities of this life, which weigh so heavily upon us, will ultimately prevail. It's "a secret" because we can't touch it or grasp it. "Do not hold on to me," Jesus said to Mary. Proclaiming the resurrection does not mean we marshal scientific data to "prove" anything. This is a secret of faith. We can't see or taste or touch Jesus. We see him with our Easter eyes, with the eyes of faith, and faith can be every bit as concrete in its impact on our lives as things that can be measured or weighed or put in the bank! This secret is one that must be told, proclaimed, shouted, and celebrated as we do today, this Easter Sunday.

As we receive this hope, we must share it with others in a world that increasingly needs hope. Let's tell the secret as we make it real in our own lives. The Easter story isn't one that we set away on a shelf after giving it a yearly reading. The Easter story becomes our story, as we affirm the great gift God has given us in the new life Jesus received and offers to us. Through this story in our lives, in the face of the worst that life can offer, we can affirm God's goodness and power.

Let me call each one of you, whether you're here every week or once a year, to commit yourself to the one whose good news we proclaim – to Jesus Christ our resurrected Lord. Make this story yours, let it renew your lives, share the story as did Mary and Peter. "I have seen the Lord," said Mary. Today, in this place, so have we. Jesus Christ transforms our lives and our world, despite the sin and suffering, despite our own failures. This new life offers us the power of hope, in Jesus Christ.

– Margaret Marcuson

Hymns
Opening: Christ the Lord Is Risen Today
Sermon: Alleluia, Alleluia! Give Thanks
Closing: Thine Is the Glory

April 7, 2013

2nd Sunday of Easter

Lessons

Semi-continuous (SC)	Roman Catholic (RC)
Acts 5:27-32	Acts 5:12-16
Ps 118:14-29 or Ps 150	Ps 118:2-4, 13-15, 22-24
Rev 1:4-8	Rev 1:9-11, 12-13, 17-19
Jn 20:19-31	Jn 20:19-31

Speaker's Introduction for the Lessons
Lesson 1
Acts 5:27-32 (SC); Acts 5:12-16 (RC)

As the popularity of the gospel message grew, so did opposition. The disciples were imprisoned and then freed by an angel. Then they were brought again before the high priest to account for their actions.

Lesson 2
Psalm 118:14-29 (SC); Psalm 118:2-4, 13-15, 22-24 (RC)

This psalm of thanksgiving rejoices in God in the wake of some unidentified act of deliverance from the threat of death

Lesson 3
Revelation 1:4-8 (SC); Revelation 1:9-11, 12-13, 17-19 (RC)

These verses are words of greeting to the churches in Asia, the area that is now Turkey. The salutation sounds much like other New Testament letters, although the content of Revelation is very different.

Gospel
John 20:19-31 (SC/RC)

This text follows right after Jesus' appearance to Mary Magdalene. Jesus appears to nearly all the disciples. These stories continue to confirm Jesus' resurrection.

Theme

Live the Easter story daily.

Thought for the Day

Easter's new life is not just for Jesus, but for all of us in our daily living.

Sermon Summary

Living out our faith may mean taking risks as we follow Jesus faithfully. But the resurrection power shown forth by Jesus means we are more able to see clearly what we are called to do, and to have the courage to do it.

Call to Worship

One: This is the day the Lord has made
All: Let us rejoice and be glad in it!
One: Jesus is risen!
All: Christ is risen indeed!
One: Our celebration of Easter life continues,
All: Let us worship and give praise to God.

Prayer of Dedication of Gifts and Self

We thank you, O God, for your many gifts – for the fellowship among us, for food, for clothing, for water to drink. We offer our gifts today to support your work in this place and in the world. Receive these gifts together with our hearts and our thanksgiving. Amen.

Hymn of the Day
New Songs of Celebration Render

Is there a better way to celebrate the season of Easter than to sing "new songs" of celebration? Erik Routley, British-born American hymnist, church music apologist, author, and teacher wrote this hymn in 1972. It is a paraphrase of Psalm 98, with grand, modern dimension. It encourages us to offer to "God who has great wonders done" the most celebrative praise possible. Here's an opportunity to use all the musical forces at your disposal in grand celebration of God this Easter season. Yes, even on "low Sunday." Routley set the text to the 16th-century tune RENDEZ A DIEU.

Children's Time: Good News!

(Bring a newspaper, a large sheet of newsprint, and a marker.)

The Sermon: Free to Serve God
Scripture: Acts 5:27-32

Easter continues! Even if the Easter candy is gone, we are still celebrating. Easter life is a year-round reality for Christians.

Our text for today tells about the preaching of the apostles, and the challenges they faced as a result. According to Acts, they met with wild success, as more and more people listened, believed, and experienced healing. The religious leaders in Jerusalem were not happy, to say the least, and arrested them. An angel of the Lord came in the night, opened the door of the prison cell, and told them to go preach in the temple.

So at daybreak the apostles entered the temple and kept on preaching – just like they were doing when they had been arrested. The high priest sent police to the prison to find them, but the temple police came back and said, "We found the prison securely locked and the guards standing at the doors, but when we opened them, we found no one inside" (Acts 5:23). At that confusing moment, someone arrived and said, "The men whom you put in prison are standing in the temple and teaching the people!" (5:25).

Once again the apostles ended up in front of the council. We can imagine what the high priest said to them! "What are you doing? We ordered you not to do this, and here you are blasting that message all over the airwaves!"

Peter replied, "We must obey God rather than any human authority" (5:29). He summed up the message they had been preaching: God raised Jesus and exalted him so he might give repentance to Israel and forgiveness of sins. And we are witnesses to it.

The leaders were furious and would have killed the apostles, except for the words of Gamaliel (Paul's teacher)."Keep away from these men and let them alone; because if this plan or this undertaking is of human origin, it will fail; but if it is of God, you will not be able to overthrow them – in that case you may even be found fighting against God!" (5:38-39)

This story in Acts is clear; the disciples, who were cowering before Easter, were different after. The Gospel of Luke vividly tells Peter's denial of Jesus. But once Peter and the others knew the reality of the resurrection and received the Holy Spirit, they were emboldened. Their experience of God's power gave them a new clarity and ability to take a stand for what they believed. The stand they took changed history.

Other Christians have found themselves able to take the same stand. German pastor Martin Niemoller preached in 1937, "We have no more thought of using our own powers to escape the arm of the authorities than had the apostles of old. No more are we ready to keep silent at man's behest when God commands us to speak. For it is, and must remain, the case that we must obey God rather than man." He preached this sermon on June 27, 1937, and was arrested on July 1 and imprisoned for eight years. (William L. Shirer, *The Rise and Fall of the Third Reich,* Simon & Schuster, p. 239.)

What about us? In what ways do we claim Easter power for ourselves? And when do we find it necessary to obey God rather than human authority? We cannot claim the power if we do not know the story – know it deeply, inside and out. We must know it not only in our heads but also in our spirits. Peter says, "We are witnesses to these things, and so is the Holy Spirit whom God has given to those who obey him" (5:32). As we live faithfully, the Spirit is present with us.

Hearing the Easter story once a year is not enough (and let me commend you for showing up the Sunday after Easter)! Hearing it once a week is not enough. I find I need to listen for God's voice every day, even if I can only sit down for a few minutes. I need to read at least one verse of scripture (or more, I hope). I need to breathe deeply and be aware of the presence of God's Spirit for at least five minutes (or more, I hope). I find these moments allow me to be more aware of God through the day. I feel more grounded, more able to make choices that are courageous rather than fearful, not only on the big issues of the day but also on how I relate to my husband, my children, and the people whom I serve and encounter.

Sometimes people talk about "seeing red" in a moment of anger. Perhaps we are called to "see gold" – to have moments of blinding clarity of what God wants us to do. As the passage in Acts describes him, Peter didn't have to agonize over whether to preach the gospel even when it had been forbidden. Peter knew what his calling was, and he stepped forward to do it.

As a young woman, I had a secretarial job. One of our firm's clients was trying to infiltrate a consumer group that was critical of their policies. I felt very uncomfortable about this, both because I felt like the consumer group was doing the right thing and because of the deception involved. So I told my boss I didn't want to work on that account. It was frightening because I did not know whether I might lose my job. Of course the risk was minimal: I was never in any real danger; I could always have gotten another job. And fortunately, my boss excused me from the project. And I grew through facing the challenge of my conscience and making a choice that I believed was right.

We can find ourselves faced with such challenges in small and large ways. The better grounded we are in our faith and the scriptures, and the better connected we are to our church community, the more prepared we will be to "obey God rather than human authority." Easter power is for all Christians who want the courage to face both the worst and the best that life can offer. Easter power is for all Christians who want to make a difference, for the sake of our risen Lord.

– Margaret Marcuson

Hymns
Opening: Crown Him with Many Crowns
Sermon: My Faith Looks Up to Thee
Closing: I Know that My Redeemer Lives

April 14, 2013

3rd Sunday of Easter

Lessons

Semi-continuous (SC)	Roman Catholic (RC)
Acts 9:1-6 (7-20)	Acts 5:27-32, 40-41
Ps 30	Ps 30:2, 4, 5-6, 11-13
Rev 5:11-14	Rev 5:11-14
Jn 21:1-19	Jn 21:1-19 or Jn 21:1-14

Speaker's Introduction for the Lessons

Lesson 1

Acts 9:1-6 (7-20) (SC)

Armed with letters from the high priest to allow him to arrest followers of the Way, Saul of Tarsus is stricken blind on the road to Damascus – an unexpected interruption to his otherwise promising career.

Acts 5:27-32, 40-41 (RC)

Peter and the apostles, enjoined from teaching in the name of Jesus by the high priest, continue to obey God in proclaiming Jesus as leader and savior.

Lesson 2

Psalm 30 (SC); Psalm 30: 2, 4, 5-6, 11-13

The psalmist offers a prayer of thanksgiving for a reversal that has transformed mourning into dancing.

Lesson 3

Revelation 5:11-14 (SC/RC)

In his vision of heaven, John hears angels, living creatures, and elders praising the Lamb as worthy of opening the scroll with seven seals, whose content is of supreme importance.

Gospel
John 21:1-19 (SC/RC)

Jesus appears to the disciples a third time after his resurrection, revealing his identity in the miraculous catch of fish and calling Peter to show his love by tending Jesus' sheep.

Theme

Transformed to discipleship by waiting

Thought for the Day

They also serve who only stand and wait.

– John Milton, "On His Blindness"

Sermon Summary

A powerful insight gained by the poet John Milton – understood through the lens of Saul's encounter with the risen Christ on the Damascus road – is that faith, of necessity, is sometimes active, but also involves waiting for God's transforming power.

Call to Worship

One: To you, O God, we cry for help.
All: From you, O God, come health and healing.
One: To you, O God, our praise ascends.
All: From you, O God, comes joy in the morning.
One: To you, O God, our souls give thanks.
All: To you, O God, we dance in joy.

Pastoral Prayer

Exaltation and worship, honor and glory, majesty and power are yours, All-Sovereign God. We, whom you have created, find our hearts lifted in praise of your otherness. To that heavenly glory, we praise you for your Son Jesus, whom you sent among us so that sin and death might be vanquished, and we might find ourselves freed from all that separates us from you and one another. Such mysteries of love, beyond our comprehension, compel us to praise nonetheless. As you were present in the abundance of the disciples' catch of fish after the resurrection, so be present with us in bounteous ways. Teach us to perceive and receive your blessings with open, grateful hearts. All these prayers we offer, in and through and under your Mercy, who is our risen Lord Jesus Christ. Amen.

Prayer of Confession

How quickly we put aside the resurrection of your Son, O God, and return to the mundane pursuits that pass for the work of discipleship. How little difference your obliterating the power of death makes, as we return to deadening ways of gluttony, greed, anger, laziness, and pride. How much we need to return to you is evident in the myriad ways we run away from you, unable to bear the brightness of the light of your truth. Forgive us, we pray, for our deliberate blindness and our unconscious resistance. Open our eyes to behold you in all your glory, and open our hearts to be ready to bring your love to all and among all in need. In Christ's name we pray. Amen.

Prayer of Dedication of Gifts and Self

God of generosity and blessing, sometimes your gifts come to us in comprehensible form, like the beauty of nature, the spectacle of the heavens, the depths of the seas. Sometimes your gifts come in packages that we wish contained instructions so that we might know how to use them. For all your gifts, we offer you our thanks and praise. Guide us to use what you provide to transform ourselves and our brothers and sisters into your faithful disciples, under your Mercy. Amen.

Hymn of the Day
You Servants of God, Your Master Proclaim

As we continue in the season of Easter, this hymn gives us further opportunity to celebrate and honor the Son. This is another of Charles Wesley's well-known hymns. It first appeared in his *Hymns for Times of Trouble and Persecution* in 1744. Although written as encouragement to those facing religious persecution in the 18th century, we can certainly use the hymn as a means of praising "God's triumphs." The principal biblical references for this hymn are Psalm 145 and Revelation 7:9-12.

Children's Time: Completely Changed

(Bring some pictures of butterflies and caterpillars and butterfly stickers.)
Show the pictures and invite the children to tell you what they know
about caterpillars and butterflies. Briefly list the differences between caterpillars and butterflies. Observe that when the caterpillar turns into a butterfly, its life is completely changed. Comment that our Bible story today
is about someone whose life was completely changed by Jesus' love.

Retell the story of Saul's encounter with Jesus on the road to Damascus. Briefly talk about the story: How do you think Saul's life changed?
Explain that Saul's life changed so much that he decided to change his
name as well. Saul became known as Paul. Soon Paul began to tell others
about Jesus. He went to many places and started many churches.

Observe that Jesus' love really makes a difference in the world. Place
a butterfly sticker on each child's hand as a reminder of the new life that
Jesus brings.

Pray, giving thanks for the difference Jesus' love makes in the world.

The Sermon: They Also Serve Who Stand and Wait
Scripture: Acts 9:1-6 (7-20)

The assignment seemed innocuous enough. Each of the students in my
tenth-grade English class had to choose an author from a preselected list
of names, then find a sonnet written by that person. We had to memorize the sonnet for recitation and learn something about the author's life.
When the list came to me, I signed my name beside that of John Milton.
Although I did not know it yet, I had embarked on an intense journey of
learning and discovery that in time would prove very exciting.

When I started the project, I must admit, I had little use for poetry.
The more I learned about him, the more unlikely John Milton seemed as a
poet a kindred spirit! Milton grew up in a home made comfortable by his
father's success as a scrivener, or law writer. He studied Latin and Italian,
as well as English, and later became a foreign language secretary to Oliver
Cromwell. Born in 1608, Milton traveled to Italy and France as a young
man and met Galileo Galilei in Florence. The vistas open to him through
wealth and political connections must have seemed truly boundless.

Milton's life was forever altered when in 1651, at the age of 43, he became blind. He who had written biting political commentary and religious
polemics turned inward to poetry. From this later period came Milton's

epic work *Paradise Lost* (1667), as well as the sonnet I chose to memorize, "On His Blindness."

The sonnet is Milton's measured reflection on the psychology of becoming blind. He struggles to find meaning by asking what God expects of him. He learns that God does not need human works; God's works proceed because they are God's works. The closing line of the sonnet is Milton's hopeful apothegm: "They also serve who only stand and wait."

John Milton could simply have given up, finding in his blindness the final break between a life of public purpose and a life of crushing disability. Instead, he owned his blindness and used it as a new way of seeing. In so doing, he became one of the greatest poets of all time.

The unanticipated consequence of my study was that John Milton became a sort of role model for me, for I, too, had struggled with impaired sight. He helped me to envision myself as transcending and exceeding my congenital visual abnormalities and leading a creative, useful, imaginative life. For this, I am forever grateful.

"They also serve who only stand and wait."

Today's lesson from Acts concerns an adult who, like John Milton, is stricken blind at the height of his powers: Saul of Tarsus. We first meet Saul in Acts 8:1, where he is present at the execution of Stephen, deacon and martyr. Two verses later, Saul is functioning as an army of one – chief of the thought police – who is "ravaging the church by entering house after house; dragging off both men and women" and committing them to prison (8:3). Saul is on the fast track to becoming Persecutor of the Year. That is, until he carries his crusade to Damascus.

Saul is not invincible, whatever his intended victims might believe. He is armed with warrants, signed by the high priest, empowering him to round up followers of Jesus' Way and extradite them to Jerusalem for trial. Suddenly, Saul is stopped – blind – his tracks. A bright light from heaven flashes around him. Saul hears a voice, identified as that of Jesus, asking, "Saul, Saul, why do you persecute me?" (9:4). Then, the voice tells him, "Get up and enter the city, and you will be told what you are to do" (9:6). Saul's companions lead him to Damascus, where he languishes for three days – blind, not eating or drinking.

Try to imagine Saul's frame of mind as he waits, helpless, in Damascus. There is no Braille for reading in Hebrew. No public works projects have made Damascus accessible for the visually impaired. There are no guide dogs, no laser surgeries. Blind is blind. How can he possibly salvage his independence? How can he persecute people he can't even see?

As promised, however, a disciple living in Damascus comes to Saul's aid. The man, Ananias, is no fool and tries to avoid the assignment; Saul's notoriety has preceded him. Ananias is told by the Lord to go to Saul anyway, because the Lord has plans for Saul. Ananias is the first to hear that Saul "is an instrument" chosen by the Lord to bring the Lord's name "before Gentiles and kings and before the people of Israel" (9:15). Ananias does his part, restoring Saul's sight. His priorities completely reversed, Saul is baptized, and the rest, as they say, is history.

For that three-day period, Saul must learn patience with his new disability. He must prepare for his blindness to be permanent. When his sight is restored, Saul completes the transformation from persecutor to proclaimer. Saul's encounter with Jesus on the Damascus road becomes a credential for his apostleship, as the only person outside the circle of the Twelve to witness a postresurrection appearance of Jesus.

"They also serve who only stand and wait."

What of us, living so far removed from Jesus' risen form? What of us, who have such difficulty acknowledging the faith we profess? Do we even recognize our many forms of blindness? Perhaps, in our perceived ignorance and failure, we are actually performing some service for our Lord. Perhaps, in patient waiting, we render glory to God. Perhaps waiting is a form of discipleship, too.

"They also serve who only stand and wait."

Thank you, John Milton, for waiting through blinded eyes for your great vision of the cost and consequence of faith. Thank you, Saul of Tarsus, for doing as you were told, remaining and waiting to see what the Lord had in mind. Thank you both for the gift of transformation that catches us up short and helps each of us, in our own small way, to be Christ's witnesses.

This is our faith, under the Mercy.

– Nancy E. Topolewski

Hymns
Opening: Christ Jesus Lay in Death's Strong Bands
Sermon: He Is the Way [New Dance]
Closing: I Want to Be Ready

April 21, 2013

4th Sunday of Easter

Lessons

Semi-continuous (SC)	Roman Catholic (RC)
Acts 9:36-43	Acts 13:14, 43-52
Ps 23	Ps 100:1-2, 3, 5
Rev 7:9-17	Rev 7:9, 14-17
Jn 10:22-30	Jn 10:27-30

Speaker's Introduction for the Lessons
Lesson 1
Acts 9:36-43 (SC)

> Tabitha, a generous woman of Joppa who has done much for the poor, dies and is miraculously restored to life.

Acts 9:13:14, 43-52 (RC)

> Paul and Barnabas travel to Antioch in Pisidia, where they convert many Gentiles by preaching faith in Jesus' life, death, and resurrection – the *kerygma* of the earliest Christians.

Lesson 2
Psalm 23 (SC)

> The "shepherd psalm" celebrates God's providential care as well as God's companioning through trying times.

Psalm 100:1-2, 3, 5 (RC)

> The psalmist invites praise of God that is grounded in the imagery of creation (God has fashioned us) and shepherding (the people of God are the sheep of God's pasture).

Lesson 3
Revelation 7:9-17 (SC); Revelation 7:9, 14-17 (RC)

> The curtain is raised in heaven, giving us a vision of heaven where the Lamb sits upon the throne and rules, surrounded by the white-robed elders.

Gospel
John 10:22-30 (SC); John 10:27-30 (RC)

Jesus' critics want him to say plainly to them who he really is. Jesus asserts that he and his father are one.

Theme
Why are we following Jesus this day?

Thought for the Day
May Christ give us eyes to see you, ears to hear you, faith to follow you, energy to stick with you, and gratitude that you have stuck with us.

Sermon Summary
The risen Christ comes to us, reveals himself to us, and calls us, but not always in ways that we can comprehend and understand. If we believe, follow, and worship Christ as Lord and Savior, it is because of his gifts to us of presence, revelation, and love.

Call to Worship
One: Let all the earth praise God with joy.
All: We come to worship God in praise and thanksgiving.
One: Let all the earth praise God with joy.
All: We come as God's people, the sheep of God's pasture.
One: Let all the earth praise God with joy.
**All: We come, blessing God's name, and celebrating God's good-
ness, love, and faithfulness.**

Pastoral Prayer
God of Good Friday, God of Easter, God of all that was, and is, and will yet be: We know that you hold our lives in your hands – from conception to death and beyond. We yearn for the day when we will join the multitudes in heaven, giving honor and praise to you for your great, glorious love. Our grateful thanksgiving belongs with those who have gone before us, whose faithfulness was not easy, safe, or assured. Hold their fidelity before us as an example of the high calling to which we aspire as followers of your Son Jesus Christ. Help us to know that in life and in death, we

are yours. We offer you these our prayers, in and through and under your Mercy, who is our risen Lord Jesus Christ. Amen.

Prayer of Confession

Your graciousness, your goodness, your loving care are around us and ever before us, O God. We know that your presence among human beings in the person of your Son is offered to heal the wounds of human sin and draw us closer to you. We speak as if we understand your nearness, but in reality, we would rather be alone with more attractive masters, who tell us it is all right to focus on personal advancement and acquisition. We shrink when you call us to account. Yet, speak those hard words that will renew our sense of purpose. Help us to return to you as those transformed, that we may once again do the work of disciples for which you have called us; through the merits and mediation of your Son, Jesus Christ our Lord. Amen.

Prayer of Dedication of Gifts and Self

We give thanks to you, God of all bounty, for the gifts with which you sustain and nourish us. In response to your extravagant generosity, we offer you our time, our abilities, our abundance, and our commitment, that what you have begun in us may be brought to fruition in your time. Help us to live as people transformed into your faithful disciples, under your Mercy. Amen.

Hymn of the Day
Crown Him with Many Crowns

English poet Matthew Bridges is remembered primarily through this hymn that he first published in 1851 in his *Hymns of the Heart*. The hymn is an imaginative search for what the "many crowns" of Revelation 19:12 may signify. Rev. Godfrey Thring, Anglican priest, did some editing of the original text, resulting in the hymn that appears in most hymnbooks today. The buoyant tune DIADEMATA was written for Bridges's text in 1868 by British composer George J. Elvey. This hymn provides an opportunity for festive celebration of the resurrected "King of kings and Lord of lords!"

Children's Time: Do You Know?

(Arrange for two or three people to bring tools of their occupation in a bag, and be prepared to come forward during the story. Examples of tools: stethoscope for a doctor or nurse, hammer for a carpenter, etc.)
I have asked some people to come and be with us today. *(Motion the volunteers to come forward).* Do you know who they are? *(Responses.)* Can you tell just by looking at them what they do on the other days of the week? I want each of these people to do something and then see if you can tell me what their job is. *(The carpenter pounds a nail into the board. The nurse or doctor listens to your* [not a child's] *heartbeat and looks at your throat.)* Now that you can see them doing their work, you know what their job is.

One time Jesus was walking in the temple and some people asked him if he really was the Son of God. Jesus said that he had told them who he was, and they didn't believe him. So, he told them to watch what he did in God's name, and they would know. Tell me some things that Jesus did. *(Responses.)* Often, in order to know about someone, we need to see what they do. How can we learn what Jesus did? *(Read the Bible. Go to Sunday school. Listen to the sermon.)* Then we can not only know who Jesus is, but maybe we can even see things that Jesus did that we can do as his followers.

Close with a prayer.

The Sermon: Show Us Plainly Who You Are
Scripture: John 10:22-30

"He's a great preacher," she said of her new young pastor. "Of course, I haven't understood most of what he's said in his sermons."

I found that rather amazing. Would any of you say that about my sermons?

I expect if you pressed her on that statement she might tell you that understanding the ideas in the pastor's sermons are not the point. She likes her new pastor, is happy to be part of his congregation, because she likes her new pastor, likes him as a person before she likes him as a preacher.

In fact, I bet that if you pressed her on this she would tell you some time when he visited her when she was in need, or some conversation with her in which he came up with just the right word at the right time, or perhaps it's not anything that specific. Perhaps it's just that when she is in the presence of her pastor she feels that she is in the presence of the living God.

I think this is the most important kind of knowledge and understanding that we ever get.

In today's Gospel Jesus' critics have had it with Jesus. It's the Gospel of John, and Jesus can be fairly evasive, ambiguous, and hard to understand in the Gospel of John. Who is this Jesus anyway?

When they have asked him, he has said things like, "I am the vine, you are the branches." Or, "I am bread, I am life, I am the way, I am the good shepherd," and on and on. What is any of that supposed to mean? It's all so symbolic, metaphorical, and figurative.

In exasperation they say to Jesus, "Show us plainly, directly, and clearly who you are."

Jesus is exasperated with them. He says that he has been teaching them, telling them, but they haven't seen and haven't heard. Then Jesus says, "My sheep hear my voice and they follow me." Sheep? We're back on the metaphorical, symbolic, and figurative. But maybe some of you know exactly what Jesus is talking about. Why are you here this morning? Why are you, despite all of your weaknesses and misunderstanding, here following Jesus?

I think it's because you have heard his voice. You may not know everything about Jesus, may not know much about the Bible, much less about theology. But you do know Jesus. In some way or another – maybe not as clearly as you might like, but clearly enough for you to follow him – he has revealed himself to you. He has spoken. And you have heard his voice as the very voice of God.

So Jesus says in our Gospel, "the Father and I are one." In other words, when you have seen and heard Jesus, you have seen and heard as much of God as you ever hope to see and hear. And that's why you are here.

"My sheep know me," says Jesus. The world may not know him. His critics and enemies may not know him. But by the grace of God (and it is by grace alone), you know him. It's a miracle. And it's a miracle that has happened to you.

That's the good news behind this rather exasperating episode. The risen Christ has come out to us, out to our doubts and misgivings, our misunderstandings and unanswered questions and called us. And we have heard. And we have followed.

Let all who have heard, and all who are following, let the church say, "Amen!"

– William H. Willimon

Hymns
Opening: Come, Ye Faithful, Raise the Strain
Sermon: O for a Heart to Praise My God
Closing: Whom Shall I Send?

April 28, 2013

5th Sunday of Easter

Lessons

Semi-continuous (SC)
Acts 11:1-18
Ps 148
Rev 21:1-6
Jn 13:31-35

Roman Catholic (RC)
Acts 14:21-27
Ps 145:8-9, 10-11, 12-13
Rev 21:1-5
Jn 13:31-35

Speaker's Introduction for the Lessons
Lesson 1
Acts 11:1-18 (SC)

When questioned about his consorting with Gentiles, Peter reports his vision of clean and unclean foods as a call to welcome Gentiles among the faithful.

Acts 14:21-27 (RC)

Paul and Barnabas return to Antioch in Syria, meeting with many disciples along the way and praying for God to strengthen them in times of persecution.

Lesson 2
Psalm 148 (SC)

This song of praise invites all of creation to join in celebration of God's glory and power.

Psalm 145:8-9, 10-11, 12-13 (RC)

The psalm bids thanksgiving for God's goodness and compassion that undergirds God's providence of all.

Lesson 3
Revelation 21:1-6 (SC); Revelation 21:1-5 (RC)

John reports his vision of the new heaven and new earth in which God dwells with mortals and makes all things new.

Gospel
John 13:31-35 (SC/RC)
> After demonstrating how the disciples are to serve one another in washing each other's feet, Jesus calls them to love one another, thereby marking themselves as his followers.

Theme
Transformed to discipleship by love.

Thought for the Day
Christian Love, either towards God or towards man [sic], is an affair of the will.

> – C. S. Lewis, *Mere Christianity*, The Macmillan Company, 1952, Book III, Chapter 9, p. 102.

Sermon Summary
One of Jesus' last instructions is that his disciples love one another – love shown in many human situations, love with the power to transform ordinariness to faithfulness.

Call to Worship
> One: Let us bless the Lord.
> **All: Let us praise God's name forever and ever.**
> One: The Lord does wondrous and awesome deeds.
> **All: Let us praise God's name forever and ever.**
> One: The Lord is faithful in words and gracious in deeds.
> **All: Let us praise God's name forever and ever.**
> One: The Lord is near to all who call upon God in truth.
> **All: Let us praise God's name forever and ever.**

Pastoral Prayer
Surprising, resurrecting God, even now, we walk past your Son's burial place, hoping to peek inside, to reassure ourselves that he has, indeed, been raised from death. We have our moments of incredulous disbelief. But the proclamation of the church is ours as well – Christ is risen, indeed. That same risen Lord bids us who have witnessed his vindication to go into the

world as his disciples, loving others as he loved us. For this inestimable blessing, we give you thanks and praise. Because the tomb is vacant, we can yearn for your heavenly city, but we also long for an end to suffering here on earth, for needs spoken and silent. (Pause). All these prayers we offer in, through, and under your Mercy, who is our risen Lord Jesus Christ. Amen.

Prayer of Confession

When your Son washed the feet of his disciples, O God, he set an example of love and service to others for us to follow. Peter and Paul and countless others have sought to be faithful to this high calling of love. It all looks so easy. Yet, when we are among those different from ourselves, and even among our own family and friends, we find ourselves holding back, as if loving others is someone else's job. Forgive our narrow and reluctant love, we pray. Open our hearts to one another, that we may become ever more faithful to your call to be loving disciples of Christ our Lord, in whose name we pray. Amen.

Prayer of Dedication of Gifts and Self

On the night before he suffered for us, O God, your Son offered his disciples the gift of love by washing their feet and instructing them to love one another. We who have received so bountifully of your gifts now offer them, and ourselves, back to you in love, that the work of faithful discipleship may continue in the world, under your Mercy. Amen.

Hymn of the Day
The Gift of Love

Appearing originally as a choral anthem, the text was written by American church musician and composer Hal Hopson in 1972. The hymn appears in some hymnal indices under its first line "Though I May Speak." The text is Hopson's paraphrase of 1 Corinthians 13:1-3. Hopson also made an adaptation of the traditional English melody O WALY WALY for the musical setting of the text. It was first set in its hymn form in 1984. At least one major hymnbook has chosen not to use Hopson's 2/2 meter in favor of the melody's original 3/4 meter, which allows the text to flow nicely in its hymn format.

Children's Time: Job Description

(Bring an example of a job description, a sheet of newsprint, and a marker.)
Explain that most people who work have some kind of a job description.
A job description lists all the things a person is expected to do at work.
Read the example you have brought. Comment that a job description can
be a very helpful thing to have. It helps a worker do her or his job well.

Comment that as followers of Jesus, we also have a job description.
Ask the children if they can guess what might be on that description.
What kinds of things do the followers of Jesus do? Explain that our job
description was given to us by Jesus and can be found in the Bible. Paraphrase John 13:31-35.

Ask the children to list some of the ways they might show love to others. Print these on the newsprint in the form of a job description. When
you have finished, read the list aloud and comment that it is easier to be a
follower of Jesus when we know what our job is.

Pray with the children, asking that God would help you show love to
others.

The Sermon: Transformation: Discipleship through Love
Scripture: John 13:31-35

On a bitterly cold February morning, my husband and I were awakened
just after dawn by a ringing telephone. Our friend and veterinarian, Dr.
Jane, was on the line. The call was not unexpected, but it still came as a
surprise, a shock. Dr. Jane told us that our ten-year-old miniature dachshund, Nadia Boulanger, had died during the night. Dr. Jane had performed surgery on Nadia three days earlier, in the hope that removing the
stones that clogged her bladder would allow her a few more months with
us. We went into the surgery with our eyes open. Dr. Jane thought it was
worth a try. We trusted in both her judgment and her skill, for she had
always dealt gently with us and with a succession of our dachshunds.

Dr. Jane was crying when she called us. "We did our best," she said,
"but our best wasn't good enough this time."

If you have ever lost a beloved pet, you know the kind of anguished
emptiness the end brings. We spent much of that bitterly cold February
day looking for Nadia in the places she used to sleep, expecting to hear

her throaty "woof" if a bird violated her air space, waiting for her to come to the kitchen table for a treat. But she wasn't there. Not in any of those places. Not any more.

That evening, we drove to Dr. Jane's office to bring Nadia home. The process of decay had already bloated her small frame. The Nadia we had known wasn't there any more. We touched her fur, stroking ever so gently. Jack took off her collar. We wrapped her for burial.

Dachshunds as a breed are scrappy little diggers, who worm and squirm and wriggle themselves into small spaces. They also like to nest, to root around in blankets and other soft things, and then snuggle down for a nap. True to her breed, Nadia had succeeded in worming and squirming and wriggling herself into empty places in our hearts, then nested there. With her death, those places were empty again.

Why do we love them so, these funny little creatures, when we know they're going to die? Why do we voluntarily subject ourselves to the anguish of losing them? After all, they're only animals – right?

Why do we love one another so, when we know we're going to die? More to the point, why does God love us so, when a consequence of the disobedience of our first ancestors is that every last one of us will die?

Part of the answer to these questions may be found in our Gospel lesson for today: "I give you a new commandment, that you love one another. Just as I have loved you, you also should love one another. By this everyone will know that you are my disciples, if you have love for one another" (Jn 13:34-35).

Coming as they do in the midst of John's report of Jesus' last hours with his disciples, these instructions carry special weight for thoughtful readers. Not quite "deathbed instructions," they nonetheless are a marker, a signpost, pointing toward where Jesus wants his followers to go. He has shown them the transforming power of love by washing their feet. Now, Jesus' words spur them on: Go and do likewise. Love one another as I have loved you.

Part of the answer, too, lies beyond the text, in the nature of love itself, as shown throughout the scriptural witness: Love that created us in God's image; love that offered the first human being the chance to name the animals; love that brought God's only Son to earth, to live and die as one of us; love that raised God's Son from death and promises to raise us, as well.

Painful as love can be, especially when it ends in death, is not love a gift, wherever and whenever we find it?

The season of Easter shows us that love's redeeming work is done – love shown to us in Christ, love that triumphs over death. This love is not cheap, but comes at a cost: the cost of spending 40 days in the wilderness, being tempted by Satan; the cost of setting his face to go to Jerusalem, waiting to be killed; the cost of losing this life, in order to find new life, resurrection life.

Sometimes the best love of all is given to us by small, insignificant, but treasured creatures who reflect the love of God in our lives. Sometimes the best love of all is what we offer them in return.

Sometimes the best love of all is the love that connects us with one another – love that, whether given or received, transforms us, makes us into different people.

Sometimes the best Love of all must die in order for us to live.

Two months after Nadia's death, we brought home an investment in love: a 13-ounce, squirming ball of downy-soft fur and needle-sharp teeth – an eight-week-old miniature dachshund, whom we named Dorothy L. Sayers. Yes, we know she is going to die someday. But in the meantime, she has joined our family, worming and squirming and wriggling herself into empty places in our hearts and nesting there. We love her with all our hearts.

This is our faith, under the Mercy.

— Nancy E. Topolewski

Hymns
Opening: Love Divine, All Loves Excelling
Sermon: Come Down, O Love Divine
Closing: Blest Be the Tie That Binds

May 5, 2013

6th Sunday of Easter

Lessons

Semi-continuous (SC)	Roman Catholic (RC)
Acts 16:9-15	Acts 15:1-2, 22-29
Ps 67	Ps 67:2-3, 5, 6, 8
Rev 21:10, 22—22:5	Rev 21:10-14, 22-23
Jn 14:23-29 or Jn 5:1-9	Jn 14:23-29

Speaker's Introduction for the Lessons

Lesson 1

Acts 16:9-15 (SC)

Called to Macedonia by a vision, Paul and Silas take their mission to the Gentiles of Philippi.

Acts 15:1-2, 22-29 (RC)

In contrast to the insistence of some in the Jerusalem church on the necessity of converts becoming Jews before embracing Christ, Paul and Silas report the fruits of their mission to the Gentiles.

Lesson 2

Psalm 67 (SC); Psalm 67:2-3, 5, 6, 8 (RC)

The psalmist invokes both God's blessing upon the community and the people's praise in response for God's just and providential works.

Lesson 3

Revelation 21:10, 22—22:5 (SC); Revelation 21:10-14, 22-23 (RC)

In a vision surely delectable to his exile on the water-poor island of Patmos, John sees the new Jerusalem basking in the glory of God and watered by the river of life.

Gospel

John 14:23-29 (SC/RC)

Jesus reminds his disciples one last time before he suffers: Live in love and draw strength and peace from his last gift to them, the Holy Spirit.

Theme

Transformed to discipleship by the Spirit

Thought for the Day

The whole offer which Christianity makes is . . . we can, if we let God have His Way, come to share in the life of Christ.
– C. S. Lewis, *Mere Christianity*, The Macmillan Company, 1952, Book IV, Chapter 4, p. 137.

Sermon Summary

In the church, as well as in horticulture, if you're planting for yourself, plant plums; if you're planting for your children, plant pecans – that is, seek out the transforming power of the Spirit over the long term.

Call to Worship

One: Let us worship God, who is gracious and blesses us.
All: Let us worship God, who calls all nations to praise.
One: Let us worship God, who judges the peoples with equity.
All: Let us worship God, who guides all the nations of the earth.
One: Let the peoples praise you, O God.
All: Let all the peoples praise you.

Pastoral Prayer

How we long, O God, for the day when we will see your Son, Jesus, face to face, when we will hear his voice speaking our names. Until that day, you have sent the Holy Spirit to be your constant, sustaining presence with us. For this inestimable gift, we lift our hearts in grateful thanksgiving. How we long, O God, for the peace the world cannot give, for calm that displaces fear. Through your Holy Spirit, be the One bearing peace to those in distress. Be the One bringing quiet to all who suffer. Be the One who enfolds us in your love and bids us not be afraid. Be the One who stands with your church in this suffering world. Be the One who hears our silent, needful petitions. (Pause). All our prayers we offer in, through, and under your Mercy, who is our risen Lord Jesus Christ. Amen.

Prayer of Confession

Your Word comes to us, O God, in words recorded in Holy Scripture. Through your Word-Made-Flesh, you bid us not to be anxious, to trust that Christ's comfort and peace will be his enduring gifts to us. But in our ignorance and pride, we look to other sources of comfort and peace. So often we keep your saving words to ourselves and hoard the overflowing bounty of your love as our exclusive property. Forgive us the arrogance of self-absorption. Free us to trust in your sustaining Spirit, even as you provide for all of your children, through all time. Transform us to be faithful, loving disciples of the risen Christ; for it is in his name we pray. Amen.

Prayer of Dedication of Gifts and Self

Gracious and loving God, we rejoice in the promise of your Holy Spirit as gift and blessing. In grateful response to all your gifts and blessings in creation, we offer you our thanks and praise. Help us to use with joy and imagination your many mercies, that we may be constantly transforming into faithful disciples of our risen Lord Jesus Christ, in whose name we pray. Amen.

Hymn of the Day
Guide Me, O Thou Great Jehovah

The author of this hymn, William Williams, was never formally ordained. However, he reportedly traveled nearly 100,000 miles over the course of 43 years, preaching the gospel in his homeland of Wales. He wrote many hymns and used them as an educational and cultural force in his ministry. Few of his hymns have been translated into English. Originally written in Welsh by Williams in 1745, this hymn was translated into English during 1771 and 1772. Williams successfully transformed the biblical story of the Israelites' march into a hymn that can still sustain the modern Christian's spiritual march.

Children's Time: Peace Be with You

(Bring a large paper heart for each child.)

Invite the children to share stories of times they were alone and afraid. Mention that in the Bible story today Jesus' followers were feeling alone and scared. They knew Jesus would not be with them for much longer.

Jesus promises the disciples that they will be given a special kind of peace to help them through the difficult times. Paraphrase John 14:27.

Ask the children if they have heard the words, "Peace be with you." Mention that the early followers of Jesus used this greeting, and we still use it in our churches today. (If you have the tradition of "passing the peace" during worship, talk about it.)

Explain that greeting someone with the words "Peace be with you" is a way of passing along Jesus' love and peace. Distribute paper hearts and invite the children to pass a heart to someone in the congregation, saying, "Peace be with you." Encourage those who receive a heart to pass it on to the next person. Watch Jesus' love and peace travel around the church.

Pray, giving thanks for the gift of Jesus' peace.

The Sermon: Discipleship by Plums or Pecans?
Scripture: John 14:23-29

Sometimes, to our immense surprise, actions taken by governments can offer entirely unintended interpretive possibilities. One such instance is the Homestead Act of 1862 and the lens it provides for viewing factors of growth and change within the church.

The Homestead Act was one of the most important pieces of legislation of the 19th century. It beckoned many hardy individuals to settle in the vast expanses of the great prairie of the American Midwest, promising the possibility of land ownership. If they could prove they were over 21 and were head of household, these pioneers could claim 160 acres from the United States government. Over a five-year period, the homesteaders were expected to build a house, make improvements, and farm the land of their tract. At the end of the five years, if they could prove they had met all the government criteria, the homesteaders paid a filing fee of $18 and were able to claim the land, free and clear. In this way, immigrants from overseas, former slaves, and many who otherwise would never have owned land were able to establish homes and farms.

The psychology of homesteading is very interesting. For the first 20 years or so, homesteaders were focused on the need to make the land arable and wrest it from the seemingly endless stands of tall, waving prairie grass. Only when those essential tasks were completed did the settlers begin to think about how they might beautify and further domesticate the prairie by planting trees.

Native trees were few and far between on the prairie. Because of the expense involved, homesteaders had to choose their trees very carefully. For many, the choice came down to plums versus pecans.

Those who chose to plant plum trees achieved a relatively quick return on their investment. Because they grow fairly quickly, plum trees soon bring a shield against the weather. Homesteaders could expect to harvest plums after a few short years. The drawback is that plum trees run to brush and bramble as they get older and must eventually be cut down, burned, and replaced.

Those who chose to plant pecan trees did not receive immediate gratification. Because pecan trees grow and mature slowly, they could not be expected to provide either shelter or fruit until long after the plum trees did. The advantage of pecan trees is that they endure, providing benefits and beauty for many years to come.

When questioned about the choice between plums and pecans, one homesteader (whose response I remember reading in a United States history text in junior high) observed, "If you're planting for yourself, plant plums. If you're planting for your children, plant pecans."

One of the most difficult tasks we face, as thoughtful Christian disciples, is finding some balance between new insight and ancient truth – between what is relevant now and what was honored in the past. The choice is, in short, between plums and pecans. When I was in seminary in the mid-1970s, theology's razor edge cut into what many would now describe as the "entitlements of dead white males." Liberation theologies – of the poor, of various racial groups, of one gender from another's political and economic domination – were the result. Such theological variants then superseded the doctrinal matters historically in the purview of Western theology, as political action replaced conciliar rumination. Now, 30 years later, it is fair to ask, What has happened to these new theologies and the individuals so passionately committed to them? What did the church catholic gain or lose, and how have the insights of liberation theologies changed the worldview of thoughtful Christians?

The 1970s also saw change in the role of language in the church. Gender-specific references to God, archaic pronouns, and grammatical constructions collided with a growing desire for inclusiveness, awakened by the liberation theologies. Language needed to reflect social change. Looking back now at all the fuss and fury, it is interesting to note that in many cases, the rich tapestry of church life has been further embroidered by new threads of language usage – a benefit that allows the church to move on in its constant self-reforming.

How do thoughtful Christians decide what is necessary for belief? Where, to cite just one example, do we place concerns about the use of electronic media in the contemporary church? How do we decide between plums and pecans?

"I have said these things to you while I am still with you. But the Advocate, the Holy Spirit, whom the Father will send in my name, will teach you everything, and remind you of all that I have said to you" (Jn 14:25-26).

As we seek some understanding of our present interpretive dilemma, the Gospel lesson for today offers help: It is God's Holy Spirit, God's Advocate, who provides the bridge between what is taught in the present and remembered from the past. It is the work of God, in and through the Holy Spirit, that keeps us alive in and for the present, as well as sensitive to the past. It is the Spirit of God that brings us all to realize that when we set aside the encumbrances of culture, ideology, and class, we can begin to see the continuity and the connections over time – the linkages between yesterday, today, and tomorrow. God's Holy Spirit enables us to hold it all together – with tension, certainly, but with creative tension.

I really like plum trees, and in terms of our life together in faith, I would not discourage planting a few. But for the sake of the church's mission and ministry, its ongoing programs, as well as our personal faith and its development and growth, I look back to the sage advice of the old homesteader:

"If you're planting for yourself, then plant plums. If you're planting for your children, plant pecans."

This is our faith, under the Mercy.

– Nancy E. Topolewski

Hymns
Opening: Ask Ye What Great Thing I Know
Sermon: Christ Is the World's Light
Closing: Holy Spirit, Truth Divine

May 9, 2013

Ascension Day

Lessons

Semi-continuous (SC)	Roman Catholic (RC)
Acts 1:1-11	Acts 1:1-11
Ps 47 or Ps. 93	Ps 47:2-3, 6-7, 8-9
Eph 1:15-23	Eph 1:17-23
Lk 24:44-53	Lk 24:46-53

Speaker's Introduction for the Lessons
Lesson 1
Acts 1:1-11 (SC/RC)

The evangelist Luke transitions the story of faith from being Jesus-centered to one of the mission of the early church. At his ascension, Jesus gives a commission to his followers to spread the good news.

Lesson 2
Psalm 47 (SC); Psalm 47:2-3, 6-7, 8-9 (RC)

This psalm celebrates God's enthronement over all creation and peoples.

Lesson 3
Ephesians 1:15-23 (SC); Ephesians 1:17-23 (RC)

As Paul opens his letter to the Ephesians, he invokes the name of Jesus as the risen and ascended one, whose power rules above anything else.

Gospel
Luke 24:44-53 (SC); Luke 24:46-53 (RC)

Jesus' ascension is not an end-all event; Christ promises to come even as his followers are reminded of all they have already witnessed.

Theme

We are empowered as witnesses to Christ's glory.

Thought for the Day

Physical absence does not mean the power, inspiration, and wisdom of a person is gone. With Christ, we have the promise of more.

Sermon Summary

Witnessing the truth of Christ, plus the power of God in our midst, makes for mission.

Call to Worship

One: Clap your hands, O people; shout to God with loud voices.

All: Why should we cause such noise?

One: Sing to God, Lord of the Most High, ruler of all.

All: Why should we sing to God?

One: It is our God who chooses us, shielding us from everything.

All: Ah, we can clap; we can shout; we can sing. For God is good indeed!

One: Give praise to our God, sing praises.

All: We bring our hands together; we raise our voices; we sing, we sing, we sing.

Pastoral Prayer

We give thanks, God almighty, for the life, teachings, sacrifice, and resurrection of your Son. We continue to be guided by all that Christ stood for in his life and ours. It is through him that we can come before you as we continue to live the life he has given us.

We give thanks, God almighty, for your ascended Son. We continue to lift our eyes to the heavens while our hearts and minds remain focused on what lies below the mountain. It is through your Son that we can be strengthened to live lives of faith in this world.

We give thanks, God almighty, for the Spirit of your Son descended upon us. We continue to live, empowered by the Spirit sealed in us in our baptism and burning in our hearts. It is through the Spirit promised by Christ that we can be emboldened by your love. Amen.

Prayer of Confession

Holy One, Christ of God, we are not worthy to tie the thongs of your sandals. We fail to hear your voice; we fail to follow your call. We are easily distracted, and we do what is more convenient for us. And yet you call us to the mountaintop from where you point to both the heavens and the earth. As we walk our journeys, you embrace us, you guide us, you walk with us. Grant us the grace to hear you, and give us the confidence to proclaim your holy name wherever we go. Amen.

Prayer of Dedication of Gifts and Self

Grant, O God, the gift of your Son, risen and ascended not just to heaven but also into our hearts. And through this gift of yours, empower us in our giving that we may be a blessing unto others. Take our lives that we may be consecrated to you as we serve our neighbors. Take our hands and let them move at the guiding of your love. Take our mouths and let them be filled with the good news of Jesus. Amen.

Hymn of the Day
Hail the Day That Sees Him Rise

This hymn by Charles Wesley first appeared in his *Hymns and Sacred Poems* in 1739. It provides a poetic commentary on Christ's ascension, as recorded in Luke 24. The "alleluias" were not part of Wesley's original text but were later added by music editors. The tune LLANFAIR, by Welsh singer Robert Williams, became identified with the text around 1817. The modern church can celebrate the ascension of Christ with this hymn. We find strong encouragement in the fourth stanza with its reminder that it is Christ who bestows "blessings on his church below."

Children's Time: Jesus Goes Home

(Bring some helium-filled balloons with long strings.)
Have a brief conversation about things the children have seen that move up into the sky and may disappear (hot air balloons, kites, rockets, fireworks, smoke from a bonfire, an eagle soaring high). Note that some of these things go up with a bang – like rockets or fireworks – while others go up very gently.

Explain that today is Ascension Day, the day we remember when Jesus returned to heaven to live with God. Retell the story of Jesus' ascension as told in Luke 24. When you come to the part where Jesus is taken up into heaven, let go of the balloons and watch them float gently up to the ceiling.

Mention that the disciples weren't sad when Jesus left because they knew that he would send the Holy Spirit to help them. The Bible tells us they went back to Jerusalem filled with great joy.

Pray with the children, giving thanks for the joy that Jesus gives.

(At the end of the service, ask a few helpers to retrieve the balloons and give them to the children.)

The Sermon: I'm Expected to Do What?
Scripture: Luke 24:44-53

Probably one of the worst things one can hear are the words "I'm disappointed in you." Certainly these words can be harsh and demoralizing to anyone. We hear the words because expectations have not been met, conclusions not reached, ends not attained. Of course, some things we just can't do. We have our bad days, failed attempts because of external factors, things that just don't fit together.

Oh, we do have great expectations placed on us. Our parents teach us many things as we grow up, and we're expected to do them: eat properly at the table, tie your shoes, brush your teeth, say thank you, clean up after yourself. We learn many things in school and we're expected to put it all together. All those math proofs add up to something useful. Science projects tell us something about life. Spelling is a way to put our thoughts into written words.

All the other training we receive helps hone our skills so we can function in particular spheres of life. We learn to work computers, strip wires, read blueprints, motivate people, take apart pistons, and recognize sounds. We learn, we observe, we question, we analyze, and we grow in understanding. And we're expected to function in this world. It should be easy enough if everything was learned well, information was absorbed, facts were set straight, practice was perfected.

One of the big concepts used these days is mentoring. Experts talk particularly about the value of mentoring youth and even young adults. Mentoring is different from teaching in that it acts more as a modeling and inspiration for life. Through mentoring one learns by experience, while being guided and encouraged, rather than as an intellectual exercise. It's a way to become all one can be for the sake of others, while seeing a wholeness of life.

That's where Jesus left his followers. Throughout his ministry, he made his disciples all they could be. And he now was sending them off for the sake of the world.

It was easy enough for the disciples to go off proclaiming Christ's good news. After all, Jesus himself was their teacher, their model, and their mentor. Of course, making Jesus into merely a mentor certainly downgrades all that he was. But there may be something to it as we look at what we see in Jesus and how we live our lives as his followers. And that was perhaps where his disciples were left. He opened their minds to understand the scriptures. He spoke about how their faith tradition was brought to fulfillment. He himself showed them what the Messiah was all about in his life, suffering, death, and resurrection. And Jesus tells them: "You've heard it; you've seen it; you understand it. Now go on and tell the rest of the world."

If only all these things actually were so easy. We know that, try as we may, things still go wrong. We may use the best of our abilities, recall the best of our experiences, find ourselves shaped by our mentors. And yet we are not always in control.

That may be the crux of things, and certainly that's the scary part: we are not in control – of things around us, sometimes even of things within us, and of things in this world. Regardless of the expectations placed on us – and no matter how much confidence we place in ourselves – ultimately we're just not in control.

Perhaps there's some wisdom in realizing and living with the fact that we're not in control. The wisdom is not in thus giving up but in trusting something else. Here, Christ had some added things to tell his followers as he sent them off. "I am sending upon you what my Father promised." That's what Jesus' disciples could take with them. They knew what they had seen, what they had learned. They were mentored along the way – their questions addressed, their mistakes corrected. The disciples knew that their message came from God. They were not in control ultimately, for they were on a mission for God. Great expectations were placed on them, but they also had a promise from God to be with them.

We are expected to do the same. Our baptism sets us on a mission, too. The joy of receiving God's grace should compel us to share that good news. There's a slight problem here, though. Jesus reminded his disciples that they had witnessed so much. They had the tools with which to spread the news. Easy enough for them! They witnessed they heard with their own ears, saw with their own eyes, touched with their own hands, walked with their own feet.

We don't have that benefit. We have not seen sight given to the blind. We have not taken bread and fish from some little boy's lunch and filled so many hungry stomachs. We have not seen the dead walk out of their graves. We have not heard words from Jesus' own mouth. We have not seen and touched the nail holes in Jesus' hands. We are not witnesses to these things.

But we are, my friends. We know of how the church has remained steadfast in its worship of God and love of neighbor for centuries. We have witnessed people turning to God, not for any self-serving reasons but because they felt touched by God. We have seen our abundance turned into gifts overflowing for others. We have seen the power of words, even the simple utterance of "I forgive you" reshaping lives and bringing wholeness to our shared humanity. We have seen utter despair – as experienced by victims of disasters or those who have lost jobs – turned into hope because good people have dared to share something of themselves. And from all this, we have seen new life emerge, one in which the gift of faith showers new joys.

Oh, I'm not saying any of this is easy or comes easily. We have our doubts. We have our setbacks. Much is expected of us and we still stumble. But as we are sent down from the mountainside, we carry a promise. Christ promises to be with us, not just here in this holy place but into all the world.

– Y. Franklin Ishida

Hymns
Opening: A Hymn of Glory Let Us Sing
Sermon: Alleluia! Sing to Jesus
Closing: A Hymn of Glory Let Us Sing

May 12, 2013

7th Sunday of Easter

Lessons

Semi-continuous (SC)	Roman Catholic (RC)
Acts 16:16-34	Acts 7:55-60
Ps 97	Ps 97:1-2, 6-7, 9
Rev 22:12-14, 16-17, 20-21	Rev 22:12-14, 16-17, 20
Jn 17:20-26	Jn 17:20-26

Speaker's Introduction for the Lessons

Lesson 1

Acts 16:16-34 (SC)

Everywhere it is preached, the gospel upsets the status quo. People complain, and Paul and Silas are imprisoned. But even in prison, the status quo is upset.

Acts 7:55-60 (RC)

Despite conspiracies against him, Stephen proclaims the good news with increased fervor. He becomes the first martyr among the followers of Jesus Christ, with many more to come.

Lesson 2

Psalm 97 (SC); Psalm 97:1-2, 6-7, 9 (RC)

The psalmist affirms God as sovereign and invites all creation to celebrate God's justice and deliverance.

Lesson 3

Revelation 22:12-14, 16-17, 20-21 (SC); Revelation 22:12-14, 16-17, 20 (RC)

Even in times yet to come, Christ proclaims that he is both the beginning and the end. Therefore, Christ's promise to come again becomes a comfort because he was, he is, and he is to come.

jail). Comment that today's story is about two followers of Jesus who were thrown into jail for helping someone.

Tell the story of Paul and Silas and their adventures in prison. Invite the children to mime the actions or stamp their feet to create an earthquake. Discuss what must it have been like for Paul and Silas to get into trouble for helping someone. Talk briefly about some of the unpopular and risky things other followers of Jesus have done to help others. If possible refer to things that have happened in your own area.

Pray with the children, asking God to help all those who take risks in order to help others.

The Sermon: Prayer, Suffering, and Cutting Corners
Scripture: Acts 16:16-34

Prayers learned in childhood have a way of slipping in and out of consciousness in later life. Their remembrance may be triggered by a word or an idea, or perhaps even a feeling. Such a prayer came to mind in the fashioning of this sermon. I can no longer recall the specifics of when or why it was learned, although I vaguely recollect it had to do with my confirmation instruction. It is a very simple prayer, at least in length. As far as content, however, it runs deceptively deep. The prayer goes as follows: "Lord Jesus: for thee I live, for thee I suffer, for thee I die."

Some might hear that as a rather curious prayer to be teaching children or youth. After all, we don't want them associating the church or Jesus with suffering or dying. They might not want to come back to church, or they might end up going to those places where you just hear the good and happy things about faith. Well, there is some truth to that – but on balance, the kind of faith we teach our children tends to be the kind of faith they possess as adults. It's a bit like what happens with the "inheritance" of religious musical preferences. My home church had a huge Sunday school program with its own youth hymnal. It contained a lot of gospel choruses that were considered, rightly or wrongly, easier to sing. Some of us couldn't wait to "graduate" to church so that we could sing out of the "real" hymnal. A lot of the kids, however, attended only Sunday school and never went to church. So they grew up assuming the choruses of the Sunday school were the be-all and end-all of religious music – and, perhaps, that the theology chorused therein was as far and as deep as it got. Care needs to be taken in passing on faith's music as well as its message, lest we create a generation semi-illiterate of the gospel's wholeness.

"Lord Jesus: for thee I live, for thee I suffer, for thee I die."

I hear in that prayer a recovery of some of the wholeness that has been lost in a time when too much of faith's focus has been centered on "what's in it for me." What have I got to gain by being faithful, or entering this or that Christian fellowship? Will I be healthier, will I be wealthier, will I be friendlier, will I be safer? *The Prayer of Jabbok,* for many in this past decade, became just such an association of believing right with living well. From the perspective of this prayer taught to children, those issues are not wrong because they are unreal or even undesirable, but because their starting point is misdirected. For the Christian faith's "magnetic north" is not self-concern, but Christ-concern. For *thee* I live, for *thee* I suffer, for *thee* I die. We start out by entrusting out lives and destinies to God in the trust of gracious love, not by striking a deal on what is most beneficial to me and mine.

Yet another part of the balance and wholeness of faith this prayer would bring to individuals and communities of faith in our day and age is the hard recognition that faith does not always come without cost. This prayer is not just about commitment when we are "living": that is, when things are going well and health is strong and security is assured. "For thee I *suffer*, for thee I *die*." Faith in and relationship with Jesus Christ remain one of those few things worthy of paying the supreme price for – and worthy of holding on to when all else is collapsing around us. Paul and Silas, the central characters in our text from Acts this morning, time and again placed their lives in jeopardy solely for the sake of the gospel. This morning's narrative of beating and torture and imprisonment bring them to the brink of losing their lives. It is not like such things ended with the closing of the biblical testimony or even the eventual acceptance of Christianity as a legitimate religion in the Roman Empire. Even the sketchiest of knowledge about the expansion of the church and the proclamation of the gospel in the centuries since then, including our own, shows that this prayer has been tested and experienced to its ultimate degree. People *have* suffered, people *have* died, simply for the sake of bearing Christ's name.

Such experiences can cause problems for all the rest of us who have never found ourselves before an inquisitioner, much less an executioner. As a result, we might be led to question the depth of our own faith. For if it is something I am to be ready to suffer and even die for, does a lack of such suffering or dying for its sake make my faith any less genuine or valid than the martyrs? My answer to that is no. Nowhere in the biblical materials or church traditions do I hear us encouraged to seek out suffering and death as proof of our sincerity. The book of Acts tells no story that comes to my mind of the apostles deliberately bringing suffering upon themselves in order to validate their faith. Their call, as our call, is to proclaim and live the gospel in whatever circumstances we find ourselves in. Indeed, Paul advises his young friend Timothy to pray that "we may lead a quiet and peaceable life" (1 Tim 2:2). So unlike those who beat themselves on the back as an expression of devotion, or who routinely deny themselves the simple gifts of food and shelter as a red badge of discipleship: we are not called to self-inflict the "cost" of our faith.

Yet, neither are we to run from such cost. And this brings up a second part to the problem of not experiencing the extreme costs of faith. For if we prepare only for the worst, we might not be ready for all the little costs that faith might be called to endure in the meantime. Peter was ready to go to the cross and offer up his own life with his Lord. But when it came down to a simple admission of truth in difficult circumstances, Peter chose to lie in order to save his own skin, not once but three times. In our text from Acts, the owners of the fortune-telling slave girl were willing to let her ply her trade nearby Paul and Silas. They didn't even stop her when her soothsaying led her to acclaim the two evangelists as servants of God. However, when Paul and Silas exorcise the spirit that possessed the girl, that's when things hit the fan. Her owners did not rejoice in her healing. They could only see it as a loss in profit, and for them the price of the gospel was too high in dollars to pay. In the freeing of their slave girl, the owners were not being challenged by the gospel to pay the supreme sacrifice – only to find a new way of augmenting their income. And they refused . . . and in their refusal, Paul and Silas very nearly end up dead.

The lesson in that for me goes back to the prayer – and the truth that the "suffering and dying" spoken of need not and most often *are* not experienced by us in the extreme. I have never in my life come close to being in a position of dying for what I believe. There have been times, however, where cutting a corner has been very appealing – too appealing, if the truth be told. Times where lashing back at someone in anger would have been, and sometimes was, my first choice. Times where a relationship stood to be adversely affected if I stood fast to my beliefs not just as a minister but simply as a Christian – and I chose, like Peter, the path of least resistance. One always wonders about the readiness to put one's life on the line if called to, for Christ and church. And yet for me, and I suspect for most of you, that is not where the real test comes. The real test of our faith's integrity comes in all the little moments, where what is at stake is not a lot of suffering – but just enough to make us uncomfortable, small enough that we think our choice of unfaith might be so minor and small as to be unimportant or go unseen.

But how does Christ understand the order of things to be? "He who is faithful in a very little is faithful also in much; and he who is dishonest in a very little is dishonest also in much." You see, the gospel has a way of turning things around, if not upside-down. For when we are worried about how we might someday do with the "big test," the "supreme sacrfice," and how that will reveal the kind of persons we really are, Christ's concern is with the daily and mundane choices. For in them, our character is more frequently if not more truly revealed than in the once-in-a-lifetime crises that may never come.

"Lord Jesus, for thee I live, for thee I suffer, for thee I die."

A common prayer, pointing us to an uncommon life. May it be a prayer illuminating every day of our lives. A prayer calling us to faith, even and especially when faith starts to cost: no matter how much, no matter how little. Lord Jesus, for thee. Amen.

– John Indermark

Hymns
Opening: When in Our Music God Is Glorified
Sermon: All Are Welcome
Closing: Take the Name of Jesus with You

past. Interdependence was necessary for the sake of survival. One may have been strong, but one needed others to live. Community was important above anything else.

Today, we identify individualism as the norm. Note the shift in emphasis in magazine titles. There was *Life;* then came *People,* then *Self.* We now have *Me.* There is a trend here, from a broader look at life to a self-centered outlook on life. We've arrived at a strange oxymoron: to be self-centered and to have an outlook on life. One has to wonder about the difference between self-esteem and self-centeredness, between self-confidence and self-help. No wonder we have a confused society in which we need to "find ourselves" by helping ourselves.

We have a popular media that does so well in taking this "self" business as a self-help matter. It sells by convincing people that they can find their own way by doing it their own way. The message to each of us is strong: You don't have to learn things from teachers, mentors, or even parents; you can do it yourself. Watch an infomercial and buy equipment touted to build up your body. Get a few books to help yourself do everything from a home makeover to a self-makeover. And if things seem too complicated, there are plenty of "Dummy" guidebooks. I do wonder which came first, general observations toward this introspection to self or a media that encourages it. Maybe it's both.

The media of the Bible tells us an old story. Way before Easter and Pentecost are two events. The serpent in the garden placed in the minds of our first parents the idea of self-centeredness. "You will be like God, knowing good and evil," said the serpent as he tempted them with the fruit of the tree. "You can help yourself know good and evil, you can be free to make your own determination. God placed the tree at the center of the garden, and now you can place yourself at the center."

There was probably some hope for humankind as God, even through punishment, protected and blessed life. But humankind could not escape a sense of self-centeredness: "Let us make a name for ourselves," they declare (Gen 11:4) as they proceed to build the tower of Babel.

There is a pattern here to what we know as sin – self-centeredness replacing God; self-help taking a front seat to trust in God; pride getting in the way of community. We don't want other powers in our lives; we'd rather do it our way. The consequences of this mindset can be devastating.

This side of Easter and Pentecost is a different story. God has already entered the picture, in person. From the quiet village of Bethlehem to the crowds on the hillsides of Galilee; from the individuals seeking healing to the masses seeking good words; the world has witnessed Immanuel, God with us.

On the cross, God suffered with us and died with us in our sins. Easter marks the ultimate breaking in of God into our lives, breaking in with the new life of the resurrection. And now, with that resurrected life, we have a further realization of Immanuel, God with us. God is now realized in the Spirit who remains with the disciples forever.

Self-centeredness is turned into life in Christ as we are sealed by that Spirit and marked with the cross of Christ forever. Self-help is turned into the interdependent spirit of the Christian community, a community that joins together in communion and service.

This comes with a promise. Jesus departed from his disciples with the promise to be with them through the Holy Spirit. And this was the power that would propel them as witnesses in "Jerusalem, in all Judea and Samaria, and to the ends of the earth" (Acts 1:8). As opposed to the self-centeredness and self-help that came in the garden of Eden and moved to the tower of Babel, the Spirit frees us to life and unity with God and one another. The Spirit is with us, in us, in this. By this we are made holy.

Certainly we can believe in ourselves. But believe in yourself as one marked with the cross. And not just any cross, but the empty cross that frees you to be the one God created you to be.

– Y. Franklin Ishida

Hymns
Opening: Gracious Spirit, Heed Our Pleading *(Njoo kwetu, Roho mwema)*
Sermon: Send Down the Fire
Closing: Spirit, Spirit of Gentleness

May 26, 2013

Trinity Sunday

Lessons

Semi-continuous (SC)	Roman Catholic (RC)
Prov 8:1-4, 22-31	Prov 8:22-31
Ps 8	Ps 8:4-5, 6-7, 8-9
Rom 5:1-5	Rom 5:1-5
Jn 16:12-15	Jn 16:12-15

Speaker's Introduction for the Lessons
Lesson 1
Proverbs 8:1-4, 22-31 (SC); Proverbs 8:22-31 (RC)

While we can point to the power and life-giving Spirit of God at work in creation, it comes down to God's wisdom even "thinking" of creation, putting everything in its right place.

Lesson 2
Psalm 8 (SC); Psalm 8:4-5, 6-7, 8-9 (RC)

The psalmist celebrates God's majesty and work in creation, while also affirming the value of humankind in the eyes of God.

Lesson 3
Romans 5:1-5 (SC/RC)

Though always undeserving, we are made right again in God's sight by faith. The Holy Spirit gives us the wisdom to understand God's unconditional love for us.

Gospel
John 16:12-15 (SC/RC)

The complete truth comes not with Christ alone but as the Spirit enters our lives as the promised advocate.

Theme

The gift of the Trinity is one that surpasses all wonders.

Thought for the Day

Three-ness, threefold-ness, three persons, three-in-one and one-in-three . . . no matter how we do it, the Trinity cannot be captured well. But then, can we ever capture God?

Sermon Summary

While the Trinity is a doctrine, it is also a way of seeing God at work in and through us. This truth is given to us as a gift.

Call to Worship

> One: Praise God the creator of all.
> **All: We sing God's praise this day!**
> One: Praise Christ the redeemer of all.
> **All: We sing as Christ's servants this day!**
> One: Praise Holy Spirit who breathes life into all creation.
> **All: We sing of Spirit's presence and power in all of life.**

Pastoral Prayer

Almighty and eternal God, you have revealed yourself as Father, Son, and Holy Spirit. You live and reign in the perfect unity of love, embracing us with your grace. Hold us firm in this faith, so that we may know you in all your ways. Enlighten us to your truth, so that we may witness to your eternal glory. Keep us in your holiness, so that we may glow with your love. For all this, we give you thanks. Amen.

Prayer of Confession

Almighty God, who created the world and deemed it good: we confess our failure in being wise stewards. You have given us the bounty of the earth, and we have plundered it. You have gifted us with wholeness, and we have fragmented this gift.

Lord Jesus Christ, who showed the world mercy even unto death: we confess that we do not follow in your path of love and forgiveness. You have shown us compassion, but we have offered poor imitations in our daily living. You have given us yourself as a new covenant, but we have relied on our own gods.

O Holy Spirit, who continues to descend upon us: we confess that we are more often ablaze with other passions. You bring unity to your church, but we are confused over even small things. You have given us wisdom, but we have been content with convenience.

Grant us your forgiveness. Amen.

Prayer of Dedication of Gifts and Self

With these gifts we give of ourselves to the world you have created, to the love you have poured out, and to the work of your holy church. Grant us your mercy that we may be strengthened to walk in your ways, even as you walk with us. Amen.

Hymn of the Day
Maker, in Whom We Live

This hymn first appeared with the title "To the Trinity" in Charles Wesley's 1747 publication, *Hymns for Those That Seek and Those That Have Redemption in the Blood of Jesus Christ.* Stanzas one, two, and three address the three persons of the Trinity. Stanza four emphasizes the undivided Trinity. The tune most generally used with this text is DIADEMATA, written by George J. Elvey in 1868. Since most congregations probably will know this tune, as used with the hymn "Crown Him with Many Crowns," it will be easier to introduce this valuable hymn of the Trinity, should it be new to the congregation.

Children's Time: Three and One

(Bring three taper or birthday candles and some rubber bands. If possible the candles should be different colors, but the same length.)

Comment that today is Trinity Sunday, a day to celebrate the three ways we know God.

Explain that the word *Trinity* comes from two Latin words. *Tri* means "three" and *unity* means "one;" the word *Trinity* means "three and one."

Hold the candles up one at a time and count them. Then put the candles together in a bundle and secure with rubber bands, with all the wicks on one end. Light the candles and comment that you now have a kind of trinity – three separate candles and one flame.

Point to each candle in turn and explain how we know God as Father, a loving parent who made and loves us; as Jesus, God's Son who came to show us God's love and God's way; and the Holy Spirit, who helps us to learn about God. Comment that we have three ways of encountering God, (point to each candle) and one God (point to the flame).

Pray with the children, giving thanks for the mystery of the Trinity.

The Sermon: Bound to the Trinity
Scripture: John 16:12-15

I once received an unsolicited email from someone in southeastern Asia. This person was struggling with faith, trying to comprehend the various religious teachings he was hearing. Specifically, he was torn between Islam and Christianity. To him, Islam made more sense; it seemed more straightforward, simpler perhaps. But he admitted he was trying to comprehend the whole notion of the Trinity. It was something that attracted him, though he was not sure what to make of it. How do you explain the doctrine of the Holy Trinity in an email response?

We know that over the years, books, treatises, lectures – whole lives – have been devoted to contemplating the Trinity. St. Patrick, for example, expounded on the Trinity, in part to highlight the different kind of God we have as opposed to the varied beliefs he countered. Patrick considered the Trinity an evangelizing tool, something to which he felt "bound" and that he could proclaim. He saw God at work through the Trinity.

Likewise, we are bound even as we continue to proclaim the faith of the church, the faith into which we were baptized. We bind ourselves as we recall our baptism. We bind ourselves every time we repeat the historic words of the Apostles' Creed or Nicene Creed. We bind ourselves as we gather in unity around the Lord's table. Unfortunately, in our haste at times to "get through" the liturgy, proclaiming our faith too often becomes just words and repeated motions.

Live it, though. Feel the life that flows from the living God, a God that surrounds us with creative power and redeeming love as we are made God's holy people. God lives in us as we live in God.

It is my hope that we can see the Holy Trinity as something that is lived. The Trinity is God living in us, and our living in God. The creative power of God, the grace-filled redeeming work of God, and the life-giving Spirit flow around us. We, as created beings, live in this grace – God in us and we in God.

The truth can seem pretty simple, but is it? We live in a created world filled with ungodly things. Famine, disasters, wars, hatred – is this the kind of world God has created for us? And what have we done about this creation as we plunder the goodness that has been entrusted to us?

Then we have humankind, more often bent on retribution than justice, hatred than forgiveness, destruction than building up. Can we truthfully say that Christ lives in us? Despite the preciousness of life that we proclaim, we live in a world where despair and hopelessness prevail in the midst of both abundance and want. Where is the Spirit of life?

There is a *Peanuts* comic strip showing Lucy walking with a sign that reads, "Jesus is the answer." Along comes Snoopy with his own sign: "What's the question?" Indeed, what is the question? The question is whether we can see God in our world, whether we can see the Trinity at work in our world and in us. The question is how to struggle with the many questions we have before us about God, about human life, about reality, about truth.

As we live in this world, there are times when we wonder whether there is a God who is almighty, loving, forgiving. Where was God in the midst of the genocide in Rwanda? Where was God as Hurricane Katrina blasted its way through Louisiana and Mississippi? Where was God in the tsunami that swept over Japan? And where is God as we struggle with issues of sexuality? Where is God as we struggle with matters of racism, sexism, classism, and all the other "-isms"?

I know it often is overused and sometimes even misused, but you probably are familiar with the poem "Footprints in the Sand" by Mary Stevenson. After walking in the sand with God, the speaker in the poem talks about seeing only one set of footprints in those moments of life that seem the lowest and saddest. God's response is that those are the times in which God carries us.

Yes, God does carry us and lives in us in so many ways. God does guide the thoughts in the compassionate words of caregivers. God does give strength to the hands of the emergency workers following disasters. God's hands are at work through the gifts of compassion shown to those who suffer. God's eyes do guide us to see the human face and soul in people around us.

When we were baptized, we put on Christ. Certainly baptism is a washing of sins. Certainly baptism regenerates us into new life. And certainly baptism makes us members of the body of Christ. We have put on Christ and we become one with Christ. As we are baptized in the name of the Father, Son, and Holy Spirit, God lives in us; the Trinity lives in us.

Living in the Trinity, we are on a mission. We are baptized into a journey. God's mission for the sake of the world becomes our journey. God walks with us as we live this life. Yes, there will be times when we stumble. There will be times when we fall back. There will certainly be times when we doubt and stray from the path. But if we look where we're going, we'll know that it's not a solitary journey.

This is what I told my email inquirer: I can walk with trust in a God who comes to me and lives in me no matter what. God's life-giving power inspires me to new life. God's redeeming love frees me to live a life of wholeness. God's Spirit burns within me, giving me a passion for life. God the Father is the answer – only through the Father do we have life. God the Son, Jesus, is the answer – only through Christ can we live free from the bondage to sin. God the Spirit is the answer – only in the Spirit do we know the truth of the world around us.

May you remember that you are sealed with the Father, Son, and Holy Spirit. Amen.

– Y. Franklin Ishida

Hymns
Opening: All Creatures of Our God and King
Sermon: All Glory Be to God on High
Closing: Blessed Be the Name

June 2, 2013

2nd Sunday after Pentecost (Proper 4 [9])
RC/Pres: 9th Sunday in Ordinary Time

Lessons

Semi-continuous (SC)	Complementary (C)	Roman Catholic (RC)
1 Kings 18:20-21 (22-29), 30-39	1 Kings 8:22-23, 41-43	1 Kings 8:41-43
Ps 96	Ps 96:1-9	Ps 117:1-2
Gal 1:1-12	Gal 1:1-12	Gal 1:1-2, 6-10
Lk 7:1-10	Lk 7:1-10	Lk 7:1-10

Speaker's Introduction for the Lessons
Lesson 1
1 Kings 18:20-21 (22-29), 30-39 (SC)
Elijah engages in a "contest" with the prophets of Baal to challenge Israel to choose the God they will serve.
1 Kings 8:22-23, 41-43 (C); 1 Kings 8:41-43 (RC)
Solomon prays at the dedication of the temple for God to hear the prayers of foreigners who come there to worship.

Lesson 2
Psalm 96 (SC); Psalm 96:1-9 (C)
The psalmist bids Israel to sing a new song to God in a psalm associated with God's enthronement as sovereign over all.
Psalm 117:1-2 (RC)
This shortest of all psalms summons praise for God's steadfast love and faithfulness.

Lesson 3
Galatians 1:1-12 (SC/C); Galatians 1:1-2, 6-10 (RC)
Paul opens his letter to the Galatian community with an open challenge to their desertion of the gospel instigated by teachers who seek to confuse them.

Gospel
Luke 7:1-10 (SC/C/RC)

> Jesus heals the servant of a centurion, an officer in Rome's occupation forces and likely a Gentile.

Theme

Sing a new song to God.

Thought for the Day

The praise that articulates this good news of [God's] enthronement is a "new song."

— Walter Brueggemann

Sermon Summary

Psalm 96 invites praise, witness, and service of God in language as inclusive as God's saving works proclaimed here. The "new" of the "new song" is not that God has changed but that we must constantly discern and celebrate God's often unexpected work in this day as in days past.

Call to Worship

> One: We gather here to praise God
> **All: For God's steadfast love and faithfulness.**
> One: We prepare here to serve God
> **All: By opening ourselves to Spirit's fashioning of our love and faithfulness.**

Pastoral Prayer

Loving God, we are grateful for the gift of this day entrusted into our hands. Help us within its opportunities and responsibilities to love as we have been loved. Remember those who walk through places shadowed with grief and death. May they find light and peace on that way. Be with those in need of strength and healing, and enable us as we are able to serve as your instruments of healing and support in their lives. Stand with those who feel alone. Guide your church that you might be the body of Christ not simply in what we say about you or about ourselves, but in the trust we keep and the compassion we exercise and the love we embody. This we would pray in the name of Christ. Amen.

Prayer of Confession

God, it is so easy to fall into ruts. To assume there is nothing new under the sun, to presume that faithfulness is simply holding to what has been. God of grace and surprise, move among us in ways old and new, in traditions that continue to grow and in change that does not forget. We need your guidance as well as your forgiveness. So walk with us now, and direct our steps in the paths you would have us take. In Jesus Christ. Amen.

Prayer of Dedication of Gifts and Self

Holy God, you open your hands wide to us: in providence, in grace, in hope. Unclench our fists, that our hands too might open to others: with gifts that provide, with forgiveness that extends grace, with support that brings hope. Use the gifts our hands place into this congregation's keeping today in such purposes – and use us to that same good and gracious ends. In Jesus Christ. Amen.

Hymn of the Day
I Was There to Hear Your Borning Cry

John Ylvisaker composed the music and wrote the lyrics for this relatively "new song" that now appears in several denominational hymnals. It celebrates God's presence at every stage and of our lives. Its closing affirmation in the imagery of the time of dying that God will have "one more surprise" ties subtly yet powerfully into Psalm 96's affirmation of the "new song" of God's saving presence in all creation and in our lives.

Children's Time: Nicodemus Drama

Singing to God

(Be prepared to teach the children a new song, with words written large on a sheet of newsprint – or arrange for a music person to be prepared to teach the new song to the children).

Welcome the children. Ask them to share the title of a favorite song. Say: do you like to just hear this song, or do you like to sing it? Invite children to say what they like about singing.

Ask children if they know a song from Sunday school or church, and if so, what it is. Give examples of songs you learned as a child in church (for example: "Jesus Loves Me"). Affirm it's good not only to have songs we all know, but that it's also good to learn new songs. Teach, or invite the volunteer, to teach the children (and maybe the congregation!) a new song. Say, isn't it great now that we have a new song to sing to God?

Offer a prayer that thanks God for songs old and new, and for the way that old and new help us to celebrate God's love for us and for all.

The Sermon: Sing a New Song
Scripture: Psalm 96

Scripture perpetuates words and ways of speaking about God: in stories, in genealogies, in teachings, in songs. At various times in history, Judaism and then Christianity made decisions about what words and ways of speaking about God would be designated as scripture, and what would not. For Judaism near the time of Christ, rabbis debated what books should be added to the Law and the Prophets – resulting in that portion of the Old Testament we call the "Writings." In third and fourth century Christianity, the great councils of the church settled on which gospels and epistles ought to be judged as the "canon" or norm of scripture. At each of those junctures, however, an important consideration always involved discerning how God spoke or revealed himself in new ways. In the first century AD, the Law and the Prophets were not enough for Judaism. New words and understandings and revelations of God rooted in Israel's experiences following the exile and returning to the land needed inclusion. For the church, the Hebrew Scriptures were not enough. New words and understandings and revelations of God rooted in Christ's life and ministry and church needed inclusion. Or, to put it in the language of our psalms this morning, new songs needed to be sung.

Particular settings in life often generate a language peculiar to them. Words employed in a surgical waiting room will vary from words shouted in the bleachers of a baseball park or whispered in the reception area of a mortuary. Certain words and ways of speaking come to have associations with those settings – which is well and good, until those words and ways become jargon, repeated from generation to generation, with little or no understanding of what they mean or why we even use them, save "that is what we have always said here." "These are our traditions" can be little more than a pious way of saying "these are our ingrained habits." Psalm 96 brings a critical word to such attitudes and lines in the sand: new songs need to be sung.

Listen for a moment to the verbs and nouns employed, some of them repeatedly, through Psalm 96: bless, ascribe, sing, song, salvation, revere, sanctuary, rejoice, exult. When we enter into the language of this psalm, we do so largely with the vocabulary of praise. Speak aloud the opening two verses of the psalm: it reads and sounds like a call to worship or the encouraging of a choir director in preparation for leading music.

The praise in this psalm has traditionally been associated, at least in its origin, with ceremonies related to enthronement or coronation, either for a new king or in a yearly renewal of covenant to God as sovereign. In more recent times, Psalm 96 has become incorporated by the lectionary not only into the readings of this Sunday in so-called Ordinary Time but also it is the designated psalm for Christmas Eve, celebrating the new song God sang in Bethlehem, the salvation chorus ringing in the night sky and enfleshed in the stable.

There is another vocabulary at work in this psalm. It is a use of language that makes clear the psalmist addresses the broadest audience possible: "peoples," "nations," "earth" occur repeatedly. And so does a tiny three-letter word: "all." The psalmist summons "all the earth" to sing to God. "All the peoples" are called to declare God's works. The psalmist bids rejoicing from "all" that fills the sea and "all the trees." Why? For God is "above all gods."

Psalm 96 does not offer a parochial vision of what it means for one people or community to engage in relationship with and praise of God. The psalmist invokes a new song, one that sings the promise of God's universal realm and sovereignty – and of the place given to all peoples and all nations in all the earth. Some might see this expansive inclusivity as part of what is new in the new song. In truth, however, the psalmist's all-encompassing vision traces back to the ancient covenant with Abraham: "In you all the families of the earth shall be blessed" (Gen 12:3).

God not only makes room for all. God also makes it an imperative that we share in that welcoming and "homecoming" for all in the presence of God who created all. Psalm 96:2 speaks of our telling God's salvation. The Hebrew verb translated as telling is *basar,* the equivalent of the New

Testament Greek word *euaggelion:* "to tell good news." *Basar* appears with frequency in Isaiah 40-55, where the telling of the promised release from exile intends to stir and renew Israel's faith – and her following of God in new ways. To be a singer of this new song is to be an evangelist, which is simply a fancy word for someone who does not hide light under a bushel. If at times the songs of God's works are new to us or others, it is because God comes revealed in new ways or by unconsidered actions. And not just in our time. We sometimes forget that the "old songs" of our faith that seem so familiar to us were at one time startling if not a bit off-putting to an earlier day's "conventional wisdom." In times of old, who would have expected waters to part or exiles to return – or the very incarnation of God to come birthed in a stable shared with livestock? God consistently acts in new and unexpected ways, and God's people are moved to add new songs to our repertoire of witness and celebration.

Now I know: we love to sing the familiar songs of faith, literally and figuratively. And that would be all we ever had to do if God had stopped speaking and working two thousand years ago. We could keep doing what we have always done, singing what we have always sung, being among those we have always been among. But God keeps springing up in new ways and among new ones, urging us to sing new songs: songs of mission and ministry, songs of justice and compassion, and yes, even songs new to our worship. Our spirits need to be open to the new songs that emerge from God's fresh actions among us: taken for the sake of creation and re-demption, as always, but actions that may take new directions – and may take *us* new directions.

Do we want to do that kicking and screaming, digging in our heels, holding our breath until we turn beet red so we can keep things the way they are . . . at least in our memory? Or do we want to "sing to the Lord a new song; sing to the Lord, all the earth"? There's that word "all" again. How will God work to bring all nations and all peoples into the choir? Faith does not take a "wait and see" attitude. Faith takes a "come and serve" – or should one say, "come and sing" – attitude. For the God who made the heavens and earth continues to recreate them. And thanks be to God for inviting us to lend our voices to the new songs as well as the old.

– John Indermark

Hymns
Opening: Gather Us In
Sermon: O Christ the Healer, We Have Come
Closing: Earth and All Stars

June 9, 2013

3rd Sunday after Pentecost (Proper 5 [10])
RC/Pres: 10th Sunday in Ordinary Time

Lessons

Semi-continuous (SC)	Complementary (C)	Roman Catholic (RC)
1 Kings 17:8-16 (17-24)	1 Kings 17:17-24	1 Kings 17:17-24
Ps 146	Ps 30	Ps 30:2, 4-6, 11-13
Gal 1:11-24	Gal 1:11-24	Gal 1:11-19
Lk 7:11-17	Lk 7:11-17	Lk 7:11-17

Speaker's Introduction for the Lessons
Lesson 1
1 Kings 17:8-16 (17-24) (SC); 1 Kings 17:17-24 (C/RC)

God sends Elijah to Sidon, which is Gentile territory, and Elijah initiates a miracle. Later, Jesus uses this story to illustrate the faith of those that Israel views as pagans (Lk 4:25-26).

Lesson 2
Psalm 146 (SC)

The psalmist praises God for creation and justice and watchful care over the vulnerable.

Psalm 30 (C); Psalm 30:2, 4-6, 11-13 (RC)

The psalmist offers praise for God's deliverance in a time of mortal danger that has transformed mourning into dancing, sorrow into joy.

Lesson 3
Galatians 1:11-24 (SC/C); Galatians 1:11-19 (RC)

This passage contains part of Paul's defense of his apostolic calling. Paul emphasizes that his call is of divine, not human, origin.

Gospel

Luke 7:11-17 (SC/C/RC)

Luke's story of the raising of the widow's son at Nain has no counterpart in the other Synoptic Gospels. In some respects, however, it is an echo of the story of Elijah in Sidon (1 Kings 17).

Theme

Faith does not deny death but embraces life in God.

Thought for the Day

By virtue of the Resurrection, nothing any longer kills inevitably but everything is capable of becoming the blessed touch of the divine hands.

– P. Teilhard de Chardin

Sermon Summary

In raising a man from death, Jesus demonstrates that the God we worship is a God of life and love.

Call to Worship

One: Praise the Lord, O my soul!

All: I will praise God as long as I live; I will sing praises to my God all my life long.

One: Do not put your trust in princes, in mortals, in whom there is no help.

All: When their breath departs, they return to the earth;

One: Happy are those whose help is the God of Jacob, whose hope is in the God who keeps faith forever; who executes justice for the oppressed; who gives food to the hungry.

All: God will reign forever. Praise the Lord!

Pastoral Prayer

God of Life, you conceive of us even before our parents know of our existence. You knit us together in our mothers' wombs and fill us with life and possibility. When we are born, you give us days to live, people to love, work to do, and the opportunity to become what you have dreamed us to be. Yet, through all the days of our lives, there is a shadow that hangs over us. Though we may be filled with breath, we know that one day it will be extinguished. Even though we understand death to be a part of life, O God, we fear it and do all we can to avoid it. Take away, loving God, our fear of dealing with death. Help us to see in it a natural completion and transition. And, help us to believe what you teach: that you are a God of life, that you love to bring new chances to those who have failed to live rightly, and that you bring new and everlasting breath to all who die in faith. Let us live in the sunlight of your love and fear not the shadow of death. We pray in the name of the one who brings new life, Jesus Christ our Lord. Amen.

Prayer of Confession
Holy One, help us when we fear death so much we end up fearing life. Raise us to take hope and courage in your presence, and then to act on the basis of our trust in you rather than our fears. In Jesus Christ. Amen.

Prayer of Dedication of Gifts and Self
Gracious God, we realize that sometimes love is as practical as sharing our time and our money for purposes that go beyond what makes life easier for us. We bring you these offerings, and ask that they might find their way in feeding the hungry in body and spirit and raising the hopes of those despairing or anxious – and bringing life to those who know all too well and near the power of death. Amen.

Hymn of the Day
At the Name of Jesus
Written by British poet Caroline Maria Noel in 1870, this hymn appeared in the enlarged edition of her book, *The Name of Jesus, and Other Verses for the Sick and Lonely.* Based on Philippians 2:5-11, the hymn is certainly not limited to being sung by "the sick and lonely." Used with the tune KING'S WESTON by Ralph Vaughan Williams, this hymn provides quite a powerful and triumphant statement of Christian faith, exalting the majestic name of Jesus Christ. By contrast, the more modern tune CAMBERWELL, written in 1960 by Michael Brierley, provides a more upbeat setting.

Children's Time: When We Are Sad

(Bring a bowl and some teardrops cut from paper.)

Show the teardrops and explain that they are tears. Scatter the tears on the floor and ask the children to name some of the things that make them sad. For each answer given, have a child pick up a tear shape and place it in the bowl. Express concern at the number of sad things the children have named. Observe that sometimes life can get very sad indeed. Comment that the Bible story today is about a time when Jesus met a woman who was very, very sad.

Tell the story about Jesus raising the woman's son. Emphasize the feelings of compassion Jesus had for the woman and her son. Comment that Jesus really cared about the sad widow and did something amazing to turn her sadness into joy. Observe that Jesus really cares about us, too. When life gets very sad for us we can know that Jesus is with us and that Jesus cares about our sad feelings. Comment that it really helps to have someone like Jesus around when we're sad.

Pray with the children, giving thanks for Jesus' loving presence with us.

The Sermon: Restoring the Natural Order of Things
Scripture: Luke 7:11-17

Perhaps the most avoided topic in our society is death. Though it occurs to every living person, we have gotten very good at isolating ourselves from it.

In an earlier age, death was understood to be a natural part of society. People were allowed to die at home, rather than in a nursing home or a hospital. After death, they were not sent off to a mortuary but kept home in bed and prepared there for visitation and burial. Once the bed had been vacated, it was put back into service for the living. How odd it would seem today to sleep in a bed that someone had died in.

People in less modernized cultures still deal with death the way we did in North America in a less antiseptic age. People of all ages come into contact with those who are sick and dying. Even children see the progression of life to death and become as familiar with it in people as they are with the deaths of house pets and farm animals.

Today, for most of us, death is kept at a distance. It usually occurs in isolated places where only specialists have to deal with it. Afterwards, when families prepare to make funeral arrangements, more specialists step in to maintain a margin of insulation around the grieving. Most of us have little to do with the death professionals. Undertakers, morticians, funeral directors: these terms – and occupations – make people nervous. One often thinks twice before shaking their hands, knowing what they have been up to in their embalming chambers. To lighten our uneasiness, we make pitiful jokes. A seminary classmate was studying for the ministry as a second career. To make money over the weekend, he would return to his first profession. He was a mortician and would do what he referred to as "quicky embalmings" for a short-staffed funeral home. "What do you do with the blood after you remove it from the body?" I once asked. "We bottle it and sell it to mosquitoes" was his practiced reply.

In Jesus' day, death was not so distant. The death rate in his day was no different than in ours: 100 percent of all people born eventually died. But, there were no professionals on hand to deal with death and burial. The body would be prepared for burial by the women (thus, the story of the women being the first at the tomb to discover the risen Jesus in Luke 23:55—24:11).

For Jesus and his large crowd of followers to encounter a funeral procession while traveling through the town of Nain would not have been in any way out of the ordinary. That Jesus would have had compassion on the mother of the dead man was also to be expected. She was a widow, and with the death of her son came a loss of income and all hope for future security. What certainly was unusual was what Jesus did when he approached the funeral bier. He spoke, "Young man, I say to you, arise." Immediately, the dead man was filled with new life. He sat up and spoke. That was not something anyone had seen happen before – nor have we since, despite the stories to the contrary that come out of Hollywood.

This episode in Luke forces us to think about death for a change. Most of the time, we can relegate death to the specialists and deal with it only as it becomes necessary. But, it is useful for people of faith to have a better relationship with things relating to death. This is true, in part, because the more familiar we are with something, the less fearful of it we will be. But, it is also true because faith is vitally about living and dying. They are inseparable. Denial of that fact is the enemy of both mental health and mature faith.

Jesus confronts death. In this story, he does not stop to worry about issues of ritual uncleanness. His compassion is stronger than religious piety. Jesus' compassion grows out of his concern for a woman whose social security program is being carried out on a funeral bier. More than an only son has died. Her own life is now in a desperate situation. The natural order of things was for the woman to give birth to a son who would care for her in her old age. She would die first, and later, his children would take care of him when he was too old to earn an income. The natural order of things was suspended in this story. Mothers should not have to bury their sons. Sons should bury their mothers. It was this imbalance that was altered by Jesus' entering the situation and loosening the grip that death had on this family.

Stories of children dying before their parents are also common in our age. The natural order of things used to allow for that to happen. Johann Sebastian Bach had 20 children by two wives. Only ten survived to adulthood. What nature took away in the form of untimely death, nature made accommodation for by the fruitfulness of human union. Today, we know how to have fewer children, and we plan to do so because most of them live. Still, tragedies occur. Every experienced pastor will be able to tell stories of the children buried under his or her pastoral watch.

What does the story of Jesus raising the man from Nain have to tell us about death upsetting the natural order of things? And, what does it have to tell us about God's relationship to the living?

This story, as the one in 1 Kings 17:17-24, points us to a powerful message of good news. Not only does the Gospel lesson make us confront the issue of death, it also engages us in consideration of life. The message of grace in both the Hebrew Scriptures and New Testament readings is that God is ultimately not interested in death. God is interested in bringing life, and new life to God's people. Giving life is the first, most important work that God does. It is, as Luther put it, God's "proper work." (God's "alien work" is to use death and the ungodly forces of the world to give evidence of God's proper work.) God first breathed the breath of life into creation in Genesis 1 (where a breath, that is, *ruach* or spirit, "from God swept over the face of the waters" [1:2]). God breathed into Adam the first breath of human life (Gen 2:7). And God breathed the Holy Spirit into the church at Pentecost (Acts 2:1-13). In the same manner, Jesus breathed new life into the young man of Nain by speaking the words, "Young man, I say to you, arise." The story indicates that bringing life is

369

what Jesus is about. He does not ignore death or seek insulation from it. He does not let the funeral procession pass by or demonstrate concerns about being among the unclean. Jesus sees death as the force contrary to God's will and acts to overcome it. In the end, his whole life will be about that one thing, overcoming the power of death and bringing new life. Jesus restores the natural order of things. He may not keep all children from dying before their parents, but he does restore the power of life over death, and the power of God over everything else in all creation.

– Clayton Schmit

Hymns
Opening: All Creatures of Our God and King
Sermon: It Is Well with My Soul
Closing: Abide with Me

June 16, 2013

4th Sunday after Pentecost (Proper 6 [11])
RC/Pres: 11th Sunday in Ordinary Time

Lessons

Semi-continuous (SC)	Complementary (C)	Roman Catholic (RC)
1 Kings 21:1-10 (11-14) 15-21a	2 Sam 11:26—12:10, 13-15	2 Sam 12:7-10, 13
Ps 5:1-8	Ps 32	Ps 32:1-2, 5, 7, 11
Gal 2:15-21	Gal 2:15-21	Gal 2:16, 19-21
Lk 7:36—8:3	Lk 7:36—8:3	Lk 7:36—8:3 or
		Lk 7:36-50

Speaker's Introduction for the Lessons
Lesson 1
1 Kings 21:1-10 (11-14) 15-21a (SC)

By remaining steadfast to his ancestral inheritance, Naboth unwittingly signs his death warrant. Jezebel plots a plan that thwarts the will of God for the faithful Naboth.

2 Samuel 11:26—12:10, 13-15 (C)

After his treachery against Uriah, David takes Bathsheba as his wife. Nathan's parable is a prelude to the harsh word the prophet delivers against King David.

2 Samuel 12:7-10, 13 (RC)

The prophet Nathan speaks a strong word of judgment against the king. This prophetic judgment illustrates that no one, not even the king, is above the law of the Lord.

Lesson 2
Psalm 5:1-8 (SC)

The psalmist lifts a prayer for God's deliverance that blends lament for those who deceive with trust in God who is trustworthy.

Psalm 32 (C); Psalm 32:1-2, 5, 7, 11 (RC)

One of the so-called penitential psalms, this song celebrates God's forgiveness while noting the debilitating effect of sin that goes unacknowledged.

Lesson 3
Galatians 2:15-21 (SC/C); Galatians 2:16, 19-21 (RC)

Paul shares his deepest theological conviction that God saves human beings by grace. We receive the gift of God's grace through faith in Jesus Christ. Thus, the law no longer has a hold on humankind.

Gospel
Luke 7:36—8:3 (SC/C/RC)

Hospitality to Jesus, the Anointed One of God, appears to take precedence over a person's past sins as Jesus forgives "a sinful woman" at a Pharisee's house.

Theme

Authentic Christians understand that real freedom comes in service.

Thought for the Day

If "the Son of Man came not to be served but to serve," then what better example can we have as followers of God's Messiah?

Sermon Summary

Paul writes to the Galatian churches about the matter of following Jewish ritual law. Paul urges these churches to remember that the only condition of their salvation is the fact that God has saved them by faith through grace. Faith in Christ is the solitary condition of salvation.

Call to Worship

One: Happy are those whose transgression is forgiven, whose sin is covered.

All: Happy are those to whom the Lord imputes no iniquity, and in whose spirit there is no deceit.

One: I acknowledge my sin to you, and I do not hide my iniquity;

All: We will confess our transgressions to the Lord, rejoicing that God forgives the guilt of sin.

Pastoral Prayer

God of everlasting peace, instill in each of us the deep desire for the grace you offer. As we gather to sing hymns of faith, help us recognize faithful ones who have not only sung these songs but also lived this faith. Let us take their faithful example as a pattern by which we, too, might be faithful. As we worship today may we join the voices of the faithful around the world and through the centuries in praise and promise. Thank you, O God, for the bounty of the earth's blessing. We pray our prayer of thanksgiving in the powerful and holy name of the one who came to give us life and give it to us in abundance, Jesus Christ. Amen.

Prayer of Confession

O God, you have freed us to be your people and we pray today that we might catch a glimpse of your promised guidance and home in you. Forgive us when we either have little inclination to follow the path you have given us or, worse, we see the path and in our fear we are reluctant to take it. We confess that we need more faith. To this end we pray that you will send us the Holy Spirit to inspire and empower us. Let us soak in the scripture and its story of salvation, so that we might be enriched by and become witnesses to your grace. In Jesus Christ. Amen.

Prayer of Dedication of Gifts and Self

As a community of faithful people, you have bestowed on us unimaginable riches and made us stewards of it all. You have placed your trust in us, O Lord of heaven and earth, and for this we are grateful. Help us manage this sacred trust; remind us that all creation belongs to you, and that you have offered it to us to use for a while. As we return today a portion of what is yours, bless both those who give and those who receive in Jesus' name. Amen.

Hymn of the Day
When Morning Gilds the Skies

The anonymous German text for this hymn appeared in *Katholisches Gesangbuch* in 1828. It was translated into English by Edward Caswall in 1854. Of course this hymn of praise is not just a morning hymn. It is well suited for any time we wish say, "Jesus Christ be praised!" It is an eternal song, as stanza four suggests, appropriate for all eras of history and people of all ages. An additional element of praise can be experienced when the hymn is sung in an antiphonal manner with the tune LAUDES DOMINI. A choir or soloist sings the first part of each line, and the congregation then responds, "May Jesus Christ be praised!"

Children's Time: Measuring God's Love

(Bring a measuring cup, a tape measure, some bathroom scales, and a watch.)
Ask the children to name each item. Explain that all these items are used to measure different things. If you want to measure time, you use a watch. If you want to measure how long or wide something is, you use a tape measure (measure the length of a child's arm). If you need to measure how heavy someone is, you stand on the bathroom scales (ask for volunteers to stand on the scales). If you need to measure the ingredients for a pie, you use a measuring cup.

Ask the children if you could use any of these things to measure God's love. Say that you think God's love is so amazing, so big, and so huge that it cannot be measured.

Recall that Paul was a leader in the early church who taught and wrote about God's love. Explain that part of his letter to the church in Galatia was about God's love for us. We can't do anything to earn God's love. God just loves us. Comment that this kind of love is too big to be measured.

Pray with the children, giving thanks for God's amazing love.

The Sermon: Freed in Christ – For What?
Scripture: Galatians 2:15-21

When my youngest son runs into a contentious person or hears an argument among adults, he sits back and with great solemnity announces, "These people have issues." What he is saying, of course, is that one or both of the parties in any argument have an agenda to push. Those who debate with passion are not disinterested persons in the discussion. To be more precise, verbal combatants advocate a strong point of view.

From our lesson today, it is clear that Paul has something that he wants to get off his chest. He writes to the Galatians. Those who know the Pauline letters understand that this audience is exceptional among all the recipients of Paul's letters. In every other case of an authentic Pauline epistle, Paul addresses his correspondence to a church, such as the church in Rome or Corinth. Where Paul does not write to an individual church, he writes to an individual person, such as the epistle to Philemon. So, who are "the Galatians" and why does Paul write to them in such strong language?

It would seem that the Galatians must be gentile Christians. They are apparently conversant with Jewish ritual practice and the Hebrew Scriptures, but it seems that the topic of circumcision is "up for discussion" in this church community. This theological business about circumcision was a major concern in the community (Gal 2:12; 5:6, 11; 6:15). The fact that these Gentiles understood Paul's nuanced argument about the circumcision rite suggests that they may have been gentile "God-fearers" on their way to becoming Christians, but also may have been contemplating participating in the Jewish faith and its rituals. In other words, "these people have issues."

Thus, the real issue in the Galatian churches is how Christians are to live within the faith. Are they to follow the Hebrew ritual law as Christians or are they freed from the strictures of the law? We might understand the issue of circumcision as a "code word" for what Paul understands as "a condition of salvation." Paul, of course, writes that "we have come to believe in Christ Jesus, so that we might be justified by faith in Christ, and not by doing the works of the law, because no one will be justified by the works of the law" (2:16).

This means that following certain Jewish rites – rites that Paul equates with "doing the works of the law"– does not bring salvation. However, Paul believes that God's grace through faith in Christ is what produces the change in a person's salvation status. Salvation comes, in other words, by faith apart from works of the law.

In every church that has ever existed, there are certain "obligations" for church membership. Some of these obligations are explicitly stated; other obligations are of a more implicit or assumed nature. For Paul, however, there is only one condition. This condition is that a person, or even a community of faith, receives the gift of salvation by faith in Christ.

Some years ago, I walked into a church to see the pastor. As I waited for him, I leafed through a brochure listing ten things a person must believe if he or she desires to be a member of this particular church. In a sense, this catalog was a laundry list of required beliefs for its members.

This catalog of approved beliefs included the church's theological position on matters such as abortion, marriage, and the virgin birth. Although the educational intent of the catalog itself was worthy, it veered from Paul's mantra that "a person is justified by faith apart from works prescribed by the law" (Rom 3:28). No matter the intention we have for adding this or that obligation to the foundational requirements of what makes a Christian and what does not, for Paul, Christ's work on our behalf is the solitary condition of salvation.

Paul never tells his readers that the law is a "bad thing." Yet, Paul is always quick to point out that "if justification comes through the law, then Christ died for nothing" (Gal 2:21). Thus, Christ's death set us free to be what God created us to be – fully human people who can choose to be servants of one another and the risen Christ.

How does one become a servant of another? Perhaps this is a question that takes a lifetime to discover. I suggest that one way to appropriate salvation by faith is to imagine that we may be the only person that another individual will encounter who can offer the promise of salvation. We have the occasion to offer Christ by way of imitating Christlike characteristics. For example, Paul wrote to the Philippian church about the "mind of Christ." Here some Christlike traits surface. Paul wrote that the mind of Christ included "taking the form of a slave" and humbling himself (Phil 2:7-8).

Clearly, Christ did things that none of us could ever or would ever want to do. But each of us can stoop to serve other people. We are free to be servants of others because Jesus Christ first stooped to be a servant to us by being "obedient to the point of death – even death on a cross" (Phil 2:8).

By being Christlike for others, we can offer the good news in non-threatening and nonmenacing ways. Rather than hand a person a laundry list of appropriate things to believe, we can offer ourselves as living witnesses of what a person with Jesus in her or his heart looks like. For people in today's world, this witness is as effective as it is faithful. After all, the invitation to the reign of God is never coercive or bullying. It is always a gracious invitation given in love. Amen.

– David Neil Mosser

Hymns
Opening: A Mighty Fortress Is Our God
Sermon: Thou Hidden Love of God
Closing: Take Up Thy Cross

June 23, 2013

5th Sunday after Pentecost (Proper 7 [12])
RC/Pres: 12th Sunday in Ordinary Time

Lessons

Semi-Continuous (SC)	**Complementary (C)**	**Roman Catholic (RC)**
1 Kings 19:1-4 (5-7) 8-15a	Isa 65:1-9	Zech 12:10-11
Ps 42 and 43	Ps 22:19-28	Ps 63:2, 3-4, 5-6, 8-9
Gal 3:23-29	Gal 3:23-29	Gal 3:26-29
Lk 8:26-39	Lk 8:26-39	Lk 9:18-24

Speaker's Introduction for the Lessons

Lesson 1
1 Kings 19:1-4 (5-7) 8-15a (SC)
Poor Elijah; after his clash with Jezebel he heads for the hills. Yet, God will not allow him to hide, but rather calls him back into service.

Isaiah 65:1-9 (C)
Grace means nothing if God does not offer it as an alternative to judgment. Israel has been idolatrous, and the prophet gives ample warning about the penalty God will exact eventually from the rebellious people.

Zechariah 12:10-11 (RC)
People in the most desperate circumstances cling to hope, and God, through the prophet, offers them this hope. Israel will be able to conquer because of God's power and not their own.

Lesson 2
Psalm 42 and 43 (SC)
Scholars view this as a single song of lament and trust, with the same structure employed in each psalm (three stanzas, concluded by a common refrain in 42:11 and 43:5).

Psalm 22:19-28 (C)
The psalmist's plea for help and deliverance flow into a song of praise for God's hearing and saving actions.

Psalm 63:2, 3-4, 5-6, 8-9 (RC)

Like Isaiah, the psalmist uses food imagery to speak of the nourishment God gives. Like water for a dry land, God refreshes the soul that thirsts for the divine presence. The psalmist is aware of God's presence night and day, and knows from life experience that God upholds, helps, shelters, and satisfies.

Lesson 3

Galatians 3:23-29 (SC/C); Galatians 3:26-29 (RC)

In this part of his epistle, Paul explains the advantage of faith over the law. Also, because of faith in Jesus Christ, all human distinctions now fade away.

Gospel

Luke 8:26-39 (SC/C)

Although people today use the word *demon* largely in an allegorical way, for people in Jesus' time demons were real. The casting out of demons was a sign of Jesus' identity.

Luke 9:18-24 (RC)

Jesus comes to give himself as a sacrifice and to call disciples to new life. The cost of discipleship will be great, but the realm of God is a place of salvation.

Theme

Christian unity: the point is not who we are, but whose we are.

Thought for the Day

Blessed be the tie that binds our hearts in Christian love; the fellowship of kindred minds is like to that above.

— John Fawcett, 1782

Sermon Summary

Christian unity is not a struggle for us to achieve against all odds some shallow uniformity. Unity in Christ is a gift already given for us to be used in humility and joy.

Call to Worship

> One: As a deer longs for flowing streams, so my soul longs for you, O God.
>
> **All: My soul thirsts for God, for the living God.**
>
> One: When shall I come and behold the face of God?
>
> **All: My tears have been my food day and night, while people say to me continually, "Where is your God?"**
>
> One: Why are you cast down, O my soul, and why are you disquieted within me?
>
> **All: Hope in God; for I shall again praise you, my help and my God.**

Pastoral Prayer

Almighty God, we gather as your people. We gather as those who live in hope. Our lives provide us many opportunities to speak words of peace and reconciliation, but often we have not the courage to do so. Make us bold not only to speak your word but also to live it. Remind us that it is by grace that we live and die. Keep the spirit of the gospel in front of us, so we are not tempted to fall back toward attempting to earn your gifts. Help us remember those in our own community who suffer through no fault of their own. Encourage us to step out in faith and assist those who need our help. Make us ever mindful that we love because Christ first loved us. We pray in the name of Jesus. Amen.

Prayer of Confession

Most merciful God, we confess that we have sinned against you and our neighbor. We have taken incalculable benefits with little gratitude. We have settled into complacency by insisting on our privileges rather than seeking the welfare of all of your children. Help us see the needs of others and then respond to them as brothers and sisters in Christ. Have mercy and forgive us, for the sake of Jesus Christ our Lord. And by that mercy and forgiveness, renew us to keep faith alive and vibrant in our community. All this we ask in Jesus Christ's sanctified name. Amen.

Prayer of Dedication of Gifts and Self

Blessed are those who can give without keeping tallies and receive without forgetting. As we offer ourselves and gifts, O God, bless these offerings and those who receive them. May these gifts be tangible signs of our relationship with you. Help us remember those who endure natural disasters, and make us mindful of their plight. We pray this in Christ's name. Amen.

Hymn of the Day
When Minds and Bodies Meet as One

This contemporary hymn explores images of unity and community in the church that reveal the nature of God. The hymnist is Rev. Brian Wren, a prolific writer of hymns and workshop leader on church music as well as professor of worship at Columbia Theological Seminary in Georgia. It first appeared in 1983 in *Faith Looking Forward,* a compilation of hymns. Peter Cutts composed the tune TRINITY CAROL for use with these words by Rev. Wren.

Children's Time: God's Children

(Bring a dark cloth, some cord, and a bowl containing a variety of large beads. Lay some of the beads on the cloth.) Invite the children to look at the beads and notice the differences and similarities among them. Express appreciation for the different beads that are available. What would it be like if there were only one kind of bead?

Comment that even though the beads are different, they are all beads. They can all be strung on a cord to make a necklace. *(Start stringing some beads onto the cord.)*

Observe that people are a little bit like beads. At first we all look different. We are different sizes and shapes. We have different colors of eyes and hair. We like different things. However, even with all our differences, all of us are God's children.

Comment that in the Bible reading today, Paul says that when God looks at us, God doesn't see the differences. To God we are all wonderful, and together we make something special. *(Hold up beads on the string and tie as a necklace.)* Express excitement that we are members of God's family.

Pray, giving thanks that we are the children of God.

The Sermon: One in Christ
Scripture: Galatians 3:23-29

The story is told of a student minister serving a Methodist church one summer. During the absence of the senior minister who was his supervisor, the young man was asked to perform a funeral service for a devoted Baptist – as the Baptist minister was also out of town. With some misgivings he conducted the service, and then worried afterward if he had done the correct thing. When the resident minister returned, the young man asked if he had violated any church policy by performing a burial service for a Baptist. "Absolutely not!" his supervisor assured him. "Bury all the Baptists you can!"

> *There is no longer Jew or Greek, there is no longer slave or free, there is no longer male and female; for all of you are one in Christ Jesus.*

When Paul wrote these words about the inherent unity that is ours by virtue of faith, you can safely assume that some of his original hearers were proponents of "burying all the Baptists you can." Except, instead of Baptists, the labels used then would have been Judaizers or libertines or one of any number of categories of folks thought not to be "true believers." From day one in the church, there have always been tensions surrounding the extent and the expression of our unity in the church as Christians. How far do we go in accommodating our understandings and beliefs with those claimed by others in the name of Christ? How do we live and work and serve with others who share the same community but differ in some of the particulars of theology?

The letter to the Galatians assumes such questions, because its affirmation of unity is not made to a single congregation already of one mind – and not even to the churches of a single community. Galatia is a region, a province in the Roman Empire. Its "church" was not a single fellowship, but a collection of assemblies located in a variety of towns populated by a diverse collection of believers. Paul's aim is to affirm their primary identity, not as churches or believers in isolation or in distinction of one from another but as a body that is one in Christ Jesus.

To the Galatian Christians, Paul frames the argument for unity as arising out of faith rather than law. That was a natural choice, as the opposition Paul faced and concluded to be divisive was a faction that sought to draw the church boundary line on the basis of observance of the law of Moses. To be a "true Christian," the argument went then, one had to keep to the law of Moses as Israel had for centuries. Otherwise, one was not truly a part of the church. Learned Pharisee that he was, Paul does not dismiss the Mosaic law or its function outright – but he does place it in perspective, viewing it as a "disciplinarian." The term "disciplinarian" referred in that era to a servant whose main function was to accompany children to school and keep them out of trouble. From age 7 till 16, the disciplinarian (the Greek term here is "pedagogue") escorted the child and supervised its conduct. But at age 16, a public ceremony formally recognizing the end of childhood and the acceptance into the adult community ended the term of the pedagogue, the disciplinarian.

So, Paul argued, was the law's function an interim one. Once the basis of community and unity for the people of Israel, the law's custodianship ended when Christ came and faith superseded observance of the law as the means to righteousness and justification. Meeting formulated prescriptions to prove oneself worthy was replaced by trust that offered oneself freely as the basis of our identity in Jesus Christ.

We are one in Christ Jesus because of whom we trust, not because our actions or worship habits or traditions fall into some lock-step precision with what someone believes should be true for all – not even when we are the "someone" presuming to make such judgments!

That is a critical point in moving from the text's concern for the unity of the church to our time's concern for and expression of that unity. We are every bit "one in Christ Jesus" in our day as were the Galatians in theirs, even and especially when outward appearances suggest the contrary. Paul's opponents sought to define that unity in a way determined by their litmus test of orthodoxy, which happened to be adherence to the law of Moses.

In our time, we do not suffer for a lack of folks who would determine for us the terms of Christian unity to the greatest precision. The fundamentalist movement arose in this country out of just such an effort, to boil down to a dogmatic checklist what unites true orthodox Christians. There have been times when the creeds of the church have been abused in just such an effort. In their own way, denominations sometimes add fuel to this fire by focusing too exclusively on their own continuity and the survival of their component congregations. And make no mistake: when individual congregations become ingrown and self-justifying, when survival and local customs become seen and used as the predominant measures for determining what is considered Christian action and belief – the unity of the church is jeopardized by parochialism.

The unity of the church is *not* something we can choose to abide by or ignore, depending on what way the wind happens to be blowing that day or how many people we can get to agree with our point of view. The unity of the church and of Christians is a *given* for us. Our faith makes it a matter of fact, a foundation upon which either we build or we flounder. Our unity is not something we are charged to create – it is a gift given for our use. We cannot create unity by coming up with a list of fundamentals or insisting we all practice the same liturgy. Our unity in Christ Jesus is far more dynamic. It is what allows us to live and serve together in community who differ from us in many ways, save in relationship with Christ. After all, in the Galatian church even after the receipt of Paul's letter, Jews continued to be Jews, Greeks continued to be Greeks, slaves continued to be slaves, free ones continued to be free, males continued to be male, females continued to be female. The outward differences remained – but these individuals and groups were bound in their diversity by unity in Christ Jesus.

Today, the unity of the church is served in the same way. I do not believe that being one in Christ requires that fundamentalists become charismatics, or that Pentecostals morph into "high-church liturgical" – or that mainline churches need to be something other than who we are. Otherwise, the advice to "bury all the Baptists you can" becomes, for all practical purposes, and with substitution of whomever we find at variance with us, an unending cycle of seeking unity on our terms rather than on God's terms. What the unity of the church *does* call forth from us is that we affirm and live as those who are one in Christ. That doesn't mean we have to become more like each other – the call is that we all become more like Christ.

We encounter the promise, and sadly at times the fracturing, of that truth at the communion table. Christ does not host "separate but equal" communions for Baptists and Methodists, UCC folk and Roman Catholics. There is but one table, even as there is but one Lord. Even as we come to this table as individuals and as a congregation, we are joined by countless others across the world – persons and communities with differences of thought and lifestyle and understanding that would make our heads dizzy. Yet, we are joined by persons and communities with whom *we are one* by virtue of the One who invites us here and accepts us as we are. The church is not one because of our agreements or our covenants, not because we share the same language or live in, much less support, the same political systems. The church is One because we serve – even as we were served at the table of communion by – one Lord, Jesus Christ. We are one here, not because of who we are, but because of *whose* we are.

– John Indermark

Hymns
Opening: In Christ There Is No East or West
Sermon: *De Colores* (Sing of Colors)
Closing: The Church's One Foundation

June 30, 2013

6th Sunday after Pentecost (Proper 8 [13])
RC/Pres: 13th Sunday in Ordinary Time

Lessons

Semi-continuous (SC)	Complementary (C)	Roman Catholic (RC)
2 Kings 2:1-2, 6-14	1 Kings 19:15-16, 19-21	1 Kings 19:16, 19-21
Ps 77:1-2, 11-20	Ps 16	Ps 16:1-2, 5, 7-11
Gal 5:1, 13-25	Gal 5:1, 13-25	Gal 5:1, 13-18
Lk 9:51-62	Lk 9:51-62	Lk 9:51-62

Speaker's Introduction for the Lessons
Lesson 1
2 Kings 2:1-2, 6-14 (SC)

> We obviously consider a double portion superior to a single portion, but how much more so with the Spirit? Elisha requests a double portion of the prophet's spirit as God transports Elijah into heaven.

1 Kings 19:15-16, 19-21 (C/RC)

> This is part of a continued story as God calls Elijah to anoint a new king over Syria and Israel. Elijah is also to anoint his successor, and finds him plowing.

Lesson 2
Psalm 77:1-2, 11-20 (SC)

> The psalmist begins with lament and then moves to a recitation of God's wondrous and saving acts on behalf of the people.

Psalm 16 (C); Psalm 16:1-2, 5, 7-11 (RC)

> This psalm of trust invokes God's protective care while asserting God as the one who brings wisdom and shows the way that leads to life.

Lesson 3
Galatians 5:1, 13-25 (SC/C); Galatians 5:1, 13-18 (RC)

> The comfort of the previous ritual law seductively tempts those freed from the law by faith in Christ. Paul urges those who are justified in faith to produce "fruit of the Spirit."

Gospel
Luke 9:51-62 (SC/C/RC)
Jesus begins his fateful journey to Jerusalem. We human beings have many excuses not to follow Jesus today, but Jesus puts into divine perspective all our feeble excuses.

Theme
Spiritual formation is seen by the fruit of the Spirit.

Thought for the Day
It is through discipline that God forms disciples for the realm of God.

Sermon Summary
Christian life is more than a destination after death. God calls us to discipleship today. One way to grow as disciples is to engage in spiritual disciplines that help to cultivate the Spirit's gifts in our lives and in Christian community.

Call to Worship
> One: Let us rejoice in the day that God has given us!
> **All: Yes, may we once again worship the God who gives life!**
> One: May we all sing and pray with a singleness of heart and mind.
> **All: We pray that the Lord will bless us with truth and light and joy. Amen.**

Pastoral Prayer
O God, in whom we live and move and have our being, bring us near to your throne of grace. As we read the Holy Scripture, may we be inspired with the same spirit that inspired those to whom you revealed your sacred message. As we sing the hymns of the faith, may these tunes and lyrics resound not only in our ears today but also in our minds and hearts through this week. May your word be spoken in sermon and broken in sacrament, so that we may discern and appropriate your ancient word for our day. We pray in the name of our great high priest, Jesus the Christ. Amen.

Prayer of Confession

We know all too well, O God, the places we have fallen short. We also know those places we would hide from or deny. Yet, we also know the promise of your gracious call that bids us turn to you in repentance. And in turning, discover your forgiveness already extended even before we see its need. We acknowledge our sin. We ask your healing and renewal to transform us and embolden us to live with faith and to forgive as we have been forgiven. We pray this in the holy name of Jesus. Amen.

Prayer of Dedication of Gifts and Self

O God of unmatched splendor, give us a spirit of sincere gratitude for your mercy. Make us mindful of your manifold blessings. Give us compassion to pass along our material blessings to those who also stand in need of life's necessities. Make us a people known for benevolence and a spirit of loving charity. We pray this and everything in Jesus' name. Amen.

Hymn of the Day
Spirit of the Living God

Presbyterian minister Daniel Iverson of Lumberton, North Carolina wrote this one-stanza hymn, perhaps better recognized as a chorus, in 1926. He wrote the words and music the day he attended the George T. Stephans evangelistic crusade in Orlando, Florida, where he heard a message on the Holy Spirit. The song's popularity began that evening when it was sung at the crusade's meeting. This short hymn can be used as a call to prayer or a prayer response. Some hymnbooks include a second stanza, written by Michael Baughen in 1982. This addition gives the hymn more of a corporate expression.

Children's Time: Growing in God

(Bring various items of clothing representing different ages from infant to adult.)
Invite the children to line up the clothes in order of size. Comment that people wear different sizes of clothing as they grow. Invite the children to name some of the clothes they can no longer wear. Talk about some of the other ways in which we grow physically. How do we know when we are growing?

Comment that we also are growing in ways that we can't see as easily. We are growing in knowledge and we are growing in our relationship with God. How can other people tell? Mention that in the Bible passage today Paul says that when we follow God's ways and love others, many good things will grow in our lives. List the fruit of the Spirit in verses 22-23.

Invite the children to name ways we can love and help others. Observe that there will be a lot of fruits of the Spirit growing in (name your community) this week.

Pray with the children, asking God to help you as you learn more about living in God's ways.

The Sermon: Spiritual Disciplines Form God's Disciples
Scripture: Galatians 5:1, 13-25

Like most of you, I am not always sure what "spiritual formation" means. Being from a Wesleyan tradition, I suppose spiritual formation has something to do with the idea of practicing spiritual disciplines. These naturally include spiritual activities such as meditation, prayer, fasting, study, almsgiving, and worship. One thing I do know is that we all need time and a means to deepen our lives in God so that we can deepen our relationships with other people and ourselves. "Our world is hungry for genuinely changed people," writes Richard Foster. Leo Tolstoy wrote, "Everybody thinks of changing humanity and nobody thinks of changing himself." Most of us know the absolute truth of Tolstoy's statement. We see it every day.

I have thought about spiritual formation quite a bit. If I had to name the goal or object of a congregation's journey of faith, then I would suggest hearing and revisiting something that the apostle Paul wrote. Clearly most Christians would confess that heaven or salvation is the aim of the Christian life, but I would like for us to stay on this side of the grave for a while. Paul got it right when he wrote, "The fruit of the Spirit is love, joy, peace, patience, kindness, generosity, faithfulness, gentleness, and self-control. There is no law against such things. And those who belong to Christ Jesus have crucified the flesh with its passions and desires" (Gal 5:22-24).

I think this is the worthy goal and object of the Christian life as we live it now.

If you are like me, your life does not always feel much like "love, joy, peace, patience, kindness, generosity, faithfulness, gentleness, and self-control." Rather, you have your problems and I have mine. Unfortunately, as members of the body of Christ, we sometimes must put on our game faces and go on. Deep in the dark night of the soul, however, we know that we need more of God than we ever manage to shoehorn into our lives. Thus we need the disciplines of the Spirit and the spiritual life just like we need the four major food groups to survive and to thrive. Spiritual formation is all about spiritual disciplines. Only by disciplining ourselves – after all, the word "disciple" does have its roots deep into discipline – can we assure ourselves of the double portion of God's grace so necessary to work with and among and for such a "stiff-necked people," as always seems our lot.

What kind of people do we do ministry with? Some years back our church's young music director tried to teach our congregation a new and beautiful hymn. One older woman came out of church that morning and stomped her foot as she said to me, "I don't come to church to learn anything!" I had to hold my tongue, although I wanted to answer her and did so to myself, "Ma'am, you may count your objective for coming to church as a total success!"

Along the way there always seem to be moments of grace or chance or serendipity that help us move on toward God and the relationships that believers claim at their baptism as people of God's reign. Sometimes events occur that remind us of why we do what we do.

Through the years the Samaritans (a group of lay ministers in our church) made visits to one family in particular in their home. After one of these weekly visits, a Samaritan came by the church office and asked if someone from the missions work group could repair Jack and Mary's front door knob that wouldn't lock. This would be a simple repair, really, probably no more than a 30-minute job.

Upon inspecting the doorknob, it was recommended that the whole doorframe be replaced, and that perhaps a new front door would be nice. When this project was completed, the workers decided to continue inside and partition off a bedroom and then paint the walls. The carpet really needed to be replaced, and how about the kitchen and bathroom.

As workers came by to complete one project, they were dreaming and planning the next project they wanted to do for the family. The end result was a complete renovation of the inside of the little house on Plum Street. There were new chairs and a couch, a new kitchen stove, new mattresses, some new windows, and a handicap-accessible bathroom. The kitchen floor was leveled so that they did not have to hold the refrigerator door shut with duct tape anymore.

Mary was so excited. "I never lived in a house as pretty as this. It's my dream house." James, who was recovering from a broken hip from a slip on the ice, returned to the house via a brand new "state of the art" wheelchair ramp. All in all, it was a project that started with a doorknob and ended up blessing the lives of all who had a part in it.

This experience with James and Mary makes me realize that even when life is hard and seems like divine testing, I am surrounded by a group of dedicated believers. Our church folk are people who want to live out the life of Christ in community. They give and live the faith. They take Paul's guidance to heart when they follow Paul's counsel to the church at Galatia: "Through love become slaves to one another" (Gal 5:13). Amen.

– David Neil Mosser

Hymns
Opening: Guide Me, O Thou Great Jehovah
Sermon: Spirit of God, Descend upon My Heart
Closing: How Firm a Foundation

July 7, 2013

7th Sunday after Pentecost (Proper 9 [14])
RC/Pres: 14th Sunday in Ordinary Time

Lessons

Semi-continuous (SC)	Complementary (C)	Roman Catholic (RC)
2 Kings 5:1-14	Isa 66:10-14	Isa 66:10-14
Ps 30	Ps 66:1-9	Ps 66:1-3, 4-5, 6-7, 16, 20
Gal 6:(1-6) 7-16	Gal 6:(1-6) 7-16	Gal 6:14-18
Lk 10:1-11, 16-20	Lk 10:1-11, 16-20	Lk 10:1-12, 17-20
		or Lk 10:1-9

Speaker's Introduction for the Lessons
Lesson 1
2 Kings 5:1-14 (SC)

> The Israelites were tempted, just as we are, to forget God's love and concern for all nations. But now a foreign official comes to Elisha, a prophet of Israel, seeking a cure for his leprosy.

Isaiah 66:10-14 (C/RC)

> God is often compared to a loving father. But here, in moving imagery, God is likened to a young mother tenderly nursing her young.

Lesson 2
Psalm 30 (SC)

> A psalm associated with the feast of Hannukah that celebrates God's transformation of a situation of mortal threat to one of joy and praise.

Psalm 66:1-9 (C); Psalm 66:1-3, 4-5, 6-7, 16, 20 (RC)

> The psalmist blends stories of God's deliverance that are both individual and community in nature, inviting all creation to sing God's praise.

Lesson 3
Galatians 6:(1-6) 7-16 (SC/C); Galatians 6:14-18 (RC)

> Some in the church at Galatia think they are superior to other members because they have undergone circumcision, a mark of Jewish identity. Paul shines the light of the cross on such mistaken attitudes.

Gospel
Luke 10:1-11, 16-20 (SC/C); Luke 10:1-12, 17-20 (RC)

Jesus has just reminded his followers of the costliness and urgency of following him. Now he sends 70 of them to proclaim the good news of God's reign.

Theme

By the life-changing power of Christ we can be and do all that God intends for us.

Thought for the Day

The way of Christ into our lives is such that grace always precedes law.

Sermon Summary

Galatians 6 is filled with exhortations concerning sowing and reaping and well-doing. But we mistake their intent if we construe them as good advice, which well-intentioned people can fulfill apart from the gospel and apart from Christ. Through Christ, we can make a difference that truly matters.

Call to Worship

One: Make a joyful noise to God, all the earth.

All: Sing the glory of God's name.

One: Come and see what God has done,

All: God's deeds are awesome!

One: Bless our God, O peoples.

All: Let the sound of praise to God be heard!

Pastoral Prayer

Almighty God, you nourish and sustain the world from day to day, and you continue to bless and strengthen and guide us more than we could dare to think or ask. Thank you for your hidden and yet faithful presence. We pray for your church, established on earth as a loving witness to your nature and purposes for the world. May your people know in a fresh way the reconciling and restoring power of Christ, so that by their lives and witness, your realm may advance in this world. We pray for those who struggle to be and do all that you would have them be and do. We sense the painful gap between our present lives and your perfect will for us. Stir us afresh by your Holy Spirit. May the living Christ be seen in our lives as we point to him as the way, the truth, and the life. We pray these things through Christ our strong Savior. Amen.

Prayer of Confession

Merciful God, we confess that we often turn from you and hurt one another. We neglect the needs of those around us; we tune out the cry of the oppressed. Heal our divided hearts, deepen our love for you and for others, and strengthen our commitment to peace and justice in our world. We offer these prayers through Christ our Lord. Amen.

Prayer of Dedication of Gifts and Self

God, you have given us all things in Christ: life, love, forgiveness, purpose. You entrust us with so many blessings. Help us to be faithful stewards of your many gifts, and may these offerings further the work of your church here and around the world, through Jesus Christ our loving Savior. Amen.

Hymn of the Day
Ask Ye What Great Thing I Know

Based on 1 Corinthians 2:2 and Galatians 6:14, the original German hymn "*Wollt ihr wissen, was mein Preis*" was written by German pastor Johann Christoph Schwedler. It first appeared in *Hirschberger Gesangbuch* in 1741, seven years after Schwedler's death. The English translation used in most current hymnbooks is the 1863 translation by British pastor and writer Benjamin H. Kennedy. At least one hymnbook has altered the first line to read, "Ask me what great thing I know." A series of soul-searching questions are proposed in the hymn. The answer to each question is, "Jesus Christ, the crucified."

Children's Time: Bearing Burdens

(Bring a sturdy plastic crate. Fill it with rocks or heavy books and place it in your worship area. The idea is to have a box that cannot be moved easily by one person.)

Gather around the crate and wonder what it is doing there. Comment that it is in the way and should be moved. Make a big show of trying to move the crate and exclaim that it is just too heavy for one person to lift safely.

Ask the children if they can think of a way to move the box. Accept all suggestions and if no one else says it, suggest that you might work together to move it. Divide the contents of the crate amongst the children and carry everything to another location. When you have finished, celebrate with a round of applause. Comment that it was much easier to carry the crate when the load was shared.

Comment that in the Bible passage today, Paul says followers of Jesus should stick together and help to carry one another's burdens – help one another when we need help. When we do this, the church will be strong. Pray with the children, asking God to help you as you help one another.

The Sermon: The Transforming Power of Christ
Scripture: Galatians 6:(1-6) 7-16

I have a little confession to make. I have a tendency to latch onto verses that reinforce my philosophy of life and affirm my way of doing things. I like passages that give us warm, fuzzy feelings without challenging us. Simon and Garfunkel, popular folksingers of the 1970s, told the truth when they sang, "A man hears what he wants to hear and disregards the rest." I could latch on to the opening words of our passage from Galatians 6 about sowing and reaping, and make them fit popular notions about life being a do-it-yourself proposition. After all, doesn't the apostle Paul declare that "you reap whatever you sow" (6:7)?

Countless sermons are nothing more than pragmatic lessons on how to solve problems, create happiness, and get ahead. Of course, Christianity is practical, and the scriptures guide us in dealing with the challenges and possibilities of everyday life. But divorced from the gospel, preaching becomes nothing more than works religion. The bookshelves in our local bookstores are lined with self-help books. People desperately pour over these volumes, attend seminars, and watch Oprah and Dr. Phil, trying somehow to attain the good life.

To be honest, we ministers are aware of these trends, and, whether we like to admit it or not, are susceptible to worldly models of success. We sometimes think of ministry as a career rather than a calling; we measure

success by things like building programs and attendance charts. We might
cloak our thinking in benign phrases such as "being seeker sensitive," and
think that our preaching must not be off-putting to visitors. After all,
didn't Paul declare that he would be all things to all people in order to save
some (1 Cor 9:22)? So marketing shapes homiletics, and we begin to hold
forth about the importance of living a good life so that we will receive
wonderful rewards here and now. Preach like that and listeners might
be inclined to nod their approval and feel reassured that they have the
resources within themselves to earn the "good life." A popular prosperity
gospel has been making the circuit for some time nowadays that asserts
precisely this, and those who preach it are packing in the crowds.

But Paul aims broadside at that kind of bootstraps theology with his
declaration, "May I never boast of anything except the cross of our Lord
Jesus Christ, by which the world has been crucified to me, and I to the
world" (Gal 6:14).

A man once announced to D. L. Moody, "Sir, I am a self-made man."
To which the famous evangelist replied, "Congratulations. You have saved
God a great responsibility."

There is brokenness in our world. The human race collectively and
individually is at enmity with God. Look at the magazines that line our
shelves at the checkout stands. They are not filled with stories about the
despair and crying needs of our inner cities. Tabloids are not going to sell
out by featuring articles about opportunities in the Peace Corps. They're
crammed with leering accounts of the escapades of the rich and famous.
Popular magazines tell us how to slim down, look younger, and get more
pleasure. Evidence for the narcissistic obsessions of our society abounds.
Luther was right when he said that, after the fall, the human race was
"curved inward upon itself." The Beatles had a song that repeated end-
lessly the line, "I, me, me, mine."

A self-centered world like ours loves to hear sermons about self-
improvement. But this is a world of urban blight, failed marriages, and
empty lives. This world will never become the realm of God apart from
the cross of Christ. Only through crucifixion can there be a resurrection.
Only by dying to self can we begin to live for others. And this happens not
by fresh resolution or greater effort. It comes through the cross of Christ.

The apostle Paul flatly asserts that something happened to him when
Jesus Christ went to the cross. Paul, too, was an accomplice in the world's
rebellion against God's way. There was a time when Paul lived for himself

and his immediate desires. But the cross changed all that. Jesus was not just a solitary martyr going to his death. Jesus died as our representative, including us in his death. When he died, we died. And when he rose, we rose. Thus Paul could make the surprising assertion that, by the cross long ago, the world was crucified to him and he to the world. All humankind is bound up together in what Jesus did on Calvary.

Paul humbly confesses that the only thing he can boast about is that Christ died for him. The great thing to which he wants to draw everyone's attention is that God incarnate, Jesus of Nazareth, donned flesh, took pain, ascended the hill, and in the mighty act of atonement, crucified the world and his former self. By faith, we can participate in what Christ did for us long ago.

If we extend our text to include the first six verses, we find three things about the Christian life. First, it is a caring life – lifting up the stumbling, bearing another's burdens, working for the good of all. It is not so much inward looking as outward looking. Second, the Christian life is a transformed life. We are no longer the same. Third, it is a Christ-centered life. The living reality of our lives is Christ. In Christ, we are new creations. It is striking that Paul declares the cross to have an ongoing impact. It is not, says Paul, merely the fact that I was crucified with Christ so that he took my place in the past. This is a fact with contemporary implications. I continue to be crucified with Christ; I continue to have victory over my selfish and sinful inclinations through the Crucified One.

Go forth, Christian friend, into your Monday morning and all the days beyond. Your life is a calling from God. Your relationships with your friends, your co-workers, and your neighbors all present opportunities to sow in fruitful ways, to make a loving difference. In due time you will reap. Lift up the stumbling one, encourage the fainthearted. Feed the hungry. In due time, you will reap a harvest through the Crucified One who died and now lives to walk every step with you.

– Daniel P. Thimell

Hymns
Opening: Joyful, Joyful, We Adore Thee
Sermon: Love Divine, All Loves Excelling
Closing: Be Thou My Vision

July 14, 2013

8th Sunday after Pentecost (Proper 10 [15])
RC/Pres: 15th Sunday in Ordinary Time

Lessons

Semi-continuous (SC)	Complementary (C)	Roman Catholic (RC)
Amos 7:7-17	Deut 30:9-14	Deut 30:10-14
Ps 82	Ps 25:1-10	Ps 69:14, 17, 30-31, 33-34, 36-37
Col 1:1-14	Col 1:1-14	Col 1:15-20
Lk 10:25-37	Lk 10:25-37	Lk 10:25-37

Speaker's Introduction for the Lessons
Lesson 1
Amos 7:7-17 (SC)

The book of Amos was written during the eighth century BCE during a time of peace and prosperity for Israel and Judah. Amos warns the people of impending judgment.

Deuteronomy 30:9-14 (C); Deuteronomy 30:10-14 (RC)

Moses promises that obeying God's laws will be accompanied by blessing in everyday life.

Lesson 2
Psalm 82 (SC)

The psalmist sounds more like a prophet by setting this song in the form of a lawsuit God brings against those who do injustice, coupled with a plea to God to deliver those vulnerable to those breaches of covenant.

Psalm 25:1-10 (C)

The psalmist cries out to God for deliverance and wisdom and then affirms God's goodness and steadfast love.

Psalm 69:14, 17, 30-31, 33-34, 36-37 (RC)

This is a psalm asking for deliverance from persecution and praising God's faithfulness.

Lesson 3
Colossians 1:1-14 (SC/C); Colossians 1:15-20 (RC)

Colossians was written to respond to those who claim that the death and resurrection of Christ are not enough to make a person right with God.

Gospel
Luke 10:25-37 (SC/C/RC)

A theological expert in the law of Moses – called here simply "a lawyer" – seeks to show up Jesus by asking him how one can earn eternal life.

Theme

Through Christ's love, we can love those rejected by society.

Thought for the Day

Christian discipleship is impossible apart from Christ.

Sermon Summary

Jesus, as Luther once said, is first gift and then example. Jesus' parable of the good Samaritan is not intended to be a short course in self-improvement but a description of how Jesus ministers to those in need, that Christ might then enable us to participate in such loving and compassionate ministry.

Call to Worship

One: To you, O Lord, I lift up my soul.
All: O God, in you I trust.
One: Make me know your ways, O Lord,
All: And teach me your paths.
One: Lead me in your truth, and teach me,
All: For you are the God of my salvation.

Pastoral Prayer

Eternal God, we come to worship your greatness, to be lost once again in the wonder of who you are. We praise you for the splendor of the stars, the warmth of the sun, and for the rain you generously send on both the just and the unjust. We thank you for your providence in clothing the lilies of the field and your children as well. We are amazed that not a sparrow falls without your notice, and are moved to know that you care about the smallest details of our lives and the lives of our neighbors. We thank you that your love is not restricted to those we deem worthy, but is generous and unconditional. We ask that the love of your Son, our Savior Jesus, would overflow from our hearts and lives into the hearts and lives of those around us. Move us to weep with those who weep, and to ache with those who are unemployed, hungry, oppressed, powerless, or hopeless. Come alongside them through us, O Holy Spirit, so that all may know God's love. These things we are bold to pray, through Christ. Amen.

Prayer of Confession

Merciful God, you know every thought of our hearts, every word that we speak, and every temptation that attacks us. We have done that which we should not do, and have failed to love our neighbor for whom you died. Forgive us our sins and transform our hearts and minds, that we may walk in newness of life, through Christ our Savior. Amen.

Prayer of Dedication of Gifts and Self

Loving God, who in Christ has already come alongside our neighbors in this country and around the world, we bring these gifts and ourselves in fresh dedication to your service. May these offerings enable your church to render loving ministry to the those who need it most, through the same Christ our strong Savior. Amen.

Hymn of the Day
Here I Am, Lord

The words and music of the hymn were written by American Jesuit Daniel L. Schutte in 1981. In the hymn we have descriptions of God, of what God has done, and of what God continues to do in response to the cry of the people. The call to join in Christian mission is presented. As in Isaiah's time, we hear God asking: "Whom shall I send?" We may respond with our heartfelt "I will go, Lord, if you lead me." The hymn lends itself to creative singing options ranging from unison singing of the stanzas and part singing of the refrain to antiphonal singing between a choir and the congregation. Rhythm instrument accompaniment can be an effective addition.

Children's Time: The Good Samaritan

(Bring a street map of your community.)

Show the map and identify some local landmarks. Explain that this is a map of your neighborhood. Talk about neighbors. Who are your neighbors? Do you ever do anything to help them, or do they do things to help you? Comment that in our Bible story today someone asks Jesus, "Who is my neighbor?"

Set the scene by explaining that Jesus often used stories to help people learn more about living in God's way. Tell the story of the good Samaritan and ask the children to identify which person was the good neighbor in this story and why.

Encourage the children to recognize that our neighbors are not only the people who live near us but anyone who needs our help. When we show care and love for others, we are being good neighbors. Have the children name some ways we might love and care for others. If you have time, talk about some of the ways your church acts as a good neighbor, both in your community and in the world.

Pray with the children, asking God to help you follow the example of the good Samaritan.

The Sermon: God's Love and Ours
Scripture: Luke 10:25-37

Sometimes the familiar can become the unknown. Some well-worn stories in the Bible elude us because we've heard them so often. The good Samaritan is a case in point. Most of us could retell the story from memory, and all of us understand the image. The good Samaritan is somebody who goes out of the way to help the fallen one – the one in need – even at great inconvenience to self. We even have good Samaritan laws to protect one who stops to render aid from liability to prosecution should something go awry in her or his well-intentioned efforts.

But if this is just a morality tale about the importance of doing good deeds, then Jesus forgot his own message. You see, the lawyer whose question occasions this parable has a prior agenda. He's not interested in Jesus or the message about God's reign. He wants to put Jesus to the test so that he can show him up. The lawyer begins by asking what he can do to inherit eternal life.

In Scotland, home improvement stores are called "DIYs:" Do-It-Yourself shops. Many then and now have thought of religion in this way, as a do-it-yourself proposition. The lawyer bought into a DIY approach, which is really self-centered religion. He was preoccupied with his piety and his destiny. He wanted another good deed on his resume, to ensure approval at the heavenly gate. His love was a self-love.

Jesus takes him on his own terms. He could have flat-out scolded him for having such a bad theology. He might have declared, as he did to Thomas in the upper room, "I am the way, and the truth, and the life" (Jn 14:6). The way to God is the way of grace. This way is constituted by Jesus, in his life, death, and resurrection for us. But Jesus always meets a person where he or she is. He begins by reviewing the law of God, encapsulated in the love of God and neighbor. Jesus even says, "Do this and you will live."

But can we, by our own strength, do these things? Can we love God with undivided hearts? Can we love others with total altruism, total unselfishness? If we could, then the cross was unnecessary. Jesus is gently showing this man that he, like the rest of the human race, is unable to be what he ought to be, to love as he ought to love, and to act as he ought to act.

At this point the lawyer starts to squirm. His selfishness and failure to love others has been exposed. If he cannot obey God's law, do God's will from his heart, then he has truly fallen short. And so Luke adds the telling observation: "But wanting to justify himself, he asked Jesus, 'And who is my neighbor?'" Most of us act with a certain measure of love and sacrifice toward those who are close to us, who love us back. We forego things and go out of our way to help our spouses, our children, and possibly our next-door neighbors.

But we find it far easier to help our daughter when her car breaks down than the anonymous stranger whose radiator is steaming on the shoulder of the interstate. In the story, the priest and the Levite have reasonable anxieties about helping this fallen man. Fred Craddock, who teaches at Candler School of Theology, notes that the body on the roadside may have been planted by thieves in order to trap somebody who stopped to help. A lot of us hesitate nowadays to render aid for fear of being carjacked or attacked. Touching a corpse would have made the priest and the Levite ritually unclean and disqualified them from ministering in the temple.

The Samaritan goes far out of his way. Craddock says that he "delayed his own journey, expended great energy, risked danger to himself, spent two days' wages with the assurance of more, and promised to follow up on his activity" *(Luke: Interpretation,* John Knox Press, 1990, p. 151). Jesus is saying, if you want to save yourself, transcend yourself. Transform yourself from a taker to a giver. Come out of your selfishness and become sacrificially preoccupied with the needs of everyone you meet.

It calls to mind another self-made man who came up to Jesus and asked how to earn eternal life. Jesus took him through the commandments and then said, looking at his sharkskin suit, Rolex watch, and Mercedes, "Sell all that you own and distribute the money to the poor, and you will have treasure in heaven" (Lk 18:22). When Jesus explained this, he added a comment, which sheds brilliant light on that episode and the encounter with the lawyer: "What is impossible for mortals is possible for God" (18:27). With humans it is impossible. A leopard cannot change its spots; we cannot transform ourselves.

Karl Barth, the great Swiss theologian, declares that in the truest sense, Jesus is the Samaritan who shows mercy to the one left for dead on the roadside. In *Church Dogmatics* (Edinburgh, T&T Clark, 1958), Barth writes that Jesus alone could act as neighbor to the fallen ones, fulfilling to the ultimate the twin commands to love God and others. But he did all that for us. In and through Christ, we can act in deeds of love and kindness. That is why the gospel of Jesus is not "good advice" but "good news."

There is a distinct ethical content to this story of the good Samaritan. The Christian life is a life of self-sacrifice and neighbor-love. But it is not undertaken autonomously. It begins at the foot of the cross and is carried out in the company of the Crucified One, by whom alone we can live such a life of love. The parable of the good Samaritan is not just a call to imitate Jesus. It's a call to participate in him.

– Daniel P. Thimell

Hymns
Opening: Praise to the Lord, the Almighty
Sermon: Won't You Let Me Be Your Servant?
Closing: Guide Me, O Thou Great Jehovah

July 21, 2013

9th Sunday after Pentecost (Proper 11 [16])
RC/Pres: 16th Sunday in Ordinary Time

Lessons

Semi-continuous (SC)	Complementary (C)	Roman Catholic (RC)
Amos 8:1-12	Gen 18:1-10	Gen 18:1-10
Ps 52	Ps 15	Ps 15:2-5
Col 1:15-28	Col 1:15-28	Col 1:24-28
Lk 10:38-42	Lk 10:38-42	Lk 10:38-42

Speaker's Introduction for the Lessons
Lesson 1
Amos 8:1-12 (SC)
The prophet Amos speaks to people who scrupulously observe the Sabbath but are guilty of blatant social injustice.

Genesis 18:1-10a (C); Genesis 18:1-10 (RC)
God has promised Abraham the blessing of a multitude of descendants, but Abraham's wife Sarah has long since passed the age of childbearing.

Lesson 2
Psalm 52 (SC)
The tone of the psalmist is unusually harsh in this judgment, made even more distinct by the voice of the words not set in the mouth of God but in that of the psalmist.

Psalm 15 (C); Psalm 15:2-5 (RC)
The psalmist answers the question of who might enter into the tent of God's presence with assertions of actions that do not take advantage of neighbor in word or deed.

Lesson 3
Colossians 1:15-28 (SC/C); Colossians 1:24-28 (RC)

This ancient hymn to Christ responds to those who think that what Christ has done is not enough for salvation.

Gospel
Luke 10:38-42 (SC/C/RC)

Jesus is invited to Martha's home for dinner and finds that Martha and her sister Mary have different priorities in their lives on that day.

Theme

Our life in Christ is the foundation for serving Christ.

Thought for the Day

Even in the midst of our busyness, we need to engage in what Brother Lawrence called "practicing the presence of Christ."

Sermon Summary

Mary's life with Jesus was more important than her life of service. Does this minimize Christian action? Hardly. But it rivets our attention on the fact that the outward journey is rooted in and sustained by the inward journey. Attending to Christ's presence among us matters.

Call to Worship

One: O Lord, who may abide in your tent?
All: Who may dwell on your holy hill?
One: Those who walk blamelessly, and do what is right,
All: Who speak the truth from their hearts,
One: Who honor those who fear the Lord.
All: Those who do these things shall never be moved.

Pastoral Prayer

Eternal and ever-blessed God, we rejoice in the order and goodness of your creation. We praise you as our creator and our redeemer. We seek to worship you, and need your strength to do so. Transform our worship into an offering acceptable to you. Remind us of the delight that comes in time spent intentionally and attentively in your presence. Cause us to see that we always live in your presence, and that by your companionship and constant help we can carry out the mission you give us in this world. O Holy Spirit, renewing all creation, transforming us from one degree of glory to another into the likeness of Christ, touch us and renew us in this hour. In Christ's name we pray. Amen.

Prayer of Confession

Forgive us, loving God, for hurrying past you in our daily lives. We crowd our lives with so many frenetic activities, many of them worthwhile, and yet we forget the one thing needful. We work hard to make ends meet, but forget the one thing needful. We spend time with our loved ones, but forget the one thing needful. We give to worthwhile causes, but forget the one thing needful. O Lord, may we never forget your presence again! Forgive us for self-preoccupation and neglecting our lives with you. Woo us to your heart all over again, and show us the joy, meaning, and purpose that come through living our lives in you. Through Christ our strong Savior we pray. Amen.

Prayer of Dedication of Gifts and Self

Gracious God, you have given us all things in Christ, and with thankful hearts we bring these gifts to further your church's ministry of worship, teaching, fellowship, and outreach, that you may be glorified. Through Christ our loving Savior, we are bold to pray. Amen.

Hymn of the Day
Be Thou My Vision

The origin of this hymn is in eighth-century Ireland. Its original title is *"Rob tu mo bhoile, a Comdi cride."* It was translated into English prose by Mary E. Byrne in 1905 and put into current hymn form by Eleanor H. Hull in 1912. It can be sung by the church as an expression of its desire that God be its vision for all current and future ministries. Perhaps the personal pronouns could be replaced by the plural pronouns "our" and "we." Also, with a little creative rewriting, each Victorian "thou" could be dropped without destroying the intent of the text.

Children's Time: Mary and Martha

(Bring a dusting cloth, broom, baking pan, and wooden spoon.)

Invite the children to recall times when they have had visitors: What sorts of things did you do to get ready? How did you help your guests feel welcome? Together look at the cleaning and baking tools and suggest ways they might be used to help get ready for guests. Comment that the Bible story today is about two sisters named Mary and Martha. They had a lot of preparations to make because Jesus was coming to their house. Tell the story of Jesus' visit with Mary and Martha.

Talk briefly about the story. Notice that each woman welcomed Jesus in her own way – Martha by working to make sure that everything was just right; Mary by sitting and listening to Jesus. Although Jesus appreciated Martha's hard work, he also wanted her to spend time listening and learning about God's love. There is a time to be busy, but it is important to take time to listen and learn about God. How might we do that?

Pray with the children, giving thanks for hands to work and ears to listen.

The Sermon: Your Life in Christ
Scripture: Luke 10:38-42

"I've been busy." That's one of our favorite self-descriptions. When asked how we've been or what we've been up to, we like to stress our high activity levels. It typifies our American culture, which has always emphasized initiative, hard work, and getting things done. We pastors are not exempt from this trend. Search committees are not terribly interested in our Christology or even our devotional lives. Committee members' attention is focused like a laser beam on church growth, community involvement, and our ability to connect with young people. Churches want their pastors to be busy.

Of course, that applies to church members, also. We applaud those who "wear several hats": serving on church council, teaching Sunday school, cooking for church dinners, and singing in the choir. At home, it's no different. How many parents set the alarm for 5:30, start breakfast, wake the kids up, get them dressed, send them off to the bus stop, dash to work, and, after school, drive them to soccer practice, and then grab a few burger combo meals in the drive-through? Late at night, as we toss in our beds, we think about how we'd really like to write that letter or call our parents or even just sit close to our children and listen to them. Then we defend ourselves by saying, "I'm so busy."

Martha was busy, too – busy sweeping the floor, baking bread, and setting the table. When Jesus knocked at the door, she ushered him to a seat, gave him something to drink, and hurried out to check on the meal. Then she noticed that Mary was just sitting out there in the living room, listening to Jesus. How ridiculous! Here she was frantically managing a three-ring circus in the kitchen, while Mary just sat around.

She marched out to the living room and complained, "Lord, do you not care that my sister has left me all the work to do by myself? Tell her then to help me" (10:40).

But Jesus did not back her up. He surprised her by saying, "Martha, Martha, you are worried and distracted by many things . . . Mary has chosen the better part, which will not be taken away from her" (10:41-42).

It's a familiar story, but we can miss the point. Jesus is not simply telling Martha to take a break. Note that Mary was not stretched out on the sofa, taking a snooze. She was sitting at the feet of Jesus. I believe that Jesus is telling us that the core of our existence is our life with him. The Christian life is an active life, a life of worship and service, a life of telling the story of God's redeeming love. And its mainspring is Jesus.

At the center of our faith is the conviction that Jesus, who was crucified, is not a dead martyr but a living savior. Death could not hold him in its icy grip. Christ rose in triumph and reigns as the head over the church, the body of Christ. Jesus is present with us today at work, at play, at home, and at the mall. He is as close to us as the air we breathe.

The Christian life is life lived in the companionship of Christ. Henry Scougal was a devout young theologian who taught at the University of Aberdeen in Scotland. He died back in 1678 at the tender age of 28. He wrote an influential little book entitled *The Life of God in the Soul of Man* (InterVarsity Fellowship, 1961). George Whitefield, one of the leading evangelists of the Great Awakening, passed on a copy to Charles Wesley in Oxford. It contributed to his conversion.

In his book, Henry Scougal laments that so few people seem to understand what true Christianity is. Some think, he writes, that Christianity is mainly orthodox notions. They imagine that all God wants is for us to have the correct mental understanding of Christianity. Others think it is a matter of external duties – obeying the laws of the Bible, keeping busy doing the right things. Still others believe that real Christianity is having the right affections and feelings toward God.

Each of these misses the point, according to Scougal. The essence of Christianity lies not in the realm of thought, performance, or feelings. Real Christianity is a union of the soul with God. The apostle Paul describes it as Christ "formed in" us (Gal 4:19).

Mary knew that. Her life with Jesus was more important than her life of service. Does this minimize Christian action? Hardly. But it rivets our attention on the fact that the outward journey is rooted in and sustained by the inward journey. Our life in Christ is the basis for our life in the world. The life of God in the human soul – that's the Christian life. Jesus makes this point when he tells the disciples that he is the vine, they are the branches, and that "apart from me you can do nothing" (Jn 15:5).

Your life in Christ is more than having devotions. It's not about "checking in" with God occasionally. It is a matter of moment-by-moment living our lives out of who we are in Christ. James Torrance, the beloved Scottish theologian and professor, emblazoned upon his students' hearts and minds this central New Testament insight. He was fond of quoting Galatians 2:19-20: "I have been crucified with Christ; and it is no longer I who live, but it is Christ who lives in me." That's the essence of the Christian life.

– Daniel P. Thimell

Hymns
Opening: Morning Has Broken
Sermon: St. Patrick's Breastplate
Closing: O Master, Let Me Walk with Thee

July 28, 2013

10th Sunday after Pentecost (Proper 12 [17])
RC/Pres: 17th Sunday in Ordinary Time

Lessons

Semi-continuous (SC)	Complementary (C)	Roman Catholic (RC)
Hos 1:2-10	Gen 18:20-32	Gen 18:20-32
Ps 85	Ps 138	Ps 138:1-3, 6-8
Col 2:6-15 (16-19)	Col 2:6-15 (16-19)	Col 2:12-14
Lk 11:1-13	Lk 11:1-13	Lk 11:1-13

Speaker's Introduction for the Lessons
Lesson 1
Hosea 1:2-10 (SC)

The prophet Hosea speaks to a people who have been unfaithful to God. They have been trying to cover their bets by worshiping both God and the old Baals, the false gods of Canaan.

Genesis 18:20-32 (C/RC)

God, the righteous judge of all the earth, is outraged by the sins of Sodom, but Abraham re-presents God's own mercy and intervenes on behalf of sinners.

Lesson 2
Psalm 85 (SC)

The psalmist hearkens back to God's past works of deliverance for the sake of calling upon God to once more bring "steadfast love and faithfulness to meet" so that "righteousness and peace will kiss."

Psalm 138 (C); Psalm 138 :1-3, 6-8 (RC)

The psalmist renders thanks and praise for God's steadfast love that answers those in need and in times of distress.

Lesson 3
Colossians 2:6-15 (16-19) (SC/C); Colossians 2:12-14 (RC)
> Some in the Colossian church have a legalistic understanding of Christianity, and the author responds by pointing out that Christ has done everything necessary to make us acceptable to God.

Gospel
Luke 11:1-13 (SC/C/RC)
> Impressed with the way Jesus prays, the disciples ask for guidance in how to pray.

Theme

Jesus gives us the heart to pray, and then teaches us to pray.

Thought for the Day

Prayer is not our best efforts to reach heaven, it is God reaching down and lifting us up into God.

Sermon Summary

When prayer is seen as an emergency measure or a natural inclination, it is not likely to be practiced in a meaningful way. But Jesus teaches us that prayer is communion with God, a communion actualized by Christ's ongoing priesthood, taking our prayers into the presence of God.

Call to Worship

> One: We gather in the presence of God's steadfast love.
> **All: God, we come seeking your restoration and healing.**
> One: We gather by the gift of God's own Spirit.
> **All: God, we come to listen, we come that we might be heard.**
> One: Let us worship and pray.
> **All: God, we come in trust that you are already here, and already ahead of us, leading the way.**

Pastoral Prayer

Almighty God, we gather in praise and adoration to confess your greatness and goodness. Father, whose love is working in all creation, we praise you. Son of God, who left the safe immunity of heaven to bring us back, we adore you. Holy Spirit, empowering us to proclaim and manifest the good news, we glorify you. Receive our worship, O God, through the ongoing ministry of Christ. We stand in awe before the life of Jesus: a life of humble service, of tender compassion, and of deep communion with you. Teach us to pray, O God! By your mighty Spirit lift us out of ourselves and our self-preoccupation to commune with you and to pour out our hearts in daily prayer. These things we would ask, through and with Jesus Christ. Amen.

Prayer of Confession

Gracious God, forgive us for prayerlessness. How seldom we seek your face! How infrequently we enter your presence! Our lives are consumed with our own wants and preoccupations. By the cross of Christ our Savior, deliver us from the dungeon of selfishness, and free us to love you and others with undivided hearts. In the name of Christ we pray. Amen.

Prayer of Dedication of Gifts and Self

Generous God, having given us all things, you give us your very self each time we commune with you. In gratitude we dedicate these offerings that the whole world might know the same joy. In Christ we pray. Amen.

Hymn of the Day
What a Friend We Have in Jesus

Although written as a personal message for his sorrowing mother, Joseph Scriven's hymn has become one of the most popular hymns around the world. Scriven was personally acquainted with great sorrow in his life. Twice he was engaged to be married and each time his fiance died prior to the scheduled wedding. The hymn was written in 1855. The hymn provides encouragement to take our personal sorrows, hurts, and other needs "to the Lord in prayer." The tune CONVERSE was written by Charles C. Converse in 1868 specifically for this text.

Children's Time: Talking to God

(Bring some newsprint and a marker.)

Talk with the children about prayer: When are some times that you pray? Do you have special prayers you use at home? Where do you pray?

Explain that we can talk to God anywhere, anytime. God is always ready to talk with us. Comment that in today's Bible story the disciples came to Jesus with a request. They had noticed that Jesus often prayed to God. They wanted to learn more about prayer, so they asked Jesus for help. Recite the prayer that Jesus taught, using the version that your congregation uses in worship.

Explain that ever since that day, the followers of Jesus have used Jesus' prayer. Comment that there are many ways to pray. We can use the prayer that Jesus taught, or we can make up our own prayers. God's not fussy! God just loves to hear from us.

Ask the children what they would like to talk to God about today. Do they want to say thank you for something? Do they want to pray for someone who is sick? Are they worried about something? List the children's suggestions on newsprint and offer them in prayer.

The Sermon: Teach Us to Pray
Scripture: Luke 11:1-13

The story is told of a doctor who had some somber news for the family of a patient. "We have done everything that is possible medically. Now, all we can do is pray." The father, shocked, asked incredulously, "Doctor! Has it come to that?"

Our world is not naturally inclined to prayer. Prayer is not normally seen as ongoing communion with God. It's a practice left for emergencies, for desperation times. We keep tabs on the weather. If serious storms are forecast, we monitor the Weather Channel, and perhaps have the foresight to stock an emergency kit with a radio, flashlight, and bottled water. If the streets begin to flood, we contemplate evacuating. But we may not turn to prayer until the evacuation routes are impassable and all human means of escape are exhausted.

Jesus did not come to proclaim an absent God who could be reached long distance in an emergency. He lived his life in daily fellowship with

God. He did pray on special occasions – in the Jordan River, when he was baptized, and in the garden of Gethsemane, when he struggled with his call to go to the cross. He spent all night in prayer prior to calling the 12 disciples. But Luke also informs us that prayer was Jesus' regular habit. In chapter five we learn that "he would withdraw to deserted places and pray" (5:16) And in our Gospel reading today, Jesus has just finished praying when the disciples request, "Lord, teach us to pray."

Harry Emerson Fosdick, the famous pastor of Riverside Church in New York City asserted that prayer is a native tendency, a natural inclination for human beings *(The Meaning of Prayer,* Association Press, 1975, pp. 1-18). If that were true, we might have expected the disciples to be regular practitioners of prayer. Instead, we find no mention in the Gospels of their prayer habits at all. It is recorded that in Gethsemane, while Jesus wrestled with apprehension and fear as he prayed to God, the disciples promptly fell asleep. They were prayerless while Jesus was prayerful.

Could it be that this is one reason we do not pray more, because it is not an inborn drive, an automatic tendency? So many sermons and devotions seem to assume that prayer is natural and that all we need are a few pointers on how to engage in it effectively. People file out of the sanctuary uplifted by such a positive message and praise the preacher for her inspiring words. Then they go home and nothing happens. Prayer is one more "ought" that is not easily complied with, so they give up.

Prayer is not natural, because prayer is centered in God and not in ourselves. We're not naturally altruistic, looking out for the needs of others. We're not automatically desirous of worshiping God. The Westminster Shorter Catechism declares in the answer to the very first question that our "chief end" is to "glorify God" and "enjoy [God] forever." That's a wonderful sentiment and it certainly accords with Holy Scripture. But there is a wide difference between what our driving purpose in life ought to be and what it actually is.

Raymond Ortlund, when he was pastor of Lake Avenue Congregational Church in Pasadena, California, said that Jesus came to make worshipers out of rebels. He's right. That's why Jesus lived our life, died our death, and rose in triumph – to free us from ourselves so that we might love God and others.

The prayer that Jesus taught, the Lord's Prayer, is not a magic formula for getting what we want out of God. The disciples were taught this prayer in response to a request humbly addressed to Jesus as Lord. "Lord, teach us to pray." It can be prayed only by those who trust in Jesus as "Lord."

The only kind of prayer natural to fallen humans is the prayer of selfishness. One little boy was overheard giving God a long list of requests as he prayed. His mother wisely advised him, "Son, when you pray to God, don't give God instructions. Just report for duty."

I don't believe the mother meant to dissuade her son from bringing requests to God. God wants us to pour out our needs in prayer. After all, Jesus tells us to ask for forgiveness, our daily bread, and help in time of temptation. I think that the mother was concerned that the boy viewed God as some sort of cosmic bellhop, an errand runner whose role is to fulfill our wishes. When we pray the prayer Jesus taught, we pray, "Thy kingdom come, thy will be done." We blurt out our worries, anxieties, and perceived needs, but we humbly lay them before the throne of God and trust that God knows best.

If prayer is not a native tendency for us, if it is not natural for us to seek and practice communion with God, should we simply give up? Far from it. Helmut Thielicke, the German theologian and preacher of a generation ago, points out that Jesus Christ is the one who teaches us to pray the Lord's Prayer: "It is fatefully significant that he is the one from whom we have received this holy prayer of all Christendom" *(The Prayer that Spans the World,* James Clarke, 1965, p. 22).

Jesus is more than a teacher, more than an inspiring example. Jesus is the one who comes as our great high priest. He practiced prayer as communion with God and comes to give us a share in his communion with God. Jesus not only offers himself as a sacrifice for us. He also inaugurates a holy priesthood and makes a realm of priests in him. As our great high priest, in the words of Hebrews 7:25, "he always lives to make intercession" for us. And Jesus gives us a share in his priesthood. When we pray as Christians, we enter into a prayer life that is always going on. We enter into the prayer life of Jesus, who always lives to pray for us. He strengthens our weak prayers. He converts our selfish prayers. He gives us the will to pray, "Thy will be done." He gives us the heart to pray and then teaches us to pray.

– Daniel P. Thimell

Hymns

Opening: I Sing the Mighty Power of God
Sermon: Lord, Take My Hand and Lead Me
Closing: Awake, My Soul, Stretch Every Nerve

Monthly Prayers for Church Meetings

by Charles Somervill

These 12 prayer devotionals, with a time for celebrations and concerns, are intended for beginning and ending your church meetings with prayer. They take about five minutes and follow the church year.

August 2012

Opening Prayer

God of all creation, from your hands we have received life and breath, spirit and senses. As you bring life to us, may we bring life to others. Remind us always how you have entrusted us as stewards of your creation, love's grace, and discipleship's call. May our wills tend faithfully to your purposes for all. In Jesus' name we pray. Amen.

Bible Reading: John 26:24-35

Prayers of Concern and Celebration

(Invite participants to suggest particular concerns or celebrations in the congregation and community.)

Let us take a moment of silence to reflect on the needs and concerns of others, as well as our own. (Pause for reflection.) Holy Lord, be present to us and to those we name in prayer, whether in words spoken aloud or in sighs of the Spirit so deep that only you can hear. Be especially present for those who pass through difficult times and places, for those who hunger, and for those who face pain of body or spirit. We pray for comfort and healing. We pray for this world: for peace where conflict rages, for justice where oppression rules, for mercy where kindness seems distant. Make us mindful so that we may be the instruments through whom your Spirit responds to these needs through Jesus Christ our Lord. Amen.

The Lord's Prayer

Depending on your tradition, offer this prayer before calling the meeting to order or as part of adjournment.

Prayer of Adjournment

Lord, thank you for the opportunity of working together as members of your body. Renew our spirits, enlighten our minds, and cast away anything that might hinder our service to you. Enable us now so that we might take on the challenges and responsibilities that you call us to face. In Christ's name. Amen.

September 2012
Opening Prayer
As we come before you, O God, we thank you for your goodness and loving-kindness, given to us and to all that you have made. Make us more aware of your mercies so that we may praise you not only with our lips but also with our lives. Lead us this day as we seek to do your will as Christ followers. Amen.

Bible Reading: Mark 7:31-37

Prayers of Concern and Celebration
(Invite participants to suggest particular concerns or celebrations in the congregation and community.)

Let us take a moment of silence to reflect on the needs and concerns of others, as well as our own. (Pause for reflection.) Loving God, hear the words we offer for those who are ill, who face isolation or estrangement. Be present to them in ways that bring healing and wholeness. Hear the words we offer this church community. May your Spirit form our ministries and shape our witness. Hear the words we offer for the world: for peace, for justice, for compassion. Mold us in word and deed as your servant people, that our faith will resonate in all that we do. We pray in the name of Christ, your Word incarnate. Amen.

The Lord's Prayer
Depending on your tradition, offer this prayer before calling the meeting to order or as part of adjournment.

Prayer of Adjournment
Giver of life, we offer thanks and praise for your vigilance over the lives of your people. Guide us to embody the words of service to which you have commissioned us. Use your powers to instill in us the need to serve as we leave this meeting, and to go into the world as your disciples. Amen.

October 2012
Opening Prayer
Thank you, O God, for the honor of serving you. We bring to you our commitment and thanksgiving for the work of your church. Receive our lives and make us willing servants who are always alert to the needs around us. Help us to dedicate ourselves anew as we seek your wisdom each decision we make. In Jesus' name. Amen.

Bible Reading: Mark 10:46-52

Prayers of Concern and Celebration
(Invite participants to suggest particular concerns or celebrations in the congregation and community.)

Let us take a moment of silence to reflect on the needs and concerns of others, as well as our own. (Pause for reflection.) O great and loving God, you enter into relationship with all people. We give you thanks for all who make our lives interesting and full. Thank you for families who love us, friends who make us laugh, children who show us the delight of discovery, youth who remind us of the importance of asking questions, and adults who demonstrate your wisdom. We pray, O Lord, for those whose relationships are troubled, those who know loss or loneliness, those who live in homes where abuse dominates them. Teach all of us to seek relationships that are healthy and show us how to reflect your love to those around us. Amen.

The Lord's Prayer
Depending on your tradition, offer this prayer before calling the meeting to order or as part of adjournment.

Prayer of Adjournment
Loving and forgiving God, you reach into our souls and see our true selves. You know where we have been faithful and where we have come up short. It is through grace and forgiveness that we leave this meeting. We ask your blessings on the things we've done or sought to change and your wisdom in pursuing things we've yet to do. Show us how we may share the love of Christ in whatever way you would lead us. Amen.

November 2012
Opening Prayer
Divine Giver, spark our desire to walk with you and to serve you with joy and thanksgiving. Grant us courage to say no to any commitment on our calendars that leaves us without time to pray, to worship, or to serve in the ministry of your church. Use our lives and our efforts as instruments of compassion and service for your glory. In Christ's name we pray. Amen.

Bible Reading: John 18:33-37

Prayers of Concern and Celebration
(Invite participants to suggest particular concerns or celebrations in the congregation and community.)

Let us take a moment of silence to reflect on the needs and concerns of others, as well as our own. (Pause for reflection.) O God, we celebrate the reign of the Christ who wipes away our tears and joins our laughter, comforts our grief, and draws us back to you. Keep us always mindful of the sovereignty that allows us to experience intimacy with Christ in the shadows of our lives, as well as in the sunlight. Whether we feel spiritually lost in a wilderness or joyously found in your presence, we thank you for your presence, your provisions, the love that shelters us, and a beloved community in which all of us are included in devotion to Christ. Amen.

The Lord's Prayer
Depending on your tradition, offer this prayer before calling the meeting to order or as part of adjournment.

Prayer of Adjournment
O God, all that we are and all that we have is yours. Energize us through your Spirit and send us forth with the realization of your grace and forgiveness. Enable us to be a blessing to others, just as you have blessed us, through Christ our Lord, Amen.

December 2012
Opening Prayer
O God, in this season we are often preoccupied and frantic, worried that each gift will not be big enough, attractive enough, and expensive enough to impress and please the recipient. Give us wisdom regarding the value of what we give to others and to you. We give to you our love and service and ask that you find acceptable the words of our mouth, the meditation of our hearts, and the work of our hands. In Jesus Christ we pray. Amen.

Bible Reading: Luke 3:1-6

Prayers of Concern and Celebration
(Invite participants to suggest particular concerns or celebrations in the congregation and community.)

Let us take a moment of silence to reflect on the needs and concerns of others, as well as our own. (Pause for reflection.) God, it is hard for some us to face this season of Advent and Christmas. Some of us are hurting so badly that we find it unreal to speak of hope. Many of our friends, grieving the absence of members of their families, feel only resentment when they hear comments about a reign of justice or peace. And frankly, when love can be such hard work, we sometimes find it easier to settle for just a little kindness and the possibility that someone might like us. So remind us again of how you came into this world to bring hope. Inspire us to love as we have been loved. Strengthen us in our forgiving so that we may know the healing and the promised peace of your coming. Amen.

The Lord's Prayer
Depending on your tradition, offer this prayer before calling the meeting to order or as part of adjournment.

Prayer of Adjournment
Come now, O God, and bless us. Look past the disarray of our celebrations and expectations and bless us. We need you, Holy One of Israel, to shine upon us, to lift us, to bring us up out of the depths and set us again on a firm, dry rock. We belong to you. And as we leave this meeting, give us the sense of your coming into our lives so that we may do your bidding and fulfill your mission. Through Jesus our Lord. Amen.

January 2013
Opening Prayer

Dear God, we thank you for your many blessings. Especially now, we thank you for the privilege of serving in the ongoing mission of the church. Keep us humble of spirit so that we might not only remember those who live with great need but also walk and serve with them as you have walked and served with us. In Jesus Christ we pray. Amen.

Bible Reading: Luke 4:14-21

Prayers of Concern and Celebration

(Invite participants to suggest particular concerns or celebrations in the congregation and community.)

Let us take a moment of silence to reflect on the needs and concerns of others, as well as our own. (Pause for reflection.) Let us recognize Christ present in this place. Let us recognize Christ in one another. Let us recognize Christ in those not present here. We are members of your body and you have called us to do your work in the world, showing forth your love and mercy until you come again. Let that work begin with us here today. Enable us to carry your work into our community, and even throughout the world. Open our eyes of faith to see you, Lord, in all the peoples of the earth. Through the power of the Spirit, enable us to be your instruments of peace, of grace, of redemption. Amen.

The Lord's Prayer

Depending on your tradition, offer this prayer before calling the meeting to order or as part of adjournment.

Prayer of Adjournment

Lord God, bless us with wisdom for the days ahead and years to come, that we might move in the direction you would have us move. Help us to meet the challenges of each moment with grace and compassion. As we leave here today, keep us open to your voice and your Spirit that we might love and serve you faithfully. In Christ's name. Amen.

February 2013
Opening Prayer
Great God, you created us and continue to sustain us in this world. We give you thanks and praise for the blessings we have received through your bountiful grace. Use our lives and the resources you have given us so that we may glorify you in all that we say and do. Unite us in our journey of faith, that we may strengthen and support one another in our mutual ministry, all to your glory. Amen.

Bible Reading: Luke 4:1-13

Prayers of Concern and Celebration
(Invite participants to suggest particular concerns or celebrations in the congregation and community.)

Let us take a moment of silence to reflect on the needs and concerns of others, as well as our own. (Pause for reflection.) We give you thanks, Holy God, for your saving purpose for the world, especially as it is revealed to us in the death and resurrection of Jesus Christ. Keep our hearts open so that we also might be an answer to the prayers we make for those who suffer pain and anguish. Help us to remain focused on Christ as we follow him in our daily lives. Enable us to do your loving will, and give us courage to follow, even when our work is difficult and the way unclear. Bless the whole church with your Spirit of wisdom and strength, so it may continue to be a faithful witness to the grace received through Jesus Christ and a beacon of hope in our troubled world. Amen.

The Lord's Prayer
Depending on your tradition, offer this prayer before calling the meeting to order or as part of adjournment.

Prayer of Adjournment
O God, we thank you for your presence in this meeting and for allowing us to participate in Christ's service. Give us faith to go where you call us. Bless the work of our ministries as we seek to be truly one with you. Give us joy in the talents and abilities you have given to us, so that we may delight in doing your will. Amen.

March 2013
Opening Prayer
We give thanks to you, O God, for Jesus' life, death, and resurrection. We are mindful and grateful for Jesus' ongoing presence with us today and with the church around the world. We ask that you strengthen our commitment and prepare us to be ever more faithful disciples as we come together now. In Jesus' name we pray. Amen.

Bible Reading: Luke 24:1-12

Prayers of Concern and Celebration
(Invite participants to suggest particular concerns or celebrations in the congregation and community.)

Let us take a moment of silence to reflect on the needs and concerns of others, as well as our own. (Pause for reflection.) Holy God, we confess that all too often we have lost sight of our intimate connection with you. As we meet together, renew us and help us to live in that connection, that we might be your voice and hands and heart. We remember friends, family, and loved ones who live with terminal illness, who endure chronic pain as their constant companion. We pray for those who bear in their hearts and minds the reminders of past hurts, betrayals, and wrongs. In your love and grace, heal them, comfort them, and strengthen them. Empower us so that in small or large ways we might be witnesses of your forgiving love. Through Christ our Lord. Amen.

The Lord's Prayer
Depending on your tradition, offer this prayer before calling the meeting to order or as part of adjournment.

Prayer of Adjournment
Lord, as we adjourn, we thank you not only for the gift of Easter but also for the daily gift of life – the sun that rises each day, the food on the table, the smiles and tears. We offer in return our very lives, our service to you, and our best intentions. Send us out, we pray, not just as hearers but as doers of your word. Amen.

April 2013
Opening Prayer
God of generosity and blessing, sometimes your gifts come to us in comprehensible form, like the beauty of nature, the spectacle of the heavens, the depths of the seas. Sometimes your gifts come in packages that we wished contained instructions so that we might better know how to use them. For all your gifts, we offer you our thanks and praise. Guide us to use what you provide and transform us into your faithful disciples. Amen.

Bible Reading: John 21:4-14

Prayers of Concern and Celebration
(Invite participants to suggest particular concerns or celebrations in the congregation and community.)

Let us take a moment of silence to reflect on the needs and concerns of others, as well as our own. (Pause for reflection.) O God, you are worthy of all our praise, for you alone are the creator of life. Thank you for the hope of Easter, not just on that one day, but today and every day. Help us to claim and live that hope through the everyday challenges of our lives and the issues we face in the world. We lift up to you today the needs of those in our midst who need that hope in a special way, for those in pain and suffering, for those struggling with the death of a loved one or wrestling with the many other crises that life can bring. Send a beam of hope into their hearts that they might be awakened to your presence. Amen.

The Lord's Prayer
Depending on your tradition, offer this prayer before calling the meeting to order or as part of adjournment.

Prayer of Adjournment
Sovereign God, as you were present in the abundance of the disciples' catch of fish after the resurrection, so be present with us in bounteous ways. Teach us to perceive and receive your blessings with open, grateful hearts, and in turn, make us available as a blessing to others. As we leave this meeting, we dedicate ourselves anew to the service of our risen Lord, Jesus Christ. Amen.

May 2013
Opening Prayer
Gracious and loving God, we rejoice in the promise of your Holy Spirit. In grateful response to all your gifts and blessings in creation, we offer you our thanks and praise. Help us to use, with joy and imagination, your many mercies. May we be constantly transforming into faithful disciples of our risen Lord Jesus Christ, in whose name we pray. Amen.

Bible Reading: Acts 1:1-11

Prayers of Concern and Celebration
(Invite participants to suggest particular concerns or celebrations in the congregation and community.)

Let us take a moment of silence to reflect on the needs and concerns of others, as well as our own. (Pause for reflection.) O God, we are thankful for your Spirit and for the peace that the world cannot give. Displace the fear of those who suffer with your calming presence. Give hope to those in distress and those who have given up. We are grateful for your gifts of food and shelter. Open our hearts and hands to view the world as a place of abundance and help us to share all we have. Give us grace to receive both blessings and challenges with gratitude. Amen.

The Lord's Prayer
Depending on your tradition, offer this prayer before calling the meeting to order or as part of adjournment.

Prayer of Adjournment
God of creation, we give you thanks for the gift of life, especially for the new life that comes through the redeeming death and resurrection of your Son, Jesus Christ. In him we live, and move, and have our being. In him we give you praise and set our eyes on the world. Through your Holy Spirit, help us to see you at work in our world. And as we leave this meeting, give us the strength to persevere in all that we do. Amen.

June 2013
Opening Prayer
Holy God, you open wide your hands to us in providence, in grace, in hope. Unclench our fists so that our hands might open to others with gifts that provide for special needs, with forgiveness that extends grace, with support that brings hope. As we gather together, we are thankful that you have entrusted us as stewards. Guide us in what we now do. In the name of Jesus we pray. Amen.

Bible Reading: Luke 7:1-10

Prayers of Concern and Celebration
(Invite participants to suggest particular concerns or celebrations in the congregation and community.)

Let us take a moment of silence to reflect on the needs and concerns of others, as well as our own. (Pause for reflection.) Loving God, open our eyes to opportunities and responsibilities to love as we have been loved. Remember those who walk through places shadowed with grief and death. May they find light and peace on that way. Be with those who are in need of strength and enable us to serve as your instruments of healing and support. Guide your church that we might be the body of Christ, not simply in what we say about you or about ourselves but in the trust we keep and the compassion we exercise. This we pray in the name of Christ. Amen.

The Lord's Prayer
Depending on your tradition, offer this prayer before calling the meeting to order or as part of adjournment.

Prayer of Adjournment
God, it is so easy to fall into ruts. We assume there is nothing new under the sun and sometimes presume that faithfulness is simply holding to what has been. God of grace and surprise, move among us in ways both old and new, in traditions that continue to grow and in change that does not forget. We need your guidance as well as your forgiveness. So walk with us now, and direct our steps in the paths you would have us take. In Jesus Christ. Amen.

July 2013
Opening Prayer
God, you have given us all things in Christ: life, love, forgiveness, purpose. You entrust us with so many blessings. Help us to be stewards of your many gifts. Inspire our service to further the work of your church, here in our community and around the world, through Jesus Christ our loving Savior. Amen.

Bible Reading: Luke 10:25-37

Prayers of Concern and Celebration
(Invite participants to suggest particular concerns or celebrations in the congregation and community.)

Let us take a moment of silence to reflect on the needs and concerns of others, as well as our own. (Pause for reflection.) Eternal and ever-blessed God, we are grateful for your transforming power and your unfailing presence. Cause us to see that by your companionship and constant help we can carry out the mission you give us in this world. Thank you that your love is not restricted to those we deem worthy but is generous and unconditional. May the love of your Son, our Savior Jesus, overflow from our hearts and into the hearts and lives of those around us. Move us to weep with those who weep and to ache with those who are unemployed, hungry, oppressed, powerless, or hopeless. Come alongside them through us, that all may know your love. These things we are bold to pray, through Christ. Amen.

The Lord's Prayer
Depending on your tradition, offer this prayer before calling the meeting to order or as part of adjournment.

Prayer of Adjournment
Almighty God, you nourish and sustain us from day to day, and you continue to bless us with more than we could dare to think or ask. We pray for your church, established on earth as a loving witness to your nature and purposes for the world. Stir us anew with your Holy Spirit. Send us forth now that we may know in a fresh way the reconciling and restoring power of our Lord Jesus Christ in our lives and in our serving. Amen.

2012-2013 Writers

Andrea La Sonde Anastos
(UCC) Littleton, CO
Oct. 31; Nov. 1, 4

Rod Broding
(ELCA) Battle Lake, MN
Sept. 16, 30

C. Welton Gaddy
(Bapt) Monroe, LA
Nov. 18, 25

Michael Gemignani
(Epis) Freeport, TX
Jan. 27

John Indermark
(UCC) Naselle, WA
Aug. 12, 26; Sept. 2; Nov. 22;
Dec. 2; May 12; Jun. 2, 23

Y. Franklin Ishida
(ELCA) Chicago, IL
May 9, 19, 26

Thomas G. Long
Bandy Professor of Preaching
at Candler School of Theology,
Emory University, Atlanta, GA
Sept. 23; Jan. 13; Feb 3; Mar. 17

William L. Mangrum
(PCUSA) Princeton, NJ
Dec. 9, 23, 24, 25

Margaret Marcuson
(Bapt) Portland, OR
Mar. 28, 31; Apr. 7

David Neil Mosser
(UMC) Arlington, TX
Jun. 16, 30

Rosemary A. Rocha
(UCC) Edina, MN
Mar. 3; 10, 24

Clayton Schmit
Fuller Theological Seminary,
Pasadena, CA
Jun. 9

Melissa Bane Sevier
(PCUSA) Versailles, KY
Oct. 7, 14, 21, 28

David P. Sharp
(PCUSA) San Jose, CA
Dec. 30; Jan 6

Jeanette B. Strandjord
(ELCA) Williams Bay, WI
Feb. 10, 13, 17, 24

Daniel P. Thimell
(UCC) Marshall, OK
July 7, 14, 21, 28

Nancy E. Topolewski
(UMC) Vestal, NY
Apr. 14, 28; May 5

William H. Willimon
(UMC) Birmingham, AL
Aug. 5, 19; Sept. 9; Nov. 11;
Dec 16; Jan. 20; Apr. 21

Monthly Prayers for Church
Meetings
Charles Somervill
(PCUSA) Granbury, TX

Four-Year Church Year Calendar

	Year C **2012**	Year A **2013**	Year B **2014**	Year C **2015**
Advent begins	Dec. 2	Dec. 1	Nov. 30	Nov. 29
Christmas	Dec. 25	Dec. 25	Dec. 25	Dec. 25
	2013	**2014**	**2015**	**2016**
Epiphany	Jan. 6	Jan. 6	Jan. 6	Jan. 6
Ash Wednesday	Feb. 13	Mar. 5	Feb. 18	Feb. 10
Passion/Palm Sunday	Mar. 24	Apr. 13	Mar. 29	Mar. 20
Maundy Thursday	Mar. 28	Apr. 17	Apr. 2	Mar. 24
Good Friday	Mar. 29	Apr. 18	Apr. 3	Mar. 25
Easter	Mar. 31	Apr. 20	Apr. 5	Mar. 27
Ascension Day	May 9	May 29	May 14	May 5
Pentecost	May 19	June 8	May 24	May 15
Trinity Sunday	May 26	June 15	May 31	May 22
Reformation	Oct. 31	Oct. 31	Oct. 31	Oct. 31
All Saints' Day	Nov. 1	Nov. 1	Nov. 1	Nov. 1

Calendars for 2012 and 2013

```
JANUARY          2012      FEBRUARY         2012      MARCH            2012      APRIL            2012
S  M  T  W  T  F  S        S  M  T  W  T  F  S        S  M  T  W  T  F  S        S  M  T  W  T  F  S
1  2  3  4  5  6  7                 1  2  3  4                    1  2  3        1  2  3  4  5  6  7
8  9 10 11 12 13 14        5  6  7  8  9 10 11        4  5  6  7  8  9 10        8  9 10 11 12 13 14
15 16 17 18 19 20 21       12 13 14 15 16 17 18       11 12 13 14 15 16 17       15 16 17 18 19 20 21
22 23 24 25 26 27 28       19 20 21 22 23 24 25       18 19 20 21 22 23 24       22 23 24 25 26 27 28
29 30 31                   26 27 28 29                25 26 27 28 29 30 31       29 30

MAY              2012      JUNE             2012      JULY             2012      AUGUST           2012
S  M  T  W  T  F  S        S  M  T  W  T  F  S        S  M  T  W  T  F  S        S  M  T  W  T  F  S
       1  2  3  4  5                       1  2       1  2  3  4  5  6  7                 1  2  3  4
6  7  8  9 10 11 12        3  4  5  6  7  8  9        8  9 10 11 12 13 14        5  6  7  8  9 10 11
13 14 15 16 17 18 19       10 11 12 13 14 15 16       15 16 17 18 19 20 21       12 13 14 15 16 17 18
20 21 22 23 24 25 26       17 18 19 20 21 22 23       22 23 24 25 26 27 28       19 20 21 22 23 24 25
27 28 29 30 31             24 25 26 27 28 29 30       29 30 31                   26 27 28 29 30 31

SEPTEMBER        2012      OCTOBER          2012      NOVEMBER         2012      DECEMBER         2012
S  M  T  W  T  F  S        S  M  T  W  T  F  S        S  M  T  W  T  F  S        S  M  T  W  T  F  S
                   1        1  2  3  4  5  6                    1  2  3                             1
2  3  4  5  6  7  8        7  8  9 10 11 12 13        4  5  6  7  8  9 10        2  3  4  5  6  7  8
9 10 11 12 13 14 15        14 15 16 17 18 19 20       11 12 13 14 15 16 17       9 10 11 12 13 14 15
16 17 18 19 20 21 22       21 22 23 24 25 26 27       18 19 20 21 22 23 24       16 17 18 19 20 21 22
23/30 24 25 26 27 28 29    28 29 30 31                25 26 27 28 29 30          23/30 24/31 25 26 27 28 29
```

```
JANUARY          2013      FEBRUARY         2013      MARCH            2013      APRIL            2013
S  M  T  W  T  F  S        S  M  T  W  T  F  S        S  M  T  W  T  F  S        S  M  T  W  T  F  S
       1  2  3  4  5                          1  2                      1  2       1  2  3  4  5  6
6  7  8  9 10 11 12        3  4  5  6  7  8  9        3  4  5  6  7  8  9        7  8  9 10 11 12 13
13 14 15 16 17 18 19       10 11 12 13 14 15 16       10 11 12 13 14 15 16       14 15 16 17 18 19 20
20 21 22 23 24 25 26       17 18 19 20 21 22 23       17 18 19 20 21 22 23       21 22 23 24 25 26 27
27 28 29 30 31             24 25 26 27 28             24/31 25 26 27 28 29 30    28 29 30

MAY              2013      JUNE             2013      JULY             2013      AUGUST           2013
S  M  T  W  T  F  S        S  M  T  W  T  F  S        S  M  T  W  T  F  S        S  M  T  W  T  F  S
          1  2  3  4                             1       1  2  3  4  5  6                       1  2  3
5  6  7  8  9 10 11        2  3  4  5  6  7  8        7  8  9 10 11 12 13        4  5  6  7  8  9 10
12 13 14 15 16 17 18       9 10 11 12 13 14 15        14 15 16 17 18 19 20       11 12 13 14 15 16 17
19 20 21 22 23 24 25       16 17 18 19 20 21 22       21 22 23 24 25 26 27       18 19 20 21 22 23 24
26 27 28 29 30 31          23/30 24 25 26 27 28 29    28 29 30 31                25 26 27 28 29 30 31

SEPTEMBER        2013      OCTOBER          2013      NOVEMBER         2013      DECEMBER         2013
S  M  T  W  T  F  S        S  M  T  W  T  F  S        S  M  T  W  T  F  S        S  M  T  W  T  F  S
1  2  3  4  5  6  7                 1  2  3  4  5                       1  2       1  2  3  4  5  6  7
8  9 10 11 12 13 14        6  7  8  9 10 11 12        3  4  5  6  7  8  9        8  9 10 11 12 13 14
15 16 17 18 19 20 21       13 14 15 16 17 18 19       10 11 12 13 14 15 16       15 16 17 18 19 20 21
22 23 24 25 26 27 28       20 21 22 23 24 25 26       17 18 19 20 21 22 23       22 23 24 25 26 27 28
29 30                      27 28 29 30 31             24 25 26 27 28 29 30       29 30 31
```